The Vākāṭakas

GONDA INDOLOGICAL STUDIES

published under the auspices of the J. Gonda Foundation,
Royal Netherlands Academy of Arts and Sciences

VOLUME V

Editor

H. W. Bodewitz, *Leiden*

Editorial Board

H. T. Bakker / D. H. A. Kolff

K. R. van Kooij / T. Vetter

Advisory Board

C. Caillat, *Paris* / R. E. Emmerick, *Hamburg*

J. Ensink, *Groningen* / R. F. Gombrich, *Oxford*

J. C. Heesterman, *Leiden* / D. Shulman, *Jerusalem*

Ch. Vaudeville, *Paris* / J. Williams, *Berkeley*

TO

THE MEMORY OF

ALAN W. ENTWISTLE

Vāsudeva image (Mondasvāmin?), Mandhal

The Vākāṭakas

An Essay in Hindu Iconology

by

Hans T. Bakker

EGBERT FORSTEN · GRONINGEN

1997

Cover design: Françoise Berserik
Cover illustration: Mātṛkā, Mandhal (Photograph: H. Isaacson)
Map on page 263: Williams, J.G. The Art of Gupta India. Empire and Province

Typesetting and layout: Adriaensen & Barkhuis

This book was printed with financial support
from the Netherlands Organization for Scientific Research (NWO)

ISBN 90 6980 100 0

Preface

In the autumn of 1986 a tour through holy places connected with the worship of Viṣṇu's *avatāra* Rāma led me to Ramtek (Rāmagiri) c. 45 km north-east of Nagpur. A thirteenth-century stone inscription of the time of the Yādava king Rāmacandra found in the Lakṣmaṇa Temple on the spur of this hill eulogized the Rāmagiri as a holy mountain, hallowed by a visit of Rāma and his wife Sītā, and this echoed Kālidāsa's description in the *Meghadūta*, where he said that its slopes were marked by Raghupati's footprints. Were it not that the separation from his beloved spoiled his sojourn, the Yakṣa of the *Meghadūta* would have enjoyed his place of exile, since his master could hardly have banished him to a more beautiful spot. Since that first visit my research has circled around this hill. For a cult of Rāma in Kālidāsa's days I could find little proof, but my investigations brought me into contact with the one-time masters of the hill, the Vākāṭaka kings of Nandivardhana. Fascinated by the monuments and the richness of the archaeological material that they had left behind, my attention began focusing itself on the history of this dynasty. I reported on my findings in several articles and for some time I had the idea of collecting these writings in one volume. However, their preliminary nature was obvious, and a comparison of the earlier publications with the later ones revealed many deficiencies and inconsistencies. I felt the need of an integral and comprehensive treatise and from this need the present book has ensued.

During my fieldwork I not only discovered the beauties of Vākāṭaka art but also the friendliness and hospitality of the people of Maharashtra. Dr S. M. Ayachit was the first friend I made. He accompanied me on my first visit to the Rāmagiri and brought me into contact with the archaeologists and historians of the University of Nagpur: Prof. Dr V. B. Kolte, the éminence grise, who ranks among the most illustrious scholars that Vidarbha has brought forth; Prof. Dr Ajay Mitra Shastri, who is the greatest living expert in Vākāṭaka history; and Dr Chandrashekhar Gupta, who with his vast knowledge of the field and unfailing assistance has greatly contributed to this book. They all became personal friends and made Nagpur for me an important and familiar city. Professor Shastri unselfishly shared with me his knowledge of the history of the Vākāṭakas, and allowed me kindly to photograph and publish the superb collection of sculptures which he had found in his excavation of Mandhal. The staff of the Nagpur Central Museum has also been most helpful; to them, Mr V. R. Verulkar, and in particular to Dr A. P. Jamkhedkar, Director of the Archaeological Survey and Museums of Maharashtra, I am much obliged for allowing me to study and photograph the Museum's collection of Vākāṭaka art. I thank the Faculty of Divinity and Religious Studies of the University of Groningen and the Netherlands Foundation for the Advancement of Tropical Research (WOTRO) for the financial support which made this fieldwork possible.

The turn my research had taken brought me to the field of ancient Indian art. In the middle of this field I found Dr James C. Harle. It is no exaggeration to say that this book owes its existence to him more than to anyone. From the very start he has been involved in the assessment and interpretation of the visual material that I collected in the course of my travels in Maharashtra. During my yearly visits to Oxford I found in him a counsellor and warm friend. Many happy days we spent together arranging and studying the photographs that were spread all over the dining-room table. He was always willing to read and to comment upon the various drafts which have preceded the text now presented, and to go through its final version. I consider it a great privilege to have been given the opportunity to profit from his scholarship, knowledge and deep insights into the history of ancient Indian art. Hawkswell Farm became my home in Oxford, and the hearty hospitality and friendship extended to me by James and Betty Harle shall always be very dear to me.

In many other ways Oxford has been important for me and for the completion of this study. The Bodleian Library, the ever friendly, helpful and professional staff of the Indian Institute, the facilities and learned serenity of this library with its wonderful view which transposes one into the fifteenth century, all these things meant that I was always looking forward to cross the Channel. In 1996 I was privileged to work in Oxford for half a year as a Spalding Visiting Fellow. I enjoyed the hospitality and scholarly ambiance of Wolfson College. The Fellowship allowed me to write a substantial part of this book and offered me the opportunity to profit from the indological knowledge which one meets there at every step. My thanks are in particular due to Prof. Dr Richard and Sanjukta Gombrich and to Prof. Alexis Sanderson, whose series of extraordinary lectures during Hilary Term 1996 on the *Levels of Initiation and Practice in the Śaivism of Abhinavagupta* was one of the high points of my stay. In Bridgestreet I found a veritable Ashram of young and brilliant indological colleagues. Drs Harunaga Isaacson and Dominic D. S. Goodall were ever available for help, discussion and criticism. The latter read the book in its final stage as its English editor. I am not only deeply obliged to him for correcting my English, but I am just as, or even more grateful to Dominic and Harunaga for their innumerable suggestions for improving the text and reconsidering the interpretation of Sanskrit passages, as well as for pointing out dubious conclusions and for referring me to other sources.

My stay in Oxford was overshadowed by the illness and death on March 28 1996 of my dearest friend Alan W. Entwistle. Alan not only introduced me to the living traditions of India; he turned my academic interest in that country into one of love. I look back on the years he lived with us in Groningen as the happiest ones of my life. His death is a deeply felt personal loss and a great loss for Indology. This book is dedicated to his memory.

The Institute of Indian Studies of the University of Groningen has gone through difficult times during the period I was working on the Vākāṭakas. I am grateful to the Department of Religious Studies – especially to my colleagues Prof. Dr Jan N. Bremmer and Dr Lourens P. van den Bosch – for safeguarding the Institute's existence. Of the small group of devoted indologists and students who make up this Institute I should like to mention in particular Yūko Yokochi, from whose research into the history of Goddess worship I have profited, and also Rob Adriaensen, who not only was my mainstay and support in the production process of this book, but whose knowledge of the Sanskrit sources has protected me from many mistakes. Egbert Forsten proved to be much more than my appreciated publisher. His friendship is dear to me and his sympathetic involvement in my work has been a great encouragement.

A small institute like ours cannot do without the support of the colleagues of sister universities. In this respect I should like to thank in particular Prof. Dr Henk W. Bodewitz of the Kern Institute of the University of Leiden who stood by me through thick and thin. Dr Ellen M. Raven of the same Institute has been so kind to go through the iconographic parts of this book; I am grateful for her many valuable suggestions. I also thank Frans H. P. M. Janssen, who has kept me up-to-date with developments in the world of Indian archaeology and who has informed me about new discoveries in the field.

All those who in one way or another have helped me in writing this book but go unnamed here may be assured of my gratitude. One real friend, however, should be mentioned: my sweet wife Aafke, the cornerstone of my existence.

Groningen, 19 March 1997

Table of Contents

Introduction 1

PART I

The History and Religion of the Vākāṭakas 7

Chapter I A Short History of the Vākāṭaka Kingdom 9
Chapter II The Hindu Religion in the Vākāṭaka Kingdom 58
Chapter III The Vākāṭaka Sites 80

PART II

A Catalogue of Vākāṭaka Hindu Sculpture 93
(Plates I to XL)

Appendices 161

I The Kevala-Narasiṃha Temple Inscription 163
II Gupta-Vākāṭaka Genealogy 168
III Outline of Vākāṭaka Chronology 169

Bibliography 173
Index 193
Index of Quotations 208
Plates 213
Maps 261

List of Plates*

frontispiece Vāsudeva image (Mondasvāmin?) found in Mandhal (cf. Plate XIX, photograph H. Isaacson)

Vākāṭaka Inscriptions

p. 125 Inscription on the book in the left hand of the Kavi image (detail of Plate XXVI, photograph Y. Yokochi)

facing p. 163 Vākāṭaka inscription in the Kevala-Narasiṃha Temple on Ramtek Hill

Vākāṭaka Sculptures

p. 213 Mandhal: male head medallion (courtesy of the Department of Ancient Indian History, Culture and Archaeology (AIHCA) of the University of Nagpur (UN))

I Mandhal: Maheśvara, *front* (courtesy of the Directorate of Archaeology and Museums Maharashtra (AMM))

II Mandhal: Maheśvara, *rear* (courtesy of the AMM)

III Mandhal: Nandīśvara (?), *front* (courtesy of the AMM)

IV Mandhal: Nandīśvara (?), *rear* (courtesy of the AMM)

V Mandhal: a Gaṇādhyakṣa, *front* (courtesy of the AMM)

VI Mandhal: a Gaṇādhyakṣa, *rear* (courtesy of the AMM)

VII Mandhal: Sadāśiva, *front* (courtesy of the AIHCA of the UN)

VIII Mandhal: Sadāśiva, A *rear*, B *right side* (courtesy of the AIHCA of the UN)

IX Mandhal: Rudra Andhakāsurasaṃhāramūrti, *front* (courtesy of the AIHCA of the UN)

* All photographs by the author unless stated otherwise.

X	Mandhal: Rudra Andhakāsurasaṃhāramūrti, *rear* (courtesy of the AIHCA of the UN)
XI	Mandhal: Naigameṣa, *front* (courtesy of the AIHCA of the UN)
XII	Mandhal: Naigameṣa, *rear* (courtesy of the AIHCA of the UN)
XIII	Mandhal: Pārvatī, *front* (courtesy of the AIHCA of the UN)
XIV	Mandhal: Pārvatī, *rear* (courtesy of the AIHCA of the UN)
XV	Mandhal: Mātṛkā, *front* (courtesy of the AIHCA of the UN)
XVI	Mandhal: Mātṛkā, *rear* (courtesy of the AIHCA of the UN)
XVII	Mandhal: Brahmā, *front* (courtesy of the AIHCA of the UN)
XVIII	Mandhal: Brahmā, *rear* (courtesy of the AIHCA of the UN)
XIX	Mandhal: Vāsudeva, *front* (courtesy of the AIHCA of the UN)
XX	Mandhal: Vāsudeva, *rear* (courtesy of the AIHCA of the UN)
XXI	Mandhal: Saṃkarṣaṇa Dhenukāsuravadhamūrti, *front* (courtesy of the AIHCA of the UN)
XXII	Mandhal: Saṃkarṣaṇa Dhenukāsuravadhamūrti, *rear* (courtesy of the AIHCA of the UN)
XXIII	Mandhal: a Vṛṣṇi Hero (Sāmba?), *front* (courtesy of the AIHCA of the UN)
XXIV	Mandhal: a Vṛṣṇi Hero (Sāmba?), *rear* (courtesy of the AIHCA of the UN)
XXV	A, Mandhal: an Ugra Head (courtesy of the AIHCA of the UN) B, Nagardhan, view of the Rāmagiri
XXVI	Nagardhan: a Kavi, *front* (courtesy of the AMM, photograph Y. Yokochi)
XXVII	Nagardhan: Viṣṇu (courtesy of the AMM)
XXVIII	Nagardhan: Gaṇeśa (courtesy of the AMM)
XXIX	Nagardhan: A, Devī Mahiṣāsuramardinīmūrti B, Lajjā Gaurī (courtesy of the AMM)
XXX	Nagardhan: A, a Bhārarakṣaka B, a Bhārarakṣaka (courtesy of the AMM)
XXXI	Nagardhan: A, Narasiṃha (miniature) (courtesy of the AMM) B, Viṣṇupada (courtesy of private owner)
XXXII	Rāmagiri: A, Varāha *enshrined* B, Varāha, *loose find* (courtesy of the AMM)
XXXIII	Rāmagiri: A, Narasiṃha, *front* B, Narasiṃha (bottom), *rear* (detail) C, Narasiṃha (*cakra*), *right side* (detail) (courtesy of the AMM)
XXXIV	Rāmagiri: A, Trivikrama, *front* (photograph Y. Yokochi) B, Trivikrama, *lower part front* (detail) (courtesy of the AMM)

XXXV Rāmagiri: A, Viṣṇu B, a Dikpāla(?) C, Makara (courtesy of the AMM)
XXXVI Rāmagiri: A, a Gaṇa B, a Nidhi (courtesy of the AMM)
XXXVII Mansar: Śiva (courtesy of the National Museum, New Delhi)
XXXVIII Ajanta: A, Vajrapāṇi (Cave 19) B, a Nidhi (Cave 21) (courtesy of the AMM)
XXXIX A, Ajanta (Cave 16): River Goddess (courtesy of the AMM) B, Paunar: Gaṅgā (courtesy of the Paramadhāma Āśrama, Paunar)
XL Paunar: A, Balarāma Dhenukāsuravadhamūrti B, Kṛṣṇa playing with the moon (courtesy of the Paramadhāma Āśrama, Paunar)

Comparative Material

XLI Mathura: A, Maheśa, *front* B, Maheśa, *rear* (courtesy of the Russek Collection (177 IMGU), photographs Russek Collection)
XLII Tala: a Gaṇa (courtesy of the American Institute of Indian Studies, Ramnagar (AIIS), photograph 92611)
XLIII Tala: A, Rudra, *front* B, Rudra, *front* (detail) (courtesy of the Directorate of Archaeology and Museums Madhya Pradesh (AMMP))
XLIV A, Tala: Naigameṣa (courtesy of the AMMP) B, Udayagiri (Cave 6): Gaṇeśa (courtesy of the AIIS, photograph 7436)
XLV Udayagiri (Cave 6): A, Viṣṇu (courtesy of the AIIS, photograph A3.63) B, Devī Mahiṣāsuramardinī (courtesy of the AMMP, photograph J. C. Harle)
XLVI Udayagiri (Cave 5): Varāha (courtesy of the AMMP, photograph J. C. Harle)
XLVII Besnagar: A, Mātṛkās, *front* B, Mātṛkās, *rear* (courtesy of the Istituto Italiano per il Medio ed Estremo Oriente (IsMEO), photograph Central Archaeological Museum, Gwalior)

Introduction

On his tour of 1873–74, the British officer of the Archæologogical Survey of India, J. D. Beglar, having arrived at the hill of Ramtek (Rāmagiri), made these observations among others:

> Continuing to ascend, there is a gate, close to which is a *bauli* [*bāulī*, tank]; ...passing then through another small gate, are seen several buildings, all modern, except, perhaps, a small temple of the Varâha Incarnation. This last is a very small open hall supported on four massive square pillars at the four corners, enshrining a large statue of Varâha. ...The statue is of the usual variety, plain and well smeared with vermilion; inscriptions, if any exist, are therefore hopelessly buried beneath the thick coat of oil and vermilion. I infer this temple to be old, and unaltered, because the four pillars supporting the roof are all alike, and the intersecting squares of the roof appear undisturbed. ...The other temples here are all modern, without exception, though some of the statues may be ancient. They are built without the remotest idea of regularity, or arrangement, either of plan, form, or material. ...Near the bungalow built by Sir R. Temple [sic] on the hill...are the ruins of another Hindu temple; a few pillars of the Mandapa exist, and fragments of statues. ...The sculpture is really a mutilated one of the Vâman Avatâr which the pujâris at the place are strangely unable to recognize. ...Two small shrines of Narasinha Avatâr have been noticed in the Gazetteer; they are quite modern and of no interest.[1]

The account is marked by the spirit of the times, in which fresh academic interest in the antiquities of India mingled with disdain for the actual living tradition. This unfortunate blend allowed Beglar to recognize some of the ancient structures on the one hand, but on the other hand it induced him to ascribe everything he did not understand to the decrepitude and ignorance of the purveyors of the culture under investigation. His report is a caveat against rash conclusions and should remind us

---

1 Beglar 1873–74, 110–113.

of how little we know, even today, of the genesis of the magnificent monument that is Rāmagiri.

The credit for first revealing the full scale, as well as for describing the antiquities, of the hill goes to the Director of the Archaeological Survey and Museums of Maharashtra, Dr A. P. Jamkhedkar. In a series of articles published more than one century after Beglar's visit Jamkhedkar reports on the discovery of at least six ancient structures that date back to the fifth century AD, to the times in which the region was under the control of the royal House of the Vākāṭakas, the southern neighbours of the imperial Guptas.[2]

In addition to the growing interest in the architectural remains on the hill the last two decades have seen the discovery and publication of a great number of inscriptions and sculptures, giving a new dimension to our appreciation of the culture of the Vākāṭakas, who formerly were mainly renowned for the artistic achievements of the Buddhist monuments in Ajanta. Since Vasudev Vishnu Mirashi's monumental *Inscriptions of the Vākāṭakas*, which appeared in 1963, the total number of known Vākāṭaka inscriptions has more than doubled. Excavations in Mandhal conducted by the Department of Ancient Indian History and Culture and Archaeology (AIHCA) of the University of Nagpur have uncovered three brick temples datable to the beginning of the fifth century, as well as a hoard of splendid, though puzzling, Hindu sculptures. The historical assessment of all these discoveries was undertaken with unremitting zeal and professionalism by Ajay Mitra Shastri.

While the historiography of the eastern Vākāṭaka kingdom has thus gained momentum, the attention of scholars concerned with the western kingdom has remained mainly focused on the Caves in Ajanta, Ghatotkaca and Bagh. A great contribution to our knowledge of the history and architecture of these caves was made during the last three decades by the researches of Walter Spink. One may say that from the middle of the sixties the kingdom of the Vākāṭakas has come to be seen as pivotal in the history of India, being essential for our understanding of the development of its art, religion and culture; as such it is on a par with the Gupta world, of which it can no longer be considered to be merely a province.

The present book builds on the achievements of many scholars, among whom those mentioned above are the most prominent. Although I disagree with them from time to time, sometimes on minor points sometimes fundamentally, I am deeply aware of my indebtedness to their work. If in this study any progress is made, this is due to two strategies which distinguish this book from most of those of my predecessors in the field.

2 Jamkhedkar 1985b, 1985–86, 1987a.

Firstly, I consider it no longer productive to concentrate exclusively on one branch of the Vākāṭakas by ignoring or marginalizing the evidence with regard to the other branch. The kings of Vatsagulma and Nandivardhana made up one family and their history is that of one family for all it is worth: divorce and rapprochement, dominance and submission, peaceful coexistence marred by fits of rivalry, occasionally erupting into downright civil war. Not only is the political history of both houses interlocked, but so is their religion and culture. An attempt will be made to show that the art of Ajanta can no longer be detached from the artistic achievements of the eastern Vākāṭakas. On the other hand there is some evidence that important religious groups migrated from Vatsagulma to the eastern kingdom.

While we thus find that northern Maharashtra, from Thalner on the Tapi river in the west to the Wainganga river in the east, made up one cultural area, we would make a serious mistake were we not to keep in mind the continuous exchange with the Gupta north, ranging from military to matrimony, from political ideology to culture, from religion to merchandise. During the first quarter of the fifth century Gupta influence, channelled through the Gupta princess Prabhāvatī, who became the virtual occupant of the throne in Nandivardhana, seems to have been at its peak, but this did not lead to cultural subordination of the Vākāṭakas. On the contrary, it fertilized the germs already there and generated a valuable culture in its own right.

The second strategy I have adopted is to utilize textual and archaeological sources in combination as far as possible. For now more than half a century, scholars of the history of Western art have become familiar with the idea that visual art is embedded in a social and cultural context which imbues it with meaning and as such may be viewed as a source which generates knowledge concerning this context; this again may result in a better understanding of the artefact itself. This synthetic method of investigation, known under the name of 'iconology,' has proved to be of great value in the research of the history of culture.[3] Iconology thus defined is a

3 Cf. Erwin Panofsky, *Ikonographie und Ikonologie*, in Ekkehard Kaemmerling (ed.), *Ikonographie und Ikonologie. Theorien, Entwicklung, Probleme*, Köln 1979, 220 f.: 'Die ikonologische Interpretation schließlich erfordert mehr als nur eine Vertrautheit mit bestimmten Themen und Vorstellungen, wie sie durch literarische Quellen übermittelt wurden. Wenn wir die Grundprinzipien erfassen möchten, die sowohl der Wahl und der Darstellung von Motiven wie auch der Herstellung und Interpretation von Bildern, Anekdoten und Allegorien zugrunde liegen und die sogar den angewandten formalen Anordnungen und technischen Verfahren Bedeutung verleihen, können wir nicht darauf hoffen, einen einzelnen Text zu finden, der mit jenen Grundprinzipien so übereinstimmt, wie Johannes 13, 21 ff. mit der Ikonographie des letzten Abendmahls übereinstimmt. Um diese Prinzipien zu erfassen, benötigen wir eine geistige Fähigkeit, die derjenigen eines Diagnostikers vergleichbar ist—eine Fähigkeit, die ich nicht besser beschreiben kann als durch den ziemlich in Mißkredit geratenen Ausdruck "synthetische Intuition" und die in einem begabten Laien besser entwickelt sein kann als in einem belesenen Gelehrten.'

branch of cultural and—applied to religious material—of religious history; it is the counterpart of philology, which contributes to the same by taking textual material as its main object of study. In order to understand the context—political, cultural, religious—the iconologist assimilates the results of philological research and utilizes them in his understanding of the visual material, which again may serve as an important source for the historiography. Since the present study focuses on this visual material as far as it belongs to the Hindu fold—brought together for the first time in the catalogue of Part II—and the understanding thereof, derived from studying its historic context, is again employed in Part I as an important source for this context, the book carries the subtitle *An Essay in Hindu Iconology*.

All the same, I sometimes found the results of philological investigations, including epigraphy, deficient or unsatisfactory. For that reason I have explored again much of the textual material relevant for the period at issue and, in addition to this corpus of well-known texts and inscriptions, I have utilized two sources which only recently have become available: the original *Skandapurāṇa* and the Vākāṭaka inscription in the Kevala-Narasiṃha Temple on Ramtek Hill. The critical edition of the former is the object of a research project at the Institute of Indian Studies of the University of Groningen;[4] the latter I have published, together with my colleague Isaacson, in 1993. Renewed study of this inscription, the value of which for the history of the Vākāṭakas and Guptas can hardly be overestimated, has led to some new interpretations and conjectures. I therefore present a revised edition in Appendix I and include again a photograph.

The method described above may be illustrated by one example. The image found in Mansar (Plate XXXVII) defies identification as one specific form of Śiva, though its identification as an image of this god is warranted by his attributes, which we know from other images and which are ascribed to Śiva in our Sanskrit sources. The site where the image was found, a hillock called Hiḍimbā Tekḍī 5 km north-west of the Vākāṭaka headquarters Nandivardhana (identified with the village Nagardhan, 6 km to the south of Rāmagiri), and also the sheer quality of the sculpture point to royal patronage. Considerations of style lead to a dating of the image in the second quarter of the fifth century and thus to a connection with the Vākāṭaka king Pravarasena II. From textual, i.e. epigraphical, evidence we know that Pravarasena, who confessed to be a Māheśvara, had a large temple complex built, which he used as an official state sanctuary, the Pravareśvaradevakulasthāna. This was probably not a *liṅga* temple, since the archaeology of the Vākāṭaka realm proves that these kings were not *liṅga* worshippers; moreover this is in conformity with the reluctance to accept *liṅga* worship which we note in the Sanskrit literature of the brahmanical elite of this period. The inference that the Mansar image was

4 See Adriaensen & Bakker & Isaacson 1994.

the idol of the Pravareśvara Temple and consequently that this temple was situated in Mansar, appears logical. Charters issued by this king also tell us that, halfway through his reign, when his dominant mother was growing older, he decided either to rename the old residence Nandivardhana after himself or to build a new one, Pravarapura. The evidence of the Mansar Śiva and its connection with the political context of its time would make it appear plausible that Pravarasena II built his new palace in the vicinity of this state sanctuary, i.e. a little to the west of Rāmagiri and Nandivardhana. It may have sealed the process in which the king broke away from his mother and her Bhāgavata milieu. The Mansar Śiva is thus an important piece of evidence in the reconstruction of the political and religious reality of the time. What does this reality contribute to our understanding of the image? It could explain why this figure, in the words of Joanna Williams, has no 'exact parallel in iconography.'[5] It represents a Śiva who appears to be more domesticated, showing a benign smile and offering life to his devotees, whereas wild traits, such as the erect phallus, third eye and weapons are absent. One could sense here the influence that the Bhāgavata environment still held over the Māheśvara faith of the king.

There is no denying that some circularity inheres in the applied methodology, but this does not, in my view, detract from its usefulness as a valuable heuristic device. The hermeneutic circle can only be broken, or rather widened, when new evidence becomes available. In this respect the latest developments are promising. Recent excavations by the Department of AIHCA of the University of Nagpur exposed a brick construction at the foot of the hillock on which the Mansar image was found (the Hiḍimbā Tekḍī), and excavations of a mound a few hundred metres to the east of this hillock by the Directorate of Archaeology and Museums of Maharashtra under the supervision of Dr Amarendra Nath have exposed a large brick structure of what seems to be a palace rather than a temple. These discoveries, which still await publication, came too late to be incorporated in this study. Prima-facie they seem to endorse this line of reasoning.

The two strategies outlined above mean that in principle all available material concerning the cultural history of the Vākāṭakas will be evaluated in the following pages. Limits are set by my own competence and the deliberate decision to leave out the specific Buddhist evidence. This implies that one will not find, for instance, an art-historical assessment of the Ajanta Caves nor a study of the iconography of the images and paintings preserved therein. The reader is referred to the publications of Walter Spink and Dieter von Schlingloff's *Studies in the Ajanta Paintings. Identifications and Interpretation*, among others. The socio-economic history of the Vākāṭaka kingdom is another subject that requires investigation by the specialist. In order to facilitate this research and to place the history and culture of the Vākātakas

5 Williams 1983, 227 n. 3.

in their geographical environment, a map has been produced which shows the natural theatre of their achievements.

It is hoped that the material brought together here may be of some use and may stimulate further Vākāṭaka studies. The dynasty deserves it.

PART I

The History and Religion of the Vākāṭakas

Chapter 1

A Short History of the Vākāṭaka Kingdom

THE ORIGINS: THE LOSS OF THE HOMELAND AND THE RECOVERY OF THE VĀKĀṬAKA KINGDOM

The second quarter of the 4th century AD saw two power blocks beginning to emerge in septentrional India, both consolidated by strategic matrimonial alliances. In the Gangetic Plain Samudragupta had ascended to the throne, inheriting Candragupta I's kingdom (comprising the regions along the Gaṅgā, including Magadha, Prayāga and Sāketa)[1] as well as the territories of the Licchavis, a patrimony to which he was entitled on account of his mother, Kumāradevī (see Appendix II). To the south of the northern plains the Vākāṭaka king Rudrasena I inherited at least parts of the kingdom of his grandfather, Pravarasena I, as well as the territories of the Bhāraśivas, a branch of the Nāga dynasty that ruled from Padmāvatī.[2] Rudrasena's father, Gautamīputra, had died before he could ascend the throne; his mother was a daughter of king Bhavanāga of the Bhāraśiva lineage, who was, it would seem, without male offspring, which made Rudrasena, like Samudragupta, a 'daughter's son heir' (*dauhitra*).[3] It seems likely, however, that both successions,

1 Pargiter 1913, 53.

2 Copper coins of an Adhirāja Bhavanāga have been found in Padmāvatī (Pawaya); see Trivedi 1957, xviii–xx, 27–37.

3 Goyal 1967, 88–94; Joshi in RGH, 112; differently Trautmann 1972. Trautmann, in rejecting Pathak and Goyal, reproaches them for paraphrasing Manu 9.132 'somewhat misleadingly' (op. cit. 7). According to Trautmann, Manu is saying that a *dauhitra*, whom Manu understands as a *putrikā-putra*—the appointed heir of his maternal grandfather who is without sons—inherits his grandfather's patrimony, but *not* that of his own father, *unless* his father has no other son. Trautmann's interpretation is problematic. First of all the text transmission of Manu 9.132 shows a significant early variant reading, attested in Bhāruci's commentary and discussed (and rejected) by Medhātithi in his commentary on this verse. If this variant were to preserve the original reading, the question of the *dauhitra*'s rights to the inheritance of his father apparently does not even occur, as the verse then seems to say that the *dauhitra*, if he inherits the whole of his maternal grandfather's estate, has to offer *piṇḍas* to his own father and his maternal grandfather. According to the reading followed by Medhātithi and later commentators, on the other hand, Manu appears to say that, in the event that his father has no (other) sons, he inherits the *whole* patrimony (*akhilaṃ riktham*), like he does of the father of his mother; in that case he is the only

that of Rudrasena and Samudragupta, were not uncontested, since firstly, enough agnate princes of Nāga stock remained to challenge Rudrasena's claims to the Bhāraśiva legacy, and secondly Rudrasena and Samudragupta had both rivals of 'equal birth' (*tulyakulaja*).[4]

Puranic and epigraphic evidence concurs with respect to the origins of the Vākāṭaka dynasty. The founder of the dynasty was Vindhyaśakti (I), who was succeeded by his son Pravarasena, 'Pravīra' according to the Puranic account.[5] This account mentions four sons of the mighty (*vīryavat*) Pravīra; two of them we know from later epigraphic evidence, Sarvasena I and Gautamīputra, the founders of the Vatsagulma and the Nandivardhana branches of the Vākāṭakas respectively. If we are allowed to believe the (later) Vākāṭaka inscriptions (of both branches), Pravarasena, said to belong to the brahmin Viṣṇuvṛddha *gotra*, ruled as a sovereign monarch (*samrāj*), during which rule he performed four Aśvamedha, a Vājapeya and several other prestigious Vedic sacrifices, a status never attained again by any Vākāṭaka king.[6]

The actual division in the dynastic line may have first evolved when the grandsons of Pravarasena I, Vindhyasena (= Vindhyaśakti II) and Rudrasena I, and their Nāga allies were confronted with Gupta power, though it cannot be altogether excluded that the branch of Sarvasena I had already split off at this stage. The Allahabad Pillar Inscription of Samudragupta testifies to the 'uprooting within a second of the staunch army of the Nāgas' (*kṣaṇād unmūlyācyutanāgasena°*, CII III, 212 vs. 7). Fleet and others have taken this to refer to two kings named Acyuta (Acyutanandin) and Nāgasena. The passage may actually have been meant as a

---

one on whom the ancestral sacrifices of both lineages to which he belongs depend. This would imply—though, admittedly, Medhātithi does not draw this conclusion—that, if his father does have other sons, he is not entitled to the whole inheritance, but to his legitimate portion only (see Manu 9.104, 156), which would entail that he remains subject to the eldest brother (Manu 9.105). Trautmann applies the laws concerning sons given in adoption (*datrima*) to the *dauhitra*, which may be based on Manu 3.11, which I, following Medhātithi, take to mean that one should not marry a brotherless maiden, if her father is not known (i.e., is dead or absent). Since the rules of royal succession usually do not acknowledge legitimate portions, as it would lead to the fragmentation of the kingdom, the elected or appointed successor (*yuvarāja*), who is in actual practice not necessarily the eldest son, does indeed, if he happens to be a *dauhitra* as well, inherit both whole (*akhilam*) patrimonies, i.e. he is a *dvyāmuṣyāyaṇa*, one having dual descent. One can agree with Trautmann that a son having obtained through marriage the qualification of *dauhitra* distinguished his descent from that of his half-brothers by virtue of which he would be more eligible as a *yuvarāja*. As history shows, however, kings were not trying to disinherit a son whom they did not want as their successor by marrying him off to a brotherless maiden (a family strategy to which Trautmann's interpretation would easily lead), but rather they arranged the marriage of that son with a *putrikā*, whom they had destined to be their own heir.

4 Trautmann 1972, 3, 10.

5 Pargiter 1913, 50; CII V, 107 f. vss. 2–6; Shastri in AV, 6 f.

6 CII V, 96 ll. 1–5; ibid. p. 12 ll. 1–4. Cf. Pargiter 1913, 50.

pun on the names of the two Rājas of Āryāvarta, Nāgasena and Acyutanandin, who are listed (in this sequence) later in the inscription, when they are said to be among the ones who have been violently eradicated,[7] a fate that also befell two other Nāga princes, Nāgadatta and Gaṇapatināga, as well as a king called Rudradeva.[8] Goyal (1967, 142) and many historians before and after him have identified this Rudradeva with the Vākāṭaka king Rudrasena I. As we saw, the grouping of the Nāgas together with the Vākāṭaka king Rudra-deva/sena does make sense, but it raises the question of the original homeland of the Vākāṭaka dynasty. If that were the region to the south of the Vindhyas, where we find the great monuments of the later Vākāṭakas, Rudra-deva/sena could not have been mentioned as the first in a list of kings of Āryāvarta, but should have been mentioned in the preceding list of kings of Dakṣiṇāpatha.[9]

A crushing defeat at the hands of Samudragupta, however, may have forced the Vākāṭakas to leave their homeland: Vindhyasena came to rule in Vatsagulma,[10] his nephew Rudrasena—or, if he did not survive the onslaught,[11] the latter's son and successor Pṛthivīṣeṇa I—in Nandivardhana.[12] The power (*śakti*) of the Nāgas, on the other hand, seems to have been curbed (*pratiṣiddha*) to such an extent that one of their young princesses could be withdrawn from her father's authority (*pitur gṛhītā*) in order to be brought up at the Gupta court. This princess, Kuberanāgā, was subsequently, probably with a view to pacifying the Nāgas, given in marriage to Samudragupta's son Candragupta II as one of his chief wives (*mahādevī*).

This hypothetical reconstruction of events is based on a new conjectured reading of verse 5 of the Vākāṭaka inscription in the Kevala-Narasiṃha Temple on Ram-

---

7 *prasabhoddharaṇa°*, CII III, 213 l. 21.

8 Coins of Gaṇapatināga were found in Pawaya (Trivedi 1957, xxii–xxiii, 49–54). We do not possess coins of Nāgadatta and Nāgasena, but the downfall of a king of Padmāvatī with the latter name is mentioned in the *Harṣacarita* (ed. Kane p. 50 ll. 18 f.): *yathā nāgakulajanmanaḥ sārikāśrāvitamantrasyāsīn nāśo nāgasenasya padmāvatyām* |.

9 CII III, 212 f. ll. 19–20.

10 The earliest Vākāṭaka inscription that has come down to us is a grant by the *dharmamahārāja* Vindhyaśakti (II), issued from Vatsagulma (CII V, 96).

11 The eulogy of Rudrasena in the later Vākāṭaka inscriptions, compared to that of his two grandfathers and son, is remarkably short, which may point to a rather infelicitous career.

12 That Samudragupta's conquest resulted in the uprooting of several of his enemies seems to be endorsed by the Vākāṭaka inscription in the Kevala-Narasiṃha Temple on Ramtek Hill (Bakker & Isaacson 1993). A renewed study of this inscription resulted in some additional readings and conjectures. I therefore present a revised edition in Appendix I. One of these new conjectures is to read *pāda* a of verse 2 as: *dūreṇa rājarṣisamudraguptaḥ* . This would imply that verses 2 to 5 are concerned with Samudragupta and verse 6 (or the verse that is possibly lost after this) introduces his son Candragupta II who married the girl who 'had grown up like a flame' (vs. 5). Consequently verse 3 refers to the kings who were vanquished by Samudragupta and brought him tribute, whereas verse 4 seems to refer to the extension of his rule to the borders of the ocean.

tek Hill.[13] Trautmann had already remarked that, 'Samudra Gupta, as we have seen, claims to have exterminated the rulers of more than one Nāga kingdom, and yet we find his son married to a Nāga princess, as if to cement the amicable conclusion of his father's wars against one of those kingdoms.'[14] Our reinterpretation of the Ramtek inscription also puts a phrase in the Poona and Ṛiddhapur Inscriptions of Kuberanāgā's daughter, Prabhāvatī Guptā, in another light: '...the daughter of Mahārājādhirāja Candragupta, who belongs to the Dhāraṇa *gotra*, who is born from a chief queen Kuberanāgā who was (herself) born in the Nāga dynasty, (this daughter) who is, as it were, the ornament of both dynasties, and who is a fervent devotee of the Lord ...';[15] 'both dynasties' should be taken to refer to the Nāgas and Guptas, not to the latter and the Vākāṭakas as is done by Mirashi (CII V, 37), since the Vākāṭakas as such are still to be mentioned and then only in passing.[16] The history of Prabhāvatī's mother, born in the Nāga House, but grown up at the Gupta court, may have induced Prabhāvatī to style herself princess of the Nāga as well as Gupta family. It seems even likely that her *gotra*, Dhāraṇa, was that of the Nāga family and not, as is usually assumed on the basis of later practice, that of the Guptas.[17] The name Dhāraṇa occurs in the list of Nāgas said to be the sons of Kaśyapa (MBh 5.101.16). The *gotra* of the Guptas, if any, is unknown, since it is never mentioned in their own inscriptions, indicating their humble origin.

The issue of the original homeland of the Vākāṭakas was taken up by A. M. Shastri at a seminar on *The Age of the Vākāṭakas* held in Nagpur 1984.[18] Shastri arrived at the conclusion that the kings Vindhyaśakti and Pravarasena ruled over the Vindhya area to the north of the Narmada river. According to the Puranic account, the mighty Pravīra, i.e. Pravarasena, ruled for sixty years from his capital Kāñcana(kā),[19] which Shastri proposed to identify with 'the modern village of Nachna or Nachna-kī-talāi in the Panna District of the Bundelkhand Division of

13 See Appendix I vs. 5; cf. Bakker & Isaacson 1993, 53.

14 Trautmann 1972, 15 n. 31.

15 CII V, 7 ll. 7–8, 36 ll. 8–9: [...] *mahārājādhirājaśrīcandraguptas tasya duhitā dhāraṇasagotrā nāgakulasambhūtāyāṃ śrīmahādevyāṃ kuberanāgāyām utpannobhayakulālaṅkārabhūtātyantabhagavadbhaktā* [...].

16 CII V, 7 l. 9, 10: *vākāṭakānāṃ mahārājaśrīrudrasenasyāgramahiṣī.*

17 Prabhāvatī's own inscriptions prove that it was possible for princesses of high birth to retain their own *gotra* after being married. Sircar 1967 I, 204–9, 236. Cf. Ashvini Agrawal, 1989, 83 f. A brahmin belonging to the Dhāraṇi *gotra* was the recipient of a grant by the Paramabhaṭṭāraka; see below n. 91 on p. 29.

18 The paper was eventually published in 1992 in the proceedings of this conference, referred to as AV.

19 Pargiter 1913, 50. Jayaswal, followed by Mirashi, proposed to emend the text *purīṃ kāñcanakāṃ ca vai* to *purikāṃ canakāṃ ca vai*, which would alter the name of the capital into Canakā; see the discussion in Shastri in AV, 7.

Madhya Pradesh.'[20] Shastri's arguments, of which the most significant are the very name of the founder of the dynasty, Vindhyaśakti, and the association of the two kings in the Puranic account with the Vindhya,[21] are well-reasoned and convincing, apart from one, viz. his identification of the Vākāṭaka king Pṛthivīṣeṇa, whom Vyāghradeva mentions in his Nachnē-kī-talāī and Ganj Stone Inscriptions as his overlord, with Pṛthivīṣeṇa I, son of Rudrasena I.[22] As will be argued below (p. 48), there are good reasons to assume that, after the death of Prabhāvatī Guptā, the old Vākāṭaka–Gupta antagonism reemerged. It will be shown that Pṛthivīṣeṇa II, in the days that Gupta power was waning, succeeded in persuading/coercing a local king to acknowledge his overlordship over the ancient homeland of his dynasty, Bundelkhand. Rudrasena I, on the other hand, may still have ruled from Kāñcana(kā) (Canakā)/Nachna.[23]

---

20 Shastri in AV, 9. For a description of the archaeological site of Nachna (24°.24′ N, 80°.29′ E) see Williams 1982, 105–114.

21 Pargiter 1913, 50. The description of the Vākāṭakas is followed by the words, *vindhyakānāṃ kule 'tīte* ..., 'After the dynasty that belonged to the Vindhyas, ...'

22 Shastri in AV, 10 f.; Shastri 1995a. Shastri carefully avoids mentioning another potential piece of evidence for the northern origin of the Vākāṭakas, which by some has been connected with the early history of this dynasty, viz. a number of seals found at the site of Bhita (Allahabad District), excavated by Marshal (ASI *Annual Report* 1911–12, 50 ff.). Two of these seals contain the name Gautamīputra, but in both cases the names are further specified by another appellation, Vṛṣadhvaja and Śivamā(e)gha. The legend of the seal of Vṛṣadhvaja Gautamīputra calls him 'Vindhyab(v)edhanamahārāja whose kingdom was graciously granted to him by Maheśvara-Mahāsena' (*śrīvindhyabedhanamahārājasya maheśvaramahāsenātisṛṣṭarājyasya*, Thaplyal 1972, 46 ff.). The neatly cut characters of this seal are datable to the 3rd or 4th century. The combination Vindhyavedhana and Gautamīputra led M. G. Pai (who proposes to read *vindhyavardhana°*) to identify this king with the Vākāṭaka Gautamīputra, grandson of Vindhyaśakti I (JIH XIV, 16 ff.). Against this identification it may be objected that the name Vākāṭaka does not occur on these seals, that Gautamīputra is never called 'Mahārāja' in the inscriptions of the Vākāṭakas, and that the names Vṛṣadhvaja and Śivamegha are unknown to the records of this dynasty.

23 This king is styled an *atyantasvāmimahābhairavabhakta*, Mahārāja of the Vākāṭakas. The religious title of Rudrasena I seems to me intrinsically different from the later general titles of Pṛthivīṣeṇa I and Pravarasena II, viz. *atyanta/parama-māheśvara*, which denote that these kings were very devout Māheśvaras (see Chapter 2). The words *svāmi* and *bhakta* preceding and following Mahābhairava suggest that a particular deity, i.e. temple image, was meant, which might be looked for in Nachna, if indeed this was the old Vākāṭaka capital. Nachna certainly is an ancient Śaiva centre with a wealth of Shaivite archaeological remains, though these date from the last quarter of the 5th century and later, when the site was under the control of the Uccakalpa king, Vyāghradeva, feudatory of Pṛthivīṣeṇa II, and his successors. They probably replaced, however, earlier constructions. The presence of the Pāśupata order would be attested by a loose sculpture found in Nachna, if that were a Lakulīśa image (Williams 1982, 113, Plate 163). However, I am not fully convinced that we are here concerned with Lakulīśa, since the deity's attribute seems to be a battle-axe, rather than a club (see below p. 100). The fragment lying next to this image is an old Viṣṇu bust, somewhat comparable to the Nagardhan Viṣṇu

On account of what has been said above, we may assume that, around the middle of the 4th century or somewhat later, after Samudragupta had firmly established his authority in Bundelkhand, a group of Vākāṭaka nobles and their entourage, along with what remained of their army, either under the command of their king Rudrasena I or his son, withdrew along the ancient southern highway that connected the central and eastern parts of the plain of the Ganges with the northern Deccan (the route of the present National Highway No. 7). They crossed the Narmada river and the Satpura Range and succeeded in carving out another kingdom for themselves in Vidarbha, in the fertile plain of the Beṇṇā or Wainganga, where they built a new royal residence, named Nandivardhana, at the foot of a prominent hill, the Rāmagiri.[24]

With Mahārāja Pṛthivīṣeṇa I (son of Rudrasena I), who is styled an *atyantamāheśvara*,[25] an era of glorious rule began, comparable to that of the legendary Yudhiṣṭhira; that is to say, if we are allowed to believe the eulogy of this king in the inscriptions of his son and grandson, according to which he was 'endowed with the following virtues among others: truthfulness, uprightness, compassion, courage, valour, good policy and conduct, magnanimity as well as wisdom, generosity towards those who well deserve it, victoriousness in the *dharma* and purity of mind.' And, the inscriptions continue, 'his son(s) and granson(s), the lineage, and the accomplishments, viz. authority and wealth, were increasing over a period of one century.'[26] Pṛthivīṣeṇa I also started the practice of making land grants in the outlying districts of his kingdom, as may be deduced from the Pāṇḍhurṇa (palimpsest) Plates of Pravarasena II.[27] However, the right to bear the title *samrāj* was lost to the Vākāṭakas forever.

The group around Sarvasena I or his son Vindhyasena, on the other hand, after having split off at an unknown stage, settled in Vatsagulma, further to the west, on the Ajanta Plateau,[28] where Vindhyasena is credited with a victory over his southern

---

(Plate XXVII), and next to that lies a fragment that Williams describes as 'a four-headed Brahmā' (op. cit. 113), but which may just as well be a Maheśvara image (cf. Plates I & II). As far as a photograph allows one to make any judgement, I am inclined to consider these loose fragments by and large contemporaneous with the Vākāṭaka material.

24 Present-day Ramtek Hill: 21°.28′ N, 79°.28′ E. Next to nothing is known about the immediate predecessors of the Vākāṭakas in Vidarbha. Local chieftains may have filled the power vacuum caused by the collapse of Sātavāhana power in the Deccan in the 3rd century AD.

25 This qualification is conspicuously absent in the Mandhal Inscription of his son, the Vaiṣṇava king Rudrasena II (Shastri & Gupta 1985, 227 l. 8), but found in all later inscriptions.

26 *satyārjavakāruṇyaśauryavikramanayavinayamāhātmyadhīmattvapātragatabha[kti]tvadharmavijayitvamanonairmalyādiguṇais samupetasya* || *va[rṣa]śatam abhivardhamānakośadaṇḍasādhanasantānaputrapautriṇa[ḥ]*, CII V, 12 ll. 9–12; cf. Shastri & Gupta 1985, 227 l. 8–10.

27 CII V, 66 l. 19.

28 Modern Basim: 20°.10′ N, 77°.11′ E, in the Akola District.

enemy, the king of Kuntala.[29]

The Period of Construction: Rudrasena II and Prabhāvatī Guptā

To judge by the archaeological and epigraphical remains, the group that had settled in eastern Vidarbha was the most prominent of the two collateral branches, at least until the middle of the 5th century; it is consequently often referred to as the 'Main Branch.'[30] A factor that undoubtedly contributed enormously to the material and cultural flourishing of the eastern Vākāṭakas is that Pṛthivīṣeṇa I concluded the peace with Candragupta II, Samudragupta's successor, who had ascended the Gupta throne at the beginning of the last quarter of the 4th century after a succession struggle (see below p. 27). Now that the Vindhyas were safely under their control and the Vākāṭakas no longer posed a direct threat to their empire, the long-term strategic interests of the Guptas required a reliable and strong ally at the southern borders of their realm. To assure this Candragupta II was prepared to give a daughter from his marriage with the Nāga princess Kuberanāgā to Pṛthivīṣeṇa I's son Rudrasena II, in the ninth decade of the 4th century.[31] The proud bridegroom leading

29 Ajaṇṭā Cave Inscription of Varāhadeva, CII V, 108 vs. 8. There is some difference of opinion as to the precise area covered by the kingdom of Kuntala. Mirashi has investigated the problem carefully and collected the data. He comes to the conclusion that in the 5th century the kingdom of Kuntala comprised the upper and central valleys of the Kṛṣṇa river (south of its Bhima tributary), including the early Rāṣṭrakūṭa capital Mānapura, but not Vanavāsī (Mirashi in SI II, 155–163). On the basis of this conclusion Mirashi argued that this kingdom was ruled by the early Rāṣṭrakūṭas of Mānapura. He suggests that the victory of Vindhyasena could thus have been over the Rāṣṭrakūṭa king Mānāṅka (EI XXXVII, 16). This would make Mānāṅka a fourth century king, and his grandson Avidheya, who issued the Pandarangapalli Grant (EI XXXVII, 20–23), a contemporary of Pravarasena II. In these Pandarangapalli Plates Avidheya says of his grandfather that 'he had frightened the countries of Vidarbha and Aśmaka by his policies': *vasa(su)dhāvidha(dhi)santrastavidabhā(rbhā)śmakamaṇḍalaḥ* [|*] *mānāṅkanṛpatiḥ śrīmān kuntalānāṃ pra[śā]sitā* [||1||*], EI XXXVII, 20 l. 1. The reading of the first hemistich, however, is far from certain.

30 I see no reason why Trautmann and others should qualify the eastern Vākāṭakas as the 'senior branch,' the Vatsagulma Branch as 'junior' (Trautmann 1972, 10).

31 Trautmann 1972, 15 n. 31: 'Was Prabhāvatī's maternal line related to Bhavanāga? The law of prohibited degrees which neither the Guptas nor the Vākāṭakas are otherwise known to have violated probably rules out too close a relationship, but it is tempting to see in Prabhāvatī's Nāga connexion the renewal of an old alliance between the Vākāṭakas and the Nāgas, as well as the start of a new one with the Guptas.' As we will see below (p. 17), the rules referred to were at least once violated and Trautmann's suggestion of a close relationship with the lineage of Bhavanāga has therefore become more feasible. At the same time it may prove that judicial hairsplitting as discussed above (n. 3 on p. 9) has only academic value in the Indian historical reality of power politics (cf. Joshi in RGH, 115).

his young Gupta princess to her new home in triumph, across the Vindhyas, along the very route that only two generations before his family had probably taken to escape the Gupta rod, must have afforded a fine spectacle. The bride, the younger sister of several brothers, 'who resembled the lustre of the moon,' and whose girlhood name evidently was Muṇḍā,[32] turned out to be a formidable lady, who became famous under the name of Prabhāvatī Guptā, a name that she may have adopted after her husband's death, when she became acting monarch.[33] She brought with her the Vaiṣṇava Bhāgavata faith and the cultural assets and sophistication of the Gupta court. To judge by her inscriptions, in which seven lines are devoted to the eulogy of her imperial origins and only one line to her Vākāṭaka husband—denoting her father Candragupta as Mahārājādhirāja, her husband as Mahārāja—she might have thought herself far above the family of her in-laws, though her marriage was actually, in Dharmaśāstra categories, *anuloma*. By emphasizing her descent from the Nāga family of the Dhāraṇa *gotra* she may have intended to make up for the obscure origins of her paternal lineage (see above p. 12).

A tragic event meant that this girl had to assume full responsibility for the royal house in which she had married. After a rule of about one decade her husband died in c. AD 405, leaving her with three boys and at least one daughter. She adopted the regency over her eldest son, the *yuvarāja* Divākarasena,[34] but apparently he too died before he was allowed to ascend the throne.[35] Her regency over her two remaining sons may have lasted one or two years more, which brought the total duration of the rule of this dowager queen to thirteen or fourteen years, from c. AD 405 to 419, an exceptionally long term by Indian standards. It seems likely that she could not have completed it, if she had not had the full and powerful back-

32 See Appendix I vs. 7 (cf. Bakker & Isaacson 1993, 53). I am now pretty certain that the syllable preceding *muṇḍa* forms no part of the name, but may be the demonstrative pronoun *sā*.

33 If Kuberanāgā was five years old when she was taken from her parental home to the Gupta court in, say, AD 355, and if she was married to Candragupta II at the age of sixteen, their wedding must have taken place in AD 366 (cf. Kane 1930–62 II, 446 f. and Altekar 1959, 58 on the marriageable age of *kṣatriya* girls). If Muṇḍā, who had at least three elder brothers, was born in the sixth year of this marriage and was wedded to the Vākāṭaka crown-prince at the age of sixteen, Rudrasena II's wedding must have taken place in AD 388. The Gupta princess may have been thirty-three when she succeeded her husband Rudrasena, whose death is usually dated in about AD 405. Cf. Goyal 1967, 107 f.

34 *yuvarāja[śrī]divākarasenajananī*, CII V, 7 ll. 9–10. The seal of these Poona Plates of Prabhāvatī, issued during the thirteenth year of her regency, runs: '[By] the enemy chastising order of the Mother of the *Yuvarāja*, who is the ornament of the Vākāṭakas and has attained royal fortune by inheritance': *vākāṭakalalāmasya [kra]maprāptanṛpaśriya[ḥ] | jananyā yuvarājasya śāsanaṃ ripuśāsa[nam ||]*, CII V, 8.

35 As we will see below Divākarasena is no longer mentioned as a son or king in the later charters of Prabhāvatī; in his stead two other sons of hers are called Mahārāja. See below p. 22.

ing of the Gupta family.[36] Evidence of the Kevala-Narasiṃha Temple Inscription endorses this supposition. Prabhāvatī Guptā had her daughter, whose name is partly illegible but may have been Atibhāvatī (vs. 24), married off to her half-brother, Ghaṭotkaca,[37] who ruled as a viceroy in eastern Malwa and Bundelkhand—that is in the land of her daughter's Vākāṭaka and Nāga ancestors—at the time her other brother, Kumāragupta, held the imperial office.[38] It may be objected that this type of maternal uncle–niece marriage would be against the law (*dharma*), but so is the rule of a dowager, and it is a fact of life, in India as well as elsewhere, that power politics remains within the precincts of the law only as long as suits its aims.[39] It thus seems that we are here concerned with an unprecedented example of matrimonial policy to consolidate matrilinear bonds (see above p. 11). Whether everyone in the Vākāṭaka family was happy at the wedding is another matter. As will be seen below, the girl's brother undertook serious steps to annul this matrimonial alliance after her husband's death.

The period in which Rudrasena II and his queen Prabhāvatī ruled the eastern Vākāṭaka kingdom, the last decade of the 4th and first two decades of the 5th century, is marked by a remarkable cultural and religious activity.

Two inscriptions of Rudrasena II himself refer to an important part of his kingdom, viz. the land that stretches along the west bank of the Wainganga (designated

---

36 When Rudrasena II died, Divākarasena, being the eldest of at least three boys and one girl, must have been between ten and sixteen years old. Prabhāvatī thus ruled when the *yuvarāja* was already between twenty-three and twenty-nine. This is quite extraordinary, even if the lower extreme were the correct age; it indicates that Prabhāvatī was more than just a regent, but was virtually wearing the royal crown of the Vākāṭakas, no doubt to the satisfaction of her Gupta relatives (cf. the succession to the throne of Sarvasena II of the Vatsagulma Branch who was only eight years old when his father died; CII V, 108 vs. 10). If our chronological reconstruction above (n. 33 on p. 16) is correct, and if we assume that Divākarasena was born in the second year of Rudrasena's marriage (i.e. in AD 390), he must have been twenty-eight when his mother issued her Poona charter.

37 Appendix I vss. 11–13 (cf. Bakker & Isaacson 1993, 53).

38 CII III, 276–279; see Bakker & Isaacson 1993, 66. The most probable date of this wedding is between Candragupta II's death (AD 415) and Dāmodarasena/Pravarasena's succession to the throne (AD 419). The former as well as the latter may have objected to this extraordinary policy of Prabhāvatī to take advantage of her three-cornered relationship that connected her with the Guptas, Vākāṭakas and the Nāgas, in whose lands Ghaṭotkaca reigned as viceroy. Atibhāvatī may have been about sixteen years old at the time of her wedding. This princess, to whom the Ramtek inscription is to be ascribed, was more proud of her Gupta affiliation than of her Vākāṭaka one. Just as in the inscriptions of her mother, the Gupta dynasty is eulogized extensively at the expense of Atibhāvatī's Vākāṭaka relatives.

39 The present case corroborates an observation made by the champion of Dharmaśāstra, P. V. Kane, to the effect that 'a very striking instance of the limits of *sapiṇḍa* relationship not being observed is the practice among certain sections of even brāhmaṇas [...] marrying their own sister's daughter' (Kane 1930–62 II, 467).

Beṇṇātaṭa in the inscriptions), in which the present-day villages of Mandhal and Deotek are situated.[40] In between Mandhal and Deotek, on the Wainganga river, lies the ancient site of Pauni, well-known for its Buddhist *stūpas* from the Sātavāhana period.[41]

In Deotek an undated palimpsest stone inscription was found, which is for the greater part illegible, but which certainly refers to a temple (*dharmasthāna*) at Cikkambu[rī]—the village Cīkmārā, within a kilometer south-west of Deotek. It would seem to have been a place of worship of Rudrasena.[42] The other inscription is a grant 'incised on a set of four [copper] plates, ... discovered while ploughing a field at Māṇḍhaḷ.'[43] The inscription is of paramount importance, not only because it is the first dated inscription of the eastern Vākāṭakas—dated in the 5th regnal year of Rudrasena (II)—but also because, in the words of Shastri,

> The grant is said to have been made at the message or command (*sandeśa*) of god Vishṇu called Mondasvāmin and described as carrying a conchshell, a wheel and a sword and resting in the *yoga-nidrā* on the body of the snake-king called Ananta in the ocean.[44]

---

40 Mandhal: 20°.57′ N, 79°.27′ E; c. 42 km south-east of Nagpur, 52 km south of Rāmagiri, c. 20 km to the west of the Wainganga river bed. Deotek: 20°.36′ N, 79°.44′ E; also c. 20 km west of the Wainganga, 47 km south-east of Mandhal.

41 Pauni: 20°.45′ N, 79°.42′ E, in the Bhandara District. A. M. Shastri remarks about this region that 'it was well-known for abundant paddy cultivation. It is interesting to note that the Bhandara region is even now regarded as the rice-bowl of Maharashtra' (Shastri in AV, 238). S. B. Deo & J. P. Joshi (eds.) 1972; see also A. Ghosh 1989, *An Encyclopaedia of Indian Archaeology* II, s.v.

42 Mirashi in SI I, 109–117; CII V, 1–4: *idaṃ rudrasenarā[jñaḥ] [sva*]dharmasthānaṃ (nam |)*. Mirashi assigns the earlier inscription on this stone to the times of Aśoka and thinks its object was to record 'the command of some lord (*Sāmi*), prohibiting the capture and slaughter,' evidently of animals (op. cit., 111, 113). In view of what has been said above, we think it very unlikely that the superimposed inscription belongs to Rudrasena I, as Mirashi thinks (CII V, 3). There is a small dilapidated temple near the place where the inscribed slab of stone was found (for a description see Cunningham's ASI *Reports* Vol. VII, 123–5). Mirashi (CII V, 3) observes: 'Though the present structure cannot date back to the fourth century A.C., to which period the inscription can be referred, it undoubtedly marks an ancient site and may have been erected when the original temple fell into ruins.'

43 Shastri in AV, 227. IAR 1981–82, 81. This Vākāṭaka inscription has been edited by A. M. Shastri & C. Gupta in 1985 in an article published in a felicitation volume offered to V. Bh. Kolte (in Marathi). The inscription has been discussed by Shastri in an English article that was published no less than three times: in the *Nagpur University Journal* 35 (1984–86), 130–164; in *Early History of the Deccan. Problems and Perspectives*, Delhi 1987; in *The Age of the Vākāṭakas*, Delhi 1992. In an article in the ABORI (1994) Shastri discusses the inscription again and mentions (op. cit. p. 114 n. 12) for the first time that the inscription has been edited by him (together with C. Gupta) in 1984 (read 1985).

44 Shastri in AV, 228. Apparently the Sanskrit text is partly illegible; I reproduce the text of this inscription (here and further below) exactly (including interspace) as it is given by Shastri &

It is evident that this refers to a Viṣṇu temple. We shall deal with the archaeological sites in the vicinity of Mandhal in Chapter 3. Here it may be observed that there existed at least three Hindu temples at Mandhal, the oldest of which may date from the last quarter of the 4th century, and we venture the conjecture that one of the later ones (beginning of the 5th century) was dedicated to 'Mondasvāmin.' We have seen above that the girlhood name of Rudrasena's wife may have been Muṇḍā, and it is tempting to assume that this Bhāgavata temple was erected by her and that she lent her name to that of the deity of the temple.[45] I do not subscribe to Shastri's view that 'there can be no doubt whatever that the Mondasvāmin known from the Māṇḍhaḷ plates of the Vākāṭaka monarch Rudrasena II was actually an Ananta-śayana image installed in the *sanctum sanctorum* and the temple was dedicated to him.'[46] No doubt the temple was dedicated to 'Mondasvāmin,' but his praise in the first sentence has no other function than to identify this deity with the supreme cosmic god Viṣṇu/Nārāyaṇa/Vāsudeva, regardless of the iconography of the idol. The iconography of the images found in Mandhal does not support Shastri's view.[47]

Gupta (1985, 227 ll. 1–2): *bhagavato ekārṇṇava – salilavistārita nāgarājñonannasya tasya vaca sphuṭaphaṭājalabhogaśāyiyoganidrāmupagatasya śaṅkhacakkrāsidhāriṇaḥ devada(de)–vasya mondasvāminassandeśāt[|*]* Since no photographs of the inscription have been published so far, these readings cannot be checked. Shastri conjectures that *nannasya* may be read as *'nannasya = anantasya*. The deity described not only rests on the coils (*bhoga*) of the serpent king but is also covered (*jālita*?) by his expanded hoods (*sphuṭaphaṭā*).

45 According to Shastri & Gupta's edition the text reads *monda°*, with dentals instead of cerebrals. However, *ṇḍa* and *nda* are mainly distinguished in the script of the Vākāṭaka inscriptions by the top of the cerebral nasal and this differentiation may have been blurred or overlooked. Since Shastri could not connect 'monda' with a 'personal name prevalent among the social elite as the founder or financier of a shrine may rightly be supposed to have been,' he proposes to connect it with a toponym by pointing to two present-day villages in the neighbourhood called Maudā and Ḍoṅgar Maudā (Shastri 1994, 115). It seems more likely, however, that the toponyms preserve the ancient name of the temple than that the temple-name derived from these toponyms.

46 Shastri 1994, 118.

47 A contemporaneous Anantaśayana relief is found in Udayagiri Excavation 13 (see Williams 1982, 46 f., Plate 39). It is quite possible, even likely, that a similar relief once decorated the Mondasvāmin temple. An early reference to 'Viṣṇu [...] as resting on the wide and spotless couch that is the single (i.e., cosmic) ocean' (*ekārṇavavipulavimalaparyaṅkatalaśāyinaḥ ...viṣṇoḥ*) is found in the inscription of the Valkhā king Bhuluṇḍa dated in the [Gupta] year 47 (=AD 365/6). This king, called 'servant of Svāmi Nārāyaṇa,' donated five villages on the southern bank of the Narmadā to the temple of this god (*deva*) who, in addition to the above qualification, is praised as 'the *guru* of the gods' etc., as 'possessed of eight arms,' as 'the one who broke the pride of Bali' etc., 'who as Varāha recovered the earth' etc. (Ramesh & Tewari 1990, 1). Just as there is no need to assume that this temple contained an idol of Varāha, so too there is no need to believe that its idol was an Anantaśayana image. Differently, however, Shastri (op. cit., 114): 'This description would show that eight armed Śeṣa-Śayana images were already well-known in Central India during the third-fourth centuries A.D. though no actual example answering this description dating from such an early age has been reported as yet.'

The same inscription further refers to the existence in the same region of two religious establishments or communities (*adhivāsa*) of the Sātvata school, which, or the members of which, apparently originated from Vatsagulma.[48] The Sātvatas were a Vaiṣṇava devotional (*bhakti*) sect promulgating the Bhāgavata mode of worship, centering around the five, later four, Vṛṣṇi or Sātvata deities: Vāsudeva/Kṛṣṇa, Saṃkarṣaṇa/Balarāma, Pradyumna, Aniruddha and Sāmba.[49] Rudrasena's ancestors had been Śaivas,[50] and he too, to judge by the wealth of Śaiva images at Mandhal, patronized this form of Hinduism. Yet, Rudrasena II is reported to have embraced—probably under the influence of his Gupta wife—the Bhāgavata faith and he describes himself as the one 'whose rule has been installed by Him whose emblem is the *cakra*, viz. the Lord.'[51]

The object of the Mandhal Inscription of Rudrasena II is the endowment or grant of a group of four villages in the eastern part of the administrative division of Padmapura,[52] but it is not entirely clear who exactly are the beneficiaries. Shastri thinks 'that the granted villages appear to have turned into an *agrahāra* (Brāhmaṇa settlement) which was placed under the Brāhmaṇas belonging to different *gotras*

---

48 The edition (Shastri & Gupta 1985, 228 ll. 17–18) reads *vātsagulmaka (kā)ryyasātvata-caraṇādhivāsadvayasya*. In the English articles discussing this passage Shastri reads *vātsa-gulmakasya sātvata°* and argues that this is a *sāpekṣasamāsa* in which *vātsagulmakasya* is intended as an adjective of *sātvatacaraṇa* and not of the entire compound, 'used in the sense of one originally belonging to and hailing from Vatsagulma' (Shastri 1994, 116 n. 17). This interpretation seems plausible, if indeed this is the reading of the text, since in the (emended) reading of the edition (*vātsagulmakāryasātvata°*) the problem would not occur.

49 See Chapter 2.

50 This is true for his Vākāṭaka as well as his Nāga forbears. The former (Rudrasena I) is described as *atyantasvāmimahābhairavabhakta* and the latter (Bhavanāga) is said to belong to a 'House that was installed by Śiva, who was pleased that its members wore His emblem, the *liṅga*, placed as a load on their shoulders' (*aṃsabhārasaṃniveśitaśivaliṅgodvahanaśivasuparituṣṭa-samutpāditarājavaṃśa*, CII V, 12 ll. 4 f.), which might be seen as an aetiological etymology of their family name 'Bhāraśiva.' As noted above (n. 25 on p. 14), Rudrasena II is silent with regard to the religious persuasion of his father Pṛthivīṣeṇa, who is called an *atyantamāheśvara* by his grandson Pravarasena II.

51 *bhagavataścakkralakṣmapratiṣṭhitaśāsanasya*, Shastri & Gupta 1985, 227 l. 11. This is changed in the inscriptions of his son into: 'whose royal fortune was obtained by the grace of Cakrapāṇi, the Lord' (*bhagavataś cakrapāṇeḥ prasādopārjitaśrīsamudayasya*, CII V, 12 ll. 13–14)—not merely because, as Shastri observes, this is 'grammatically more acceptable,' but because Pravarasena, who had again embraced the Śaiva faith of his ancestors, thought it politically more acceptable; for as a Māheśvara he could not officially declare that the rule of his father, or of his House for that matter, had been installed by Viṣṇu. For similar reasons Rudrasena II may have left out the religious affiliation of his father (see n. 25 on p. 14).

52 Selluddraha, Accabhallikā, Saragrāmakā and Aragrāmakā, which are situated to the west of Kurudumbhaka, to the north of the two Śaṅkhikas, to the east of Bābbaikā and to the south of Phukudumbhaka (Shastri & Gupta 1985, 228 ll. 15–17). The locations of these villages are uncertain; cf. Mahajan in AV, 73 f.

and *charaṇas* and engaged in study.'[53] The inscription (in the sentence quoted in the preceding note) states that the usual privileges and exemptions applicable to *agrahāra* villages were accorded to (*vitarāmaḥ*) the learned brahmins 'thereof' (*cāsya*), that is of the land granted; that land, i.e. the four villages, was apparently (already) inhabited/possessed by the members of two Sātvata religious communities who hailed from Vatsagulma. These two communities are mentioned in the sentence that describes the four villages, which precedes the statement about the privileges granted. The learned brahmins, including those who were members of the two Sātvata communities, may therefore have been the donees in the sense that they were exempted from taxes etc.[54]

About the other religious centre, the sacred compound on the Rāmagiri, which may have developed somewhat later than the one in Mandhal—say during the first quarter of the 5th century—we are chiefly informed through the inscriptions of (or related to) queen Prabhāvatī, that is after Rudrasena II's demise.[55] The hill to the north of Nandivardhana developed, it would seem, into a sort of official state sanctuary, dedicated to Viṣṇu and his *avatāras*.

A pavilion enshrining the footprints of Viṣṇu occupied the spur of this hill. The hill had been associated with a visit of the epic hero Rāma and his wife Sītā, either before the Vākāṭakas had arrived or during the period at issue. The *atyanta-bhagavadbhaktā* Prabhāvatī, who professed 'to meditate on the feet of the Lord,'[56]

---

53 Shastri in AV, 228. This interpretation is based on the following sentence of the text as edited by Shastri & Gupta 1985, 228 ll. 18–20 (faithfully reproduced, including interspaces): *ucitā(tāṃ)ścāsya brāhmaṇānā(nāṃ)nānāgotracaraṇāta(nāṃ)ya sa[dyā]ya* [**svādhyāya°*, in note] *niratānā (nāṃ) pūrvvarājñānumatām(n) cāturvve(rvvai)dyāgrahāra maryyādāparihārānvitarāmaḥ [|*]* Shastri 1994, 115 f. has a rather cryptic interpretation: 'The inscription states that the land earlier granted to the two monasteries of the Sātvata school originally belonged to Vatsagulma …' What originally may have belonged to Vatsagulma is the Sātvata school or its members, but not the land granted.

54 The last part of the sentence that begins with the description of the location of the four villages (the fourth one being Aragrāmakā) runs: […] *aragrāmakānāmagrāmaḥ vātsagulmaka (kā)ryyasātvatacaraṇādhivāsadvayasya| apūrvvadatyā(ttyā) udakapūrvvamatisṛṣṭaḥ [|*]* (op. cit. ll. 17–18). The clause, *apūrvadattyā udakapūrvam atisṛṣṭaḥ*, occurs in many Vākāṭaka inscriptions and means that the land had not earlier been granted and was donated after an oblation of water. The genitive *°dvayasya* depends, it would seem, on the preceding four *grāmas* and signifies that these villages were in one way or another connected with the two Sātvata communities. For Shastri's paraphrase, 'barring the land earlier granted in favour of a couple of monasteries of the Sātvata school originally belonging to Vatsagulma' (Shastri in AV, 228), I see no ground.

55 CII V, 35 (Ṛiddhapur Plates); Bakker & Isaacson 1993 (Kevala-Narasiṃha Temple Inscription); Shastri in AV, 233 f. (Miregaon Charter), 239 (Māṇḍhaḷ Plates of Pṛthivīsheṇa II).

56 *bhagavatpādānudhyātā*, CII V, 36 ll. 10–11, which may as well be interpreted as 'whose rule was sanctioned/favoured by the Lord.'

issued two charters from 'the soles of the feet/footprints of the Lord of Rāmagiri.'[57] Elsewhere (Bakker 1992b) we have argued that two other temples arose on the hill during this period. The shrine of Varāha, the boar *avatāra* of Viṣṇu, which still stands today (Plate XXXII A), may have been erected by Rudrasena II and/or his spouse to transfer merit to the former's father, king Pṛthivīṣeṇa I, paying tribute by way of metaphor to Pṛthivīṣeṇa's recovery of the Vākāṭaka kingdom, analogous to Varāha's rescue of the earth (*pṛthivī*).[58] And the so-called Rudra-Narasiṃha Temple, enshrining a large image of Viṣṇu's man-lion incarnation, may have been erected by Prabhāvatī to transfer merit to her deceased husband. The enshrined god, seated in *mahārājalīlāsana*, the relaxed, gentle but sovereign pose of a king—his right knee pulled up, supporting lightly the right arm that holds the *cakra*, the symbol of royal power, dignity and sovereignty—may have been consciously reminiscent 'of the illustrious Mahārāja of the Vākāṭakas, Rudrasena II,' 'whose rule was installed by Him whose emblem is the *cakra*' (Plate XXXIII C).[59]

THE PERIOD OF CONSOLIDATION AND BLOOM: DĀMODARASENA AND PRAVARASENA II

After her long rule as regent for her sons, Prabhāvatī Guptā continued to play an important role in the affairs of the kingdom. This follows from charters of land donations made in the nineteenth and twentieth regnal year of her son Pravarasena II. In these inscriptions she describes herself as the 'Mother of the Mahārājas of the Vākāṭakas, the illustrious Dāmodarasena and Pravarasena.'[60] Evidently, after the early death of Divākarasena, two sons remained, but the expression quoted above was long a mystery and often taken as referring to one king only, viz. Pravarasena II, because no inscriptions of Dāmodarasena have come to light. That we are actually concerned with two kings follows from an inscription dating from the twentieth regnal year of Pravarasena, newly found in Miregaon. The seal attached to this charter has been preserved and reads, '[By] the enemy chastising order of the illustrious Prabhāvatī Guptā, the mother of *two* valorous kings of the

---

57 *rāmagirisvāminaḥ pādamūlād*, CII V, 35 l. 1; Shastri in AV, 233 (Miregaon Charter).

58 Bakker 1992b, 12 f. Prabhāvatī may have got the idea of this metaphor from her father, who had a Varāha image carved in the Udayagiri Cave 5 near Vidiśā (Plate XLVI). Cf. Asher 1983.

59 *vākāṭakānāṃ mahārājaśrīrudrasenasya* (CII V, 7 l. 9) and above n. 51 on p. 20 (cf. below p. 52). Bakker 1992b, 14; Bakker & Isaacson 1993, 69.

60 *vākāṭakānāṃ mahārājaśrīdāmodarasenapravarasenajananī*, CII V, 36 l. 10; Shastri in AV, 233, reporting the contents of the Miregaon Charter of the Reign of Pravarasena II, Year 20, which is not yet published.

Vākāṭakas.'[61] This new evidence allows us to conclude that, either Dāmodarasena ruled only for a short period, or was in one way or another incapable to exercising his royal rights. Since his mother styles him 'valorous king,' the latter option is less likely; we therefore have to assume that Dāmodarasena held the royal office for a short period before his younger brother Pravarasena II ascended the throne of Nandivardhana.[62]

Pravarasena II ruled for at least twenty years with his mother at his side (AD 422–443), a mother who, no doubt, will have ensured that relations with the mighty northern neighbour, her brother Kumāragupta, remained good. To judge by the six charters that we have of the king himself pertaining to this period, the eastern Vākāṭaka kingdom enjoyed a period of peace and prosperity. Pravarasena boasted to have established the conditions of the Kṛtayuga on earth by the grace of Śiva (Śambhu),[63] and there are no references to military campaigns. If the sites where the inscriptions were found are any indication of the actual extent of the kingdom, we may roughly demarcate the boundaries, giving their distances from the present city of Nagpur: in the north Siwani, on the Seoni Plateau on the upper course of the Wainganga (140 km N), in the east the left (east) bank of the Wainganga river (c. 100 km E), in the south the Penganga/Wardha river till its confluence with the Wainganga (180 km S), and in the west Chammak on the Chandra River (160 km W). Thus the eastern Vākāṭaka kingdom seems to have been confined to the Nagpur and Wainganga plains, and their fertile soil was the source of its wealth.

It would seem though, that Pravarasena II did not strike his own coinage; his charters are all concerned with land grants, and excavations have not exposed urban settlements of any consequence.[64] We may therefore safely assume that we are concerned with a small-scale rural exchange economy in which long distance trade played a minor role.[65] As far as can be known the economic surplus was used, apart from maintaining the royal court and its administration, to build religious establishments and temples.[66] The endowment of brahmins with tax free land on the periph-

---

61 *vikrāntayor jananyās tu vākāṭakanarendrayoḥ | śrīprabhāvatiguptāyāḥ śāsanaṃ ripuśāsanam* ||, Shastri in AV, 233.

62 A reasonable guess of the duration of Dāmodarasena's reign would be about three years, from AD 419 to AD 422.

63 *śambhoḥ prasādadhṛti(ta)kārtayugasya*, CII V, 12 l. 15–16.

64 Shrimali 1987, 22 ff.

65 Shrimali 1987, 4 ff.

66 In addition to religious centres such as Mandhal and Rāmagiri, which feature prominently in Vākāṭaka history, reference is made to the 'feeding house' (*sattra*) of the *pādamūla* of Mahāpuruṣa, to which a donation was made on the request of Nārāyaṇarāja (CII V, 60 ll. 22–23), and to a temple (*devakulasthāna*) of Pravareśvara (CII V, 65 l. 1), evidently a Śiva temple built by Pravarasena (see p. 87).

ery may have served to spread and reinforce the dharmic (Sanskritic) religious and social order from which the Vākāṭaka kings derived their authority.[67] The cultural elite and members of the administration obviously had their base in a landed aristocracy. This could partly account for the robust, solid quality of their art, marked, particularly in its early phase (Mandhal), by an undeniable indigenous flavour (see below p. 107).

A charter dating from Pravarasena's sixteenth regnal year, found in Mandhal, bestows one third of the resulting merit (*puṇya*) upon the mother of Narindarā[ja], who may be identified with Pravarasena's son and successor Narendrasena. If this identification is correct, this mother, called Ājñākabhaṭṭārikā, but whose descent is not mentioned, may have been Pravarasena's chief queen.[68] In most of Pravarasena's inscriptions the donations are said to aim at increasing the 'religious merit, life, power, victory and rule' of the king himself,[69] but in his Patna Museum Plate, which is incomplete and consequently of unknown date, all the merit is said to accrue to the queen mother (*mātṛbhaṭṭārikā*).[70] When the latter issued her Miregaon charter from the 'soles of the feet/footprints of the Lord of Rāmagiri' in the twentieth regnal year of her youngest son, 'in order to increase her own religious merit (*puṇya*) here on earth and hereafter,'[71] she must have been quite old, presumably in her early seventies, and it seems reasonable to assume that she died not long afterwards.

---

67 Bakker 1992a. The Chammak Plates of Pravarasena, which were found at and refer to the western periphery of the eastern Vākāṭaka realm, may illustrate this. It records that 'The village named Charmāṅka (*consisting of*) eight thousand—8000—(*nivartanas*) of land, according to the royal measure, (*situated*) on the bank of the (*river*) Madhunadī in the *rājya* of Bhōjakaṭa, has, at the request of Kōṇḍarāja, the son of Śatrughnarāja, been given to a thousand Brāhmaṇas of various *gōtras* and *charaṇas*' (CII V, 26, 24 ll. 18–20). Carmāṅka is modern Chammak (21°.13′ N, 77°.28′ E) and the Madhunadī may be identified with the river called today Candra(bhāgā). Bhojakaṭa, the eponymous capital of the province (*rājya*), is possibly referred to in the *Harivaṃśa* (1.88.32), as pointed out by Mirashi (CII V, 23). It has been 'identified with Bhātkulī, a village about 8 miles from Amarāvatī where there is still a temple of Rukmin' (ibid., p. 23). The chief (*rājan*) of this outlying region, who evidently was subordinate to the Vākāṭaka king and whose name refers to his tribal background, viz. the Koṇḍs or Gonds, proved his worth to the sovereign by allowing a thousand brahmins to settle on his land (cf. Kauṇḍarāja in the Paṭṭan Plates, CII V, 61 l. 45).

68 Shastri in AV, 231 has doubts about this: 'However, there can be no certainty about it as the relegation of just one-third of the merit to Narindarāja's mother Ājñākabhaṭṭārikā and the casual manner in which the mother and the son are mentioned seem to negate this conjecture' (cf. Shastri in EI XLI (1975–76), 72).

69 *ātmano dharmāyurbalavijayaiśvaryavivṛddhaye*, CII V, 12 ll. 22–23.

70 CII V, 71 l. 7.

71 That these phrases are found in the Miregaon charter is inferred from Shastri's description of it to the effect that, 'The inscription is similar in all respects to Prabhāvatīguptā's Riddhapur Plates except technical details like the names of the donees and the donated village etc.' (Shastri in AV, 233). Cf. CII V, 36 l. 13.

There are indications that the death of the extraordinary queen mother in about AD 443 marked a significant change in Vākāṭaka policies, policies which, to the taste of ambitious princes, may had tended too much towards subservience to Gupta will. A shift towards a more autonomous stance may already have been imminent for some time though. Pravarasena II had not followed his parents in their choice for the Bhāgavata (Sātvata) faith. Instead he claimed, like his Vākāṭaka forbears, to be a great devotee of Maheśvara (Śiva), a *paramamāheśvara*, who by Śambhu's grace carried the lance (*śūla*) instead of the *cakra*.[72] Somewhere in between his eleventh and sixteenth year of government he had started to issue his charters no longer from Nandivardhana, but from Pravarapura. It is commonly assumed that this implied a change in the seat of government, and consequently Pravarapura is identified by many Vākāṭaka historians, who all follow Mirashi in this respect, with the archaeological site of Paunar on the banks of the river Dham.[73] A. P. Jamkhedkar has argued, with reason, that the etymological relation between Paunar and Pravarapura is problematic, and the present author has argued that a change of name would not automatically imply a shift of 'capital.' There seems to have been no particular reason for Pravarasena to move the 'capital' to another part of his kingdom, but his self-esteem may have increased along with the growing prosperity of his realm and may have induced him either to rename the residency after himself or to build a new palace in the vicinity of the old one (in the Mansar-Ramtek-Nagardhan area).[74]

In an inscription dating from Pravarasena's twenty-third regnal year, i.e. soon after Prabhāvatī's death, we encounter the first evidence that the Vākāṭaka king had entered into the territories of the Gupta empire—whether with or without military objectives remains to be seen. The so-called Indore Plates were issued from the royal camp in Tripurī, the ancient capital of the Dahala country on the northern bank of the Narmada river.[75] Mirashi linked this information with a problematic verse in the Bhitari Stone Pillar Inscription of Skandagupta, in which this king records how he, still during the reign of his father Kumāragupta, had rescued the shaken fortunes of his family by vanquishing and subduing his enemies (CII III, 315 vs. 4). These ene-

---

72 CII V, 12 l. 16; *śambho[ḥ] prasādadhṛti(° ta°)śūla(° lā°)yudhasya*, ibid. p. 71 ll. 1–2. We shall argue below (p. 87) that, as a counterpart of the Vaiṣṇava Rāmagiri, Pravarasena erected his own state sanctuary (*sthāna*) on a prominent hillock near the present-day village of Mansar, which mirrored, as it were, the Ramtek Hill situated 5 km to the east; this sanctuary (*devakula*) dedicated to Śiva was named Pravareśvara.

73 Paunar: 20°.47′ N, 78°.41′ E, c. 70 km south-west of Nagpur.

74 Cf. Bakker & Isaacson 1993, 68.

75 Identified with the hamlet Tewar, c. 10 km south-west of Jabalpur City, 23°.8′ N, 79°.51′ E. Mirashi in IRP I, 69, 72 l. 1: *tripurīvāsakā[t*]*. For the meaning of the term *vāsaka* see also below n. 199 on p. 56.

mies, Mirashi argued, may have been the Vākāṭakas.[76] Mirashi (ibid.) also pointed out that verses 4 to 8 in fact 'refer to three different struggles in which Skandagupta was involved.' In reaction to Mirashi's theory, G. S. Gai, though accepting the reading of the Bhitari inscription proposed by Divekar and Mirashi, rejected Mirashi's conclusions, mainly because, 'There is absolutely no evidence either in any records of Kumāragupta I or of Pravarasēna II to indicate that there was rivalry between them.'[77] This statement, however, is to be reconsidered in the light of the Vākāṭaka inscription in the Kevala-Narasiṃha Temple on Ramtek Hill, about which more below.

The Bhitari inscription continues with a verse describing the glory won by the young prince (vs. 5) and then, in the next verse (vs. 6), records how he, when his father had gone to heaven, established the fortunes of his family once more (*bhūyas*), by vanquishing his enemy, which made his mother weep like Kṛṣṇa made Devakī weep after he had killed his enemy (viz., his uncle Kaṃsa). Thus rescuing his faltering dynasty, he conquered the earth on his own and was duly praised for it (vs. 7). These verses have often—and rightly so—been taken to mean that there had been a war of succession after Kumāragupta's death. It appears likely that Skandagupta, who fails to 'identify his mother in a context where we are entitled to expect it' was not born of a *mahādevī*.[78] The comparison in the Bhitari inscription with Kṛṣṇa makes one look for an uncle who was more entitled to the throne than a bastard son; thanks to the Ramtek inscription we are now certain that the viceroy of Vidiśā, Ghaṭotkacagupta, until recently only known from his Tumain inscription of AD 435–6, a seal found in Basarh, and two gold coins,[79]

---

76 Mirashi in IRP I, 70 f.; cf. Mirashi in JESI (1980), 86 ff. The interpretation of this verse is controversial. Fleet in CII III (1888), 53–54, ll. 10–11 reads *samuditaba[la]koṣān puṣyamitrāṃś ca [j]itvā*, taken as a reference to the tribe of the Puṣyamitras. Fleet admitted in a note that the second syllable of the name was damaged. Mirashi (IRP I, 70), following a proposal of Divekar, conjectures the reading: *samuditaba[la]kośā[n yuddhy a]mitrāṃś ca [j]itvā*, that is 'after having vanquished in battle (*yudhi*) his enemies whose wealth and power had increased,' a reading accepted in the revised edition of CII III (p. 315 vs. 4).

77 Gai in JESI V (1978), 100. Shastri (AV, 235) agrees with Gai and adds an important argument, viz., 'had the Gupta-Vākāṭaka relations become that inimical during Pravarasena II's reign as Mirashi would have us believe, the reference to the matrimonial alliance with the Guptas, which is certainly indicative of cordial relations, would have been dropped in subsequent records.' For this argument see also below p. 27 and n. 203 on p. 57.

78 Trautmann 1972, 9.

79 ASI *Annual Report* 1903 04, 107; EI XXVI, 117; CII III, 276–279, 294–296. Two gold coins of Ghaṭotkacagupta are found as yet. One is in the St Petersburg Collection (Allan 1914, p. liv, pl. XXIV.3), the other was published by Ajit Ghosh in JNSI 22 (1960), p. 260 f., Pl. 9.6. With regard to the St Petersburg coin Thaplyal 1972, 67 remarks that, if this coin was issued by the Ghaṭotkaca of the Tumain Inscription, 'he might also have unsuccessfully contended for the imperial crown against Skandagupta.' This assessment is based on the affinity of the Ghaṭotkaca coins with the Archer coins of variety B struck by Skandagupta (Raven 1994, 15 n. 1.31).

was the uncle of Skandagupta, albeit a paternal, not a maternal uncle as Kaṃsa was of Kṛṣṇa.[80]

Although history does not repeat itself, geographical patterns of spheres of influence may repeatedly produce power struggles that are structurally akin. Eastern Malwa, with its important centres of Vidiśā and Airikiṇa (Eran), had been earlier the scene of an uprising against the authority of the imperial centre, viz. when Candragupta II ousted his rival Rāmagupta after the death of Samudragupta.[81] In these struggles the viceroys of Vidiśā may have been supported by Nāga feudatories who had not yet forgotten their defeat by Samudragupta and were awaiting their chances. Verse 2 of Skandagupta's Junagaḍh Rock Inscription may allude to this, when it refers to Skandagupta as the one 'who forged an order with an effigy, namely, Garuḍa, which rendered, devoid of poison, the Serpent Rulers [i.e. the Nāgas] who uplifted their hoods in pride and arrogance.'[82] The Ramtek inscription further informs us, as we saw above, that the rival uncle was married to a Vākāṭaka princess, his niece (*bhāgineyī*) to be precise,[83] and that, after his death,[84] her brother, who can hardly be other than Pravarasena II, the cousin of Skandagupta, brought her home by force.[85] It is conceivable that Pravarasena came to the aid of Ghaṭotkaca and his Nāga allies and/or, taking advantage of Skandagupta's elimination of his uncle and the former's protracted struggle with the Hūṇas—who are Skandagupta's adversaries mentioned in the next (two) verse(s) of the Bhitari inscription (vss. 8 (9))—tried (after an earlier unsuccessful attempt in his 23rd regnal year?) to establish his authority in the region to the north of the Narmada, the not yet forgotten homeland of his paternal and maternal

---

80 If he had been a maternal uncle his claim to the throne would have been weaker than that of a bastard son.

81 There is evidence that Vidiśā was Rāmagupta's stronghold, see EI XXXVIII, 46–49; cf. Gupta 1974–79 I, 290–296; Joshi in RGH, 121.

82 Bhandarkar's translation (CII III, 302) of *[na]rapati[bh]ujagānāṃ mānadarpotphaṇānāṃ pratikṛti[ga]ruḍājñā[ṃ] nirviṣī[ṃ] cāvakartā* ||2||. The Sanskrit (and translation) is problematic; one would expect something like *°ājñayā nirviṣīkartā*. I agree with Bhandarkar (in CII III, 302 n. 3) that this simile probably alludes to the Nāgas, but unlike him (CII III, 81), I assume that they were Ghaṭotkaca's allies rather than his adversaries; and I think that Mirashi (IRP, 76) is wrong on this point, although he rightly saw, unlike Bhandarkar, that Skandagupta's inscriptions refer to three separate struggles. The issue was taken up again in G. S. Gai's *Presidential Address* (JESI XVII (1991), 6 f.), in which he repeated his earlier statement, on which his rejection of Mirashi's 'three separate struggles theory' was based, to the effect 'that none of the records of Pravarasēna II nor of his successors indicate hostile relationship between the Vākāṭakas and Guptas during Pravarasēna's or Kumāragupta's time.'

83 Appendix I vss. 11–13; cf. Bakker & Isaacson 1993, 66 f.

84 Appendix I vs. 17; cf. Bakker & Isaacson 1993, 67.

85 Appendix I vs. 17: *bhrātā balāt svaṃ gṛham ā(ni)nāya*; cf. Bakker & Isaacson 1993, 67.

ancestors.[86] In any case, the expedition to bring back his sister led his army into Bundelkhand and eastern Malwa.

Before embarking on these highly risky campaigns across the Narmada, Pravarasena may have secured the borders of his realm. About this we possess little information; our only indication is that the Vākāṭaka king allied himself with the ruler of Kuntala—the traditional enemy of Vatsagulma (see above p. 15)—since his daughter-in-law, Ajjhitabhaṭṭārikā, was a daughter of a king of Kuntala.[87] The dramatic events told in the Ramtek inscription, if they indeed coincided with Skandagupta's war of succession, must have taken place in AD 454–5, since also the Junagaḍh Rock Inscription of Skandagupta makes, as we have seen, an allusion to these troubled times, while the contents of this inscription implies that Skandagupta had established his imperial authority before the month of Prauṣṭhapada in the Gupta year 136, i.e. August 455.[88] The expedition may have exhausted Pravarasena and he probably died soon thereafter. This would explain why we do not find allusions to these events in the Vākāṭaka king's own inscriptions, the last one of which dates from his thirty-second regnal year (c. AD 454). The fact that Skandagupta in his inscriptions refers to anonymous enemies (*amitrāṃś*) rather than mentioning them by their names, as indeed the Hūṇas are mentioned, may have been dictated by internal political considerations: after all it was his uncle and cousin who had driven him into dire straits. With this internecine struggle half a century of peace, stability and prosperity in the eastern Vākāṭaka realm seems to have come to a close.

The Period of Expansion and Internal Strife: Narendrasena and Devasena and Hariṣeṇa

In the second half of the sixth decade of the fifth century Narendrasena succeeded his father Pravarasena II to the throne of the eastern branch of the Vākāṭakas. His aunt, the unfortunate widow of Ghaṭotkacagupta, was back in Nandivardhana.

86 The upheaval in the western part of the Gupta kingdom is also apparent from the fact that from the time of Kumāragupta's death the issuing of charters by the Gupta feudatories ruling in Valkhā (Anūpa), south of Malwa, is disrupted; these rulers had in their many inscriptions, which are dated in the Gupta era, referred to the grace of the Paramabhaṭṭāraka. About this time, or shortly afterwards, this region came under the sway of Vatsagulma (see below n. 132 on p. 39).

87 CII V, 81 ll. 30–31, where Pṛthivīṣeṇa II is said to be the son of Narendrasena and Mahādevī Ajjhitabhaṭṭārikā, the daughter of the Kuntalādhipati. Opinions differ as to who this Kuntala king may have been (see e.g. Mirashi in SI I, 186 and M. J. Sharma in AV). The princess could have been a daughter of Avidheya (see above n. 29 on p. 15).

88 CII III, 299 vss. 2–3; see above p. 27. Cf. A. Agrawal in RGH, 172.

The army of the Vākāṭakas had proceeded to eastern Malwa during or shortly after the succession struggle that followed the death of Kumāragupta. It is almost certain that Narendrasena was no friend of Skandagupta. The serious disruption of Gupta–Vākāṭaka relations had obviously an unbalancing effect on Narendrasena's dominion. No inscriptions of this king have so far been found. In the inscriptions of his son Pṛthivīṣeṇa II, however, it is stated that his authority was acknowledged by the rulers of Kosalā, Mekalā and Mālava.[89] This has been taken by historians as an empty boast, but in view of the events described in the preceding section there might have been more truth in it than has so far been believed possible.

In Mekalā at this time a new dynasty was beginning to assert itself, which traced its descent back to the legendary Pāṇḍu; its kings styled themselves Pāṇḍavas belonging to the Lunar Race (*somavaṃśa*). The first two kings of this lineage, Jayabala and Vatsarāja, are called Rājan and Nṛpati, not yet Mahārāja, in the inscriptions of the last known member of the dynasty Śūrabala.[90] In Kosala also a new dynasty had come to power at this juncture, called, for the want of a dynastic name, Śarabhapurīya, after the capital Śarabhapur. Mahārāja Narendra, son of the founder of this lineage, Śarabha, refers in his Kurud Plates to the Paramabhaṭṭāraka, who had earlier granted a village to Bh(ā)śrutasvāmin, which grant Narendra reconfirmed in favour of this brahmin's son Śaṅkhasvāmin for the sake of the increase of merit of the Paramabhaṭṭāraka.[91] This has commonly been interpreted as an acknowledgement of the sovereignty of the Guptas, i.e. of Kumāragupta, over Kosala, and the early Pāṇḍavas of Mekalā may initially have been Gupta feudatories as well. It can no longer be excluded though that, with the Gupta empire shaking to its foundations in the sixth decade of the fifth century, these countries temporarily shifted their allegiance to the Vākāṭakas, however nominal this may have been; at least, the Vākāṭaka king Pṛthivīṣeṇa II wanted his subjects to believe that his father's overlordship was recognized by their rulers.

The first years of Narendrasena's reign may still have been successful, capitalizing on the legacy of his father and grandmother. We surmise that the inscription in the Kevala-Narasiṃha Temple on Ramtek Hill dates from the period in which Narendrasena took over from Pravarasena (c. AD 456/7).[92] It records that the wid-

89 *kosalāmekalāmālavādhipati[bhi]r abhyarcitaśāsanasya pratāpapralātārisanasya* (i.e. °*praṇatāriśāsanasya*) *vākāṭakānāṃ mahārājaśrīnarendrasenasya*, CII V, 81 ll. 27–30.

90 EI XXVII, 132-145 (CII V, 82–88); JESI III, 183–193; Shastri 1995 II, 73–85. See Bakker 1994, 3 f.

91 EI XXXI, 263–268; Shastri 1995 II, 8–11. See Bakker 1994, 7–11. The original charter of the Paramabhaṭṭāraka, issued after a bath in the Ganges, had been written on palm-leaf but had been burnt. The original donee, the brahmin Bh(ā)śrutasvāmin, is said to belong to the same *gotra* as Prabhāvatī and her mother, viz. Dhāraṇa (Dhāraṇi); see above p. 12.

92 From the contents of the Kevala-Narasiṃha Temple Inscription it cannot be deduced whether Pravarasena II was still alive or whether his son was already ruling when the temple was being

ow of Ghaṭotkacagupta, returned to her paternal home, erected a temple for the merit of her mother Prabhāvatī, naming the enshrined deity after her, Prabhāvatīsvāmin.[93] This probably refers to the Narasiṃha Temple in which the inscription is found (Plate XXXIII).[94] Not far from this temple is the earlier Rudra-Narasiṃha Temple. The images of both temples are almost identical. Side by side they may have called to the minds of their contempories the conjugal unity that once was the mortal couple Rudrasena and Prabhāvatīguptā.[95]

Two more temples, known today as Bhogarāma and Trivikrama, are, for stylistic reasons, to be dated to approximately the same period as the near-by Kevala-Narasiṃha Temple. It is possible that their construction was also commissioned by Prabhāvatī's daughter Atibhāvatī. Her inscription appears to refer to one or two other temples (vss. 27 to 31), but the fragmentary state of the text does not warrant any conclusion in this respect.[96] Despite the uncertainty about whether Atibhāvatī was involved in their construction or not, it is plausible that these two temples were built for similar purposes as the Narasiṃha Temple. The Bhogarāma Temple, with its two parallel *garbhagṛhas*, may have been dedicated to Saṃkarṣaṇa/Balarāma (= Bhogarāma) and Vāsudeva/Kṛṣṇa; the merit of its construction may have gone to the two brothers, the 'valorous kings' Dāmodarasena and Pravarasena (see above p. 22).[97] The Trivikrama Temple, of which only the *maṇḍapa* and the image remain (Plate xxxiv), was possibly built for the spiritual benefit of the eldest brother of Atibhāvatī, Divākarasena, the *yuvarāja* who never became king.[98]

---

built.

93 Appendix I vs. 21; cf. Bakker & Isaacson 1993, 54, 69.

94 It has to be admitted that this is not entirely certain. The inscription, as far as we can read it, does not refer to Narasiṃha explicitly. The *maṅgala* verse that opens the inscription praises, according to our present reading, Viṣṇu as the one whose body swells at the occasion of Bali's sacrifice (i.e. Viṣṇu Trivikrama or Vāmana) and as the one who is viewed with fear and trembling by the wives of the demons (Appendix I vs. 1; for a translation see p. 145). The erection of the Prabhāvatīsvāmin temple, however, is only one of the recorded deeds of the princess; it is followed by several others pious acts, one of which is the building of the storage reservoir Sudarśana (see below). It may be of significance that the (almost contemporaneous) Junagaḍh Inscription of Skandagupta, which records the reparation of the Sudarśana reservoir in Girinagara, also opens with an invocation of Viṣṇu as the god who takes the royal fortune away from Bali (CII III, 299 l. 1).

95 Bakker & Isaacson 1993, 69; Bakker 1992b.

96 Reconstruction of verse 30 especially remains highly problematic and what has been said about it in Bakker & Isaacson 1993, 63, 69 appears to me now even more speculative than at the time of writing. The conjectured reading of 30a, proposed in our earlier publication, has therefore not been inserted in the revised edition in Appendix I.

97 Bakker 1992c; Bakker 1992b.

98 Bakker 1992b. The eastern part of the Rāmagiri appears thus to have been a kind of memorial monument of the Nandivardhana dynasty, comprising altogether at least five temples: four dedicated to the oldest triad of Viṣṇu's *avatāras* (Varāha, Narasiṃha (2 ×), Trivikrama), and

One more devout act of Atibhāvatī is reported in the Narasiṃha Temple Inscription, namely the construction of a storage reservoir, called Sudarśana, in the village Kadalīvāṭaka, which in all probability is identical with modern Kelāpur, 2 km north of the hill, situated in the basin of the rivulet Sura. The reservoir near Rāmagiri might have been named after the first construction of this kind known to us, viz. the one in Girinagara (Junagaḍh), with the repair of which Skandagupta's inscription is concerned. The Rāmagiri reservoir may have served, next to irrigation purposes, as a water storage for the nearby residency Nandivardhana/Pravarapura. The inscription further informs us that in connection with the reservoir in Kadalīvāṭaka a beautiful (*sudarśana*) image of a god was installed.[99]

At this juncture of Vākāṭaka history the spotlight turns to the western branch in Vatsagulma. After the one and only inscription of Vindhyasena (above p. 11) and a reference to Vatsagulma as the original home of two Sātvata communities in Rudrasena II's Mandhal Inscription (above p. 20), a period in which our sources are silent began, during which period of half a century two kings ruled, as we can infer from later inscriptions: Pravarasena II (not the same as the king of that name of the eastern branch) and Sarvasena II.[100] The latter king was succeeded by Devasena. To

---

one dedicated to the two elder Sātvata brothers (Balarāma, Kṛṣṇa), who were also included in the lists of Viṣṇu's incarnations. D. R. Bhandarkar surmises something similar with respect to the Gupta dynasty and the monuments in Bhitari: 'In fact, Bhitarī is studded with so many large mounds that it is not impossible that it was the mausoleum or *pratimā-gṛiha* of the Gupta family' (CII III, 83; cf. ibid. p. 237).

99 Appendix I vs. 24; cf. Bakker & Isaacson 1993, 54, 69 f.

100 A. M. Shastri 1991 proposes to identify this Sarvasena II with the king of that name who is said in the Mudigere Plates of the Kadamba king Siṃhavarman, son of Viṣṇuvarman, to have honoured Siṃhavarman by consecrating him after he was earlier anointed (*abhiṣikta*) by a certain Maisada (Maisava?): *tad anu sarvasenamahārājena mūrddhā[bhiṣekeṇ]ābhyarcitaḥ tatsvarājyapañcame vatsare pauṣamāse tithau daśamyāṃ sa śrīmān kadambānāṃ mahārājaḥ siṃhavarmā* (text based on quotation in Shastri op. cit. 317 and M. J. Sharma in AV, 54). M. J. Sharma (ibid.) proposes to identify this king with the son of Hariṣeṇa, who, he conjectures, might also have been called Sarvasena. The latter suggestion may have been prompted by the chronological difficulties to which Shastri's identification gives rise. About the son of Hariṣeṇa, however, we know next to nothing (see below n. 135 on p. 40); if indeed he succeeded his father to the throne of Vatsagulma, he seems to have been hardly in the position to anoint a far-off Kadamba king. The earliest date suggested for the commencement of Siṃhavarman's reign by B. R. Gopal is AD 490 (*Corpus of Kadamba Inscriptions*, by B. R. Gopal, Sirsi 1985, p. xxx (quoted from Shastri 1991, 318; Gopal's publication was not available to me)). Shastri argues that this date should be reconsidered. Chronological problems apart, Shastri's identification appears to be inconsistent with the subordinate position held by Sarvasena II (see below). On the other hand it should be observed that Sarvasena II's interest in the Kadambas may have been raised by the circumstance that Pravarasena II of Nandivardhana had established a matrimonial alliance with the rulers of Kuntala (above p. 28), the northern neighbours of the Kadambas and old enemies of Vatsagulma (above p. 15).

him we owe the only inscription that provides a firm chronological basis for the Vākāṭaka dynastic history, since his Hisse-Borala Inscription is dated in the year 380 of the Śaka Era, i.e. AD 457–8. It was discovered near the remnants of a dam in the vicinity of the eponymous village, c. 10 km south of the capital Vatsagulma (Basim). It records 'the construction of a water storage (*saras*) called Sudarśana by a noble called Svāmilladeva for the welfare of all living beings.'[101] The man under whose supervision the construction was built, the *karmopadeṣṭṛ*, was called Bappaka.

Discussing this inscription Shastri (AV, 247) concludes 'that Svāmilladeva, who was responsible for getting this inscription engraved and, of course, for the excavation of the lake recorded in it, hailed from Gujarat where the Śaka Era had been in use ever since its initiation.'[102] Shastri assumed that the idea of constructing the Sudarśana artificial lake was brought to Vatsagulma by Svāmilladeva from the reservoir with that name in Girinagara in the Junagaḍh District of Gujarat. In the light of the Kevala-Narasiṃha Temple Inscription, however, another possibility should be considered, viz. that Svāmilladeva knew of, or had even been involved in the construction of the Sudarśana reservoir in Kadalīvāṭaka near Rāmagiri a few years earlier.[103] A noble (*ārya*) Bappa is, as is a certain Svāmideva (see n. 103 on p. 32), among the donees of the Chammak Plates of Pravarasena II (11th regnal year).[104]

---

101 *vākāṭakānāṃ śr[ī]devāṣanasya* (*devasenasya*) *rājñaḥ ājñākareṇa svāmilladevena āryeṇa asmin kāle pratiṣṭhāpitaṃ nāmnā sudarśanaṃ saraḥ sarvasattvahitāya*, EI XXXVII (1967–68), 3. Much has been written about this inscription and its date, which is apparently also given in astronomical terms (see i.a. Kolte 1965; Gokhale and Gai & Sankaranarayanan in EI XXXVII (1967–68), 1–4, 5; Shastri 1970; Mukherjee 1980; Shastri in AV, 246 f.).

102 The only inscription that mentions the Śaka Era explicitly before the Hisse-Borala Inscription is 'the Wāḷa (Thane District, Maharashtra) inscription of the Bhoja-Maurya chief Suketuvarman' of the Śaka year 322. (Shastri in AV, 247). In a note (op. cit. 265 n. 145) Shastri adds, 'In the *Report* (p. 13) itself [i.e. *Annual Report on Indian Epigraphy 1950–51*, No. B 36, not available to me] the record is said to have been found at Vala in Saurashtra and to refer to Suketuvarman as *Dharmmamahārāja*. On palaeographical grounds it is dated about the sixth century A.D.' The first inscription mentioning the Śaka Era after our inscription is that of Vikramendravarman II (Śaka 488 = AD 566), for which see below p. 46. Mirashi in IRP, 171 observed that, 'the era [i.e. Śaka Era] was not current anywhere in Western Mahārāshṭra, Gujarāt and Koṅkaṇ, the home province of the Traikūṭakās, in the period from A.D. 250 to A.D. 620.' This statement is to be qualified in the light of the evidence discussed in Shastri 1996.

103 A Svāmideva Ārya is known to us from the Chammak Plates of Pravarasena (11 regnal year) as one of the thousand brahmins who were endowed with land at the western perimeter of the eastern Vākāṭaka kingdom, that is the land adjoining the territory of the Vatsagulma Branch (CII V, 25 l. 57; see above n. 67 on p. 24). He is said to belong to the Gautama *gotra*. Another Svāmideva, said to belong to the Vatsa *gotra*, is known as a donee from the Yawatmal Plates of Pravarasena (year 26), EI XLII (1977–8), 34 l. 11.

104 CII V, 25 l. 53. This Bappa is said to belong to the Bhāradvāja *gotra*. Another Bāppārya, son of Goṇḍārya, belonging to the Vājikauśika *gotra*, is known from the Indore Plates (CII V, 40 ll. 15–17).

This Bappa, or the Bappaka of the Hisse-Borala Inscription for that matter, might have been Pravarasena's officer Bāppadeva, who was *senāpati* during the period that lasted at least from c. AD 440 to 448.[105] After Pravarasena's death he may have entered the service of Devasena. If so, this may be taken to point to a drain of members of the establishment, officials and craftsmen, from the eastern to the western Vākāṭaka realm. This surmise appears to be confirmed by our archaeological evidence (see p. 42). The barrage near Vatsagulma, which probably served a similar double function as the Sudarśana construction near Nandivardhana, may be seen as just the beginning of this shift from east to west.[106]

We encounter Svāmilladeva also in the Bidar (Hyderabad) Plates of Devasena (regnal year 5), where he either makes or executes a land grant,[107] and then again in the Thalner Plates, as the liaison officer (*dūtaka*) of Devasena's son, Hariṣeṇa.[108] Little historical information can be culled from Devasena's Bidar Plates, apart from the fact that the growing importance and self-confidence of the western kingdom under Devasena seems to have found expression in the title that this king reserved for himself, viz. Dharmamahārāja, which was denied to his two predecessors, who are only called Mahārāja.[109] This fact combined with the total absence of inscriptions of these two preceding kings, Pravarasena II and Sarvasena II, lead us to the

---

105 Siwani, Wadgaon and Yawatmal Plates, 18th, 25th and 26th regnal years of Pravarasena II; CII V, 31 l. 35, 56 l. 42; EI XLII (1977–78), 34 l. 18. Whether he is the same as the Boppadeva whom we find as the engraver of Hariṣeṇa's Thalner Plates dating from his 3rd regnal year (Mirashi in IRP, 87 l. 27) is doubtful, since a career from well-endowed landowner to a high-ranking officer called *senāpati* and subsequently to superintendent of public works (*karmopadeṣṭṛ*) seems feasible, but to end this career as a scribe would imply rather a demotion.

106 How much our knowledge of the Vākāṭaka cultural history has progressed during the last two decades can be illustrated by a remark made by Walter Spink in his publication of 1981, p. 111: 'Furthermore, it is remarkable that no remains of brick or stone structures—nor more than a single piece or two of stone sculptures—have ever been found in the huge areas which the Vākāṭakas directly controlled in the fifth century.' It would seem, however, that for one reason or another the discoveries in the eastern Vākāṭaka realm after Spink's now obsolete observation have had little impact on this scholar's later views on the (art) history of this period.

107 JESI XIII (1986), 74 l. 12; cf. Shastri in AV, 265 n. 149.

108 Mirashi in IRP, 87 l. 26.

109 The two founding-fathers of the Vākāṭaka dynasty, Vindhyaśakti and Pravarasena I, are also given the title of Dharmamahārāja (JESI XIII (1986), 73 f. ll. 1, 4–5). The Bidar Plates are an iron replica of the original copper-plate set, which was made by a craftsman in the Bidar District (Karnataka). The whereabouts of the original set and the place where it was found are not known. A. M. Shastri attaches great value to these plates, because they apparently came to light in Bidar, which led him to the following speculation. 'If the plates originally belonged to the Bidar region, they would indicate an extension of the dominions of the Vatsagulma Branch of the Vākāṭakas into northern Karnataka' (Shastri in AV, 250). Admittedly Vatsagulma was traditionally more orientated towards the south than Nandivardhana (see above p. 15), but it is doubtful, even if the plates were originally found in the Bidar District, whether it can be inferred from them that Devasena had extended his rule towards Karnataka.

assumption that they were subordinate to the eastern kingdom during the reign of Rudrasena II, Prabhāvatīguptā, Dāmodarasena and Pravarasena II, i.e. during the first half of the fifth century.

The increasing prosperity of the western branch may also be deduced from the Ajaṇṭā Cave Inscription of Varāhadeva, in which it is said that Devasena entrusted the actual government of his kingdom to his chief minister, the father of Varāhadeva, Hastibhoja.[110] As we will see, the time was about to come when the Vākāṭakas of Vatsagulma turned the tables on their eastern relatives.

We assume with Spink that Devasena's son Hariṣeṇa ascended the throne of Vatsagulma in about AD 460.[111] Soon after his enthronement Hariṣeṇa initiated a policy of expansion. His first (and only surviving) inscription, dating from his third regnal year, was found in the region to the west of his kingdom, in Thalner, ancient Sthālakanagara, on the Tapi river.[112] This region might till then have been subordinate to the king of Trikūṭa, possibly Dahrasena, ruling further to the west in Aparānta (North Konkan).[113] It would seem that Dahrasena himself became soon afterwards within the reach of Hariṣeṇa, that is, if the latter's minister Varāhadeva is not aggrandizing his king and patron too much when he proclaims in his Ajaṇṭā Cave Inscription (verse 18) the superiority gained by Hariṣeṇa vis-à-vis the kings of Kuntala, Avanti, Kaliṅga, Kosala, Trikūṭa, Lāṭa, and Āndhra, though he admits that they too were well-known for their courage.[114] Ever since Bühler conjectured that a Sanskrit equivalent of the word *conquered* must have stood in the illegible part of this verse,[115] it has been interpreted as proclaiming a kind of *digvijaya* of Hariṣeṇa and this again has opened the floodgates of speculation.[116]

It is, however, far from certain whether the verse should be read in this sense. Nowhere else in the available sources concerning Hariṣeṇa, nor in those of his supposed antagonists for that matter, do we find any confirmation of this putative extraordinary military achievement, which is most unlikely ever to have taken place in historic reality. The verse rather seems to suggest that the Vākāṭaka

---

110 CII V, 108 vss. 11–16.

111 Spink 1976–77, 58, repeated in most of this author's later publications.

112 Thalner in the Dhule (or West Khandesh) District of Maharashtra, 21°.10′ N, 74°.55′ E.

113 Mirashi in IRP, 83–85, 164 ff.; CII IV, 22–25. cf. Shastri in AV, 252 f.

114 *sa kuntalāvantikaliṅgakosalatrikūṭalāṭāndhra°* ⏑–⏑ *°jānimān*[|] ⏑–⏑––⏑⏑ *śauryaviśrutān api svanirdeśaguṇāti°* –⏑– [||18||], CII V, 108 ll. 14–15. Sircar (Sel. Ins. I, 453) reads, –⏑ *nairdhṛtān* instead of *śauryaviśrutān*.

115 Bühler in ASWI IV (1883), 127; cf. CII V, 110.

116 Mirashi in CII V, xxxi, 'It would thus seem that Hariṣeṇa became the undisputed suzerain of the entire country extending from Mālwā in the North to Kuntala in the south and from the Arabian sea in the west to the bay of Bengal in the east.' Spink 1991, 92, 'Hariṣeṇa's vast imperium, which by the mid-470s had stretched from sea to sea, …' &c.

king was outdoing or putting to shame all the surrounding kings. This suspicion receives some support from the text as far as it is legible in Plate LVII of Bühler's publication (ASWI IV). On the basis of what I can read and conjecture this verse says that, 'He (i.e. Hariṣeṇa), [stands above] these foreign kings of Kuntala, Avanti, Kaliṅga, Kosala, Trikūṭa, Lāṭa and Āndhra, renowned for their valour and courage, their own names [...].'[117] Although Hariṣeṇa's imperialist exploits thus seem to lack sufficient epigraphic basis, the verse at issue underlines his expansionist ambitions, and one of the first victims thereof might have been his eastern kinsman Narendrasena.

Before investigating the evidence for this last statement, however, we will consider once more the verse discussed above for what it does not say. It does not mention those territories for which we have some positive evidence that they had come under Hariṣeṇa's sway, viz. Aśmaka and the eastern Vākāṭaka kingdom. Hariṣeṇa, or his minister in his stead, did not mention them, first of all because the inscription probably does not refer to his conquests, as we have just argued. Moreover, to specify them as such may have been thought embarrassing, as it might have cast doubt on Vatsagulma's pretension that they formed an obvious part of the kingdom.

As usual, Mirashi and Sircar differed on the area designated Aśmaka. We accept Mirashi's well-reasoned conclusion to the effect that the fifth-century country of Aśmaka lay south of the Godavari river, north of the upper course of the Bhima, comprising the present-day Ahmadnagar and Bhir Districts. It adjoined the heartland of the western Vākāṭakas to the north; in the south it bordered on the kingdom of Kuntala.[118]

That Hariṣeṇa had some sort of control over Aśmaka is suggested by the fact that, under his rule, a prince (*nṛpati*), who prides himself on having grown very rich after he (and his brother) 'had attacked repeatedly (?) rich countries such as Aśmaka,'[119] is permitted to excavate a rock sanctuary (*maṇḍapa*) and adjacent hall

117 *sa kuntalāvantikaliṅgakosalatrikūṭalāṭāndhra⟨videśa⟩jān imān*| ⟨*narādhipān vikrama*⟩*śaurya-viśrutān api svanirdeśa* ⏑ – ⏑ *dhiṣṭhi*⟨*taḥ*⟩, ASWI IV, Plate LVII ll. 14–15. The syllables *guṇāti* read by Mirashi seem to me very uncertain. It also seems that we are concerned with a case of haplography, since I can count only four visible *akṣaras* and there is space for only five, while the metre requires six syllables after *nirddeśa*. Though the last three *akṣaras* of the verse might read *dhiṣṭhitaḥ* (I am moderately certain of *dhiṣṭhi*, *taḥ* is supplied) it is conceivable that the intended reading is *°dhitiṣṭhati*. In the translation above we have therefore added 'stands above' between square brackets. Even if one considers the verse after *svanirddeśa* as hopeless, the particle *api* beginning the last *pāda* directly followed by *sva°* suggests that the reflexive pronoun refers to the foreign kings and not to *sa* (i.e. Hariṣeṇa) at the opening of the verse. This again suggests that the intended meaning is that Hariṣeṇa somehow obliterated these kings' own names (*svanirdeśa*) as a result of his superiority. In any case there is little in the verse that refers to a military conquest.

118 Mirashi in SI II, 160–163.

119 *...[nīyocchrita]m aśmakādi[kam]* [|*] *[kṛ]tārthasatvā(ttvā)[v a]bhibhūya bhūyasā rarājatuś candradivākarāv iva*, CII V, 125 l. 10. Mirashi's reading of *pāda* c is not supported by what

of worship (*gandhakuṭī*) in the Sahya Mountain, i.e., Ajanta Cave XVII (in which the inscription is found), and Cave XIX.[120] The precise implication of the word *abhibhūya* ('subdued') is not clear to me. One could argue that, if indeed Aśmaka belonged to Hariṣeṇa's kingdom, he would not allow to have it plundered. Maybe we are nearest to the truth if we assume that Hariṣeṇa considered Aśmaka primarily as a source of revenue.

Hariṣeṇa's sovereignty is explicitly stated in verse 21 of the Inscription in Ajaṇṭā Cave XVII: 'while the moon among kings, Hariṣeṇa, protected [the earth], for the good of his subjects.'[121] Who the afore-mentioned prince and his brother are is not clear. Their pedigree is given in the inscription and from that we know that they were the sons of Kṛṣṇadāsa and [Ati]candrā. They are compared to Pradyumna and Sāmba, the two sons of Kṛṣṇa.[122] The names of the two princes appear to be given in verse 9cd, which is translated by Mirashi as, 'The elder (*of them*) bore the title of a king, while the second bore the appellation Ravisāmba.'[123] The 'name' of the elder brother is odd: Dharādhipa (i.e. 'Lord of the Earth,' 'King').[124] After the younger brother had died, the elder one made generous gifts, among which Caves XVII and XIX, thus 'illuminating the entire earth with the rays of his fame which were white like the beams of the moon.'[125]

---

one can actually see in the Plate published in ASWI IV, Pl. LVI No. 4 (in Plate XXVII of CII V one does not see very much). Bhagvanlal and Bühler read, ... *nu tābhyām abhibhūya bhūyasā*.

120 *gāmbhīryaguṇair upetam | niveśitāntarmunirājacaityam ekāśmakaṃ maṇḍaparatnam etat*, CII V, 127 l. 24 and *anyāṅgadeśe 'sya diśi pratīcyām acīkarad gandhakuṭīm udārām*, ibid. l. 27.

121 *paripālayati kṣitīndracandre hariṣeṇe hitakāriṇi prajānām*, CII V, 126 l. 21.

122 *[pradyu]mnasāmbapratimau kumārau* |, CII V, 125 l. 9, vs. 9ab.

123 *dharādhipākhyāṃ prathamo babhāra, dadhre dvitīyo [ra*]visāmbasaṃjñām* ||, CII V, 125 l. 9, vs. 9cd, 128 (the printed text actually reads *dharādhipārakhyāṃ*, which must be a typographical error). The second part of the name of the younger brother, 'Sāmba,' appears to be a sort of surname, which also occurs in the names of two of his ancestors (Harisāmba and Śaurisāmba). His name makes the comparison with Sāmba, son of Kṛṣṇa, and the sun (*ravi/divākara*) apposite.

124 The first word was not recognised as a name by Bühler (ASWI IV, 129) who read *ekādhipatyaṃ* (i.e. 'sovereignty'), although the context seems to require a name here if anywhere. The comparison with sun and moon would suggest a name that designates the moon. The name 'Tārādhipa,' however, is not born out by the form of the first syllable, which, though uncertain, conforms most to Mirashi's reading *dha*. There is something mysterious about this verse. The *communis opinio* is that the name of the elder brother has been lost, but I can't see a better place in the inscription where it could have occurred than in this hemistich 9cd. Maybe the brother, in a fit of unlikely modesty, did not want to have his name explicitly mentioned, the reasons for which we can only guess. One of the possible guesses may be that the donation was entirely intended for the good of his deceased brother. If I am allowed one more guess, I would suggest that a possible name of the elder brother may have been Somasāmba. 'Soma' was in use as a personal name in Vākāṭaka circles, as the pedigree of Varāhadeva proves, in which the father of a handsome prince called Ravi was named Soma (CII V, 116 vss. 6–7).

125 *yaśoṃśubhiś candramarīciśubhrair jagat samagraṃ samalañcakāra*, CII V, 126 l. 20.

Mirashi proposed to identify the prince who sponsored the excavation of these caves with the rulers of Ṛṣīka, a country that he situates to the west of the Vākāṭaka realm proper, viz. in Khandesh (where Hariṣeṇa's Thalner Plates were found). The country of Ṛṣīka features prominently in Mirashi's and Spink's reconstructions of the history of the Vākāṭakas, yet it does not feature in any inscription pertaining to this period that I know of. The confusion created by introducing Ṛṣīka in Vākāṭaka history is illustrated by the fact that Spink, contrary to Mirashi, identifies this country with the region of Ajanta itself, while Sircar and Sankaranarayanan situate it far in the south in the Mahbubnagar–Nalgonda region, the homeland of the Viṣṇukuṇḍins.[126]

Mirashi, followed by Spink with considerably less reservations, derives the role of the feudatories of Ṛṣīka from Daṇḍin's *Daśakumāracarita*, the eighth *Ucchvāsa* of which both authors treat as a reliable description of the historic events that led to the downfall of the House of Hariṣeṇa—as if it were a roman à clef, in which Puṇyavarman represents Hariṣeṇa, Vasantabhānu the king of Aśmaka, Ekavīra the king of Ṛṣīka etc.; yet, the eastern Vākāṭakas are conspicuous by their absence. We do not accept this hypothesis for the simple reason that Daṇḍin's work was composed a century or more after the events it putatively describes and, more importantly, is primarily a literary, not an historical work.[127] At best it could be seen as a kind of Alexander Romance, valuable in itself, though no historian would use it as his primary source for Alexander's life and deeds. That is not to say that there might not be echoes of historical reality in the romance of prince Viśruta, but they can only be used by the historian if they are supported by independent evidence.

---

126 Mirashi in SI I, 168; CII V, 123 f.; Spink 1976–77, 55; Sircar in Sel. Ins. I, 205 n. 5; Sankaranarayanan 1977, 301.

127 Lienhard 1984, 234 dates Daṇḍin, author of the *Daśakumāracarita*, 'before the middle of the seventh century'; considerably earlier Kuiper 1979, 229: 'c. 550 A.D.?' S. K. De (in Dasgupta & De 1947, 214): 'The *Daśakumāra* is imaginative fiction, but it approaches in spirit to the picaresque romance of modern Europe, which gives a lively picture of rakes and ruffians of great cities.' Recently a new attempt has been made to prove the historicity of the tale of prince Viśruta. In an article with the somewhat awkward title, *An Analysis of Daṇḍin's Daśakumāracarita and its Implications for Both the Vākāṭaka and Pallava Courts*, in JAOS 1995, Robert DeCaroli argues that Daṇḍin's story was meant as a metaphor that should have served to caution the young Pallava king Narasiṃhavarman II. To make the metaphor effective Daṇḍin 'peppered' his text with accurate historical information (op. cit. 671, 677). Unfortunately the author, who wholly relies on secondary literature, has not taken the trouble to investigate the historical sources that could corroborate or cast doubt on his contention. Actually, by viewing Daṇḍin's story as a metaphor, DeCaroli generalizes the contents of the eighth *Ucchvāsa*, turning its characters into stereotypes that would fit many a king and many historical situations. In other words, contrary to the author's intention, his 'analysis' implies, if anything, that there is less historicity in Daṇḍin's tale than he and some of his American colleagues might have hoped.

In his treatment of the inscription in Cave XVII, Spink goes one step further than Mirashi when he identifies the elder brother called 'King' with the donor of Cave XX. In the latter cave a very fragmentary donative inscription is found which seems to feature the name Upendra, who, possibly, is the son of a man whose name might have begun with Kṛ.[128] One of the ancestors (the great-great-great-great-grandfather) in the pedigree of Ravisāmba and his anonymous brother is called Upendragupta; hence Spink conjectures that the elder brother might have been named after him, in which case the name of the father in the inscription of Cave XX, whose name might have begun with 'Kṛ,' should be read as 'Kṛṣṇadāsa.' However, the inscription in Cave XX is in such a bad condition that hardly any reliable information can be derived from it; moreover, Cave XX is not Cave XVII or Cave XIX. It is difficult therefore to consider Spink's theory as any more than ingenious speculation.[129]

Summarizing, we may say that Hariṣeṇa had some sort of control over the country of Aśmaka. A prince, who patronized the excavation of Ajanta Caves XVII and XIX may have been installed by Hariṣeṇa as its governor. With regard to verse 18 of Varāhadeva's Ajanta Cave (XVI) Inscription, we conclude that, contrary to what this verse until now has been taken to mean, it specifies precisely those countries that were not under Hariṣeṇa's direct control; their rulers however were put to shame by his excellence. And to judge by the monuments built under his rule, Hariṣeṇa's minister Varāhadeva was perfectly justified in the praise of his king.

Another region that evidently formed part of Hariṣeṇa's dominion was that in which the Bagh Caves are found. This region formed part of Anūpa, which by all accounts appears to have been the country to the north of the Satpura Range, which forms the watershed between the basins of the Tapi and Narmada. The Narmada river flows through it and on its right bank lay the ancient capital Māhiṣmatī (modern Maheshwar).[130] To the north-west of Maheshwar, about 90 km as the crow flies, are the Bagh Caves. Anūpa thus adjoined Avanti (Western Malwa) to the north and in the south bordered on the heartland of the western Vākāṭakas. As has been shown by Spink, the caves near Bagh are closely related to those of Ajanta in style and date.[131] Like Aśmaka, Anūpa is not mentioned in Hariṣeṇa's putative *digvijaya*,

128 *[...] ya[ṁ] maṇḍapa [...] pautrasya [Kṛi] [...] putrasya Upendra[sya] [...] sya dharmma-haga (?) [...] trasya jayatāṁ [...]*, Chhabra in *Ajanta* IV, 113 f.

129 Still a mere footnote in his article of 1975 (143 f., n. 2), the theory attained the status of established fact in later articles; e.g. Spink 1981a, 119: 'When, in *c*. A.D. 471 Upendragupta, the Rishīkan king, dedicated his beautiful *vihāra*, Cave 17, he makes a particular point of stating that he had subjugated the neighbouring province of Aśmaka...'

130 For a summary of the archaeology of this site see Ghosh 1989 II, s.v.

131 Spink 1976–77. Spink conjectures, on the basis of the *Daśakumāracarita*, that Anūpa was ruled by one of Hariṣeṇa's sons, called Mitravarman in Daṇḍin's work. I find the art-historical and iconographic reasons presented by Spink for dating the Bagh Cave in Hariṣeṇa's time rather than

and like Aśmaka it may have served as a buffer between hostile neighbours (Kuntala and Malwa) and the Vākāṭaka kingdom proper.[132]

In sum, it would thus seem that Hariṣeṇa, probably in an early stage of his career, had managed to extend his authority in the west towards West Khandesh (Thalner), in the south towards the upper course of the Bhima (Aśmaka), and in the north towards the borders of Avanti (Bagh). We shall now turn our attention towards the eastern border of Hariṣeṇa's kingdom.

As has been observed above, we do not possess charters of Pravarasena II's son and successor to the throne of the eastern Vākāṭaka kingdom, Narendrasena, and this may be more than mere chance. Information about what happened to this king must be culled from the inscriptions of his son Pṛthivīṣeṇa II. In these inscriptions Pṛthivīṣeṇa II describes his father as one whose authority was acknowledged by the rulers of Mekalā, Kosalā and Mālava and we have tried to give a plausible explanation for this claim above (p. 29).

Another phrase in Pṛthivīṣeṇa II's inscriptions has long puzzled its decipherers, but its proper reading and understanding has been offered by A. M. Shastri on the basis of an inscription of Pṛthivīṣeṇa II (year 10) found in Mandhal. In this it is clearly said of Narendrasena that 'the royal fortune of his house, to which he initially had succeeded, was taken away from him by a kinsman who possessed virtue.'[133]

---

a century earlier convincing. A chronological problem is apparently created by the Bagh Plates of king Subandhu (CII IV, 19–21), which tell us that this king provided the means to restore and maintain the caves. Another inscription of the same king is dated 167 in an unnamed era. Mirashi took this as the Kalacuri-Cedi era which would yield a date of AD 417 for this king (CII IV, 17–19). Spink argues that the era probably was that of the Guptas, which would yield a date of AD 486/7 (Spink op. cit. 57; cf. *inter alios* Williams 1982, 182 n. 7; Goyal 1967, 297 f.; Shastri 1994, 113).

132 Before this region was brought under Hariṣeṇa's sway it was ruled from Valkhā by kings who recognized the overlordship of Samudragupta, Candragupta II and Kumāragupta, all three referred to as Paramabhaṭṭāraka. Their last known charter, dated in the [Gupta] year 134 (= AD 452/3), was issued by Mahārāja Nāgabhaṭa. A hoard of copper-plate inscriptions of these kings was found in Bagh and has been published by K. V. Ramesh & S. P. Tewari 1990. It thus appears that, either under the final years of the reign of Devasena or the first of that of his son, the Anūpa region (Valkhā) was temporarily brought under Vākāṭaka control. After the fall of Hariṣeṇa, another regional king, Subandhu, reinstated the practice of issuing charters dated in the Gupta era (see above n. 131 on p. 39). Ramesh and Tewari identify Valkhā with 'modern Balkhar situated to the south of the Narmmadā and removed from Mahesvar, lying on the northern bank of the Narmmadā, by about 8 kilometres as the crow flies. Mahesvar (District Nimar) is a well-known archaeological site. It is likely that at some unknown time political importance shifted from Valkhā to Bagh in the vicinity of which the present hoard was unearthed. It is even possible that the modern name Bagh is also derived from Valkhā. Bagh, lying to the north of Narmmadā, is separated from Balkhar by a distance of about 50 kilometres as the crow flies.' (op. cit. p. xxiv f.)

133 *pūrvādhigataguṇavad(dā)yādāpahṛtava[ṃ]śaśriya[ḥ]*, EI XLI, 177 l. 17; Shastri in AV, 242.

Shastri (ibid.) comments that 'The word *dāyāda* ['kinsman'] primarily means "heirs to property," i.e., sons or brothers in relation to each other with a claim to inheritance.... *Dāyāda* has, however, a secondary meaning also, *viz.*, a distant relative or kinsman (*Amarakośa* III 3.89), and if this were the intended meaning, it may well refer to a feud between the two branches (Nandivardhana and Vatsagulma) of the Vākāṭakas during Narendrasena's reign, in which Narendrasena was defeated and lost the kingdom or a major portion thereof.' *Dāyāda* in the wider sense is synonymous with *sapiṇḍa*, that is to say it refers to relatives who offer sacrifices to the same ancestor. Hariṣeṇa and Narendrasena were *sapiṇḍas* at sixth remove; both performed *śrāddha* rites for Pravarasena I and Vindhyaśakti.[134] At first sight one may wonder that in Pṛthivīṣeṇa II's inscription this relative is described as 'possessed of virtues' (*guṇavat*), but, after all, he was a member, albeit a distant one, of his own family.

After having at first briefly enjoyed the legacy of his father and grandmother, Narendrasena thus lost his sovereignty, a twist of fortune that is reflected in the archaeological remains of both kingdoms.[135] While we possess in the eastern realm a wealth of material dating to the first six decades of the fifth century and very little that unequivocally belongs to the subsequent decades, it is in the 460s that the western Vākāṭaka kingdom is beginning to create its stunning artistic production, some of the caves of Ghatotkaca, Bagh and Ajanta, for which the Vākāṭakas until recently were mainly known.

We must be brief on these wonders of the age. First of all, because so much has already been written about them. Secondly, because their assessment is only partially relevant for the political history which concerns us here and their description is, by and large, beyond the scope of this book, since the caves belong to the Buddhist, not the Hindu tradition. That this should be so is already remarkable in itself. By all we know of Hariṣeṇa he was a Hindu; nevertheless, the material remains of his reign that we possess are almost all directly linked to the Buddhist faith. In this con-

134 *Śrāddha* rites are performed for seven generations of patrilinear ancestors.

135 An alliance struck between the king of Kosala, his eastern neighbour, and Hariṣeṇa might have contributed to Narendrasena's misfortune, if Hariṣeṇa had indeed succeeded in arranging the marriage of his son with a princess of Kosala, possibly a daughter of the Śarabhapurīya king Narendra. However, this information is derived only from Daṇḍin's *Daśakumāracarita*—rather a problematic source (see above p. 37)—in which it is said (p. 202): 'His (i.e. Bhāskaravarman's) mother (i.e. Vasundharā, wife of Anantavarman) was born of Sāgaradattā—daughter of Vaiśravaṇa, a merchant from Pāṭaliputra—and the king of Kosala, Kusumadhanvan': *pāṭaliputrasya vaṇijo vaiśravaṇasya duhitari sāgaradattāyāṃ kosalendrāt kusumadhanvano 'sya mātā jātā iti* |. Mirashi and Spink identify Anantavarman, son of Puṇyavarman, with the son of the Vākāṭaka king Hariṣeṇa. Mirashi in SI I, 174 is certainly wrong, however, when he takes *'sya* in the passage quoted above to refer to Anantavarman. The pronoun refers to the latter's son, Bhāskaravarman, whose mother hailed from Kosala (cf. *Daśakumāracarita* p. 208.).

nection it may be relevant that not a single one of these caves contains a dedicatory inscription by the king himself. Spink has argued at great length that Ajanta Cave I is the 'royal cave,' patronized by Hariṣeṇa himself, but he is at pains to explain the absence of any positive evidence for this. We are encouraged to believe that the great emperor Hariṣeṇa, whose dynasty in the heyday of its power 'had hardly a rival in the world in terms of either its political or its artistic achievements,' at the very moment that 'there was hardly two weeks' more work to do, and that on the murals alone,' died 'from a heart attack or a stroke, or (considering the perverse machinations of the Aśmakas) it may have been by poison or the knife.'[136] And no one among the mourners—no doubt due to the 'shock wave [that] surged through the site'—had the presence of mind to inscribe the *praśasti* on the wall, on which work must already have begun to rush it to completion before the great occasion of the official conveyance of the *vihāra* to the *saṅgha*, which was due within a fortnight!

In fact, questioning Hariṣeṇa's patronage of Cave I is raising the question whether all the Mahāyāna Caves of the site were excavated by and large during his reign. Spink has with increasing eloquence and tenacity argued that they were. Yet, we are not fully convinced that this is so of all the caves. In particular the caves at both outer ends of the crescent, Caves I and XXVI, XXVII, may be of a later date. The matter should be left to art historians to settle. As far as historical and epigraphical evidence goes, I do not see a reason why all work should have come to a halt almost immediately after Hariṣeṇa's death.[137] The inscriptions found in Cave XXVI and on 'the back wall of the Chapel between Caves XXVI and XXVII'[138] actually seem to testify against Spink's assumption. The first inscription records the donation of the cave by a Buddhist monk, Buddhabhadra, who was a close friend of the minister of the king of Aśmaka, Bhavvirāja, in whose honour the cave was excavated.[139] No word of Hariṣeṇa's overlordship nor of any other ruler apart from that of Aśmaka. This strongly suggests that this complex was excavated after the Aśmakas had gained full control over the region, i.e. after Hariṣeṇa's death. The other inscription is of still later date. It belongs to one Nan(n)arāja born of the Rāṣṭrakūṭa family in Dakṣiṇāpatha. He is to be dated either at the end of the sixth or, less likely, at the end of the seventh century AD.[140]

On the other hand, there are numerous features that connect the Ajanta Caves with artistic/iconographic forms developed in the eastern Vākāṭaka kingdom; this

---

136 Spink 1991, 69, 82.

137 See the discussion in e.g. Williams 1982, 181–187.

138 *Ajanta* IV, 121.

139 *Ajanta* IV, 115 f. vss. 9–13.

140 See Chhabra in *Ajanta* IV, 121 f. Nannarāja was possibly a descendant or distant relative of Mānāṅka who had struck terror in the countries of Vidarbha and Aśmaka (see n. 29 on p. 15).

is in particular true for what I consider the core of the Mahāyāna Caves, viz. those caves from which one has a full view of the gorge of the Waghora river, Caves XVI, XVII and XIX. Their connection with the reign of Hariṣeṇa is substantiated by epigraphic evidence and in that respect they are unique.[141] It cannot be our aim here to give a full art-historical assessment of the continuity and discontinuity of the art and architecture of the eastern and western Vākāṭaka kingdoms. To underpin our hypothesis of a drain of officials and craftsmen from Nandivardhana towards Vatsagulma during the early reign of Narendrasena a few observations should suffice.

It is not true that the eastern Vākāṭakas did not experiment with the excavation of caves and temples in rock. Two excavations are found below the pathway that leads to the top of the Rāmagiri on the southern side of the hill. The first one is a little temple, known as Kapaṭarāma or Guptarāma.[142] The second one is a reclusory of ascetics, known as the Siddhanātha Cave, 100 m further along the track from Guptarāma. It consists of two little rooms excavated in the rock. Pseudo-capitals of the cross-bracket type, similar to free standing constructions on top of the hill, 'support' the roof (Bakker 1989b, 92 f.). And there appear to have been caves in a hillock in Mansar, 5 km west of Rāmagiri. S. Deo tells us that Mansar contains, among other things, rock-cut caves, 'though now completely filled up, [which] are supposed to have been yielding, some years back, a few sculptures. It is not possible to know where these antiquities are.'[143]

Leaving aside these caves, which admittedly pale into insignificance compared with those in Ajanta, there are architectonic relationships between the free standing stone temples on the Rāmagiri and for instance Ajanta Cave XVI. Both Narasiṃha Temples have a shrine chamber, in which the large cult image, tightly enclosed by four pillars (*catuṣkī*), is encircled by a narrow circumambulation path (*pradakṣiṇāpatha*) running between these pillars and the temple wall. These two temples may therefore represent the earliest specimens of the so-called *sāndhāra* class. In front of the shrine chamber is a hall or *maṇḍapa*, the roof of which is supported by a quadrangle of four pillars.[144] This plan resembles that of Cave XVI in some respects. The latter cave has a shrine chamber in which the large Buddha figure is positioned between four pillars and also here there is a narrow path to circumambulate the

---

141 The only construction outside Ajanta that we can certainly assign to Hariṣeṇa's reign is the so-called Ghaṭotkaca Cave at Gulwada, 17 km west of Ajanta, on account of the dedicatory inscription by Varāhadeva (CII V, 112–119).

142 EITA II.1, 70, Plate 127.

143 Deo 1975–76, 275. I saw two shallow cave excavations on the northern slope of the Hiḍimbā Tekḍī. They did not seem to be 'filled up.'

144 EITA II.1, Fig. 27, 28.

image.[145] The size of the Buddha figure, just as those of the Narasiṃha images (or that of Varāha) on Rāmagiri, gives the impression of being out of proportion with respect to the *catuṣkī* that encloses it. It was evidently designed to have the maximum visual effect on the beholder. The *maṇḍapa* in front of the shrine chamber of Cave XVI also contains a quadrangle of pillars, increased to twenty because of the size of the hall. Just as in the Narasiṃha temples there is not (yet) an antechamber (*antarāla*) between shrine and hall, and I doubt whether it had ever been the original intention of the architect to provide one.[146] The front of the cave consists of a verandah or porch. Its façade consisted originally of six pillars as in Cave XVII.[147] This verandah may be compared to that of the Bhogarāma Temple on Rāmagiri, which has a colonnade of six pillars with unequal intercolumniation and plain bracket capitals.[148] And like the Ajanta Cave, in which, 'The roof of the front aisle is cut in imitation of beams and rafters,'[149] the façade of the Bhogarāma Temple shows an

---

145 Fergusson & Burgess 1880, 304 f., Plate XXXIII.1. 'Of these four No. XVI is certainly the earliest and in some respects the most elegant.' ... 'The gigantic statue of Buddha sits with his feet down and the hands in what is called the *dharmachakra mudrâ*... There is a passage quite round the image; and on each side are octagonal pillars screening off side aisles...' Cf. Spink 1966, 140 f.: 'Indeed, the plan of the shrine of Cave 16 must have been suggested by the somewhat similar arrangement of the traditional chaitya hall, where the worshipper could enter down the left aisles and, keeping the sacred chaitya on his right, move behind and around it in his ritual of *pradakshina* and exit on the other side.' Differently Spink 1975, 153 f.: 'What seems to have occurred is this: when this new and grandiose type of image was conceived, the architects decided to design a fitting architectural setting for it—a "pavilion" of a type no previous image had ever had. Therefore they created this special pillared chamber, in the center of which this new and compelling image sits with an almost regal grandeur. The fact that one *could* if one wished, circumambulate the image, is merely the result of (and not the reason for) the particular architectural form used.' Spink's altered view on the history of Cave XVI should be reconsidered in the light of the Rāmagiri temples. See also the discussion in Williams 1982, 184 f. Incidentally, I fail to see why the Buddha seated in *pralambapādāsana* is necessarily a late feature, in view of the fact that this pose was already fully developed half a century earlier, as, for instance, the (less ponderous) Besnagar Mātṛkās illustrate (Plate XLVII). A third-century Buddha image sitting in *pralambapādāsana* is known from Nāgārjunakoṇḍa (Weiner 1977, 62 Pl. 43). Weiner (op. cit.) argues for the relatively late date of Buddha images sitting in this posture in Ajanta. She argues that cave *vihāras* without *antarāla* in which the Buddha shrine is directly connected with the *maṇḍapa* (as is the case in Cave XVI) are a comparatively late development. Apart from the fact that her arguments show a high degree of circularity, the thesis proposed by Weiner (and Spink) has lost much of its plausibility in the light of the Rāmagiri evidence.

146 Spink 1975, 159: 'It seems likely that the *original* plan was to include—as in nearly all other caves at the site—an antechamber fronted by two pillars with an inner image chamber beyond (*text fig. 1*)' (see ibid. p. 167).

147 Fergusson & Burgess 1880, 304, 'Its verandah, 65 feet long by 10 feet 8 inches wide, had six plain octagonal pillars with bracket capitals and two pilasters, of which all are gone except one.'

148 EITA II.1, 70, Fig. 29. 'Pillars of the mukhamaṇḍapa are simple, Rucaka, with a short octagonal constriction of the upper part.' See op. cit. Plate 124.

149 Fergusson & Burgess 1880, 304.

imitation of a wooden roof construction.

As regards style and iconography there are also links with the sculptures of Rāmagiri, though here, of course, limits are set by the different Buddhist and Hindu affiliations of the sites. Actually these connections were the first to be noticed: 'The resemblance is unexpectedly striking between the Ramtek dwarves and the colossal guardians of Ajantā cave 19 in pose, body-type, and head-dress.'[150] And not only with the two guardian figures of Cave XIX, but with many of the minor figures that adorn Ajanta's friezes and pillars. One example should do. The doorjamb of the Kevala-Narasiṃha Temple shows eight *gaṇas* or *nidhis*, of which the two lower ones carry money bags on their shoulders from which they shower coins; comparison is invited with an almost identical representation on a doorjamb in Cave XXI.[151] Finally, every visitor of both sites will be struck by the similarity of decorative motifs on pillars dados and architraves, though the Ajanta ones are generally more elaborate, indicative of a later date and of the greater wealth of their donors. I do not want to argue that the art of Ajanta can be fully explained by its counterpart in the eastern Vākāṭaka kingdom, far from that, but a stream of artisans moving from Nandivardhana to Vatsagulma was certainly one of the creative forces that contributed to the development of the Caves, a development that can no longer be studied without taking the findings of the last two decades in eastern Vidarbha into account.

Yet, the material remains of the western Vākāṭakas breath a totally different atmosphere from those of their eastern relatives. The inscriptions speak no longer of kings who are praised for their upright, reliable and solid rule, paragons of the *dharma* as it were, but instead of a world of courtiers, in which ministers took over the day-to-day worries of government in order to allow the king to become 'free from care' so that he could engage 'himself in the enjoyment of pleasures, acting as he liked' (CII V, 110 vs. 16). No longer is the king compared with the righteous Yudhiṣṭhira, but in his person he resembles the gods, like 'Indra, Rāma, Hara and Cupid' (CII V, 110 vs. 17). This world of sensuous pleasures and sophisticated refinement is the one we find in the Ajanta murals. They reflect the very world of leisure and affluence that enabled their donors to be magnanimous. The excavation and decoration of these caves must have been a heavy drain on the economic resources of the kingdom. That this was at all possible indicates that its economic basis and organisation was very different from that of the eastern kingdom.

As we have seen, the prosperity of Nandivardhana was rooted in a rural small-scale economy. The sudden development of the economic potential of Vatsagulma

---

150 Williams 1983, 226. Compare Plates XXXVI A and XXXVIII A, and below p. 151.

151 Compare Plates XXXVI B and XXXVIII B.

must have had other causes. Possession of arable land played a less significant role. The western kingdom seems to have comprised considerably less thereof than its eastern neighbour anyway; we possess only one land grant of Hariṣeṇa. On the other hand this king had been a conqueror from the beginning. By incorporating the eastern Vākāṭakas in his realm he probably secured a sufficient supply of grain and rice. His northern, western and southern expansion brought him in control of a long stretch of the principal north-south caravan route, which ran from Ujjain (Malwa), over Māhiṣmatī (Anūpa), along Ajanta, toward Pratiṣṭhāna (Paithan) on the Godavari into Aśmaka. As we saw above, Cave XVII and XIX were probably financed by plundering Aśmaka (and other 'rich' countries).[152]

And along with the riches that were thus amassed new ideas poured into the kingdom. In a way, one could say, the Vākāṭaka kingdom was opened up to the real world. As I have stated above, the art of eastern Vidarbha alone could not explain the artistic explosion in Ajanta. Influences from all sides must have been absorbed, among which those from the Gupta North were paramount. The religion of the rich merchants, the manifestations of which one meets everywhere along the great trade routes, was Buddhism. Buddhist patrons became connected with the Vākāṭaka court, as exemplified by Varāhadeva. The king himself seems to have taken only a marginal interest in these by-products of his policy. He allowed his courtiers to improve their balance of merit and demerit by spending parts of their earnings or spoil on lavishly decorated Buddhist monasteries. In this respect the inscription in Cave XVII is most revealing. However, in view of the absence of any sign to the contrary, we assume that Hariṣeṇa contented himself by being at the apex of this prolific political organisation.

The Collapse of the House of Hariṣeṇa and the Reestablishment of the Eastern Vākāṭaka Kingdom

Narendrasena's alliance with the royal house of Kuntala, to which he was related through his wife Ajjhitabhaṭṭārikā, had not brought him the support that his father might have hoped for. The rulers of Kuntala, probably bound by Hariṣeṇa's aggressive policy in the country of their northern neighbours, Aśmaka, evidently were of no immediate help to their Vākāṭaka in-laws when these ran into difficulties. As we have seen, Narendrasena lost his sovereignty but not his life. Scheming to recover his lost fortune he might have sought for other possible allies in the south and

152 How this type of economy could have done without coinage of its own is a problem that I am happy to leave to economic historians.

apparently found these in the burgeoning dynasty of the Viṣṇukuṇḍins. He arranged the marriage of one of the daughters of his house with the son of Mahārāja Govindavarman Vikramāśraya, Mādhavavarman II Janāśraya.[153] The Tummalagūḍem Plates that contain this information are dated in the year 488 of the Śaka Era, i.e. AD 566. A. M. Shastri has established on account of this and other evidence that Mādhavavarman II must have ruled between the *termini post* and *ad quem* of AD 470 and 528.[154] Until Mādhavavarman II, the Viṣṇukuṇḍins were petty kings in the Guntur District of Andhra Pradesh who had extended their rule to the Mahbubnagar and Kurnool Districts. Govindavarman and his wife, Mādhavavarman's parents, were both Buddhists and patronized a Buddhist *vihāra* in Indrapura.[155] The ascension to the throne by Mādhavavarman initiated a new period. The dynasty went over to Hinduism and became devoted to Śrīparvatasvāmin, the god that is now known as Mallikārjuna, situated on a hill overlooking a deep gorge of the Kṛṣṇa river.[156] Like the father of the Vākāṭakas, Pravarasena I, and the father of the Bhāraśivas, Bhavanāga, Mādhavavarman is credited with the performance of many Vedic sacrifices, including eleven Aśvamedhas.[157] His great fame is said to have spread over the earth like a stream that sprung from his unequalled virtues.[158] We shall see below to where this stream reached.

In the north too the political scene was rapidly changing around AD 470. The last Gupta emperor whom we know to have still held the entire empire together,

---

153 The Tummalagūḍem Plates (set II) of Vikramendravarman II inform us that the grandfather of this king, Vikramendravarman I, was a son of Mādhavavarman II and a Vākāṭaka princess, *vākāṭakamahādevīsuta* (JIH 43 (1965), 734 ll. 9–10). This is confirmed by another charter of this king, in which he proudly declares that his grandfather was born as an ornament of two dynasties, the Viṣṇukuṇḍins and the Vākāṭakas, *viṣṇukuṇḍivākāṭakavaṃśadvayālaṃkṛtajanman* (EI IV, 196 l. 10).

154 Shastri 1987, 122–131. See also below n. 194 on p. 55. Though we nowhere find the name of the father of this Vākāṭaka princess, the most plausible candidate, in view of the above dates and the subsequent history, is Narendrasena.

155 JIH 43 (1965), 740 ll. 21–24; ibid. p. 736 ll. 28–31. The *vihāra* was built by this queen and named after her Paramabhaṭṭārikāmahāvihāra.

156 Nandikotkur Taluk of the Kurnool District (AP), 16°.5′ N, 78°.53′ E. The legend connected with this sanctuary might not be completely irrelevant for our history. It tells of a princess called Candrāvatī, who is said to have been a daughter of Candragupta. This princess came to the south and offered a garland of jasmine (*mallikā*) to the deity of Śrīparvata, hence the name of the deity Mallikārjuna (White Jasmine), a manifestation of Śiva. The *Report on Epigraphy for 1914–15* (Southern Circle), p. 91 quotes this legend from a Sthalamāhātmya. Lakshman Rao 1924, 52 refers to a 'Telugu poem of the 13th century' that refers to this legend. If indeed a daughter of Narendrasena was married off to Mādhavavarman, his bride was a great-great-granddaughter of Candragupta II.

157 JIH XI (1924), 59 ll. 11–13.

158 *ananyanṛpatisādhāraṇadānamānadayādharmadhṛtimatikṣāntikāntiśauryaudāryagāṃbhīryaprabhṛtyanekaguṇasaṃpajjanitarayasamutthitabhūmaṇḍalavyāpivipulayaśāḥ*, JIH XI (1924), 59 ll. 9–11.

Skandagupta, had died in the second half of the sixties. No sons of him are known and the rule of the dynasty appeared to have returned to the hands of the legal heirs of Kumāragupta I, offspring of the latter's son Pūrugupta. The later historiography of the imperial Guptas is notoriously confused, which probably reflects the situation within the empire itself during the last quarter of the 5th century.[159] Skandagupta may have been succeeded in the heartland of the empire by Narasiṃhagupta Bālāditya I[160] and Kumāragupta II, of whom we have a dedicatory inscription dating from AD 473.[161] With another son of Pūrugupta, Budhagupta, stability seems to have returned to some extent.[162] His earliest inscription dates from AD 477. The pillar inscription at Eran, dated AD 484, reveals however, in the words of Joanna Williams, 'the condition of the empire to the west. Although this calls Budhagupta *bhūpati* or Lord of the Earth, he is here eclipsed by more local potentates. One Suraśmicandra, who ruled between the rivers Yamuna and Narmada, is compared to a Lokapāla (divine World-guardian), a simile hitherto reserved for Samudragupta in Gupta inscriptions. Furthermore, the local ruler Mātṛviṣṇu is styled Mahārāja and is in fact the subject of the entire eulogy, he whose "fame extends up to the shores of the four oceans."'[163] While thus the old antagonism between Vidiśā and the centre had once again surfaced and the latter's control over Eastern Malwa had been reduced to being merely nominal—this time for good—the Guptas also lost control over parts of Bundelkhand in the same period.

In Nachna (the old capital of the Vākāṭakas according to Shastri, see above p. 12) and nearby Ganj two inscriptions were found that belong to a king named Vyāghradeva, who acknowledged the overlordship of the Vākāṭaka king Pṛthivīṣeṇa II, son of Narendrasena. This Vyāghradeva probably ruled sometime between 470 and 490, since two inscriptions of his son by his wife Ajjhitadevī, Jayanātha, are dated in the Gupta years 174 and 177 (i.e. AD 493, 496).[164] Historians have

159 See the discussion in Gupta 1974–79 I, 169–182.

160 Known from gold coins of 71% (Altekar 1957, 266–71) and two Nalanda clay seals and the seals of his son Kumāragupta (CII III, Nos. 44–46). Bhandarkar names the latter Kumāragupta III and thinks he is different from Kumāragupta II of the Sarnath Stone Inscription (cf. Goyal 1967, 323 f.; Gupta 1974–79 I, 179–182).

161 CII III, 321 f. Sel. Ins. I, 328 f.

162 D. R. Bhandarkar (CII III, 82) argues that Pūrugupta was another name of Skandagupta and that Budhagupta was thus the son of Skandagupta. No real arguments for this identifiction are given, except a rather dubious one, namely that it 'simplifies the chronology of the later Imperial Guptas.' Cf. Gupta 1974–79 I, 172 f. Bhandarkar's edition of the Bihar Stone Pillar Inscription of Budhagupta (CII III, 348) is an example of how an inscription should not be edited.

163 Williams 1982, 66; CII III, 339–341.

164 CII III (1888), 118 ll. 4–5, pp. 122, 131, 136. We accept Mirashi's view as the most plausible, viz. that 'Vyāghradeva probably belonged to the Uchchakalpa dynasty' (CII V, xxviii). This dynasty is referred to as that of Uccakalpa on account of the place of issue of their later charters.

expressed doubt about this allegiance to the Vākāṭakas, since Vyāghradeva's successors dated their inscriptions in the Gupta Era. Moreover, to the east of their territory, in Baghelkhand, epigraphical evidence testifies to the rule of a Varman dynasty, a king of which, Harivarman, acknowledged the suzerainty of Budhagupta in an inscription dated in the Gupta year 168 (= AD 487–8). This inscription was found in Sankarpur in the Sidhi District.[165] We, however, do not see anything incongruous in this situation. In a time that imperial power was evidently on the wane, allegiances were quickly pledged and just as easily broken. The distance between the findspots of the inscriptions of Vyāghradeva and Harivarman (Ganj and Sankarpur) is 160 km as the crow flies and the respective territories of both kings were separated by difficult terrain, criss-crossed with several rivers, including the Son, and the Kaimur Range.[166] I fail to see why rulers in Baghelkhand could not still acknowledge explicitly the nearest major power, the Guptas, while further to the west, where Gupta power was less influential, at the same time rulers could opt for a possible other allegiance that looked more promising.

The actual boundary line between land that still was to some extent nominally under Gupta sway and that of a ruler who no longer recognized the authority of the Gupta king, i.e. Vyāghra(deva), seems to have run between the territories of the latter king and those of his neighbour Mahārāja Hastin of the Parivrājaka House. Though Hastin (AD 475–510) dates his inscriptions in years in which Gupta kings were in power,[167] he fails to mention any Gupta king by name in his three inscriptions. That the kingdoms of Vyāghradeva and Hastin were contiguous follows from a marker erected jointly by Vyāghradeva's grandson Śarvanātha and king Hastin in Āmbloda—probably identical with the site where it was found, Bhumara, c. 22 km east of Nachna—in AD 508.[168] The fact that in this inscription, and in this inscrip-

---

Most of these inscriptions were found in Khoh, in the Nagod District, the earliest one in Kārītalāī, 35 km north-east of Muḍwārā (Murwara).

165 JESI IV, 62–66. Sankarpur is a hamlet c. 3km south-west of the Gopad river, a tributary of the Son (24°.5′ N, 81°.55′ E).

166 Shastri in AV, 11 blurs the actual topographical situation when he writes, 'The recently discovered Shankarpur (Sidhi District, Madhya Pradesh) copperplate grant of *Mahārāja* Harivarman dated in Gupta year 168 clearly shows that the Baghelkhand region, where Nachna and Ganj are situated, was ruled by Harivarman as a feudatory of the Gupta emperor Budhagupta in 487–88 A.D.' Nachna and Ganj are not situated in Baghelkhand, but in Bundelkhand.

167 CII III (1888), 95 ll. 1–2, *guptanṛparājyabhuktau*.

168 CII III (1888), 111. Bhumara is a village c. 16 km north-west of Uchahara in the Nagod District (24°.26′ N, 80°.41′ E). Williams 1982, 104 observes, 'Traditionally interpreted as a boundary stone, this has been recently reconsidered by D. C. Sircar, who suggests that it concerns a village within the Parivrājaka kingdom that was also a *jagir* (economic holding) of the Uccakalpa Śarvanātha. This would imply a somewhat subordinate status for the Uccakalpas at this point. Territorially, the boundary between the two kingdoms cannot have been far from this point, for Nāchnā lies some 25 kilometers to the west.'

tion alone, Hastin refrained from mentioning the 'reign of Gupta kings,' may be taken as a sign of recognition on his part that at this junction one was leaving the sphere of Gupta influence. The situation in Bundelkhand-Baghelkhand appears to have been similar to that one and a half millennia later under the British Raj, during which a part of this region was divided in petty principalities and a part was 'British Bundelkhand.' That Vyāghradeva's successors payed what at best is lip-service to Gupta authority (only by using, not naming its era), instead of to the Vākāṭakas, has a very simple reason: in the 6th century there were no more Vākāṭakas. Moreover, a date in the Gupta era would no longer have amounted to much ('a phrase that could hardly have evoked more than a distant memory')[169] and might have had above all practical reasons. I therefore consider it almost certain that the Pṛthivīṣeṇa in Vyāghradeva's inscriptions is the second Vākāṭaka king of that name (for an additional argument see below p. 52).[170]

We have anticipated the course of events in order to clarify the policies pursued by Narendrasena, which can only be assessed by their subsequent effects, since we do not possess authentic documents of this king. To the arguments in favour of Vyāghradeva's acknowledgement of Vākāṭaka suzerainty rather than that of the Guptas, to which his neighbours were inclined, another, admittedly speculative thought may be added, namely that Narendrasena gave one of his daughters in marriage to the king that ruled in the ancient homeland of his dynasty. This is suggested by the similarity of the rather unusual (Prakrit?) names of Narendrasena's chief queen, Ajjhita(bhaṭṭārikā), and that of Vyāghradeva's chief queen, Ajjhita(devī).[171]

We have no means to decide exactly in which year Pṛthivīṣeṇa succeeded his father Narendrasena. This happened, as we shall see below, at least two years before the death of Hariṣeṇa, which we date, with Walter Spink, in about AD 477–478. On the other hand the kings or crown-princes to whom Narendrasena may have given his daughters in marriage both ascended to their respective thrones in the beginning of the eighth decade of the fifth century at the earliest. To date Narendrasena's death therefore in the mid-470s is a plausible guess. During the last fifteen years or so of

169 Williams 1982, 103.

170 This does not entail that monuments of this area pertaining to this period are necessarily Vākāṭaka in style (Williams 1982, 94, 'thus surely in terms of style, eastern Bundelkhand was at this point part of the Gupta world'), though, now so many new Vākāṭaka monuments have been discovered since Joanna Williams wrote, a new scrutiny may reveal some Vākāṭaka influence; the *sāndhāra*-type Pārvatī Temple at Nachna and some loose finds there (Williams 1982, Pl. 163) may be cases in point.

171 CII III (1888), 118 l. 5. Also in Prakrit the name Ajjhita makes little sense. It could go back to a Dravidian name (though the aspiration makes this problematic too), since Ajjhitabhaṭṭārikā came from the south, from the kingdom of Kuntala.

his life he had to put up with a checked control over his hereditary kingdom, but he may have made some friends. Hariṣeṇa, on the other hand, expanded his sway as no Vākāṭaka king before him, but he made no friends, apart perhaps from some who were totally dependent on him. He thus neglected an important *aṅga* of the traditional science of politics (Nītiśāstra), the acquisition of friends (*mitralābha*), and this was to cost his family dearly.

As argued above (p. 37), we cannot consider Daṇḍin's *Daśakumāracarita* as a reliable historical source for the events which happened at Hariṣeṇa's death, but the fact is that with his demise the House of the western Vākāṭakas virtually ceased to exist. Whether Hariṣeṇa was actually overthrown and killed by his enemies or whether the latter were biding the opportunity of a weak successor is impossible to determine, but the inscription in Ajanta Cave XXVI indicates that the Aśmakas had taken over control of important parts of the Vatsagulma kingdom.[172] A similar event apparently happened in the northern part of Hariṣeṇa's kingdom, when the Anūpa country asserted its independence under a king called Subandhu. We accept with Goyal, Spink and Williams (versus Mirashi) that this king ruled in Māhiṣmatī in AD 486/7 and that he, in about the same time, had restoration work carried out on the Bagh Caves (see above n. 131 on p. 39). Here the opposite seems to have happened as in Bundelkhand where Vyāghradeva shifted his allegiance to Pṛthivīṣeṇa, who had reinstated the power of the eastern Vākāṭakas. Subandhu accepted the Gupta Era, which may indicate that he, like his northern neighbours ruling in Avanti (Western Malwa), considered himself within the margins of Gupta influence rather than within that of the Vākāṭakas.[173]

That Pṛthivīṣeṇa II indeed seized the opportunity to reinstate Nandivardhana's power not only follows from Vyāghradeva's allegiance to him, but from his own records, in which he proudly claims that he was 'the resurrector of the sunken family.'[174] This 'resurrection' took place between the second and tenth years of Pṛthivīṣeṇa II's rule, since he does not yet mention this achievement in his earlier charter dating from the second year of his reign. At that time Hariṣeṇa was probably still alive and hence Pṛthivīṣeṇa II had not thought it opportune, naturally enough, to

172 *Ajanta* IV, 114–118.

173 Goyal 1967, 299, 'Further, the fact that the Maitrakas of Vallabhī continued to owe their allegiance to the Gupta emperor even in the sixth century, strongly suggests that the rulers of western Malwa, situated as it is to the east of Surāshtra, had not assumed complete independence in the last quarter of the fifth century A.D. Actually, there is absolutely nothing in the inscriptions of the king Gauri to indicate that he or Ādityavardhana were not within the sphere of Gupta influence, however weak.'

174 Māṇḍhal Charter of Pṛthivīṣeṇa II, year 10; EI XLI, 177 l. 21, *magnavaṃśoddhartṛ*, a phrase repeated in his Māhūrzarī Plates, year 17 (ABORI LIII, 193 l. 26). In the inscription of his tenth regnal year Pṛthivīṣeṇa also makes mention for the first time of the fact that his father had lost his royal fortune to a relative (see above p. 39).

mention that his father had lost his royal fortune to his relative (see above p. 39), nor did he mention his father's claim of having been honoured by the kings of Kosalā, Mekalā and Mālava.[175] It is impossible to prove, but all the same very likely, that Pṛthivīṣeṇa II was involved in the events that led to the downfall of Vatsagulma. A militant spirit in the new king is already discernible in the seal of the charter that he issued in the second year after his succession and in the fact that he ventured to make a land grant on his own at all. Until this time the inscriptions of the eastern Vākāṭakas had been remarkably free from military swank, but that was going to change. The seals attached to Pṛthivīṣeṇa II's charters state his intentions right from the beginning by making it perfectly clear that here we are concerned with a king who is 'desirous of conquering' (*jigīṣu*), i.e. 'whose rule is victorious' (*jayaśāsana*).[176] And like his majestic great-grandmother, whom he still might have known, he issued his first public charter from the state sanctuary (*sthāna*) of Rāmagiri.[177]

The basis of this resilient spirit may have been laid by Narendrasena. Pṛthivīṣeṇa II was strengthened in his attempt to 'raise his sunken family' by relying on the support—which he could justifiably hope for if our hypothesis is correct—of his two brothers-in-law, Vyāghradeva in the north and Mādhavavarman II in the south. We do not possess data which allow us to assess how Pṛthivīṣeṇa II's alliance with Vyāghradeva worked out. On the other hand, there is substantial evidence, that his alliance with the Viṣṇukuṇḍins had eventually a great impact on his kingdom. Obviously Mādhavavarman was quite a different person and in quite a different situation from his brother-in-law by marriage, Vyāghradeva.

Mādhavavarman Janāśraya had an exceptionally long reign; the last of four inscriptions of his that we possess is dated in his regnal year 48.[178] Two of the remaining three are also dated in the last part of his rule, the Velpuru Pillar Inscription, being the earliest one, is dated in his 33rd regnal year, that is to say in AD

---

175 Neither does Pṛthivīṣeṇa II in the charter of his second year call his father Mahārāja, but he describes himself as the 'good son of Narendrasena' (*narendrasenasatputra*). The whole inscription is still in low key, but for the seal which announces his intentions (see below). Shastri (AV, 239) thinks that this is 'due to negligence on the part of the composer of the grant,' but this does not seem very plausible, if the beginning of the inscription, *dṛṣṭam*, has any meaning at all. Alternatively, Shastri suggests that the 'post-Pravarasena II *praśasti* or draft was not yet standardised at the time of this charter.' That may be so, but our reconstruction of the history of events provides good reasons why it was not. The differences between the first and later inscriptions of Pṛthivīṣeṇa II are pregnant with historical significance.

176 Shastri in AV, 289 f. describes two coins with legend *jaya* (Figs. 70 IIIA and IIIB) which he tentatively ascribes to the Vākāṭakas, possibly Pṛthivīṣeṇa II.

177 EI XLI, 165, 169.

178 Polamuru Plates (Set I), EI XXIII, 88–99. According to Sankaranarayanan 1977, 10 ff. this inscription belongs to Mādhavavarman IV, but the *biruda* 'Janāśraya' points against this.

503 at the earliest,[179] whereas the Khanapur Plates (found in the Satara District of Maharashtra) do not mention a year.[180] It seems quite likely that the information contained in these inscriptions and in those of his grandson and great-grandson, which credit Mādhavavarman II with conquests unto the Narmada river, all relate to the final twenty years of his reign when the eastern Vākāṭaka kingdom had collapsed.[181] All the same, the backing of such a potentially powerful ally may have bolstered Pṛthivīṣeṇa II's campaign to reassert his sovereignty in Nandivardhana at the close of the seventies of the fifth century and it may have contributed to the fall of the House of Hariṣeṇa.

The Twilight of the Vākāṭakas: Pṛthivīṣeṇa II's Rule Struggle and Fall

Pṛthivīṣeṇa II professed to be a Vaiṣṇava, declaring himself 'a great devotee of the Lord, a store, as it were, of energy and forbearance.'[182] His return to the religion of his great-grandfather and -grandmother by placing Vākāṭaka kingship once again under the gracious protection of the Lord (Bhagavat) whose emblem is the *cakra*, becomes iconographically visible in the two stone inscriptions of his feudatory Vyāghradeva, which both depict the eight-spoked wheel (*cakra*), the symbol of Pṛthivīṣeṇa II's overlordship.[183] At a deeper level it may symbolize Pṛthivīṣeṇa II's nostalgic endeavour to restore the glory of olden times, when the

179 EI XXXVII (1967–68), 125–130. This interesting inscription is 'engraved on two sides of the lower part of a white marble pillar, about 2.75 metres in height, now set up in the front *maṇḍapa* outside the entrance into the Rāmaliṅgasvāmin temple in this village [i.e. Velpuru]' (op. cit. 125). It records (op. cit. 130 ll. 13–16) the installation of an image of Dantimukhasvāmin, Vināyaka (i.e. Gaṇeśa).

180 EI XXVII, 312–318. That this inscription is equally late may be inferred from the fact that Mādhavavarman Janāśraya assumed the title *sārvabhauma*, 'emperor' (op. cit. 316 l. 3). The region where the inscription was found, the Satara District, indicates that at the time of issue Mādhavavarman was in the possession of great parts of Maharashtra.

181 Shastri 1987, 135, 'As we have seen above, Mādhavavarman came to power not later than the eighth decade of the fifth century A.D. And he must have taken a few years to consolidate his position at home prior to embarking upon a career in distant territories. His conquest of Maharashtra may, therefore, be placed about the close of the fifth or early in the sixth century AD, immediately after the fall of the Vākāṭakas.' See also below p. 57.

182 EI XLI, 177 l. 20, *atyantabhāgavatasya teja[ḥ*]kṣamā(sa)ṃnidhānabhūtasya*. We do not have information about the religious affiliation of his father Narendrasena.

183 CII V, Plates XXI and XXII. See also below p. 90. This is one more reason to assume that we are here concerned with Pṛthivīṣeṇa II, since Pṛthivīṣeṇa I was a Śaiva (see above p. 14). One wonders whether the same symbol was not also engraved on the Deotek Stone Inscription of Rudrasena II, CII V, Plate I. See above p. 22.

kingdom was flourishing and enemies poised to tear it apart were nowhere to be seen. The fact that his first charter was, after more than thirty-five years, issued again from Rāmagiri may be viewed in the same perspective.

For the time being everything went well. Pṛthivīṣeṇa's military prowess proved itself and the eastern Vākāṭakas were again their own masters in Nandivardhana during a period that lasted from about 478 to 492. The charters issued by Pṛthivīṣeṇa II in his tenth and seventeenth regnal years betray, however, that the spirit of the times had changed. In the *praśasti* of the Mandhal Plates (year 10) we not only find a reference to Narendrasena's superiority vis-à-vis the kings of Kosalā, Mekalā and Mālava; Pṛthivīṣeṇa II also found it necessary to exhume two old epithets of Pravarasena II, which, as far as we know, the latter himself had once used in his Siwani Plates (year 18) but never again thereafter—attributes such as 'he who follows the path marked out by earlier kings,' and 'he who exterminated all his enemies by his excellent policies, power and valour.'[184] In the Mahurjhari Plates (year 17) the composer of the *praśasti* understood that Narendrasena, despite his failures, 'chastised his enemies who bowed down before him by virtue of his prowess.'[185]

The latter Plates were issued from Pṛthivīsamudra, which has led to considerable controversy. Kolte, who edited these plates, thinks that this refers to (again) another capital, situated further to the west because of the threat from the side of the Nalas in the east, and he proposes to identify it with the village now called Samudrapura in the Hinganghat Taluk of the Wardha District.[186] A. M. Shastri argued against this and proposed to identify the place with Mahurjhari where the plates were found and thinks that this may have been a holy place.[187] Though I consider it unlikely that Pṛthivīṣeṇa II shifted his capital—which, I think, was still Nandivardhana[188] —and find the reason alleged for it rather illogical in military terms, it is certainly true that by this time a serious threat had built up to the south-east of the kingdom.

In the last quarter of the fifth century, in the remote, until today mainly tribal area of the Bastar District of Madhya Pradesh and adjacent Khammam District (Andhra Pradesh) and Koraput District (Orissa), local chiefs—naming themselves

---

184 CII V, 30 ll. 14–15, *pūrvarājānuvṛttamārgānusāriṇaḥ sunayabalaparākramocchinnasarvadviṣaḥ*; cf. EI XLI, 176 f. ll. 14–15, ABORI LIII (1972), 193 ll. 17–18. Cf. the Mandhal Plates of Rudrasena II: *sakaṅ*[*saṅka*, H.T.B] *lpābhidyo(yo)gaparākkramopajitānvarttamānānājñāpayāmaḥ [|*]*, Shastri & Gupta 1985, 228 l. 29. Pṛthivīṣeṇa II's Mandhal Plates (year 10) were issued, not from Rāmagiri, but from the (other) state sanctuary (*sthāna*) on the bank of the river Beṇṇā (Wainganga), which possibly refers to Mandhal where the inscription was found (*beṇṇātaṭasthāna*).

185 ABORI LIII (1972), 193 l. 23, *pratāpapraṇatā(ri)[śā*]sanasya*.

186 Kolte 1971–72, 67 ff. Kolte in ABORI LIII (1972), 191.

187 Shastri in AV, 245 f.

188 See Bakker & Isaacson 1993, 68 f. n. 62.

after Nala, the famous epic king of Niṣadha (*nalanṛpavaṃśaprasūta*)—had established a petty kingdom. To their north in Dakṣiṇa Kosala the Śarabhapurīyas were ruling. To their south and west the kingdom of the Viṣṇukuṇḍins was expanding. Their capital Puṣkarī has recently been identified with the site Garhdhanora, where excavations led by the Directorate of Archaeology and Museums Madhya Pradesh (Museum of Raipur) in 1989–90 have brought to light several temples and three (standing) Viṣṇu and one sitting Narasiṃha image.[189] The pose of the latter image is similar to that of the Rāmagiri images, though it lacks the latter's sophistication.

The founder of the Nala dynasty was Bhavadattavarman, whose copper plate inscription was found along with that of Prabhāvatīguptā in Riddhapur. The grant recorded in this charter was apparently made during a pilgrimage of this king and his wife to Prayāga, but it was issued from Nandivardhana. The charter was engraved on copper plates by Arthapati Bhaṭṭāraka, who was 'favoured by the grace of his grandfather's feet.'[190] Arthapati, Bhavadatta's grandson, had the charter published and executed in his 11th regnal year.[191] The above phrase 'favoured by the grace of his grandfather's feet' served to authorize his acting posthumously on his grandfather's behalf. The land donation was made by Bhavadatta 'in order to invoke blessing upon his and his wife's matrimony,'[192] and if this means 'asking for sons' the present and other plates prove that the grant had the desired effect. The pilgrimage to Prayāga may have been undertaken to the same end. It must have taken place in the early years of Bhavadatta's kingship, before he became embroiled with the Vākāṭakas, through whose kingdom and that of their northern feudatory he probably travelled.

---

189 Personal communication of the deputy director of the Raipur Museum Dr G. K. Chandrol and Dr L. S. Nigam (see also Nigam 1994). Garhdhanora: 20°.5′ N, 81°.34′ E, 4 km west of Keskal, 20 km south of Kanker in the Bastar District (Raipur Division) of Madhya Pradesh, and 270 km south-east of Nandivardhana as the crow flies. In Keskal another large Narasiṃha image has been found; this village is to be identified with the Keselakagrāma mentioned in the Keśaribeda Plates of Arthapati (EI XXVIII, 16 l. 3), rather than the spot where the inscription was found, Kesarabeda in the Koraput District of Orissa (19°.45′ N, 82°.5′ E).

190 EI XIX, 103 l. 24, *āryakapādaprasādānugṛhītena*.

191 Krishnamacharlu, the editor of the grant, takes this date to refer to the eleventh regnal year of Bhavadatta himself, which is rejected by Sircar (EI XXVIII (1949–50), 13). Sircar's objection seems to be justified by the fact that another charter of Arthapati (EI XXVIII, 17 l. 14) was also written by the officer Culla, who is mentioned in the Rithapur Plates in the same Āryā verse that mentions the date: *yā caikādaśe* [i.e. *yaikādaśe*, H.T.B.] *'tha varṣe kārttikamāsasya bahulasaptamyām | svamukhājñā [sā] likhi(tā) rahasi niyukte(na) cullena* || (EI XIX, 103 l. 20–21). For the expression *rahasi niyuktena* compare the Keśaribeda Plates of Arthapati were Culla is called *rahasyādhikṛtena*, which, according to Sircar, refers to a 'Privy Councillor' (EI XXVIII, 16).

192 EI XIX (1927–28), 102 l. 6, *mama cācapī (cāpi?) bhaṭṭ(ā)rikāyāś ca d(ā)mpatyasyāsmākam anugrahārtham*.

It is commonly deduced from this piece of evidence that Bhavadatta ousted Pṛthivīṣeṇa II from his capital and temporarily ruled proudly from Nandivardhana in about AD 493. This seems to me, however, far from certain. Bhavadatta may have had this intention, but his plans foundered. When his grandson, at least twenty-three years later,[193] i.e. after AD 516, executed the grant of his grandfather he may have done so, because he himself was master of Nandivardhana at that time, thinking it a worthy tribute to the ambitions of his grandfather. Arthapati may have seen the opportunity to capture Nandivardhana after the death of the Viṣṇukuṇḍin king Mādhavavarman II, who ruled over Vidarbha after the fall of the Vākāṭakas (see below).[194]

Nevertheless it seems that Pṛthivīṣeṇa II came under heavy attack from the Nalas. After a serious initial setback, he appears to have reassembled his forces and probably summoned the help of his brother-in-law Mādhavavarman II, to whom, as to Pṛthivīṣeṇa II, the growing power of the Nalas must have been a matter of mounting concern. Mādhavavarman's involvement in the struggle with the Nalas may also be inferred from his Polamuru Plates (Set I), in which he declares that 'he crossed the Godavari for conquest in the east,' [195] which alludes to the territories of the Nalas in the Bastar District to the east of the Godavari river. How much the power had increased during Bhavadatta's reign may not only be inferred from his success against the Vākāṭakas; there are strong indications as well that the Nalas seriously disturbed the status quo in Dakṣiṇa Kosala. Here we notice a disruption in the lineage of the Śarabhapurīyas, and it was from them probably that Bhavadatta got the idea of issuing his own gold coins.[196] A successful counterattack was launched, the Nalas were driven back, and their capital Puṣkarī was raided, as may be inferred from an inscription of Bhavadatta's son [Skanda?]varman: 'the illustrious king [Skanda?]varman—the good son of king Bhavadatta, the foremost of the lineage of the illustrious Nalas who had destroyed his enemies by his valour—after having wrested back the royal fortune which had been lost and had fallen into (the hands of) others, and after having (re)populated the deserted

193 We possess an inscription of Bhavadatta's son, [Skanda]varman, from his 12 regnal year, while Arthapati/Bhavadatta's Rithapur Plates date from the eleventh year (of Arthapati's reign).

194 Shastri 1987, 135 observes, 'The Viṣṇukuṇḍin rule over Maharashtra, however, did not last long. Neither has any record of any successors of Mādhavavarman II been discovered anywhere in Maharashtra nor do we come across any allusion to their hold over this area except for the description of Mādhavavarman III as the lord of Trikūṭa.' If we accept the *terminus post quem*, AD 470, as the actual year of Mādhavavarman's accession to the throne, his death may have occurred shortly after his last known inscription, which dates from his regnal year 48, i.e. AD 518 (see above p. 46).

195 Rao 1924, 60 ll. 21–22, *prāgdi[g]jigīṣayā pra(sthi)taḥ godāvarīm atītaran*, which is corrected by Sankaranarayanan 1977, 181 n. 15 to *prasthitaiḥ* +++ *atitaradbhiḥ*.

196 Bakker 1994, 9; Mirashi in JNSI XI, 109 f.

(capital) Puṣkarī, has established this temple/footprint of Viṣṇu, desiring welfare for himself and acting for (the good of) his father, ancestors and mother—† having established hope of obtaining merit (for them)†.'[197] Bhavadatta may have been killed in this war and it evidently took his son twelve years to put his dynasty on its feet again. Pṛthivīṣeṇa II, on the other hand, revelled in his victory, calling himself 'the rescuer of his House which had sunken *twice*' in his unfinished Bālāghāṭ Plates,[198] which were issued, at least that was the intention, from his camp (*vāsaka*) Vembāra, identified by Mirashi with Bembal in the south-eastern corner of the Vākāṭaka kingdom, on the western bank of the Wainganga, which may be considered his eastern line of defence.[199]

It proved to be a Pyrrhic victory. In order to withstand the Nalas Pṛthivīṣeṇa II probably had to accept a greater presence of the Viṣṇukuṇḍins in his realm. There is abundant evidence that Mādhvavarman II or his countrymen stayed in Vidarbha, especially in the south. This evidence has been collected and dealt with by A. M. Shastri (1987, 132–137). A hoard and several loose base metal coins were found in Paunar on the river Dham. Though recent research of Shastri and Gupta have made a case to assign some of these coins to the Vākāṭaka kings themselves, notably Pṛthivīṣeṇa II, there can be little doubt that the majority of them were struck by the Viṣṇukuṇḍins, initially perhaps in collaboration with their Vākāṭaka in-laws, in order to finance their combined war effort against the Nalas.[200] The archaeological remains of this site likewise point to Viṣṇukuṇḍin influence (we shall deal with the remains in Paunar in Chapter 3). Viṣṇukuṇḍin coins were also reported from Nagara in the Gondia Tahsil of the Bhandara District, where excavations revealed a

197 EI XXI (1931–32), 155 ll. 2–5, *śrīnalānvayamukhyasya vikramakṣapitadviṣaḥ* | *nṛpater bhavadattasya satputreṇānyasaṃsthitām* ||2|| *bhraṣṭām ākṛṣya rājarddhiṃ śūnyām āvāsya puṣkarīm* | *pituḥ pitāmahānāṃ ca jananyāḥ kri(kṛ)tinā [tataḥ]* ||3|| *kṛtvā dha[rmā]rthanebhyāśān(m) idam ātmahitaiṣiṇā* | *pādamūlaṃ kṛtaṃ viṣṇo [rājñā] śrī[skandava]rmaṇā* ||4||. I do not understand *pāda* 4a, which was evidently no problem for Krishnamacharlu who translates 'with the hope of obtaining religious merit for his father etc.' (EI XXI, 157).

198 CII V, 81 l. 33, *dvimagnavaṃśasyoddhartuḥ*. Due to their unfinished character the Balaghat Plates do not contain a regnal year, but they must be later than the Mahurjhari Plates of Pṛthivīṣeṇa II's 17th year, because in the latter plates he still is 'the rescuer of his House which had sunken,' scil. once (*magnavaḍ(ṃ)śoddhartur*, ABORI LIII (1972), 193 l. 26). Hence we assumed above that the Nala attack must have taken place about eighteen years after Pṛthivīṣeṇa II's accession to the throne, i.e. in about AD 493.

199 Bembal: 19°.55′ N, 79°.45′ E, 50 km east of Chandrapur, c. 190 km due west of Garhdhanora, the supposed capital Puṣkarī of the Nalas (see above p. 54). The term *vāsaka* in the meaning of '(military) camp' we also encounter in the Indore Plates of Pravarasena II (*tripurīvāsakāt*, Mirashi in IRP, 72 l. 1), which we, following Mirashi, interpreted as referring to Pravarasena's intrusion into Gupta territory (see above p. 25). The only other Vākāṭaka charter that was issued from a *vāsaka* is the Wadgaon inscription, which was issued from the Hiraṇyānadīvāsaka (CII V, 54 l. 1), a camp on the Erai river.

200 See below p. 90. Shastri and Gupta in AV, 142–145, 285–294.

huge brick temple complex.[201] The question seems justified whether Pṛthivīṣeṇa II had not let in the Trojan horse. The conquest of Mādhavavarman, whose kingdom, according to the inscriptions of his descendants, adjoined the waters of the Revā river (i.e. the Narmada),[202] took place, according to A. M. Shastri, 'immediately after the fall of the Vākāṭakas. In view of the pride felt by his [i.e. Mādhavavarman's] successors in his marriage with a Vākāṭaka princess, it is unlikely that he himself contributed to the collapse of the Vākāṭaka power.'[203] In any case, if the Viṣṇukuṇḍins did not themselves have a hand in the fall of the Vākāṭaka kingdom, they were quick to turn it to their profit. How long Pṛthivīṣeṇa II's rule continued after the battle with the Nalas is difficult to say, but probably not very long, in view of the fact that the Balaghat Plates remained unfinished. The new masters of Vidarbha, the Viṣṇukuṇḍins, did not allow any of Pṛthivīṣeṇa II's descendants to raise his voice, for nothing of the Vākāṭakas was ever heard again.

---

201 Shastri 1987, 134. For this temple, about which I have serious doubts whether it was built by the Vākāṭakas and which for that reason I have left out of this study, see EITA II.1, 64 f.

202 JIH 43 (1965), 734 ll. 8–9, *revāsaritsalilavalayavibhūṣaṇāyā bhuvo bhartur mahārājaśrīmādhavavarmaṇaḥ*.

203 Shastri 1987, 135. The argument does not carry much conviction, for the Vākāṭakas too kept their *praśastis* unchanged till the very end, irrespective of the fact that they had intruded into Gupta territory and even had established feudatory relations within it. The emphasis on the descent of one of the ancestors from another mighty dynasty of the times may, in addition to enhancement of one's own status, have been regarded as a justification of asserting certain rights, if not of territorial expansion into the realm of one's in-laws. Cf. also Prabhāvatī's emphasis on her Nāga descent, above n. 38 on p. 17 and p. 11.

Chapter 2

The Hindu Religion in the Vākāṭaka Kingdom

The two forms of Hinduism that are reflected predominantly in the material remains of the Vākāṭaka kingdom are those in which either Maheśvara (i.e: Śiva) or Bhagavat (i.e. Viṣṇu) is the principal focus of worship. The devotees of Maheśvara call themselves Māheśvaras, those of the Bhagavat Bhāgavatas. The kings of the eastern Vākāṭakas were either Māheśvaras or Bhāgavatas. The Vatsagulma kings call themselves Dharmamahārāja, without being more explicit about their religious orientation.[1] They were, at least indirectly, great patrons of the Buddhist *saṅgha*, though we do not possess indications that they themselves were Buddhists. The title Dharmamahārāja may therefore be interpreted as a general one indicating an oecumenical attitude towards the religions represented in their kingdom. The large majority of the images described in the catalogue below pertain either to the Śaiva or the Vaiṣṇava pantheon and, with a few exceptions from Ajanta which are included for the sake of comparison, they all belong to the Nandivardhana kingdom.

There are good reasons to assume that the stone images that have been found are not a faithful reflection of the variety of religious cults in the Vākāṭaka realm. They represent the 'higher,' brahmanical forms of Hinduism. Within the villages, however, local cults of folk deities and mother goddesses may have been of equal or greater importance, as they still are today. When they were acknowledged and received patronage from the elite, they were accommodated to the general forms of Hinduism that we know from Sanskrit literature. Thus we have an image of Devī, the slayer of the buffalo demon (Mahiṣāsuramardinī, Plate XXIX A) and of a Mātṛkā goddess (Plate XV), two goddesses who may have had long histories before they were eventually acknowledged in Sanskrit literature, in which they appear comparatively late. A female deity that was never admitted to the circle of 'higher' Hinduism is the fertility goddess commonly designated Lajjā Gaurī. She is repre-

1 The *biruda* Hāritīputra given to Pravarasena I in Vindhyaśakti II's Basim Plates and in Hariṣeṇa's Thalner Plates cannot be taken to mean that this king was a Buddhist, though Hāritī is a folk deity (Mother Goddess) who became particularly prominent in the Buddhist fold. A series of Vedic sacrifices was also ascribed to this Pravarasena. The same *biruda* was adopted by the Hindu Cālukya kings (Mirashi in IRP I, 82; CII V, xxxvi n. 5).

sented in our catalogue by a stone tablet (Plate XXIX B); her cult must have been widespread, since many similar plaques have been found in Vidarbha and all over Maharashtra and beyond; we noticed a shrine in which such an icon was still in worship in a street in Pauni. In an earlier publication (Bakker 1992a) we have argued that also for instance the cult of Narasiṃha on the Rāmagiri may have been rooted in the local worship of a lion deity that was elevated to the Vaiṣṇava pantheon, a process in which political motifs played a role. Through recognition and patronage (e.g. by means of temple construction) of local deities, large groups of the population were assimilated to the culture of the elite, while at the same time, by promoting 'higher' or Sanskritic forms of worship, the brahmanical world-view, which was the ideological basis of the Vākāṭaka rule, was spread broadly through the populace.[2] The limitations of our survey may finally be illustrated by three splendid Buddhist bronzes, found at the site of Nandivardhana (Nagardhan), testifying to the fact that the Buddhist Mahāyāna religion was not exclusively found in the Vatsagulma kingdom, but was present in the eastern kingdom as well.[3]

For the understanding of the images illustrated in this work we shall briefly discuss the underlying religious beliefs of the Bhāgavatas and Māheśvaras in so far as these can be reconstructed on the basis of early Sanskrit sources.

The Bhāgavata Faith

Vaisnavism, as represented in the images found in eastern Vidarbha, seems to have been focused on two originally quite different sets of deities, which were eventually synthesized; and indeed the archaeological remains of Rāmagiri reflect the initial phase of this fusion (see p. 64).

The first set of deities seems to go back to a cult of deified human heroes. It comprises the Pañcavīra, the 'Five Heroes,' about whom the *Vāyupurāṇa* remarks: 'Learn about the gods who are of human nature, whose praises are sung (by me): Saṃkarṣaṇa, Vāsudeva, Pradyumna, Sāmba and Aniruddha, they are praised as the five heroes of the race.'[4] The 'race' referred to is that of the Vṛṣṇi clan of the Yādava tribe, whose origins may have been the region around Mathura. These five deities are also said to belong to the race of the Sātvata. The devotees of these gods

2 Bakker 1992a, 89.

3 Jamkhedkar 1985a.

4 *manuṣyaprakṛtīn devān kīrtyamānān nibodhata| saṃkarṣaṇo vāsudevaḥ pradyumnaḥ sāmba eva ca| aniruddhaś ca pañcaite vaṃśavīrāḥ prakīrtitāḥ||*, VāP 97.1–2.

are named Sātvatas after them and their belief, the Sātvata religion.[5] The earliest evidence of the enshrinement of these five deities for the sake of worship comes from the Mora Well inscription (near Mathura) of king Śoḍāsa (AD 10–25), which records the installation in a stone temple of the 'images of the exalted five heroes of the Vṛṣṇis.'[6] Vidiśā (modern Besnagar) and Padmāvatī (modern Pawaya), which played such prominent roles in the Gupta/Vākāṭaka history, as we have seen, appear to have been other centres of Sātvata worship. On the basis of epigraphical and archaeological evidence, Banerjea argued convincingly that at least three deities, Saṃkarṣaṇa, Vāsudeva and Pradyumna, had their respective shrines there.[7] Vāsudeva is understood as the patronymic of Kṛṣṇa, and Saṃkarṣaṇa is taken as another name of Balarāma, Kṛṣṇa's elder brother;[8] Sāmba and Pradyumna are the latter's sons and Aniruddha his grandson, son of Pradyumna. The Sātvata religion is part of and sometimes seems to coincide with the Bhāgavata faith. In his Mandhal inscription Rudrasena II refers to the existence of two settlements or communities of the Sātvatas (*sātvatacaraṇa*), and this may well be the first epigraphical attestation of this school as such (see above p. 20).

The *Nārāyaṇīya* section of the *Mahābhārata* gives us more information on an early stage of the Bhāgavata religion and cult.[9] In this connection mention is made of the Sātvata *dharma*, also referred to as Pāñcarātra: Kṛṣṇa was a local prince, head of the Vṛṣṇi clan of the Yādavas, and said to belong to the people of the Sātvatas. However, in the *Nārāyaṇīya* the name of Kṛṣṇa is not prominent, but the bearer of the name Vāsudeva is the central figure of a religion which was explained to his true devotee (*bhakta*) Nārada by Nārāyaṇa himself in Śvetadvīpa:[10] Vāsudeva, also called Hari, is the Supreme Soul, the internal ruler of all. His religion is the Bhāga-

---

5 MBh 12.336.31 (cf. 12.322.19), *tataḥ prāvartata tadā ādau kṛtayugaṃ śubham | tato hi sātvato dharmo vyāpya lokān avasthitaḥ ||*. In MBh 1.210.12 Kṛṣṇa Vāsudeva is named Sātvata. Bhandarkar 1913, 8–13.

6 *bhagavatāṃ vṛṣṇīṇāṃ paṃcavīrāṇāṃ pratimāḥ śailadevagṛ[he sthāpitāḥ]*, Sel. Ins. I, 122.

7 Banerjea 1956, 104.

8 The exact connection between Vāsudeva and Kṛṣṇa, and how they came to be associated with each other, if indeed they were ever completely separate personalities, is a matter of considerable obscurity. Later mythology states that Kṛṣṇa was the son of Vasudeva (presumably derived in retrospect from the supposedly patronymic Vāsudeva) and Devakī (given as the name of the mother of an apparently different Kṛṣṇa in *Chāndogya Upaniṣad* 3.17.6). The process of identification of the two deities just as that of their two respective brothers, Saṃkarṣaṇa and (Bala)rāma/Baladeva, appears to have already been completed in the second century BC when Patañjali used these names for one and the same pair of brothers (*Mahābhāṣya ad* P. 2.2.24, 2.2.35, 4.1.114). In *Mahābhāṣya ad* P. 3.1.26 and 3.2.111 Patañjali says that Vāsudeva killed Kaṃsa; the *pāda*, '*asādhur mātule kṛṣṇaḥ*,' ascribed to Patañjali by Jaiswal 1967, 66 (cited from Raychaudhuri 1936, 37, 51) I could not find with the help of Pathak's *Word Index*. Cf. BhG 7.19, 19.57, 11.50, 18.74. See Jaiswal 1967, 51 ff.; Bhandarkar 1913, 3 f.

9 MBh 12.321–339.

10 MBh 12.326.1 ff. Laine 1989, 193–202.

vata faith, a devotional (*bhakti*), monotheistic (*ekāntika*) belief system (*dharma*), in which the Bhagavat, Vāsudeva, is the principal object of ritual (*sātvatavidhi*). The world evolves from him through his forms (*mūrtis*), Saṃkarṣaṇa etc.[11] This devotional movement distanced itself from traditional Brahmanism in that it took issue with the animal slaughter involved in Vedic sacrifices, a practice of *ahiṃsā* which greatly pleased the Lord, though not the other gods.[12] In MBh 12.327.78 the Bhagavat answers the gods upon their question where to go in the Kali age when only a fourth of the *dharma* remains,

> O best of the gods, where the Vedas, sacrifices, asceticism, truthfulness and self-discipline prevail along with a *dharma* of 'no killing (of animals),' that is the land that should be visited; may *adharma* not tread on you.[13]

In MBh 12.332.13–18 the Sātvata path to Vāsudeva, a theological variant of the early Sāṃkhya, is described. The sinless devotees go, without merit and demerit (*puṇyapāpavivarjita*), along the good path to the sun (after death, though an esoteric interpretation is possible).[14] The sun (*āditya*), which destroys all darkness, is called the gate. It burns their bodies and, invisibly (*adṛśya*), having become atom-like, they enter the deity, i.e. Āditya. Leaving him again they stay in the body of Aniruddha. Then having become *manas* they enter Pradyumna. Leaving him they enter Saṃkarṣaṇa, the *jīva*; after having left their *triguṇa* nature behind them, they finally enter the Kṣetrajña, that is Vāsudeva.[15]

---

11 MBh 12.326.17–46. Cf. Bhandarkar 1913, 4–13; Gonda 1977, 8 f.

12 MBh 12.323.10–11.

13 MBh 12.327.78, *śrībhagavān uvāca* | *yatra vedāś ca yajñāś ca tapaḥ satyaṃ damas tathā* | *ahiṃsādharmasaṃyuktāḥ pracareyuḥ surottamāḥ*| *sa vai deśaḥ sevitavyo mā vo 'dharmaḥ padā spṛśet* ||78||.

14 Cf. *Kauṣītaki Upaniṣad*, 1.3–4.

15 *ye hi niṣkalmaṣā loke puṇyapāpavivarjitāḥ* |
teṣāṃ vai kṣemam adhvānaṃ gacchatāṃ dvijasattama |
sarvalokatamohantā ādityo dvāram ucyate ||13||
ādityadagdhasarvāṅgā adṛśyāḥ kenacit kvacit |
paramāṇubhūtā bhūtvā tu taṃ devaṃ praviśanty uta ||14||
tasmād api vinirmuktā aniruddhatanau sthitāḥ |
manobhūtās tato bhūyaḥ pradyumnaṃ praviśanty uta ||15||
pradyumnāc cāpi nirmuktā jīvaṃ saṃkarṣaṇaṃ tathā |
viśanti viprapravarāḥ sāṃkhyā bhāgavataiḥ saha ||16||
tatas traiguṇyahīnās te paramātmānam añjasā |
praviśanti dvijaśreṣtha kṣetrajñaṃ nirguṇātmakam |
sarvāvāsaṃ vāsudevaṃ kṣetrajnaṃ viddhi tattvataḥ ||7||
samāhitamanaskāś ca niyatāḥ saṃyatendriyāḥ |
ekāntabhāvopagatā vāsudevaṃ viśanti te ||18|| (MBh 12.332.13–18; cf. MBh 12.326.35–43).

We see that the place of the fifth Vṛṣṇi deity Sāmba is taken by Āditya, the sun, to which Sāmba in another, mythological context is closely related. For reasons not satisfactorily explained Sāmba was, when the above religion evolved into the Pāñcarātra system, expelled from the pantheon, while the four remaining *mūrtis* developed into hypostases of Vāsudeva's emanations (*vyūhas*) in the process of world-creation. Banerjea, however, has collected evidence that, before he became exclusively associated with the cult of the sun, that is of Sūrya, Sāmba was worshipped in his own right, along with the other Vṛṣṇis, in images of which the iconography anticipates that of Sūrya.[16] Of the four or five Sātvata deities Vāsudeva (Kṛṣṇa) and Saṃkarṣaṇa (Balarāma) were singled out for special worship. Quite a few early inscriptions and images testify to the worship of these two, and their images are found in Mandhal too (Plates XIX to XXII). A third image found here may also have belonged to this group of Sātvata or Vṛṣṇi heroes (*vīras*) and, possibly, represents Sāmba (Plate XXIII).

The Sātvata worship was integrated into the Bhāgavata religion in two ways: as noted above, four of the five deities were eventually transformed into abstract functions in an intricate theology that became known as the Pāñcarātra, and therewith lost their immediate devotional appeal to worshippers; simultaneously, the two main deities, Balarāma and Kṛṣṇa, were accommodated to another ramification that developed in the Bhāgavata fold, namely that of Viṣṇu's appearances (*vibhavas*) or descents (*avatāras*) to earth. It is this doctrine that is reified in the temples of the Rāmagiri. They lead us to the second set of Vaiṣṇava deities.

The same *Nārāyaṇīya* section that provided us with some valuable information about the Sātvatas contains several lists of Viṣṇu's manifestations (*prādurbhāvas*). The idea of god Kṛṣṇa/Vāsudeva, identified with Viṣṇu,[17] incarnating in human form to save the world was first expressed in the *Bhagavadgītā*, in the famous verses where Kṛṣṇa says,

> For Me have passed many births, and for thee, Arjuna; These I know all; thou knowest not, scorcher of the foe. Tho unborn, tho My self

16 Banerjea 1944, 129 f., 'The early iconographic texts refer to his images, and I shall try to show in this paper whether extant images of this god who was originally a human being can be recognised among a class of sculptures of the Kuṣāṇa period from Mathurā. These are seated figures, some shown riding in a chariot drawn by four horses, while in the case of others the chariot is either completely absent or faintly suggested only. These figures are usually dressed according to the mode of the northerners (*udīcyaveśa*), and hold in their two hands either lotus flowers (not very distinct in many cases) or a mace, a sword and other indistinct objects. They are either described by modern scholars as so many images of Sūrya or statues of some Kuṣāṇa kings, according as their attributes are clearly recognisable.'

17 BhG 11.24, 11.30.

> is eternal, tho Lord of Beings, resorting to My own material nature I come into being by My own mysterious power. For whenever of the right a languishing appears, son of Bharata, a rising up of unright, then I send Myself forth. For protection of the good, and for the destruction of evil-doers, to make a firm footing for the right, I come into being in age after age.[18]

That the highest god could assume different forms on different occasions was already known from the Brāhmaṇas in which Prajāpati is said to have assumed the forms of a tortoise (→ Kūrma) and a boar (→ Varāha).[19] These incarnations became eventually associated with Viṣṇu, but the earliest incarnations around which a devotional cult developed were without doubt the ones mentioned in the *Nārāyaṇīya* 12.337.36, viz. Varāha, Narasiṃha, Vāmana (i.e. Trivikrama) and the 'man incarnations,' referring to Rāma Dāśarathi, Kṛṣṇa and his brother Balarāma,[20] and Bhārgava Rāma (i.e. Paraśurāma).[21] Sanctuaries were built on the Rāmagiri that were dedicated to most of these deities; of Varāha, Narasiṃha and Trivikrama we still possess the idols (Plates XXXII to XXXIV), of Kṛṣṇa/Vāsudeva and Balarāma/Saṃkarṣaṇa the temple, known as Bhogarāma, is preserved, and Rāma Dāśarathi's connection with the hill—though not a proof of his cult in its own right, which was first to develop many centuries later—is indicated by its name, 'Hill of Rāma,' and the contemporaneous *Meghadūta* (vss. 1 and 12, see below p. 85). Only Paraśurāma is missing, for his divine power seems to have been looked upon as something of the past, suggested in the *Rāmāyaṇa* 1.75.11–12 where we read,

> Then, while the world was stupefied and Rāma (Dāśarathi) held the eminent bow, that Rāma, son of Jamadagni, gazed at Rāma, being bereft of his power: the son of Jamadagni was stupefied because his power (*vīryatva*) was nullified by the ardour (*tejas*) (of Rāma Dāśarathi).

As has been observed above, the cult of Narasiṃha may have been grafted on a folk deity and so may that of Varāha. The figure of Trivikrama goes back to Vedic origins and pertains to Viṣṇu as cosmic deity. It became connected with the myth of his dwarf incarnation (Vāmana) who wrested the world from king Bali's oppressive rule by striding through the universe in the three steps that Bali in his ignorance

---

18 BhG 4.5–8, translation by Franklin Edgerton.

19 ŚBr 7.5.1.5, 14.1.2.11; TaiBr 1.1.3.5 ff.; TaiSa 7.1.5.1; cf. ŚBr 1.8.1 (the fish that saves Manu).

20 He is designated Sātvata in MBh 12.326.851*.

21 MBh 12.337.36, *vārāhaṃ nārasiṃhaṃ ca vāmanaṃ mānuṣaṃ tathā| ebhir mayā nihantavyā durvinītāḥ surārayaḥ* ||.

had allowed the dwarf to take. The myths connected with these three deities, all concerned with the rescue of the earth from evil forces, lent themselves perfectly to royal allegory, an opportunity not lost upon the kings of Nandivardhana nor upon their Gupta counterparts.[22]

The background of the two human *avatāras*, Kṛṣṇa and Balarāma, is a different one as we saw above. The Bhogarāma Temple with its two *garbhagṛhas* next to each other may originally have been dedicated to the two Sātvata brothers. The figure of Balarāma (Saṃkarṣaṇa) had been from early times onwards connected with serpent worship and snakes play an essential role in his iconography; the word *bhoga* preceding *rāma* should hence be taken in its meaning 'coil of a snake,' and the 'Rāma with the coils' can only be Balarāma.[23] The temple today is in the possession of the Manbhaus sect and they have installed an image of their god Kṛṣṇa in one of the cellas.

The affiliation of Rāma Dāśarathi with the hill is less transparent. The worship of Rāma as the major form of or as identical with Viṣṇu did not develop until the eleventh century.[24] The name 'Rāmagiri' on the other hand, which appears in the inscriptions of Prabhāvatī Guptā, indicates that it was associated with the hero of the *Rāmāyaṇa* from the fifth century onwards. The tradition that the hill was visited by Rāma who left his footprint is known from *Meghadūta* 12 and is corroborated by the thirteenth century Yādava inscription in the Lakṣmaṇa Temple on the hill, which says that the mountain had been 'touched by the lotus-feet of the illustrious Rāma' (vs. 83), hence it is called the 'Mountain of Rāma' (Rāmagiri).[25]

---

22 The Trivikrama/Vāmana symbolism is expressed in the opening verse of the Kevala-Narasiṃha Temple Inscription: ⟨*ba*⟩(*l*)⟨*i*⟩(*ma*)*khasamayaidhitāṅga*(*śo*)⟨*bho*⟩(Appendix I vs. 1); and Skandagupta's Junagaḍh Rock Inscription: *śriyam abhimatabhogyāṃ naikakālāpanītāṃ tridaśapatisukhārthaṃ yo baler ājahāra*| (CII III, 299 vs. 1). The Narasiṃha symbolism is found on some coins of Kumāragupta ('Lion-slayer Type'), the obverse of which has the following legend (Allan 1914, cxviii, 77, 155): 'Like Narasiṅha in presence, the lion-Mahendra is eternally victorious' (*sākṣād iva narasiṅho siṅhamahendro jayaty aniśam*).

23 Bakker 1992c and 1992b.

24 Bakker 1987; Pollock 1993.

25 Bakker 1989a, 485 (vs. 85): *rāmasya girāv iha*. The same inscription in verse 86 identifies the Rāmagiri with the hill on which Śambūka practised *tapas* and was beheaded by Rāma: "Here the *śūdra* saint Śambuka [sic] had reached the abode of Murāri after having been killed by the sword Candrahāsā [sic] which was wielded by Rāmacandra; and on this eminent mountain he became well-known as Dhūmrākṣa, the 'smoky-eyed' " (Bakker 1989a, 493). The inscription, as far as legible, does not mention the name Śaivala. The *liṅga* sanctuary of Dhūmrākṣa or Dhūmreśvara, considered as the *bhūmipālaka* of the hill, is still pointed out today. In a forthcoming article I have evaluated this tradition, which may have its starting point in an old Yakṣa shrine, which, possibly, inspired Kālidāsa to situate the Yakṣa of his *Meghadūta* on this hill. There are several indications that the famous poet was well acquainted with the actual Rāmagiri (Bakker, *forthcoming b*). Possibly the first attestation (4th century AD?) of a hill called 'Rāmagiri' is found in Vimalasūri's *Paümacariya*: Rāma (also called Padma) and his retinue stayed on a hill

The temples of Viṣṇu's *avatāras* mentioned so far are all situated a few hundred meters to the east of the main temple complex on the spur of the hill. Though the latter complex, dedicated to Rāma and his brother Lakṣmaṇa, dates from the Yādava period (13th century), it can be taken for certain that the main sanctuary of the hill in the fifth century, the Rāmagiristhāna, occupied the same spot. In one of her inscriptions Prabhāvatī seems to give some additional information regarding the nature of this main sanctuary, when she declares that the charter was issued from the 'soles of the feet of the Lord of Rāmagiri,'[26] which echoes an earlier charter by her in which it is said that the grant had first been offered to the 'soles of the feet of the Lord.'[27] With regard to a tablet containing a pair of footprints that was found at the foot of the hill in Nagardhan and is described below (Plate XXXI B) I advanced the hypothesis that the footprint icon may represent a miniature version of the sanctuary on top of the hill (Bakker 1991). If this conjecture is correct, we could answer the question as to how the *rāmagirisvāminaḥ pādamūlam* sanctuary, in which Prabhāvatī Guptā worshipped, should be conceived. It might have been a square enclosure giving access to a square platform on which an altar containing the footprints of the Bhagavat, the Lord (*svāmin*) of Rāmagiri, was installed, squared in by a low railing or wall, rather than being enshrined in a temple.[28] This sanctuary may have been replaced in Yādava times by the Rāma temple that is still crowning the hill. The legend that connected the hill with a visit of Rāma makes it plausible that these footprints were conceived, by some at least, as those of Viṣṇu's incarnation Rāma as depicted in the *Rāmāyaṇa*.

The concept of a hill-top imprinted by the feet of Viṣṇu is not only repeatedly found in the *Mahābhārata*,[29] its actual occurring in the religion of the Bhāgavatas is also attested by the Meharauli Pillar Inscription of Candra.[30] This inscription is the subject of extensive scholarly debate, which in my view has not led to a refutation of Sircar's most plausible interpretation that 'the pillar was made for Candragupta II about the end of his life; but the record was engraved by Kumāragupta soon after his father's death.'[31] On account of this interpretation we feel confident in conclud-

---

called Vaṃśagiri near the city of Vaṃśasthapura. Because the king of that city erected many Jaina shrines on that hill on Rāma's advice, that hill became known as 'Rāmagiri': *rāmeṇa jamhā bhavaṇottamāṇi jiṇindacandāṇa nivesiyāṇi | tattheva tuṅge vimalappabhāṇi tamhā jaṇe rāmagirī pasiddho* ||16|| (*Paümacariya* 40.16). See Mirashi 1968.

26 *rāmagirisvāminaḥ pādamūlāt*, CII V, 35.

27 *bhagavatpādamūle nivedya*, CII V, 7.

28 This would endorse the view that the expression *pādamūla* should in some cases be taken literally, in its sense of 'sole of the foot,' i.e. 'footprint,' and not as a metaphor for 'temple' as argued by Sircar in Sel. Ins. I, 512 n. 2.

29 MBh 3.81.86–87, 3.130.7–8, 5.109.19, 7.57.32, 12.29.31. See Bakker 1991.

30 CII III, 257–259; Sel. Ins. I, 283–5.

31 Sel. Ins. I, 284 n. 4; Papers of a symposium on this pillar were published by M. C. Joshi and S.

ing that the *paramabhāgavata* Kumāragupta, brother of Prabhāvatī Guptā, erected a lofty column (*dhvaja*) of Bhagavat Viṣṇu on a hill (*giri*) that was believed to contain a footprint (*pada*) of this god and was hence called Viṣṇupada.[32] The tree-like object that is depicted between the two footprints on the tablet found in Nagardhan, if it reflects a similar object once standing near or in the footprint sanctuary on the spur of the Rāmagiri, may have expressed the same symbolism as the *dhvaja* on the Viṣṇupada, viz. that of the cosmic pillar (*skambha*), the world tree that rose out of the primordial hill, along which Viṣṇu took his strides to separate heaven and earth.[33]

The Māheśvara Faith

> Certain (*kecana*) Māheśvaras disapproved of the doctrine of the Vaiṣṇavas, a (doctrine of) dependence on another's will as indicated by such terms as "servitude" (*dāsatva*) (used therein), doing so on the ground that this doctrine does not furnish what we desire, namely the end of suffering (*duḥkhānta*). Preferring (to take as their goal) absolute sovereignty (*pāramaiśvarya*), they accept as authoritative the following inference: Those souls whom others (the Vaiṣṇavas) consider to be released cannot be released, because they are dependent upon another (viz. God) (*paratantratva*), and because they lack absolute sovereignty just as we do (in the present life). (On the other hand) souls which are (truly) released must be possessed of the qualities of

---

K. Gupta 1989. The issue was taken up again by V. C. Pandey in RGH, 155–164.

32 *prāptena svabhujārjitaṃ ca suciraṃ caikādhirājyaṃ kṣitau candrāhvena samagracandrasadṛśīṃ vaktraśriyaṃ bibhratā| tenāyaṃ praṇidhāya bhūmipatinā bhāvena viṣṇo(au) matiṃ prāṅśur viṣṇupade girau bhagavato viṣṇor dhvajaḥ sthāpitaḥ* [||∗], Sel. Ins. I, 284 f.; cf. CII III, 259.

33 Kuiper 1983, 49, 'From a purely mythological point of view Viṣṇu, who by his position in the center must also in Vedic belief have been immediately associated with the cosmic pillar (*skambhá*), must have ascended along the pillar at the beginning of the year and descended in the second half of it but, owing perhaps to the fact that the texts are primarily concerned with the beginning of the new year, they do not contain any reference to such a belief. [...] On the other hand there is clear evidence of Viṣṇu's connection with the mountains: he is 'dwelling' or 'standing' on the mountain(s) and 'regent of the mountains.' [...] he stands on the summit of the mountain (*Ṛgveda* 1.155.1). [...] Later art represents him standing on Mount Mandara, and arising from it as the cosmic pillar. In the middle of the seventh century A.D. an artist at Māmalapuram portrayed the god, while taking his three strides, as being the supporting pillar of the universe.'

> an absolute sovereign (*parameśvara*), because despite the fact that they are individual souls they lack all seeds of (future) suffering, as in the case of the highest Lord (Maheśvara). Accordingly these Māheśvaras take to the Pāśupata scripture, a system which sets forth the five categories (*pañcārtha*) as their instrument for achieving the highest goal of men.[34]

Sāyaṇa Mādhava's (c. AD 1350) opening statement of the chapter in which he deals with the system of the Pāśupata according to Nakulīśa (*Nakulīśapāśupatadarśana*) makes a number of things clear. First that not all Māheśvaras are Pāśupatas. The Pāśupatas were ascetics who, after having undergone initiation (*dīkṣā*), were committed to the *pāśupatavrata*, i.e. to observe a life in accordance with the Pāśupata scriptures, a career which was beyond the pale of organized society (termed 'the Outer Path,' Atimārga).[35] The majority of the Māheśvaras on the other hand were probably householders (*laukikas*) who, like the Vaiṣṇavas, contented themselves with worshipping Maheśvara (Śiva) and supporting the order, thereby, in the view of their world-renouncing brethren, abstaining, at least in their present life, from the possibility to realize complete autonomy (= release from all suffering, *duḥkhānta*).[36] The relationship between the majority of the Māheśvaras and the (Nakulīśa)-Pāśupatas may therefore have been similar to that between the laity and the monks of the Buddhist order. Mādhava's statement, secondly, seems to entail that the Māheśvaras on the whole set greater store by ascetic values than their Vaiṣṇava counterparts. The *Nārāyaṇīya* section of the *Mahābhārata* informs us that there were five different doctrines or schools (*jñāna*): in addition to the Vaiṣṇava school (here termed Pāñcarātra) and the Sāṃkhya, Yoga and Vedic traditions, there was the Pāśupata, which was promulgated by Śrīkaṇṭha, the son of Brahmā, the

---

34 Sāyaṇa Mādhava, *Sarvadarśanasaṃgraha*, Chapter 6, p. 161 ll. 1–6, translated by Minoru Hara 1958, 12 f.

35 Sanderson 1988, 132. MBh 13.15.4 pictures the outward appearance of the initiate who has gone through a *dīkṣā* ceremony: he carries a staff, his head is shaven, he has *kuśa* grass (in his hand), he is clad in bark (or rags), he wears a girdle and is anointed with ghee: *dine 'ṣṭame ca vipreṇa dīkṣito 'haṃ yathāvidhi | daṇḍī muṇḍī kuśī cīrī ghṛtākto mekhalī tathā* ||4||.

36 The more mundane objectives of the common devotee may have been succinctly summed up in Kṛṣṇa's request to Śiva and Umā in MBh 13.16.2, 6. 'I wish firmness in the *dharma*, in war (the ability) to kill the enemies, the utmost fame and greatest power, dedication to yoga, nearness to you, and hundreds of hundreds of sons': *dharme dṛḍhatvaṃ yudhi śatrughātaṃ yaśas tathāgryaṃ paramaṃ balaṃ ca | yogapriyatvaṃ tava saṃnikarṣaṃ vṛṇe sutānāṃ ca śataṃ śatāni* ||2||; 'I wish freedom of anger towards the brahmins, grace from my father, a hundred sons, and the utmost enjoyment, attachment to my family, and grace from my mother, the obtainment of tranquility and skillfulness': *dvijeṣv akopaṃ pitṛtaḥ prasādaṃ śataṃ sutānām upabhogaṃ paraṃ ca | kule prītiṃ mātṛtaś ca prasādaṃ śamaprāptiṃ pravṛṇe cāpi dākṣyam* ||6||.

consort of Umā and lord of the *bhūtas* (beings/spirits), the unwavering Śiva.[37]

The Pāśupata sect that considered Nakulīśa (Lakulīśa) as its preceptor was probably only one of the order's divisions,[38] and it was itself again split in four subdivisions each headed by a disciple of Lakulīśa.[39] The latter was seen by his followers as the 28th and last incarnation of Maheśvara, who had assumed a human body by animating a corpse in the cremation ground of Kāyārohaṇa (Kārohaṇa), modern Karvan in the Baroda District, Gujarat.[40] This myth might ultimately go back to a trick of an accomplished *yogin* and it is generally assumed that Lakulīśa was a historical figure.

On account of an inscription on a pillar found in Mathura which is dated in the Gupta year 61 (= AD 380) it has been inferred that Lakulīśa lived in the second century AD. At the time of the inscription there had been nine Masters (*ācāryas*) since Kuśika. The inscription records the installation of two cult objects, named after two of the earlier *ācāryas* (Kapilavimala and Upamitavimala) as 'Upamiteśvara' and 'Kapileśvara,' in a sanctuary of the order that seems to have been some sort of memorial shrine of the gurus of the Kuśika lineage (*gurvāyatana*).[41] The inscription was made to beseech the Māheśvaras to protect the sanctuary and to offer worship there.[42] The pillar on which the inscription was engraved shows a large trident (*triśūla*) with a stocky naked figure at the bottom whose right hand rests on a staff (*daṇḍa*) and who may represent the guardian god (*bhagavat*) Daṇḍa, a supreme leader (*agranāyaka*) of Rudra's host of *gaṇas*, personifying the latter's *daṇḍa* or authority (*rudradaṇḍa*); he is saluted in the last line of the inscription.[43]

The 'five categories' referred to in the quotation from Mādhava are, (1) 'the effect' (*kārya*), which is the visible and invisible world comprising knowledge, the

---

37 *umāpatir bhūtapatiḥ śrīkaṇṭho brahmaṇaḥ sutaḥ | uktavān idam avyagro jñānaṃ pāśupataṃ śivaḥ* ||62||, MBh 12.337.62. It has been argued that Śrīkaṇṭha refers to a historical person of that name, who could have been Lakulīśa's teacher (see H. Chakraborti in the Introduction to his translation of the *Pāśupatasūtra*, 1.9; Pathak 1960, 4 ff.).

38 Sanderson 1988, 132 ff.

39 VāP 23.223; Cintra Praśasti in EI I, 281 vss. 14–16: Kuśika, Gārgya (Garga), Kauruṣya and Maitreya (Mitra). SP_{Bh} 167.128–149: Kauśika (in Ujjayinī), Gārgya (in Jambūmārga), Mitra in (Mathurā) and *kuruṣveva sugotrajaḥ* (?) (in Kānyakubja).

40 VāP 23.220–24.

41 Sel. Ins. I, 278.

42 *[atha*] māheśvarāṇāṃ vijñaptiḥ kriyate sambodhanaṃ ca* (|*) *yathākā[le]nācāryāṇāṃ parigraham iti matvā viśaṅka[ṃ] [pū]jāpuraskāra[ṃ] parigrahapāripālyaṃ [kuryā]d iti vijñaptir iti*, Sel. Ins. I, 278 ll. 11–14; cf. Sircar in IHQ XVIII (1942), 271–75. Sircar, following D. R. Bhandarkar, thinks that 'the lower part of the Liṅga-shaft called *Upamiteśvara* was so shaped as to represent the figure of Upamita, while the figure of Kapila was made in the lower part of the other Liṅga called *Kapileśvara*. Apparently the teachers were represented as bearing a Liṅga on the head' (Sircar op. cit., 275; Bhandarkar in EI XXI (1931–32), 6 f. (cf. CII III, 239)).

43 Sel. Ins. I, 279 l. 17; Kreisel 1986, 252. Banerjea 1968, 52 (following Bhandarkar) identifies the naked figure as Lakulīśa (by equalling *daṇḍa* with *lakuṭa*).

means of knowledge (i.e. the organs and the material world associated with them),[44] and the *paśus* (living beings dependent on God); (2) 'the cause' (*kāraṇa*), which is God (Paśupati); (3) '*yoga*,' which is the connection with God through the psychic faculties; (4) 'prescribed behaviour' (*vidhi*), which entails the Pāśupata observance (*vrata*); (5) 'end of suffering' (*duḥkhānta*). The 'prescribed behaviour' of the Pāśupatas knows five stages, in the first of which 'the ascetic lived by a temple of Śiva. His body was smeared with ashes and he was to worship the deity in the temple by dancing and chanting, boisterous laughter, drumming on his mouth (*huḍḍukkāra*), and silent meditation on the five *mantras* of the *Yajurveda*, the five *brahmamantras*, which in course of time became personified as the five faces of Śiva.'[45] The task of the wider circle of Māheśvaras was thus an important one. They should erect the temples, enshrine the idols, maintain and worship them and support the ascetics who were living in and around them. The duties and rewards of these laymen are described in the *Śivadharma*, a corpus of texts that, for the greater part, still awaits editon and exploration. Abhinavagupta may have put it in a nutshell, 'Those who are without initiation and knowledge but are fully devoted to the worship of *liṅgas*, they will attain to the City of Rudra, (high) within the Cosmic Egg, and they will never (fall back) to lower stages.'[46] Despite the emphasis on *yoga*, asceticism and some transgressive practices and notwithstanding their aim and claim of absolute sovereignty, the Pāśupata ascetics, and *a fortiori* the Māheśvaras at large, operated within a theistic system, as is illustrated by Kauṇḍinya's *Bhāṣya* on *Pāśupatasūtra* 5.40.

> Those who reach release through Sāṃkhya and Yoga attain the 'supreme state,' (yet) they are then no longer aware of their own self nor of another self, as if in a state of unconsciousness. But there is knowledge for him (who has attained the (Pāśupata) ultimate goal), since the *sūtra* says: 'He whose vigilance does not fail shall attain the end of sorrows thanks to the grace of God.'[47]

An important idea in the theology of the Māheśvaras, which features in their

---

44 For this part of their view of the world the Pāśupatas, like their Bhāgavata (Pāñcarātra) counterparts, rely heavily on the philosophy of the Sāṃkhya school.

45 Sanderson 1988, 133. The other stages are, (2) moving about in public pretending to be mad etc., (3) retreat in a cave for meditation, (4) living in the cremation ground until death, (5) completion (*niṣṭhā*), i.e. the end of suffering.

46 *dīkṣājñānavihīnā ye liṅgārādhanatatparāḥ* ||157|| *te yānty aṇḍāntare raudraṃ puraṃ nādhaḥ kadācana* |, *Tantrāloka* 8.157 f. Jayaratha ad loc. explains *liṅgārādhanatatparā iti śivadharmottarādiprakriyayā* (I owe this reference to A. Sanderson).

47 *sāṃkhyayogamuktāḥ kaivalyagatāḥ svātmaparātmajñānarahitāḥ saṃmūrchitavat sthitāḥ* | *asya tu jñānam asti* | *yasmād āha — apramādī gacched duḥkhānām antam īśaprasādāt* ||40|| *iti* |. R. Ananthakrishna Sastri's edition, p. 140.

praxis (see above) and eventually came to inform the iconography of their images, is that of the five *brahmamantras*. This very old tradition, ultimately reaching back to the *Taittirīya Āraṇyaka* (10.43–47), associates five mantras, i.e. five cosmic aspects or functions with Sadāśiva; the first word of each mantra is explained by the commentator Sāyaṇa as the name of a face (*vaktra*) of God (Parameśvara), viz. Sadyojāta, Vāmadeva, Aghora, Tatpuruṣa, and Īśāna. These five aspects, known in the scriptures of the Śaiva Siddhānta as 'the five Brahmans,' are conceived of as being comprised in or as being the embodiment of Sadāśiva, an idea also reaching back to the *Taittirīya Āraṇyaka*, which concludes the fifth formula of Īśāna with the words *sadāśivom*, glossed by Sāyaṇa as *sa eva sadāśiva om*. The highest aspect, Īśāna, embodying Śiva's grace, is homologized with the fifth element *ākāśa*. The other Brahmans are also associated with the elements, in such a way that they form two correlated series of decreasing subtlety.[48]

Like the Bhāgavata, the Māheśvara faith of the fourth and fifth centuries was an entwining of various religious strands. At the end of the Vedic period the idea of a personal supreme God, the cause of fear and bliss, who grants desires and delivers those who know him from all fetters (*pāśa*) and who is called the 'Great Lord' (Maheśvara), 'was propounded truly by the wise Śvetāsvatara, thanks to his *tapas* and the grace of God, to those who had proceeded beyond the stages of worldly life,' in a text that may be considered as the earliest treatise of the Māheśvara faith, the *Śvetāśvataropaniṣad* (6.21). This God is said to be the Great Lord of Lords, the Master of Masters, who, though transcendent, is known as the Ruler of the world who should be worshipped; He is the highest, pure *brahman*, the magician who issues the past and future, all that is propounded in the Vedas, in short the natural world of phenomena.[49]

This supreme god is grafted on the older Vedic deity Rudra, who was beyond the pale of the neatly organized, sacrificial world of the brahmins and who was more feared than loved and needed to be propitiated; hence his euphemistic appellation

---

48 See e.g. Abhinavagupta's *Parātrīśikālaghuvṛtti* p. 7 ll. 18-21 (I owe this reference to A. Sanderson); the same correlation is given in VDhP 3.48.1–3: *sadyojātaṃ vāmadevam aghoraṃ ca mahābhuja | tathā tatpuruṣaṃ jñeyam īśānaṃ pañcamaṃ mukham ||1|| sadyojātaṃ mahī proktā vāmadevaṃ tathā jalam | tejas tv aghoraṃ vikhyātaṃ vāyus tatpuruṣaṃ matam || 2 || īśānaṃ ca tathākāśam ūrdhvasthaṃ pañcamaṃ mukham |*.

49 *chandāṃsi yajñāḥ kratavo vratāni bhūtaṃ bhavyaṃ yac ca vedā vadanti | asmān māyī sṛjate viśvam etat tasmiṃś cānyo māyayā saṃniruddhaḥ* |4.9| *māyāṃ tu prakṛtiṃ vidyān māyinaṃ tu maheśvaram | tasyāvayavabhūtais tu vyāptaṃ sarvam idaṃ jagat* |4.10| [...] *tam īśvarāṇāṃ paramaṃ maheśvaraṃ taṃ devatānāṃ paramaṃ ca daivatam | patiṃ patīnāṃ paramaṃ parastād vidāma devaṃ bhuvaneśam īḍyam* |6.7| [...] *tapaḥprabhāvād devaprasādāc ca brahma ha śvetāśvataro 'tha vidvān | atyāśramibhyaḥ paramaṃ pavitraṃ provāca samyag ṛṣisaṅghajuṣṭam* |6.21|, *Śvetāśvataropaniṣad* 4.9–10, 6.7, 6.21 (ed. Limaye and Vadekar).

'the auspicious one' (*śiva*). In the *Ṛgveda* (2.33) he is called the bull (*vṛṣabha*), the terrifying one (*ugra*), who carries bow and arrows, but he is also called the lord of medicines (ṚV 1.114.5). The *Vājasaneyī Saṃhitā* styles him the Lord of Cattle (Paśupati).[50] This Rudra or Paśupati is sung in the so-called *Śatarudrīya* of the *Taittirīya Saṃhitā* (4.5.1–11). He is depicted as roaming on the mountains,[51] the leader of the armies, lord of the foot-soldiers and warriors,[52] who pierces his enemies and is the master of the thieves.[53] He is also spoken of as the master of the hosts (*gaṇapati*) and as *vrātapati*, possibly an allusion to a group of Indo-aryans that was outside brahmanical Vedic society, viz. that of the Vrātyas.

In this early source we already encounter several of the characteristics and epithets that will inform the iconography of the Rudra/Maheśvara/Paśupati of the times of the Vākāṭakas, such as those which emphasize his wildness, by describing him as being 'deformed' (*virūpa*), 'all-formed' (*viśvarūpa*), stocky (*hrasva*, *vāmana*), as a hunter, carrying bow and arrows that embody his wrath, as having a reddish brown colour,[54] but with blue neck (*nīlagrīva*) and white throat (*śitikaṇṭha*); he is also called 'Blue-red' (Nīlalohita).[55] His hair is said to be either wound up in the form of a shell on the top of his head (*kapardin*), an epithet already given to Rudra in ṚV 1.114.1, or straight (*pulasti*, = matted?), or shaven/bald.[56] He is a real Lord of Spirits (Bhūteśvara), commanding thousands of Rudras who dwell on earth, Bhavas in the great ocean and in the air, Śarvas beneath the earth, and spirits living in trees.[57] Though these awesome features predominate, he is also said to wear the sacred thread (*upavītin*) and a turban (*uṣṇīṣin*),[58] indicative of his royal dignity in the terrestrial realm.

Several visions of this god are described in the *Mahābhārata* in which new, iconographically significant characteristics are added. Upamanyu saw the *bhagavat* Maheśvara,[59] standing immovable as a post (*sthāṇu*), possessed of eighteen arms, with Pārvatī at his side and surrounded by singing, dancing and jumping companions, which seems to be a clear reference to Pāśupata practice.[60] He had three eyes and was wearing a crown adorned by the crescent moon and a white

---

50 *Yajurveda* IX.39, XXXIX.8.
51 TaiSa 4.5.1, 3.
52 *senānī, pattipati, satvapati*, TaiSa 4.5.2.
53 *stenapati*, TaiSa 4.5.3.
54 *aruṇa, tāmra, babhru*, already in ṚV 2.33.
55 These colours might reflect the phenomenon of lightning and thunder with which he was associated as appears from his epithets such as *meghya, vidyutya, dundubhya* (TaiSa 4.5.7).
56 *vyuptakeśa, śipiviṣṭa*, TaiSa 4.5.5.
57 TaiSa 4.5.11.
58 TaiSa 4.5.2–3.
59 Laine 1989, 202–211.
60 MBh 13.14.115–118.

garland strung together by golden lotuses and adorned with jewels. His weapons had assumed bodily form: the bow called Pināka, a seven-headed serpent; the arrow, the terrible Pāśupata weapon, with which he destroyed the Triple City (of the Asuras), a one-footed, thousand-headed, majestic body.[61] Among the other attributes mentioned are the lance (*śūla*) and the axe (*paraśu*), given to Paraśurāma to kill Kārtavīrya and the *kṣatriyas*.[62] To his right stood Brahmā, to his left Nārāyaṇa, near to him Skanda with the spear (*śakti*) and in front of him Nandin carrying the *śūla*, another Śaṃkara as it were (*dvitīyam iva śaṃkaram*).[63] Upamanyu sings the praise of the God who is said to wear a garment made of the skin of a black antelope, and whose appearance is bright (*śukla*), as he is wearing white clothes and smeared with white ashes (*śuklabhasmāvalipta*).[64]

After having been initiated by Upamanyu, Kṛṣṇa also had a vision of Śiva,[65] adding again other characteristics, among which the crown (*kirīṭa*), the mace (*gadā*), a tiger-skin (*vyāghrāja*), the staff (*daṇḍa*) and sharp fangs (*tīkṣṇadaṃstra*), beautiful armlets (*śubhāṅgada*), a *yajñopavīta* consisting of snakes (*vyāla*), and matted hair (*jaṭila*).[66] He is said to be surrounded by *gaṇas*, *pramathas* and eleven Rudras and riding the bull.[67]

From these and other descriptions of Maheśvara/Śiva in the (late) *Anuśāsanaparvan* of the *Mahābhārata* it emerges that the god of the Māheśvaras was no longer only an archetype of those excluded from brahmanical society and of world-renouncers, but had developed into a catholic cult figure with a fully-fledged iconography of its own. Yet it is not exactly the deity that we encounter in the art of the fourth and fifth centuries. Two aspects seem to be underexposed: his life-sustaining and gracious nature (though he is said to grant every desire when he is duly propitiated), symbolized in the images *inter alia* by the *varada-* and *abhayamudrā* and his holding of the vessel (*kalaśa*) with ambrosia (*amṛta*), and his marked sexuality, expressed by his erect penis (*ūrdhvaliṅga*).

With regard to Śiva's phallic aspect some more information is given when Vyāsa reveals Śiva's nature in a famous eulogy in *Droṇaparvan* 173.

> When his phallus stands in perpetual celibacy and people worship (*mahayanti*), (then) is he known as Maheśvara. Seers, gods, Gandhar-

61 MBh 13.14.119–126.
62 MBh 13.14.131–140.
63 MBh 13.14.141–146.
64 MBh 13.14.150–153.
65 Laine 1989, 212–217.
66 MBh 13.15.11–12.
67 MBh 13.15.13–14. After another hymn sung by Taṇḍi (MBh 13.16.13–65), the famous hymn of the thousand names (*Śivasahasranāmastotra*) follows in MBh 13.17.30–150.

> vas and Apsarases also adore his phallus, and then also it stands erect. Therefore that Great Lord (Maheśvara) rejoices when his (phallus) is worshipped; Śaṃkara becomes happy and gratified and he is certainly delighted.[68]

A veiled reference to the four-faced *liṅga* may have been implied in the myth of the nymph Tilottamā told in the *Ādiparvan.*[69] This myth explains why Maheśvara, referred to as Sthāṇu ('Post'), has four faces.[70] They emerged from his body, caused by his desire to watch the beautiful nymph when she made his *pradakṣiṇā*. This myth is taken up in the *Anuśāsanaparvan*,[71] where significant iconographic features are added. Again the text stops short of explicitly referring to Śiva's *liṅga*; it explains how Śiva assumed a quadruple form (*caturmūrtitva*).

> Wherever she with beautiful teeth (i.e. Tilottamā) came into my vicinity, there, O Goddess, emerged a lovely head of mine. Wishing to watch her, I assumed a quadruple form with the help of *yoga*. Having become four-faced, while showing my own *yoga*, I exercise sovereignty with my eastern face, with my northern one I sport with you, O blameless one (Umā); my western face is gentle and conveys happiness to all living beings; my southern face, which has a terrifying appearance and is fierce, crushes creatures.[72]

---

68 *nityena brahmacaryeṇa liṅgam asya yadā sthitam* | *mahayanti ca lokāś ca maheśvara iti smṛtaḥ* ||83|| *ṛṣayaś caiva devāś ca gandharvāpsarasas tathā* | *liṅgaṃ asyārcayanti sma tac cāpy ūrdhvaṃ samāsthitam* ||84|| *pūjyamāne tatas tasmin modate sa maheśvaraḥ* | *sukhī prītaś ca bhavati prahṛṣṭaś caiva śaṃkaraḥ* ||85||, MBh 7.173.83–85. This passage is taken over in *Anuśāsanaparvan* 146.15–18. Apart from some minor variants, an explicatory *śloka* is inserted after verse 83 (= MBh 13.146.16), which disturbs the syntax, since the relative pronoun *yo* in 16a has no clear antecedent. It is the first and only verse in the *Mahābhārata* that unequivocally refers to the *liṅga* as a particular cult object different from an (ithyphallic) iconic idol: 'One worships the image of the magnanimous one (i.e. Śiva), or otherwise his phallus (*liṅga*); he who always worships his phallus shall obtain great prosperity (*vigrahaṃ pūjayed yo vai liṅgaṃ vāpi mahātmanaḥ* | *liṅgaṃ pūjayitā nityaṃ mahatīṃ śriyam aśnute* ||16||). Compare also MBh 13.14.99–102.

69 MBh 1.203.22–26.

70 That the appelation 'Sthāṇu' may have a phallic connotation emerges from the ambiguous explanation in MBh 7.173.92: 'When he stands erect, he burns (/destroys), and when he is standing (erect), living beings are born, and because he always bears the mark of standing (/his phallus is always standing), therefore is he known as "Post." ' (*dahaty ūrdhvaṃ sthito yac ca prāṇotpattisthitaś ca yat* | *sthitaliṅgaś ca yan nityaṃ tasmāt sthāṇur iti smṛtaḥ* ||92||).

71 MBh 13.128.1–6.

72 *yato yataḥ sā sudatī mām upādhāvad antike* | *tatas tato mukhaṃ cāru mama devi vinirgatam* ||3|| *tāṃ didṛkṣur ahaṃ yogāc caturmūrtitvam āgataḥ* | *caturmukhaś ca saṃvṛtto darśayan yogam ātmanaḥ* ||4|| *pūrveṇa vadanenāham indratvam anuśāsmi ha* | *uttareṇa tvayā sārdhaṃ ramāmy aham anindite* ||5|| *paścimaṃ me mukhaṃ saumyaṃ sarvaprāṇisukhāvaham* | *dakṣiṇaṃ bhīmasaṃkāśaṃ raudraṃ saṃharati prajāḥ* ||6|| (MBh 13.128.3–6).

The same myth is told in another early Śaiva source, the original *Skandapurāṇa* (SP_{Bh}62.1–26). Here explicit reference is made to Śiva in his *liṅga* form.[73] From this *liṅga* four faces emerged when Tilottamā made her circumambulation, the eastern one lustrous, with lips gracious as the bimba fruit (*prasannabimbauṣṭha*) and with three eyes (*tryakṣa*), the southern one dark as a water-laden cloud, with a terrifying voice (*bhīmanisvana*) and dreadful teeth (*karāladaśanodbhāsin*),[74] the western one perfect (*anuttama*) having three eyes, and the northern one very full (*susaṃpūrṇa*) and very gracious (*suprasanna*).[75]

From the textual evidence presented above it becomes apparent that the concept of a fourfold form of Śiva was well established in Vākāṭaka times. This concept could be applied to his representation in a *liṅga* (Sadāśiva), where it became eventually assimilated to the concept of the five Brahmans, or to an anthropomorphic manifestation (Maheśvara). The distinction between Sadāśiva and Maheśvara is made by art-historians on the basis of a fundamental distinction in Śiva's iconography, viz. his aniconic or semi-aniconic representation in the *liṅga* or *mukhaliṅga* on the one hand ('Sadāśiva'), and iconic representation in a more or less anthropomorphic idol ('Maheśvara') on the other. The highest fivefold manifestation of the transcendent Parameśvara, i.e. Sadāśiva, is still beyond the world of (gross) phenomena; he is, as we have already noted, embodied in the five *brahmamantras*. The Maheśvara level of God is structurally connected with the higher fivefold manifestation of Sadāśiva but, less subtle than this, it unfolds in forms which can be represented in space and time and which allow identification with personal forms of Śiva known from (later) mythology such as Bhairava, personifying his *ugra* or terrifying aspect. The quadruple form that we find in the *Mahābhārata* evolved into the fivefold Maheśvara division, a process in which these forms, like those of Sadāśiva, were homologized with the five elements, which was believed to make the highest, fifth form invisible, since it is associated with *ākāśa*.

We shall argue below that the theological distinction referred to by us as 'Sadāśiva' and 'Maheśvara' was known to the Māheśvaras of Mandhal who designed the images found there, since it seems to be implied in their iconography. However, the archaeological evidence strongly suggests that the Vākāṭakas, like the composers of the *Mahābhārata*, had a preference for the anthropomorphic forms. Of the multi-headed images found in Mandhal the faces in eastern, western and northern directions are all very similar and could be described as gracious (*prasanna*) or gentle (*saumya*); the southern head is well distinguished in one case,

73 'There arose amidst these celestials a *liṅga*, solid, massive, a bundle of *tejas* as it were,' *atha liṅgaṃ samuttasthau teṣāṃ madhye divaukasām | susaṃhataṃ susaṃśliṣṭaṃ samūhas tejasām iva* ||12|| (SP_{Bh} 62.12).

74 For a full quotation see below p. 123.

75 SP_{Bh}62.16–24.

in the eight-faced, four-headed image (Maheśvara, Plate II), and conforms to Śiva's ferocious aspect. It remains open to question, however, whether the quadruple form of Śiva had already become standardized in an iconographic set of (five) deities as specified in the *Viṣṇudharmottarapurāṇa* (3.48.3–6)—viz. Sadāśiva, Mahādeva, Bhairava, Nandivaktra, Umāvaktra, though the deities implied in these names are separately represented in Mandhal.

Resuming the issue of *liṅga* worship again, we observe that, although arguably the earliest textual reference to *liṅga* worship is found in the *Gṛhyapariśiṣṭasūtras* of Baudhāyana (3rd–4th centuries AD?),[76] and abundant archaeological evidence testifies to *liṅga* worship all over India from the beginning of the Christian era,[77] there is very little to prove that *liṅga* worship was patronized in the Vākāṭaka kingdom, this notwithstanding the fact that the kings must have been very well acquainted with the *liṅga* cult, as they repeated in their inscriptions that their Bhāraśiva ancestors were favoured by Śiva because they wore his emblem, the *liṅga*, on their shoulders.[78] The Śiva images of Mandhal show his ithyphallic mark decently covered by a *dhotī* (Plates I to VIII), except for the Rudra image (Plate IX), a mark indicating his complete control over the senses and sexual drive, rather than his lustful character.[79] As has already been indicated and will be shown below (p. 103), the same symbolism that underlies the *caturmukhaliṅga* was applied in the Sadāśiva image of Mandhal (Plates VII and VIII), though in an unusual iconic way and as such far removed from the original sexual and fertility connotations.

The overall impression is, to conclude, that the Māheśvara worship of the elite in the Vākāṭaka kingdom was iconic, not aniconic or semi-aniconic. This state of affairs seems to confirm that phallus worship was only reluctantly accommodated into the brahmanical circles of Śaivism and that, when it was, it was by being transformed into a sophisticated theology. The *Ṛgveda* had warned against the worshippers of the penis (*śiśnadeva*),[80] in the *Mahābhārata*, apart from the few places referred to (see n. 68 on p. 73), it does not feature and also in the *Pāśupatasūtras* and its commentary there is no evidence for *liṅga* worship; on the contrary, this text describes the Śiva sanctuary in iconic terms.[81] The Vākāṭakas on the whole seem to

---

76 When Śiva is worshipped in an image there is an eye-opening rite, when in a *liṅga* there is not: *hiraṇyena tejasā cakṣur vimocayet tejo 'sīti | liṅge cen nivartate cakṣuṣor abhāvād | Pariśiṣṭasūtra* II.16 (see Harting 1922, 7 ll. 16 f.); cf. ibid. II.17 (Harting 1922, 10 l. 23).

77 The best survey is that of Kreisel 1986, 44 ff. Jamkhedkar reports the finding of a *liṅga* in the Nagardhan area (Jamkhedkar 1985a, 18).

78 See above n. 50 on p. 20; cf. above n. 42 on p. 68. I presume that this refers to a tattoo or applied design in the form of a *liṅga* on the upper arm.

79 See MBh 7.173.83 quoted above n. 68 on p. 73.

80 ṚV 7.21.5; 10.99.3

81 Kauṇḍinya does not refer to *liṅga* worship but *ad Pāśupatasūtra* 1.9 mentions as one of the marks (*lakṣaṇas*) of the image (*mūrti*) of Sadāśiva the *ūrdhvaliṅga*: 'The "image" (*mūrti*) is

have been too orthodox to take up with this popular form of devotion, which would soon, however, cast off all disreputableness.

Archaeology has revealed two major sites of Māheśvara worship in the eastern Vākāṭaka kingdom, Mandhal and Mansar.

Of the three temples exposed in Mandhal two at least seem to have been dedicated to Śiva. The older (?) one is referred to as MDL-II, situated c. 800 m south of the village. In its neighbourhood (?) three Śaiva images were found in the field, which are now preserved in the Nagpur Central Museum (Plates I to VI). Under the floor of the other structure, referred to as BHK-I, c. 1.5 km south of the village, nine images (and three heads) were found, kept in the Museum of the Department of AIHCA of the Nagpur University; five of these images and one of the heads belong with certainty to the Śaiva pantheon (Plates VII to XVI). We surmise that the three images found in the field pertain to the temple at MDL-II. Whether the other five images and the loose head (Plate XXV A) originally all belonged to the temple in which they were found is not certain but not unlikely. The iconography of these images is without close parallel and is only partly understood.

On admittedly rather vague stylistic grounds we are inclined to date the images found in the field (Nagpur Central Museum) somewhat earlier than the group of BHK-I, with the possible exception of the *ugra* head, which might be slightly older than the rest of the images in the University Museum. Two two-armed images, one pertaining to the group found in the field and one to the set of BHK-I, are closely related in respect of their iconography (compare Plates I–II and VII–VIII). The major difference appears to be that the older one has one tier of four *yogin* heads, the other has two such tiers. Both images have bald faces on the upper-arms and two turbaned faces on the thighs. We conjecture that the eight-faced image (Maheśvara) was the main idol of MDL-II, the twelve-faced one that of BHK-I. We shall discuss the iconography in detail below; here it may suffice to note that in both cases the basic structure, although elaborated in a most unusual fashion, seems to conform to what has been called the 'Grundtyp der Śivadarstellung':

> Der śivaitische Bilderkult läßt sich bis in den Beginn der kunst- und religionsgeschichtlich bedeutsamen Phase zurückverfolgen, in der zur Kennzeichnung der gnädigen, 'bhaktischen' Gottheit die Geste des huldvollen Grüßens eingeführt wird. Dieses Bildelement erscheint

---

that visible object (*rūpa*) that is seen by him who, with his face turned north, stands to the south of the deity at the edge (i.e., entrance) and that is characterized by a Banner of the Bull, (the two figures of) Nandin and Mahākāla with lances in their hands, an erect penis, etc.' (*mūrtir nāma yad etad devasya dakṣiṇe pārśve sthitenodaṅmukhenopānte yad rūpam upalabhyate vṛṣadhvajaśūlapāṇinandimahākālordhvaliṅgādilakṣaṇam*, Sastri's edition p. 15).

> an Kultfiguren gegen Ende des letzten Jahrhunderts v. Chr. und ermöglicht, zusammen mit einem weiteren göttlichen Attribut, dem Nektar- oder Wassergefäß (*kalaśa*, auch *ghaṭa* oder *kamaṇḍalu*), die Gestaltung einer standardisierten, allen zum Bilderkult tendierenden Glaubensgemeinschaften zugänglichen Form des Götterbildes, das dann durch spezifische Kennzeichen differenziert wird.[82]

The two other images found in the field may be identified as two acolytes belonging to the inner circle of Maheśvara, representing his vigorous nature. It will be argued below (p. 98) that the one with the four arms and heads, who carries the *daṇḍa* (or *śūla*?), may represent Nandīśvara (Plate III). If he had the function of a sentinel, this would explain that his rear face, which would have been turned towards Maheśvara, has a pleasant smiling expression (Plate IV). The other sturdy four-armed figure, who probably carried an axe may represent another superintendent of the *gaṇas*, a Gaṇādhyakṣa (Plate V). These two four-armed images, both showing an energetic, striding stance, may have guarded the temple of MDL-II. In view of the north-south orientation of this temple the main idol probably faced north. If we apply this orientation to the eight-faced Maheśvara image it follows that its rear head, which alone has a moustache and looks grim, would face south and hence may represent his destructive aspect (Plate II).[83]

The twelve-faced image (Sadāśiva) may have been the main idol of the temple of BHK-I, in which it was found (Plates VII–VIII). In addition to the stylistic argument, it would seem that also from the points of view of developing theology and artistic expression it appears plausible that first the Maheśvara image with eight faces (MDL-II) was designed and afterwards its iconographically and technically more complicated counterpart, this image with twelve faces. The intricacy of the iconography of this image suggests that the iconographic programme of the temple as a whole might have been equally grandiose. If the four other Śaiva images, to which an image of Brahmā and the *ugra* head may be added, really belonged to the same temple complex, this programme may have virtually encompassed Śiva/Mahādeva's family; present are: his wife Pārvatī (Plate XIII), his son Brahmā (Plate XVII), his alter ego Rudra (Plate IX), said to be born as Brahmā's incestuous son,[84] Naigameṣa (Plate XI), who is a form of his son Skanda, and a Mātṛkā (Plate XV), mother of Skanda, who iconographically seems to be linked with the Naigameṣa image. Skanda himself is conspicuous by his absence (unless Naigameṣa represents

---

82 Kreisel 1986, 88 f.

83 Our hypothetic reconstruction of the iconographic programme of this temple would thus structurally conform to the description in Kauṇḍinya's commentary (the *vṛṣadhvaja* is missing), although the orientation of the MDL-II temple seems to have been the other way round. Kauṇḍinya's description of the image as facing south seems to be atypical (see n. 81 on p. 75).

84 Bakker 1996, 9 ff.

him), but we don't know whether the set that was found is complete or not. Of the three loose heads one has clearly a terrifying (*ugra*) countenance with strands of matted hair combed backwards over a protruding occiput (Plate XXV A). Its mouth is open, showing fangs, and the whole face is one intended to inspire great fear. The third eye is carved horizontally on the forehead.[85] The other two heads are too much damaged to allow an interpretation.

In short, it would thus seem that the Śiva and Viṣṇu temples (BHK-I & II) of Mandhal enshrined more or less the major family members of both gods, Mahādeva and Vāsudeva. The religious sophistication of the Māheśvaras that is evident in the Mandhal images matches that of the Bhāgavatas and the artistic accomplishment of the craftsmen of the local workshop duly paid tribute to it. These sculptures in stone must have continued a long tradition in wood.

A high point in the artistic achievements of the Māheśvaras, and arguably in Vākāṭaka sculpture as a whole, was recovered from the debris on a hillock, called Hiḍimbā Tekḍī, five kilometers due west of the Rāmagiri near a village called Mansar. Bricks scattered all over the hill indicate that a temple once crowned its top. Though this hillock, like the Boṃgī Huḍkī in Mandhal (see p. 80), to which it bears some resemblance, is nowadays (locally) associated with Buddhism, there can be little doubt that the 5th-century brick temple was a Hindu one.

Among the rubble a splendid four-armed Śiva image was found in 1972, which is presently on display in the hall of the National Museum in New Delhi (Plate XXXVII). The red sandstone of the image points to the adjacent Rāmagiri, where images carved out of the same kind of stone have been found (Plates XXXIV and XXVII to XXX), and towards which the deity must have looked, if the temple on the hill faced east. Stylistically the image is a trait-d'union between the stocky (*vāmana*, *hrasva*) Śaiva images of Mandhal and some of the *yakṣas/bodhisattvas* of Ajanta (Plate XXXVIII A). As such a trait-d'union it is closely akin to some *gaṇa* sculptures from the Rāmagiri/ Nagardhan area.[86] The subtle modelling of the flesh is so similar to that of one of the Bhārarakṣakas found in Nagardhan (Plate XXX A), that we conjecture that both images hail from the same workshop (see below p. 135).[87] We therefore think it safe to date the image to the reign of Pravarasena II, that is in the second quarter of the fifth century AD.

---

85 This may be indicative of an early date, since 'Aghora/Bhairava' heads with horizontal third eye are (apart from a Nepalese tradition) only known from Kuṣāṇa sculptures (Kreisel 1986, 96, 71, Abb. 14, 60b). The Māheśvaras of the Vākāṭaka kingdom reserved the iconographic feature of the third eye for the ferocious forms of Śiva (see below n. 6 on p. 96).

86 Cf. Williams 1983, 228.

87 For the stylistic development compare Plates IX, XIX (Mandhal), XXVI, XXX (Nagardhan), XXXVI A (Rāmagiri), XXXVIII A (Ajanta). Cf. Deo 1975–76, 277, Plates 39–40.

The Mansar Śiva shows the advancement made since Mandhal, not only in artistic expression, but also in the views of the Māheśvaras. Here we meet a god whose serene smile truly expresses his 'love for his devotees.' In a way, the Śiva of this image has become domesticated; gone are his wild traits, his weapons and his ithyphallic mark and one may detect here the subtle influence of the Bhāgavata religion. The image combines in an asymmetric but harmonious way two principal, though opposing aspects of the god of the Māheśvaras, viz. life and death, represented on the one hand by the life-renouncing Pāśupata *yogin* who conquers death in the cremation ground, symbolized by the skull on his head, and on the other hand by the life-affirming Ruler of the World, who graciously bestows blessing upon his subjects, a precious gift presented in his right hand that reaches out towards his devotee.[88] Because this God, possibly named 'the All-highest' (Pravareśvara),[89] 'is the very great one among the gods and because he has the great (world) as his domain and because he protects the great universe, he is traditionally known as the Great God, Mahādeva,'[90] a definition that we think appropriate to the deity represented by this Śiva image, which may be viewed as an epitome of the Māheśvara faith of the Vākāṭakas.[91]

---

88 For these two aspects see p. 96 ff.

89 See below p. 88.

90 *devānāṃ sumahān yac ca yac cāsya viṣayo mahān/ yac ca viśvaṃ mahat pāti mahādevas tataḥ smṛtaḥ* ||8||, MBh 13.146.8.

91 Kreisel 1986, 64: 'In der Bildgestaltung kommt freilich zum Ausdruck, daß Mahādeva als zentraler Aspekt die Funktion des höchsten Gottes übernimmt und nicht nur Teilaspekt der fünffachen Manifestation, sondern die dominierende Repräsentation Śivas im Bilderkult ist.'

Chapter 3

The Vākāṭaka Sites*

MANDHAL

Nine out of the twelve Mandhal sculptures discussed above were found at a site called Bholāhuḍkī Tekḍī (BHK-I) in the vicinity of the village of Mandhal which is situated c. 42 km south-east of Nagpur. Apart from some diggings in Mandhal village itself (MDL-I), altogether three sites have been excavated: (1) MDL-II, c. 800 m south of the village; (2) BHK-I, a site between two hillocks, the Bholāhuḍkī Tekḍī in the east and the Boṃgī Huḍkī in the west, situated c. 1.5 km south of the village; (3) BHK-II, the Boṃgī Huḍkī directly to the west of BHK-I.

> Excavation revealed that the two brick structures exposed earlier [BHK-I and MDL-II, H.T.B.] represent remains of temples datable to the Vakataka period (fourth-fifth century A.D.). One of these temples at BHK-I was raised on a rectangular platform, measuring 18.0 × 10.60 × 1.20 m [orientated east-west]. In the middle of the platform were found traces of what appears to have been a small shrine, represented by an altar (2.10 × 0.95 m) with three courses of bricks, a semicircular brick platform to its west and a fragment of a wall possibly going round the altar. A flight of steps on the north leading to the platform, a brick-built cistern (2.30 × 2.50 × 1.59 m) on the east of the platform and a couple of brick chambers on the west were also exposed. [...] Excavation in BHK-II, a small hillock locally known as Bongi Hudki, brought to light remains of yet another temple. The temple, built on a massive platform (11.70 × 14.70 m) had a *garbhagriha* (4.50 × 5.60 m) and *mukha-mandapa* (4.00 × 3.30 m).[1]

---

* Only those Vākāṭaka sites are described that have yielded images that are included in the present catalogue.

1 IAR 1976–77, 39. Jamkhedkar 1988, 64 remarks about the temple at BHK-I that 'the brick structure at Bhōlā Huḍkī, though of inferior quality and built entirely of brickbats, has some notable features. The main shrine above the rectangular platform has a central altar (6 ft.11 in. × 3 ft.), approached by steps from the north and south. The main approach on the north had two cham-

The brick temple of BHK-I lies to the east, at the foot of the hillock on which BHK-II is situated, separated only by a 'few yards' (*kuch gaj*). The platform on the hillock on which the latter temple was raised was partly built into the surface of the rock, which was levelled by 32 layers of brick at the southern side.[2] The report in IAR 1975–76 had already mentioned that,

> The bricks used were of two sizes,[3] viz., 44 × 23 × 8 cm and 40 × 24 × 8 cm. The ceramic industry of the period is represented by a red ware, comparable to that found in Paunar in the Vakataka levels. Associated finds include: a dozen sculptures of the Hindu pantheon, all broken and stylistically belonging to the Gupta-Vakataka period; an earthen pot containing three sets of copper plates, one of Pravarasena II and the rest of Prithivisena II of the Vakataka dynasty. The sculptures and the pot containing the copper plates appear to have been deliberately buried under the floor of the structure. (IAR 1975–76, 36)

The same report noticed that the Mandhal site 'on an earlier occasion' had yielded 'three Saiva images of the Gupta-Vakataka period while digging pits for planting saplings by the Forest Department.'[4] In his *Epigraphia Indica* publication of the same year (1975–76) Shastri adds some information to this. The finding 'in the course of an efforestation programme' happened in July 1974: 'These sculptures representing Lakulīśa, Ashṭamūrti and Sadāśiva forms of God Śiva are now deposited in the Central Museum, Nagpur.'[5] The 'dozen sculptures of the Hindu pantheon' found in BHK-I include the nine images kept in the Museum of the Department of Ancient Indian History and Culture and Archaeology (AIHCA) of the University of Nagpur as well as three heads of male deities, kept in the same museum, and evidently belonging to this group.

---

bers and a rectangular cistern. Slightly away from the main structure can be noticed a pathway 6 ft. 7 in. wide forming a sort of pradakṣiṇāpatha around the structural complex.' About the temple at BHK-II this author only says that 'nothing remains except the plinth' (op. cit. p. 63). Jamkhedkar is completely silent about the images found. The first report of the excavations in IAR 1975–76, 36 mentions, in conformity with Jamkhedkar's description, that steps were found 'on the north and south' of the BHK-I temple. The second report in IAR 1976–77, however, only speaks of a 'flight of steps on the north' and omits the southern steps altogether, as does the excavation report of Shastri 1977–78. Neither Shastri nor the IAR reports mention this so-called '*pradakṣiṇāpatha*.' See also below n. 8 on p. 82.

2 Shastri 1977–78, 144.

3 According to Shastri 1977–78, 145, the size of the bricks of site MDL-II is 44 × 23 × 8 cm.

4 IAR 1975–76, 36.

5 Shastri 1975–76, 68. The details of the iconography of these three image will be discussed below (Plates I–VI), a discussion that has led us to designate these three sculptures as 'Gaṇādhyakṣa,' 'Maheśvara,' and 'Nandīśvara (?).' See also above p. 76.

Apart from some minor fragments,[6] altogether twelve images and three heads were found in Mandhal, which are all, stylistically speaking, very similar. They may have been sculptured in the same workshop at about the same period. Shastri's preliminary excavation report (1977–78) describes only eight images, kept in the Museum of the AIHCA, omitting the 'Vṛṣṇi Hero' image (Plate XXIII) and the three heads. This excavation report gives some extra details with regard to the lay-out of BHK-I.[7] According to this report the 'cistern' or *jalakuṇḍa* is situated NE of the platform, whereas the 'couple of brick chambers' or *pujārī athavā sevak kā nivās* is situated opposite it in the NW.

The brick construction found at MDL-II measures 11.5 × 10.0 m and is 'orientated north-south, with a couple of projections on the west' and with an 'alignment of stones dressed on the exterior' (on the northern and southern sides). This temple was 'originally built of massive brick walls; it was first reconstructed in the late Vakataka period or shortly thereafter. Once again, around twelfth century A.D., it was provided with rubble wall raised on the remains of the earlier stone wall.'[8]

It is much to be regretted that no final comprehensive excavation report has appeared, which could have shed more light on the lay-out of these brick temples (even a map or plan would work wonders!). Consequently we grope in the dark when we try to establish the exact provenance and original function of these images.

It would seem plausible a priori, that the three images found in 1974 and the 'dozen' found in BHK-I belonged to different temples. If this supposition is correct, the Nagpur Museum triad of sculptures probably belonged to the original brick temple at site MDL-II. The eight-faced idol, designated 'Maheśvara,' may have been its main idol (Plate I–II). This temple may be dated in the last quarter of the fourth

6 See n. 11 on p. 84.

7 '[...] adhiṣṭhān [BHK-I] par pahuṃcane ke lie uttar diśā meṃ īṭoṃ kā ek sopān-mārg thā | iske uttar-pūrv meṃ īṭoṃ kā banā ek jalakuṇḍa thā, jiskā ākār 2.30 × 2.50 mīṭar aur gahrāī 1.59 mīṭar thī | yaḥ pūrṇataḥ surakṣit sthiti meṃ milā hai | iske ṭhīk sāmne (adhiṣṭhān ke uttar-paścim meṃ) do īṣṭkānirmit kakṣoṃ ke avaśeṣ upalabdh hue | inmeṃ saṃbhavataḥ mandir ke pujārī athavā sevak kā nivās rahā hogā | is sthal ke utkhanan meṃ anya vastuoṃ ke atirikt vividh Hindū devī-devatāoṃ kī ek darjan sundar prastar-mūrtiyāṃ evaṃ Vākāṭakoṃ ke tīn dānapatra prāpt hue haiṃ jinkī carcā āge yathāsthal kī jāyegī |,' Shastri 1977–78, 144.

8 IAR 1976–77, 39. About this temple Jamkhedkar (1988, 63) notices: 'Half a mile from the village on the bank of the Varhaḍī Talāō are the remains of a shrine that appears to have been crudely rebuilt during the Yādava period. The square *garbhagṛha* had 8 ft. 2 in. thick walls preceded by a balustrade, 14 ft. 9 in. long flanking a flight of steps. The brick-built plinth was encased in blocks of buff sandstone. Excavations yielded a bull in the mature style of the Vākāṭaka period.' When I visited this site I saw indeed an image of a bull and a *liṅga* pedestal (*yoni*), but both were certainly of a much later date (Yādava period or still later). Nothing is known of a 'bull in the mature style of the Vākāṭaka period.'

century AD.[9]

Three sculptures of the set found in BHK-I appear to pertain to the Vaiṣṇava pantheon: Vāsudeva (Plate XIX–XX), Saṃkarṣaṇa (Plate XXI–XXII) and the one representing another, unidentified Vṛṣṇi Hero (*vīra*), possibly Sāmba (Plate XXIII–XXIV). As suggested above (p. 19), these three images, or only the Vāsudeva image, may have belonged to the Mondasvāmin Temple, mentioned in the Mandhal Plates of Rudrasena II, which, in our view, is to be looked for in Mandhal. The temple on top of the hillock Boṃgī Huḍkī appears, as far as its lay-out is concerned—a *garbhagṛha* with a narrower *mukhamaṇḍapa* in front, orientated west-east—to be structurally most akin to the Vaiṣṇava temples on top of the Rāmagiri.[10] It may therefore be considered as a likely candidate for being this Viṣṇu sanctuary. If its identification with the Mondasvāmin Temple is correct and the latter's name indeed refers to Prabhāvatī Guptā as conjectured above (p. 19), it may date from around AD 400.

The majority of the images found in BHK-I, however, are not Vaiṣṇava, but Śaiva, and at least one of the three loose heads that are kept in the Museum of the Department of AIHCA is Śaiva as well. Stylistically speaking, these three heads conform to the other Mandhal images. As we have suggested above, these images may all or partly have belonged to the temple in which they were found. They suggest a date for this temple that is roughly contemporaneous with the Vaiṣṇava one.

The sacred compound of BHK-I must have been by any standard a most extraordinary one. The sculptures that may have belonged to it are all carved in the round with much attention paid to the reverse side. This indicates that the images were standing free and could be circumambulated. The 'small shrine' in the 'middle of the platform' may have housed the Sadāśiva image, the most imposing of the set (Plate VII–VIII). Other images may have encircled the central shrine in a structure that once covered the main platform (*jagatī*), or they may have occupied a place along the flight of steps and the reservoir. The two 'chambers' may have contained images as well, that is to say, these rooms may actually have been minor shrines. As has been noted above (n. 1 on p. 80), according to Jamkhedkar's report, this temple complex was encircled by a *pradakṣiṇāpatha*. No doubt a well-thought-out and intricate iconographic programme underlaid the whole sacred structure of Bholāhuḍkī; reconstruction of it, as long as so many pieces of the puzzle are missing, would lead us beyond well-reasoned speculation into pure guess-work.

---

9 Cf. Shastri 1977–78, 145 who dates this site on account of the earthenware findings between the third and fifth centuries: 'in bhāṇḍoṃ kā pracalan kāl sādhāraṇataḥ īsvī tīsrī-pāṃcvī śatābdī mānā jātā hai |'.

10 See EITA II.1, p. 66, Fig. 27.

NAGARDHAN

The village of Nagardhan lies 6 km due south of Ramtek Hill (Rāmagiri) in the midst of paddy fields. The area around this village and the adjacent Hamlapuri is now commonly identified with the site of the Vākāṭaka residence ('capital') Nandivardhana. Of this residence no traces remain. Over the last twenty years, however, a wealth of loose archaeological findings have been reported from here, the majority of which pertain to the Vākāṭaka period. They are partly stored in the Nagpur Central Museum and partly in private collections. In 1989 the then keeper of this museum, Mr V. R. Verulkar, informed me that during archaeological explorations a (mud?) wall was found between Nagardhan and Hamlapuri of about 1 km in length.

Among the most spectacular finds in this area is the image of a seated man with an open *pothī* in his left hand (Plate XXVI). The image is locally dubbed 'Kālidāsa,' and I have earlier argued that this possibility cannot be fully excluded (Bakker 1993b). Though I still am of the opinion that the image represents a 'human' sage (*kavi*), I now think it less likely that he represents the historical poet, who probably was well-known in Nandivardhana and whom we have to date in the same period in which the image was made (first half of the 5th century AD). A portrait statue of an ordinary, though celebrated contemporary would be highly exceptional in the Indian context.

Half-way between Nagardhan and Hamlapuri is a little (modern) open shrine in which a Vākāṭaka image of Gaṇeśa is installed (Plate XXVIII). Several other images of the same red sandstone and similar fluid style were reportedly found in its vicinity; the major ones are, next to two Bhārarakṣakas (Plate XXX), a Mahiṣamardinī image (Plate XXIX A) and a head of Viṣṇu (Plate XXVII). They may all date from the first half of the fifth century AD, when the site was the theatre of the royal court of Prabhāvatī Guptā and her son Pravarasena II. It may be coincidence, but it is nevertheless remarkable that sculptures of the same deities are found grouped together in niches in the verandah of Cave VI in Udayagiri.[11] Iconographi-

11 For an overall picture see Williams 1982, Plate 35. The Gaṇeśa image of Udayagiri Cave 6, situated in the south-eastern side wall of the verandah (Plate XLIV B) faces a worn Saptamātṛkā relief in the opposite wall (not illustrated; see Panikkar 1997 [1996], Pl. 20). In niches in the rear wall of the verandah (facing NE), on either side of the entrance, are images of two Dvārapālas and Viṣṇu (Plate XLV A); the Mahiṣamardinī image (Plate XLV B) is beside the Viṣṇu image that is illustrated, to the viewer's right side of the entrance. The similarity of the iconography of this Mahiṣamardinī image of Udayagiri and that of Nagardhan decides the dispute over the date of the Udayagiri image in favour of Harle and Williams who had argued for an early date (see Williams 1982, 42 n. 68). The remarkable coincidence extends to the site BHK-II in Mandhal, which we tentatively identified with the site of the Mondasvāmin Temple, where reportedly two little Gaṇeśa images and a little Mahiṣamardinī image were found, presently kept in the Museum of the Department of AIHCA of the University of Nagpur (see n. 97 on p. 129 and n. 106 on

cally these sculptures are close to the Nagardhan images, but their style is more typical of early Gupta sculpture. An inscription above the Viṣṇu and Mahiṣamardinī images records that Udayagiri Cave VI was donated by a feudatory of Prabhāvatī's father Candragupta II in AD 400–01.[12] Evidently there was an iconographic programme underlying Cave VI, which is however no longer understood—we do not even know whether the cave was Vaiṣṇava or Śaiva.[13] In view of the Udayagiri evidence we venture the conjecture that also the red sandstone images of Nagardhan belonged to one sacred compound. As in the case of the Varāha image and, perhaps, of the Viṣṇupada on the Rāmagiri, inspiration for it might have come from the Gupta North.[14]

The Buddhist presence at this site in this period is attested by three splendid bronzes.[15]

RĀMAGIRI (RAMTEK HILL)

Travelling along the National Highway No. 7, either coming down from the Satpura Range heading towards the Deccan or going up to the North from Nagpur, one cannot miss the magnificent sight of the white temples glittering in the sun on the top of a steep hill that suddenly rises about 150 m above the Wainganga Plain (Plate XXV B). This hill, today known as Ramtek (Hill) or Ramtekri, has been identified by V.V. Mirashi with the Rāmagiri celebrated in Kālidāsa's *Meghadūta*.

> A *yakṣa*, who had neglected his duties, had lost his powers by his master's curse—heavy to bear, since he had to live separated from his beloved for one year; he took up his abode in the hermitages on the Rāmagiri, where the trees (spread) a cooling shade and where the waters were hallowed by the bathing of Janaka's daughter. (1)
> [...]
> After having embraced that lofty hill, you, (O cloud), should take

p. 132).

12 CII III, 242–44.

13 Williams 1982, 41 n. 64: 'It is impossible to determine whether this cave [i.e. Udayagiri Cave VI] is Vaiṣṇava (with Gaṇeśa attendant, as at Deogarh) or Śaiva (with Lakulīśa perhaps in the central *candraśālā* and with the two Viṣṇu images attendant upon the greater glory of Śiva).' See also below n. 99 on p. 130.

14 See above p. 22 and p. 65 and *ad* Plates XXXII A and XXXI B.

15 Jamkhedkar 1985a. One of these (Fig. 1) is typically Gupta, the other two may have been imported from Andhra (Figs. 3 & 4). In addition to these three images some bronze fragments were found among which a pedestal inscribed with a dedicatory inscriptioṇ (Figs. 17–20).

> leave of your dear friend that, on its slopes, is marked by Raghupati's footprints, venerated by mankind; every time when you and he meet, shedding of warm (tear)drops born from long separation betray your affection. (12)

There is abundance evidence to support Mirashi's theory, which we have accepted as the most plausible identification of the poet's 'lofty hill.'[16]

This hill and the buildings it contains have been described in various publications. The reader may be referred to R. B. Hiralal's *Visit to Ramtek*,[17] R. V. Russell's *Nagpur Gazetteer*,[18] V. V. Mirashi's *Meghadūta meṃ Rāmagiri arthāt Rāmṭek*,[19] and the same author's Introduction to Volume V of the *Corpus Inscriptionum Indicarum*, or earlier publications of the present writer. The best and most up-to-date archaeological description of Vākāṭaka temples on the hill is found in a chapter of the *Encyclopædia of Indian Temple Architecture* by A. P. Jamkhedkar.[20]

The sacred complex of Rāmagiri of Vākāṭaka times seems to have been spread over three areas. The first and main compound, we assume, was situated at the western spur of the ridge, today occupied by the 13th-century temples of Rāma and Lakṣmaṇa. In view of the prominence of this site it must also in the fifth century have contained the main sanctuary, the Rāmagiristhāna, abode of the 'Lord (*svāmin*) of Rāmagiri' and the spot where Viṣṇu or his incarnation of Rāma was believed to have left his footprint.

The second area lay 250 m to the east, at the entrance of the ridge where the two arms of the horseshoe-shaped mountain diverge. A slightly curved line running north-south connects the three oldest sanctuaries, those of Varāha and the two Narasiṃhas, which all face west; the Varāha shrine is situated due east of the main sanctuary on the spur. A little to the south-west of Varāha, north-west of Rudra-Narasiṃha, lies the temple of Bhogarāma, the only one that faces east, overlooking the horse-shoe. The Trivikrama Temple, which again faces west, lies somewhat out of the centre, c. 200 m north-east of Varāha on the northern arm of the horse-shoe. As has been argued above this compound may have been designed as a kind of memorial of the kings of Nandivardhana.

Finally, about 250 m due south of the main complex, c. 100 m below the top of the hill, are the little rock-cut temple of Kapaṭarāma (also known as Guptarāma) and the recluse cave of Siddhanātha. Their architectural features prove that they pertain

16 Mirashi 1959, 1964, and in CII V, liii ff.

17 Hiralal 1908.

18 Central Provinces District Gazetteers Nagpur District. Bombay 1908, 332. Revised Edition, Maharashtra State Gazetteers, Bombay 1966, 764–66.

19 Nagpur 1959.

20 EITA II.1, Chapter 3, II.2, Plates 101 to 129.

to the Vākāṭaka period. In the vicinity of the rock temple a heavily mutilated four-armed standing image was found, which can be identified as Viṣṇu (Plate XXXV A). It may have been the original idol of Guptarāma, though its stiff hieratic style sets it apart from the other sculptures of Rāmagiri. This temple presently houses a *liṅga* and Śiva's *vāhana*, the bull, both dating from the Bhonsle period (18th century).

MANSAR

Five kilometers due west of Rāmagiri is an ancient site, named Mansar after the adjacent village. The site comprises a large pond, with rock formations and some (modern) temples on its western and a steep hillock rising at its eastern end. A high bank along the south side of the pond connects both ends. A few hundred metres to the east of the hillock is another mound. According to S. B. Deo,

> The present site seems to contain at least a *stūpa*, rock-cut caves and brick structures. A number of stone sculptures lie around. The caves, though now completely filled up, are supposed to have been yielding, some years back, a few sculptures. It is not possible to know where these antiquities are.[21]

None of the sculptures referred to appear to have emerged, but a superb Śiva image was 'retrieved from a brick debris by Shri Bishan, a local mine contractor' (Plate XXXVII).[22] The brick debris is found on and at the foot of the hillock to the east of the pond, known as the hill of the goddess Hiḍimbā, Hiḍimbā Tekḍī. On the rock face of this hillock is an undeciphered inscription in shell script.[23] A set of five copper plates was also discovered in the neighbourhood (CII V, 73). Only one of these plates could be retrieved from the finders. Contents, style and palaeography point to Pravarasena II as its commissioner.

If the brick temple on the Hiḍimbā Tekḍī matched the quality of the Śiva image, it must have been a magnificent one. It would make Mansar and the Hiḍimbā Tekḍī a fully fledged Śaiva counterpart of the Vaiṣṇava Rāmagiristhāna opposite it in the east.

In this connection we would venture an hypothesis. After initially issuing his charters from Nandivardhana, just as his mother did, Pravarasena made the majority of his land donations in his residential abode Pravarapura which, as we

21 Deo 1975–76, 275.
22 Sarma in AV, 219.
23 Mirashi 1959, 22.

have argued (above p. 25), might have been either a new palace in the vicinity of Nandivardhana, or the old residency renamed. Two of his charters were issued from *vāsakas* (Tripurī and Hiraṇyānadī), which appear to have been army camps (see above n. 199 on p. 56). Two other charters were issued from *sthānas*, which were religious places. One was connected with water (Narataṅgavāristhāna),[24] the other was the temple (*devakula*) of Pravareśvara ('the All-highest').[25] The Pravareśvara temple was an important one, not only because, as the name indicates, it was founded by Pravarasena II. Firstly, it appears to have possessed lands. This may be inferred from the designation of a donee, Sūryasvāmin of the Kāśyapa *gotra* of the Taittirīya *śākhā*, as a resident of the 26th village (*vāṭaka*) of Pravareśvara.[26] Secondly, like the Rāmagiristhāna and the Beṇṇātaṭasthāna (Mandhal?), the temple of Pravareśvara was a state sanctuary (*vaijayika dharmasthāna*).[27] In view of the evident importance of Pravareśvara and the extraordinary quality of the Śiva image found in Mansar, which one would assume could only be produced with the support of royal patronage, we tentatively identify the temple on the Hiḍimbā Tekḍī with the Pravareśvaradevakulasthāna. It may have been Pravarasena's equivalent of the sanctuaries of his (Vaiṣṇava) father and mother in Mandhal and on the Rāmagiri.

AJANTA

Descriptions of the site of Ajanta have been published so often that they need no repetition here. The reader may be referred to James Fergusson & James Burgess, *The Cave Temples of India*,[28] G. Yazdani (*et alii*), *Ajanta*,[29] and the publications of Walter Spink. We assume with the latter author that the excavation of the Mahāyāna

---

24 CII V, 50 l. 1.

25 *pravareśvaradevakulasthānāt* [|*], CII V, 65 l. 1. Pṛthivīṣeṇa II issued his Mandhal Plates, second regnal year, from Rāmagiristhāna, the sanctuary on the Rāmagiri; his Mandhal Plates, tenth regnal year, from Beṇṇātaṭasthāna, the sanctuary on the bank of the Wainganga, which may refer to the site were the plates were found, Mandhal.

26 *pravara(re)śvaraṣadviṣa(ḍviṃśa)tivāṭakava(vā)stavyataittiri(rī)yakāśyapasagotra[sū]ryya-svāmina(ne) datta[m*]* [|], CII V, 19 ll. 14 f.; cf. CII V, 19 ll. 13 f. One or more sanctuaries on the Rāmagiri seem also to have had landed property, probably in the vicinity of the village Kadalīvāṭaka, which was mentioned in connection with the building of the Prabhāvatīsvāmin Temple (Bakker & Isaacson 1993, 70).

27 The precise implication of the qualification *vaijayika dharmasthāna* is not known. It seems to refer to a royal estate where official functions could be performed. The Narataṅgavāristhāna did not have the status of *vaijayika dharmasthāna*, but the army camps (*vāsakas*) and residency(ies) Nandivardhana/Pravarapura did.

28 London 1880.

29 London 1930–1955, 4 vols.

caves started in the 460s under the reign of Hariṣeṇa, but we do not subscribe to his opinion that all Mahāyāna caves were executed within twenty years or less. The caves that with certainty pertain to the period of Hariṣeṇa's rule are XVI, XVII and XIX, situated in the centre of the curving scarp of the gorge of the Waghora river. They represent two monasteries (*vihāras*) and one *caitya* or congregation hall (*gandhakuṭī*).

Though this site is distinguished from the other sites described in that it belongs to the Buddhist tradition, its architecture, style and iconography have several features in common with other Vākāṭaka artefacts (see above p. 42 f.). It is true that the magnificent paintings in some of the caves make them outstanding monuments of Indian art, yet the quality of their sculpture on the whole does not reach the sophisticated subtlety and fresh originality of that of the Eastern Vākāṭaka kingdom.

Paunar

Paunar in the Wardha District is a small village on the right (i.e. south) bank of the river Dham, 70 km south-west of Nagpur. It has several mounds testifying to a longstanding occupation of the site. Excavations were carried out in 1967 under the supervision of S. B. Deo of the Department of AIHCA of the University of Nagpur. The site chosen for digging (PNR-I) was at the north-eastern side of a mound locally known as Qilā ('Fort'), the top of which is crowned by a mosque and at the base of which remains of a massive fortification wall are found.[30]

> The excavations were undertaken with a view to ascertain, if possible, the proposed identification of Paunār with ancient Pravarapura, the capital of the Vākāṭakas. It may be stated here that though the remains of the Vākāṭaka-Gupta period—i.e. Period III—were varied, greater in number and rich in conception as compared to those in any other period, the excavations have not brought to light any positive evidence to suggest that Paunār is ancient Pravarapura. However, it is beyond doubt that Paunār seems to have enjoyed its days of prosperity during the Vākāṭaka period.[31]

With respect to the findings of Period III the excavators report,

> The constructions of this period were characterised by well-planned foundations, use of brick and brickbats, construction of ring wells, the

30 Deo & Dhavalikar 1968, 1–4.
31 Deo & Dhavalikar 1968, 114 f. Cf. Gupta in AV, 119–153.

> employment of tiles on a large scale and floors of compact clay sometimes mixed with fine gravel. [...]
>
> The houses were well built, beautiful red pottery came into use, coins of the Vishṇukuṇḍins were possibly in circulation. Beautiful beads of semi-precious stones, bangles of shell and precisely made plaques and sculptures of Brahmanical deities like Gaṇeśa were used.[32]

Period III is defined by layers 4 and 5. Two coins, which were assigned to the Viṣṇukuṇḍins, 'were found in the top horizons of layer (4) of Period III' (op. cit. 13). The evidence seems to confirm that (red) brick was widely used as building material throughout the Vākāṭaka period (cf. Mandhal and Mansar) and that the Viṣṇukuṇḍins settled in the south of Vidarbha in the last phase of the kingdom under the reign of Pṛthivīṣeṇa II. Viṣṇukuṇḍin presence is further corroborated by the (surface) finding of a copper pot containing a large number of copper/bronze coins.

> The motifs on the obverse depict either bull facing right or a lion with one of the fore paws upraised and the tail curled up, whereas the reverse shows either an axle in relief with a crescent and a pellet at the four corners, or a conch shell, or a vase on stand, all in a circle with radiating strokes.[33]

On account of these motifs these coins were assigned by the excavators to the Viṣṇukuṇḍins. Recently, examination by A. M. Shastri and C. Gupta has led to the hypothesis that some of these coins have to be assigned to the Vākāṭaka kings, notably Pṛthivīṣeṇa II (see above p. 56). The legend of one of these coins reads *śrīmahārājapṛthivī*, another shows a *cakra*, which, as we have seen (p. 52), appears to have been the royal emblem of Pṛthivīṣeṇa II, and two others again contain the legend *jaya*, which reminds us of the seals of Pṛthivīṣeṇa II's inscriptions reading *jayaśāsana* (p. 51).[34]

The major findings in Paunar, however, did not emerge from the excavation, but were recovered during the building of the Paramadhāma Āśrama of Vinoba Bhave on the left (northern) bank of the Dham. Moreover a good number of surface finds are reported by Gupta (AV, 145 ff.), most of them now in private collections. The sculptures and panels found 'while digging in the fields round Śrī Vinōbājī's *āśrama*' are preserved in the Ashram.[35] They attest to the existence of several sanctuar-

---

32 Deo & Dhavalikar 1968, 9, 115.

33 Deo & Dhavalikar 1968, 14.

34 Shastri in AV, 285–294, Figs. 70 I, IIIA and IIIB and 72 VIII. Gupta in AV, 144 remarks, 'As there were cordial relations between the Vākāṭakas and the Vishṇukuṇḍins the possibility of exchange of their coins cannot be ruled out. The need to study these coins from this point of view is strongly felt.'

35 CII V, lx.

ies on the bank of the river, among them at least one large Viṣṇu temple. From the beginning, however, there has been controversy over their iconography and date. Mirashi, who was the first to give a systematic interpretation of the panels, thought they depicted scenes of the *Rāmāyaṇa*.[36] This view has proved to be untenable and it is now generally believed that the majority of the panels (if not all) represent *līlā* scenes of Kṛṣṇa and his associates (Plate XL). With the refutation of Mirashi's *Rāmāyaṇa* interpretation this scholar's theory to the effect that there existed a Rāma cult in the days of Pravarasena II and that this king built a great Rāma temple in his new capital Pravarapura on the bank of the river Dham is to be relinquished.

Actually, considerations of style would rather suggest that many of the findings preserved in the Ashram, including the panels, are of a later date and it may even be doubted whether they belong to the Vākāṭaka period at all. Walter Spink ascribes them to 'a period (c. A. D. 500) of Viṣṇukuṇḍin rule over Vidarbha.'[37] Joanna Williams, comparing the panels with those of Deogarh and Ajanta, remarks that,

> the artists of Deogarh and Pavnar differ substantially. For some panels in the Pavnar group, a later date and affinities to the south (Rāṣṭrakūṭa sculpture, for example) are tempting. Yet the analogy between the seated figures in Plate 18 [not illustrated here] and the paintings on the porch of Ajantā Cave 17 are equally great. Without surface detail, one can go no further.[38]

The Viṣṇukuṇḍins, whose homeland, as we have seen, was the region to the north of the Śrīśaila Hills (the present Mahbubnagar District, AP), became, when their kingdom began to emerge at the end of the 4th century, heirs to the artistic tradition of Amaravati and Nāgārjunakoṇḍa (3rd century AD), the sculptural style of which is outlined by Huntington as follows.

> The sculptural style at Nāgārjunakoṇḍa, like that at Amaravati, is known from the carved stone slabs that were part of the veneer of the major *stūpas*, as well as from free-standing images. By and large, the Nāgārjunakoṇḍa carvings are closely tied to the latest sculptures from Amaravati in style as well as range of subjects. If anything, the compositions of the reliefs are often more animated, the figures *more lithe and slender*, and the spatial arrangements more sophisticated.[39]

It is this legacy that we may recognize in the slender, natural but sensuous figures of Paunar; it may account for the stylistic undercurrent that is responsible for the

36 Mirashi in SI II, 272–282.
37 Spink 1981a, 123 n. 8.
38 Williams 1983, 230.
39 Huntington 1985, 180 (italics mine).

'South-Indian flavour' that art-historians savour when they examine these sculptures.

To substantiate this contention one would wish to see other specimens of unquestioned Viṣṇukuṇḍin origin, but here serious difficulties are encountered. Apart from the much contested cave temples at Uṇḍavaḷḷi and Mogalrājapuram, there seems hardly to have survived any artistic testimony of the Viṣṇukuṇḍin dynasty.[40] Whether or not the above-mentioned caves are to be ascribed to the Viṣṇukuṇḍins, and if so, whether there are stylistic features apparent that may link them to Paunar, are questions that should be decided by art-historical research.[41] It should be observed, however, that nothing in these caves comes near to the refinement of the Gaṅgā image of Paunar (Plate XXXIX B).

To wind up, it may be repeated that Paunar has turned out to be a site that has yielded a rich harvest of sculptures. For the present work we have selected only three specimens from the dozens that are preserved in the Paramadhāma Āśrama. A more extensive survey—which is, however, not complete either—the reader may find in Chandrashekhar Gupta's article *Paunar under the Vākāṭakas* (AV, 119–153). Our reason for being so reluctant is that, unlike Gupta, we think that the majority of the sculptures postdate the Vākāṭaka period proper. The foundations of the religious building activity in Paunar, however, may have been laid in the last decade of the reign of Pṛthivīṣeṇa II, when Vākāṭakas and Viṣṇukuṇḍins together seem to have held sway over this region. This would explain the conflated stylistic features that mark most of the findings. The art of Paunar thus appears to represent a southern tradition which blended with that of the Vākāṭakas and in which their spirit lived on.

---

40 Sankaranarayanan 1977, 146–150.

41 A good point of comparison may be *inter alia* the large image of Viṣṇu Anantaśayana in the cave temple of Uṇḍavaḷḷi (Longhurst 1924, 29, Pl. XII; Pattabiramin 1971, Pl. XXIV–XXVI; Nigam 1987, 347, Pl. 37) and the Viṣṇu Anantaśayana image that is found in a (modern) Rāma temple next to the Ashram discovered in Paunar along with the other sculptures (Mirashi 1954, 8, Fig. VIII; Soundara Rajan 1980, 181, Fig. 31; Jamkhedkar 1985b, 84, Pl. 126; Jamkhedkar 1991a, 205, Pl. 95; C. Gupta in AV, 149).

PART II

A Catalogue of Vākāṭaka Hindu Sculpture

PLATES I to XL

Plates I & II
Maheśvara, Mandhal
(I *front*, II *rear*)

Mandhal. Nagpur Central Museum, no. A 93. Red-brown sandstone. 61 × 43 × 26 cm. Last quarter of 4th century AD. Found, together with two other images (Plates III–VI), in the fields in the vicinity of the village of Mandhal. Lit.: Jamkhedkar 1991a, 199, Pl. 76, 77; Joshi 1984, 53.

Throughout the history of Indian culture, one of the ways of expressing metaphysical hierarchy in spatial dimensions is by superimposing horizontal layers or tiers, the highest tier representing the highest, the lowest tier the lowest principle in the hierarchy. When this stratification is projected on the human body, as is done, for instance, in the famous Puruṣa Hymn of the *Ṛgveda*, the feet represent the lowest, the head the highest rank.[1] This general principle of spatial order should offer the key to solve the riddle posed by some of the images found in Mandhal. One of the most intriguing among these images is the figure of a standing male, who carries one tier of four heads with matted hair on one neck. A second tier is represented by two shaven faces on the two upper arms.[2] Two more faces are situated on the thighs, constituting the third tier. Within each tier the heads or faces are virtually identical, with the exception of the addorsed head.[3]

The principal characteristic that distinguishes each tier from the other is the hair/head-dress. The heads of the lowest, i.e. third tier are covered by the cloth of the *dhotī*, which trims the foreheads with three lines. Though no other wrappings of the turban are visible, we are probably justified in denoting these two heads as *uṣṇīṣin*. The head of the second tier (on the upper arm) is bald or shaven (*muṇḍa*). The four heads of the first tier wear an ascetic coiffure. These heads are connected by a headband (*bhālapaṭṭa*), which binds strands of matted hair smoothly combed back over the joint cranium.

The image is two-armed. The right arm is broken off at the shoulder. Its left hand holds the water/elixir vessel (*kalaśa*) from which a stalk (*nāla*) emerges.[4] The

1 Mainly two ways of spatial ranking are employed in Śaiva thought: vertically, the path from top to bottom is one of decreasing purity; horizontally, purity decreases along the radius proceeding from a centre. Cf. Davis 1991, 44.

2 Because the right arm is missing, only one face has been preserved in this image, but the Sadāśiva image (Plate VII & VIII) proves that the right arm possessed a face like the left arm.

3 For the significance of faces on the joints of the (human) body see p. 107.

4 We are probably concerned with a bottle-gourd (Lagenaria siceraria (Mol.) Standl.) that is used as a water vessel (*alābupātra*) and has the iconographic function and symbolic meaning of the *kalaśa*, viz. container of *amṛta* and source of all that grows. Cf. the Pārvatī image from Patur in the Nagpur Central Museum (Divakaran 1984, 284, Pl. 244; Jamkhedkar 1991b, 90, Fig. 8).

right hand may have been raised in *abhayamudrā* like, for instance, the Maheśa-mūrti of the Russek Collection (Plate XLI), and have held the rosary. The deity is without ornaments. The elongated ear lobes are pierced. Only the head on the reverse has a vertical third eye. The image is without *upavīta*. The *dhotī* is rolled into a ribbed belt (*kaṭibandha*) which undergirds the big-bellied trunk; it covers the (*ūrdhva*)*liṅga*.

The three tiers possibly point to a theological conception that involves a sequential manifestation in three arrays of diminishing subtlety: *yogin*, *brahmacārin* (*muṇḍin*), and *uṣṇīṣin*. The *uṣṇīṣin* represents Śiva's manifestation in this world (*sakala*), on which the turban (*uṣṇīṣa*) bestows royal dignity. The *brahmacārin*, the religious aspirant (*dīkṣita*), stands half-way between this world and the reality of the *yogin*; his shaven head (*muṇḍin*) indicates his detachment.[5] The ascetic or *yogin* form of Śiva, recognizable by its matted hair, exercises sovereignty over the mundane reality, as represented by the lower two levels, and ultimately transcends it (see also below p. 102).

The four heads of the first tier conform to some extent to the description of the quadruple form of Śiva (*caturmūrtitva*) in *Mahābhārata* 13.128.3–6. All four show his *yoga* as symbolized by the matted hair. Iconographically the most significant distinctive feature is the addorsed head, which looks grim, has a moustache and third eye.[6] It may represent his 'southern face, which has a terrifying appearance and is fierce, and which crushes creatures' (see above p. 73). As such it symbolizes the destructive aspect/function of Śiva.[7] If this interpretation is correct, it follows that the obverse head must have been facing north. According to the *Mahābhārata* description this northern head faces Umā in sport. We can no longer assess whether it had a distinctive joyful expression, because it is mutilated. The eastern and western faces, said 'to excercise sovereignty' and 'convey happiness' respectively, are iconographically hardly distinct from each other in the image at issue.[8] The assumption that the image as a whole faced north makes it plausible

5 The *dīkṣita* is described as *muṇḍin* in MBh 13.15.4 (see above n. 35 on p. 67).

6 As far as can be assessed, the addorsed head of the image at issue and that of the Rudra image (Plate IX) are the only Śiva heads among the Vākāṭaka sculptures that have a vertical third eye (*tryakṣa*). The loose *ugra* head found in Mandhal has an horizontal third eye (Plate XXV A). From this evidence it emerges that the Māheśvaras in the Vākāṭaka kingdom reserved the iconographic feature of the third eye for the *ugra* forms of Śiva. It is conceived as the eye which emits the destructive rays of Śiva's anger. Cf. Kreisel 1986, 96–98.

7 This aspect became later associated with the figure of Bhairava (VDhP 3.48.5, 11). It should be observed, however, that Bhairava as such, as being a specific embodiment of Śiva, is not mentioned in the *Mahābhārata*, *Purāṇapañcalakṣaṇa*, *Vāyupurāṇa*, or *Pāśupatasūtras* and their commentary (see also von Stietencron 1969). On the other hand, a deity named Mahābhairava is already attested in the Vākāṭaka inscriptions as the focus of devotion of Rudrasena I (above n. 23 on p. 13).

8 Cf. Kreisel 1986, 64: 'An dieser Stelle sei vermerkt, daß seit der Guptazeit die Catur-

that it once was the main idol of the temple excavated in MDL-II which was orientated north–south.

Because the image represents the High God of the Māheśvaras in an anthropomorphic (iconic) form, symbolizing his emanation in space and time, we propose to designate the image 'Maheśvara.'[9]

PLATES III & IV
NANDĪŚVARA (?), MANDHAL
(III *front*, IV *rear*)

Mandhal. Nagpur Central Museum, no. A 92. Red-brown sandstone. 55 × 50 × 25 cm. Last quarter of 4th century AD. Found, together with two other images (Plates I/II & V/VI), in the fields in the vicinity of the village of Mandhal. Lit.: Bhattacharya 1989, 63; Jamkhedkar 1991a, Pl. 73, 74; Joshi 1984, 52.

This four-armed image with four heads (in one tier) resembles in some respects the Maheśvara image, though it is without faces on the arms and thighs. The legs are broken off at the knees, the top right arm has disappeared almost completely, the top left arm is preserved until the elbow. The right forearm is akimbo (*kaṭihasta*), holding up at the wrist something that resembles a large paw, but which might actually be the clumsily carved right lower hand of the deity himself (cf. the left hand of the Naigameṣa image, Plate XI). The left (lower) hand holds either the shaft of the lance (*śūla*), or a stick or staff (*daṇḍa*).[10] The two upper hands may have held

mukhaliṅga-Köpfe in der Ost- und Westrichtung sich bis zur Kongruenz angleichen und somit die Möglichkeit bieten, je nach Ausrichtung der Kultstätte den einen wie den anderen als Haubtaspekt Śivas zu betrachten. Dieser dürfte in jedem Fall richtiger als Mahādeva zu bezeichnen sein und nicht der kanonisierten literarischen Version entsprechend Tatpuruṣa oder Sadyojāta. Der als Nandivaktra bezeichnete Kopf wäre dem gemäß der jeweils rückwärtige ...'

9 This name has little more pretension than to conform to a (later) convention and denotes a generic type rather than a particular form (see above p. 74). Alternative names are possible throughout. Shastri 1975–76, 68 refers to this image as 'Ashṭamūrti' because it has altogether eight faces. *Aṣṭamūrti*, however, seems not to be a particular iconographic category of Śiva images (cf. Gonda 1970, 42). MBh 13.146.6 reserves the name 'Maheśvara' for Śiva's most terrifying form in which he destroyes the world: *yāsya ghoratamā mūrtir jagat saṃharate tathā* | *īśvaratvān mahātvāc ca maheśvara iti smṛtaḥ* ||6||. MBh 7.173.83–85 (≈ MBh 13.146.16–18) and 13.14.101 connect the name 'Maheśvara' with the ithyphallic nature of Śiva (see above n. 68 on p. 73), a feature found in the image at issue.

10 The *daṇḍa*, which we take as a stick or ascetic staff rather than a club (*lakuṭa*/*laguḍa*/*lakula* or *gadā*, cf. Kreisel 1986, 103). MBh 13.15.11 calls Śiva *daṇḍapāṇin*, though usually Yama is referred to by this epithet. According to VDhP 3.48.11–13 the *daṇḍa* symbolizes death (*mṛtyu*)

other weapons. The waist is wrapped in a *dhotī*, visible on the reverse. A slender belt skirts the hips and passes around the back. An erect penis (*ūrdhvaliṅga*) is distinguishable underneath the *dhotī*. Unlike Joshi (1984, 52), we were unable to discover traces of a *yajñopavīta*, though two parallel oblique lines run across the breast (probably due to imperfections in the stone). The trunk is not paunched; it carries four heads, which are encircled by a broad headband; the joint matted hairdo is more flattened than that of the first tier of the Maheśvara image (Plates I & II). As in the latter image, the four heads have ears in common. The front face is badly mutilated but nevertheless creates the impression of being slightly protruding. Whether it had a third eye is difficult to determine, but the other three faces do not have one, nor do they have moustaches. The countenances of the two lateral heads are somewhat different, sterner than the faces of the Maheśvara image. The countenance of the addorsed head shows a beatific smile.

The conception underlying this sculpture is evidently different from that of the Maheśvara image. The aim seems not to be to divulge different levels or stages of Śiva's epiphany, but rather to represent one form of his. The matted hair and absence of ornaments indicate that we are concerned with a *yogin*. The figure shows a striding stance, which, combined with the *daṇḍa* or *śūla*, suggests that he had a protective function. In this respect he may be compared to the guardian god Daṇḍa at the bottom of the pillar found in Mathura (see above p. 68). However, his possession of four arms and heads point to an higher deity. The foremost of Śiva's acolytes, who resembles him (*dvitīyam iva śaṃkaram*), who is the captain of his guard and leader of his hosts (*gaṇas*), is Nandīśvara or Nandin. He is described as resting upon a lance (*śūla*) or carrying a golden staff (*vetra*).[11] His four heads and *ūrdhvaliṅga* may signify his impersonation of Śiva, and he is accordingly described as four-faced (*caturvaktra*) and carrying the lance (*śūlapāṇi*) in the (much later)

---

and is, together with the *mātuluṅga* (see n. 98 on p. 129), an attribute of Bhairava: *daṇḍaś ca mātuluṅgaś ca karayor bhairavasya tu* ||11|| *mṛtyur daṇḍo vinirdiṣṭo mātuluṅgas tathā kare* | *jagadbījasya sarvasya ye rājan paramāṇavaḥ* ||12|| *taiḥ pūrṇaṃ bījapūratvaṃ bhairavasya kare smṛtam* |. However, the attribute may just as well be the lance; compare the weapon held in the right hand of the Rudra image (below Plate IX).

11 Rām. 7.16.13–14: *so 'paśyan nandinaṃ tatra devasyādūrataḥ sthitam* | *dīptaṃ śūlam avaṣṭabhya dvitīyam iva śaṅkaram* ||13|| *taṃ dṛṣṭvā vānaramukham avajñāya sa rākṣasaḥ* | *prahāsaṃ mumuce tatra satoya iva toyadaḥ* ||14||. MBh 13.14.144: *purastāc caiva devasya nandiṃ paśyāmy avasthitam* | *śūlaṃ viṣṭabhya tiṣṭhantaṃ dvitīyam iva śaṅkaram* ||144||. Kumārasaṃbhava 3.41: *latāgṛhadvāragato 'tha nandī vāmaprakoṣṭhārpitahemavetraḥ* | *mukhārpitaikāṅgulisaṃjñayaiva mā cāpalāyeti gaṇān vyanaiṣīt* ||41||. The confusion of Nandīśvara (Śiva's effigy and doorkeeper) and Śiva's *vāhana*, the bull (*vṛṣabha*), which eventually resulted in their merging, may have started with an intermediate anthropomorphic figure with the head of a bull. The earliest archaeological evidence of such a (conflated) figure reported by Bhattacharya 1977, 1556 f. is found in Aihole and Badami (6th and 7th centuries AD).

Haracaritacintāmaṇi, though there he is said to be six-armed.[12] The description of a four-armed Nandin in the *Viṣṇudharmottarapurāṇa* also only partly agrees with the present image. This text ascribes to him the trident (*triśūla*) and dart (*bhindipāla*).[13]

In brief, we shall probably never be certain which deity exactly the sculptors of Mandhal had in mind when they made this image. On account of the arguments considered above we tentatively propose identifying him as Nandīśvara, who may have stood in front of Maheśvara as a servant. This interpretation has at least the advantage that the beatific smile of the addorsed head makes sense: it was directed to his Master. The latter may have been represented by the Maheśvara image (Plate I), the main idol of the MDL-II temple.

PLATES V & VI
A GAṆĀDHYAKṢA, MANDHAL
(V *front*, VI *rear*)

Mandhal. Nagpur Central Museum, no. A 94. Red-brown sandstone. 60 × 45 × 27 cm. Last quarter of 4th century AD. Found, together with two other images (Plates I–IV), in the fields in the vicinity of the village of Mandhal. Lit.: Jamkhedkar 1991a, Pl. 69; 1991b, 87, Pl. 1, 2.

This sturdy figure has been identified as a '*gaṇa*' by Jamkhedkar (1991b, 87). The image is four-armed, its left rear arm is intact until the elbow, the right rear arm has completely broken off. Tresses of matted hair on top of the head, parted in the middle, turn into long snail-shell curls which cascade down on to the back; the crown is covered by a flower rosette, a feature regularly found in Vākāṭaka sculpture as well as in some Gupta images. The elongated pierced ear lobes are decorated by earrings which rest on the shoulders.[14] The image wears a collar (*ekāvali*) around a neck that

---

12 Haracaritacintāmaṇi 4.74–76: *rudro bhava caturvaktraḥ ṣaḍbhujaś chagaladhvajaḥ* ||74|| *pramathaprathamaḥ piṅgaśmaśrukeśavilocanaḥ* | *vyāghracarmāmbaradharas trinetro vṛṣavāhanaḥ* ||75|| *śūlapāṇir mayā tulyo bhava sarvatra putraka* |. See also Granoff 1979, 66 nn. 3 and 4.

13 VDhP 3.73.15cd–17: *nandī kāryas trinetras tu caturbāhur mahābhujaḥ* ||15|| *sindūrāruṇasaṅkāśo vyāghracarmāmbaracchadaḥ* | *triśūlabhindipālau ca karayos tasya kārayet* ||16|| *śirogataṃ tṛtīyaṃ tu tarjayantaṃ tathā param* | *ālokamānaṃ kartavyaṃ dūrād āgāmikaṃ janam* ||17||.

14 Cf. the Viṣṇu panel at Ramgarth Hill described by Berkson 1978, 226: '[...] the earrings on the Viṣṇu figure at Ramgarth Hill resemble the earrings on an unidentified Mātṛkā at Pathari [cf. the Mandhal Mātṛkā, Plate XV, H.T.B.]. The ears protrude, the lobes have been bored, and the fleshy parts descend to the shoulders, supporting the earrings. Gupta sculptors were fond of this

is marked by three lines (*kambugrīva*), jewelled bracelets, and a *yajñopavīta*. The *dhotī* is wrapped tightly around the thighs, indicated by two parallel double lines, and twisted around the waist into a *kaṭibandha*, showing an *ūrdhvaliṅga* beneath. The end of the cloth turns over the left side of the girdle and is firmly held by the left (lower) hand. The left knee is slightly bent, which gives this figure a special vigorous air (*vikrama*).

Identification of this image will to some extent depend on the interpretation of the only attribute that is (partly) preserved and is held in the right lower hand. Jamkhedkar thinks (op. cit. 87) it to be a sword. This might be the case, but it seems also possible that the figure carries a kind of club (*lakuṭa*) which rests against his right shoulder and of which the top has broken off. The latter interpretation would point, of course, to the figure of Lakulīśa, but there are hardly any other signs that could justify such an identification.[15]

To solve the problem, the attribute of the image may be compared with that of a sculpture found in Nachna, illustrated in Williams 1982, Pl. 163. As we have noted above (n. 23 on p. 13), this sitting figure described by Williams as 'Lakulīśa,' does not seem to be that deity, because his left hand holds a battle-axe rather than a club. Since the broken-off attribute in the right lower hand of the image at issue also broadens where it rests against the shoulder (as in the Nachna image), it is probably a similar weapon, perhaps the axe (*paraśu* or *paraśvadha*).

The image does not represent a *yogin* as such, but rather calls to mind a stalwart warden. His mouth, though mutilated, seems to be slightly open (*karāla*), which adds to his deterrent nature. Like the image of Nandīśvara (?) (Plates III–IV), we may here be concerned with a figure from Śiva's entourage, whose staunch posture was meant to impress. We shall therefore refer to this image as Gaṇādhyakṣa, i.e., 'superintendent of the *gaṇas*.'

The original *Skandapurāṇa* gives a description of the Gaṇādhyakṣas when they arrive for Nandīśvara's consecration (SP 23.5 ff.). The first and foremost *gaṇapa* who arrives is Diṇḍi. He is described as having, among other features, an open mouth, contracted brows, fangs, three eyes, his head covered by thousand twisted locks, a girdle and *upavīta* of snakes, an erect penis, while he is loudly laughing and carrying the battle-axe (*paraśvadha*).[16] This early (6th–7th century) literary

---

device and used it often.'

15 Judging from the sign at the pedestal of the image, this identification has been proposed by the staff of the Nagpur Museum. According to U. P. Shah (1984, 100) four-armed Lakulīśa images make their appearance in the 6th century AD.

16 *tataḥ karālavadano bhṛkuṭībhūṣitānanaḥ | śaṅkhahārāmbugauraś ca daṃṣṭrī sragvī trilocanaḥ ||6|| jaṭāsahasrordhvaśirā jvālākeśo mahāhanuḥ | agnyaṅgārakanetraś ca bhujagābaddhamekhalaḥ ||7|| vidyujjihvo mahākāyas tathā caivordhvamehanaḥ | sarpayajñopavītī ca paraśvadhadharas tathā ||8|| bhujagābaddhamauñjiś ca bhujagair eva kaṅkaṇaiḥ | aṭṭahāsaṃ sṛjānaś ca aśanīpātasaṃnibham ||9|| diṇḍir ity eva vikhyāto gaṇapaḥ samadṛśyata |*

description of a *gaṇapa* agrees in some respects with the image at issue, though certainly not in all—something that could hardly be expected. A major difference is that our Gaṇādhyakṣa has four arms, a feature that seems to indicate that the deity was intimately related to Śiva himself.[17] The question must therefore remain open as to whom among Śiva's acolytes this image represents. Whoever he is, however, he may have had a guardian function in the Maheśvara Temple of MDL-II.

PLATES VII & VIII
SADĀSIVA, MANDHAL
(VII *front*, VIII A *rear*, VIII B *right side*)

Mandhal. Museum of the Dept. of AIH-CA, University of Nagpur. Red-brown sandstone. 89 × 50 × 30 cm. c. 400 AD. Found under the floor of brick temple of BHK-I. Lit.: Jamkhedkar 1991a, 199, Pl. 78; Joshi 1984, 54; Sarma 1992, 221–224; Shastri 1977–78, 146.

This image reflects in many respects the Maheśvara image described above (Plates I & II). It is better preserved, though, and its portion below the neck is distinguished from the Maheśvara image by the fact that it wears a necklace (*graiveyaka*), bracelet with a jewelled clasp (*ratnavalaya*), and a simple *upavīta*. The *kaṭibandha* is twisted instead of ribbed. As the image seems to be complete, it can be observed that the lower and upper legs are actually contracted to the space occupied by the two faces on the thighs (the feet-cum-pedestal was found separately and added to the image afterwards).[18] The major difference with respect to the Maheśvara image is found above the neck: on top of the four-headed tier that corresponds to the first tier of the Maheśvara image is placed another tier of four heads resulting in altogether eight heads on one neck.[19]

ātmanaḥ sadṛśānāṃ ca koṭībhir daśabhir vṛtaḥ | *gaṇapānāṃ sureśānāṃ yogināṃ dīpta-tejasām* ||10||, SP 23.6–10.

17 Cf. the four-armed Śaiva image from Mandasor, about which Williams 1982, 142 f. remarks that it resembles the *gaṇas* and attendants in other examples fom the area, yet 'while four-armed *gaṇas* are known, I am tempted to identify this as Bhairava (with animal in the lower right hand) or possibly Vīrabhadra.'

18 See the photograph in Shastri 1977–78.

19 The earliest depiction (2nd–3rd century AD) of a deity with two tiers of (each three) heads on one body may be the figure of Kārttikeya (Kumāra) on some Yaudheya coins (Allan 1936, CXLIX f., 270, Pl. XXXIX.21). Cf. the six-headed Kṛttikā figure on a Gandharan stele published by Sherrier 1993, pl. 48.1a.

The heads of the uppermost (first) tier are aligned with the intermediate (*antardeśa*), those of the second tier with the cardinal directions, supposing that the front of the image faced to one of the main quarters, probably east. The heads of the two upper-tiers differ from the faces of the two lower tiers by their moustaches, some of which are twisted upwards,[20] others downwards.[21] The heads of the second tier (from the top) are somewhat bigger than those of the first. This leaves the former without intermediate space, whence each head of the second tier has its ears in common with those of the two adjacent heads. The tresses of a high ascetic coiffure (*jaṭājūṭa*) with a parting in the middle are gathered up by a hair-ribbon (*keśabandha*) and rise above each head of the second tier, filling the intermediate space between the four heads of the first tier. This produces the effect of a column out of which the latter heads emerge. The top heads are, as in the Maheśvara image, connected by a headband (*bhālapaṭṭa*), which binds strands of matted hair.

The theological conception underlying this image is evidently more complicated than the one embodied in the Maheśvara image. The quadruple form of Śiva has been adapted to a vertical as well as horizontal structure, whereby the four aspects, as indicated in the *Mahābhārata* description (MBh 13.128.3–6), are blurred or indistinct. The four vertical levels, however, may be aligned with the concept of the emanation of the transcendent God in four hypostases, an idea that we primarily know from Pāñcarātra theology, where it is known as the four Vyūhas (*caturvyūha*).[22]

---

20 Notably the whiskers of the head on the reverse in the second tier.

21 Notably the moustache of the head that faces to the left on the reverse in the first tier.

22 SP_{Bh}33.9 praises Deva (Śiva) as follows: (obeisance to) *caturvyūhāya devāya trinetrāya bhavāya ca | caturmukhāya śuddhāya jālāntaravicāriṇe* ||9||. Cf. KūP 1.11.26–27; ŚiP (VāyavīyaS) 10.29; LiP 1.18.22 (*caturvyūhātmane*). The concept of a Śaiva *caturvyūha* is problematic (Srinivasan 1984, 42 f.). Mostly reference to this concept is made in discussing the Śiva figure on a pillar in the Muktādevī Temple in Mūsānagar (Srinivasan ibid.; Joshi 1984, 56). Kreisel (1986, 144 f.) remarks about this figure that the main aspect of this image is 'Uṣṇīṣin, der als sitzende Mittelfigur drei weitere Aspekte als verkleinerte Halbfiguren aus Schultern und Kopf entläßt. Er ist ithyphalisch dargestellt [...]. Gestik, Attribut und Schmuck entsprechen der Form des ikonographischen Grundtyps der Śivafigur [see above p. 76]: die rechte Hand ist in huldvollen Grußgeste erhoben, die linke trägt ein kleines rundbauchiges Gefäß (*kalaśa*). [...] Über dem kopf des Uṣṇīṣin erscheint die Halbfigur des Yogin mit langer Asketenfrisur, deren mittlere Strähnen wahrscheinlich abgebunden sind. [...] Die zwei seitliche emanierenden Halbfiguren, die im selben Größenverhältnis wie der Yogin dargestellt sind, lassen sich im jetzigen Erhaltungszustand nicht mehr detailliert beschreiben. Die Gestalt über der rechten Schulter hält in beiden erhobenen Armen rundliche Objekte (?), der Kopf trägt eine leicht erhöhte Frisur. [...] Die entsprechende Figur über der linken Schulter hält die rechte Hand über den Kopf, die linke liegt in Brusthöhe. Ob sie ein Objekt trägt, ist ungewiß. Am Kopf erhebt sich eine runde Schmuckscheibe, die als seitliche Kokarde eines deutlichen Stirnbandes interpretierbar ist. [...] Illustriert werden soll jedoch nicht eine (freistehende) Kultfigur, sondern die theologische Konzeption der Aspekte Śivas. In diesem Sinne kommen sämtliche Aspekte in Frontalstellung zur Abbildung, ohne daß ein nicht darstellbarer rückwärtiger Kopf anzunehmen wäre.

The two tiers of *yogin* heads, which are superior with respect to the *brahmacārin* and *uṣṇīṣin* and are consequently placed above them, may refer to the distinction of Sadāśiva and Maheśvara (see above p. 74): as the ruler and creator of the world, god, in a way, forms part of it, which corresponds to his embodiment called Maheś(var)a; transcending this embodiment, and nearing his absolute nature (*para*), is his reality as Sadāśiva (*sakala–niskala*).[23] Or, as described by Srinivasan:

> Out of the cosmic essence that is Para Śiva (i.e. the *liṅga*), the body of god begins to reveal itself and the head projects first. There follows a series of projections leading towards full manifestation. When the full figure is revealed, that is Maheśa. That figure can be described with five heads in the *āgamas*. [...]
>
> Maheśa's five heads are clearly depicted, but those of his predecessor are not. Theoretically there should be structural parity between Maheśa and Sadāśiva since the former is the latter, fully revealed. Indeed, Sadāśiva, just like Maheśa, is described with five heads in the *āgamas*, and the Pañcamukha Liṅga is his theoretical cognizance. [...] the Four-headed Śiva Liṅga is understood to stand for a Pañcamukha Liṅga, since the fifth head, in the center, is rarely represented.[24]

The interpretation that we propose of this complex Mandhal image is that it represents Śiva's manifestation on four levels, the eight heads of the upper two tiers jointly representing his two forms as Sadāśiva and Maheśvara, thus expressing the 'structural parity' of these two concepts. As a deviation from the common representation of Sadāśiva in the *caturmukhaliṅga*, the sculptor of the Mandhal image made the four (visible) heads (Brahmans) of Sadāśiva emanate from the central 'column' that is formed by the tied up hair of the heads of the second tier. The horizontal headband, which encircles the heads of the top tier, may be seen as reminiscent of

---

Die Viergestalt Śivas ist somit als eigenständige Konzeption aufzufassen. Sie geht einher mit der Entstehung der [...] Caturmukhaliṅga-form.' Although Kreisel avoids speaking of *caturvyūha*, his description could be taken as illustrating this concept, which is, though not widespread, not totally unknown to Śaiva literature (see above). We may here be concerned with a borrowing from Vaiṣṇava theology which never caught on in Saivism as it was superseded by the concept of the *caturmukhaliṅga*.

23 This distinction is broadly in keeping with the Śaiva Siddhānta tradition (see e.g. Brunner 1963 (= SŚP I), X f., XXIX; Srinivasan 1990; Davis 1991, 121). Granoff (1979, 75) and Kreisel (1986,143) do not distinguish between Śiva's manifestation as Sadāśiva and Maheśa, although the latter author reserves the term Maheś(var)amūrti for iconic (i.e., *sakala*) representations of Śiva. However, it cannot be denied that there is a good deal of conflation of the concepts of Maheśvara and Sadāśiva in the iconography of the semi-aniconic *caturmukhaliṅga* and, as the present image shows, in the iconic representation of Śiva as well.

24 Srinivasan 1990, 109. Cf. Davis 1991, 121.

the *pārśvasūtra*, the vertical hair parting of the *brahmasūtra* of the *liṅga*. The *liṅga* rising above four heads of a Maheśvaramūrti is not unknown.[25] The early Gupta Maheśamūrti in the Russek Collection (177 IMGU) in particular seems to come close to the conception underlying the Mandhal image (Plate XLI).[26] There is however only one other image known to me, in which this 'top *liṅga*' is again furnished with four (?) heads, viz. the 'rare lifesize sculpture of chatushpāda-Mahāsadāśiva [...] exhibited in the Archaeological Museum, Khajuraho.'[27]

It is uncertain whether the concept of the fivefold form of Sadāśiva (the five Brahmans) had already, in the period under consideration, influenced the idea of the quadruple form of Śiva Maheśvara so much that also the latter concept had come to involve a fifth, invisible head, homologized with *ākāśa*. For this we do not find support in contemporaneous texts, but the later *Viṣṇudharmottarapurāṇa* (3.48.3–6) seems to attest it. It calls the fifth head of Śambhu—a name taken as equivalent to our 'Maheśvara'—which represents his highest aspect (or from the point of emanation his origin), 'Sadāśiva.'[28] If this idea existed in the theology of the Māheśvaras of Mandhal, then the four heads of the first tier could be conceived of as the differentiation (corresponding to the Brahmans) of the apex of the second tier, Sadāśiva. The image would thus be the visual representation of the two interlocking concepts of Sadāśiva and Maheśvara.

The eight heads do not differ much in their physiognomy, which could in all cases be described as that of the *yogin*; notably the image does not seem to feature the terrifying aspect, which we found in the Maheśvara image. The faces all look rather neutral in that they all have forceful though composed expresssions, are adorned with moustaches, but, and this is remarkable, none has the third eye.[29] Identifica-

---

25 See Kreisel 1986, 147–150, Abb. 65, 66, 67(?), A20.

26 See also Kreisel 1986, 211 f.

27 B. N. Sharma 1976, 21, Pl. XXVIII. Sharma (ibid.) remarks about this image, 'His heads arranged horizontally in two tiers remind us of the figures of Skanda-Kārttikeya depicted on some early Yaudheya coins and a dome like projection above suggests the Īśāna aspect of the deity. His surviving lower right hand is held in gift-bestowing attitude and the four legs are arranged as in the image of Sadāśiva carved on the Kaṇḍariyā Mahādeva Temple at Khajuraho (Pl. V). The sculpture can be dated to the Chandella period, 10th century AD.' Compare also the so-called '*caturmukhaliṅga*' of Kāmān (11th century: Maxwell 1984, 78, Pl. 61), and the 'Sadāśiva with six heads' (Desai 1984, 150 f., Pl. 160).

28 *vibhāgenātha vakṣyāmi śambhor vadanapañcakam ||3|| mahādevamukhaṃ jñeyaṃ pūrvaṃ śambhor mahātmanaḥ | netrāṇi trīṇi tasyāhuḥ somasūryahutāśanāḥ ||4|| dakṣiṇaṃ tu mukhaṃ raudraṃ bhairavaṃ tat prakīrtitam | paścimaṃ yan mukhaṃ tasya nandivaktraṃ tad ucyate ||5|| umāvaktraṃ ca vijñeyaṃ tasya devasya cottaram | sadāśivākhyaṃ vijñeyaṃ pāvanaṃ tasya pañcamam ||6||*, VDhP 3.48.3–6.

29 Kreisel 1986, 119: 'Allerdings kann der Schnurrbart allein weder in der Kuṣāṇa- noch in der Guptazeit als hinreichendes Kriterium zur Interpretation der Aspekte gelten.' As we have seen above (n. 6 on p. 96), the third eye was only given to those forms of Śiva that are ferocious (*ugra*). The present image does not feature that aspect.

tion of any of these eight heads with one particular aspect, form or face of Sadāśiva and Maheśvara is not warranted by the evidence of the image.[30]

It follows from this analysis that Sadāśiva, Śiva's first and foremost manifestation in the cosmos, is the constituting principle that underlies this image—not conceived as aniconic as usual, but embedded in an intricate iconic structure. We therefore propose to refer to this image as 'Sadāśiva.' For the ordinary devotee, not educated in Māheśvara theology, the image will above all have inspired awe and he will have perceived chiefly its anthropomorphic Maheśvara aspect, embodied in the two-armed figure holding the vessel with the elixir (*amṛta*) in his left hand, while the right hand might have held the rosary in *abhayamudrā*. In this way the cryptic Mandhal figure, although elaborated in a most unusual fashion, conforms in its basic structure, like the Maheśvara image, to what Kreisel described as the 'Grundtyp der Śivadarstellung' (see p. 76).

Although, admittedly, we cannot give a special metaphysical explanation of the doubling of the faces on arms and thighs—this may have been prompted by reasons of symmetry—the above-proposed interpretation has the advantage of explaining most of the aspects of the sculpture, making it a meaningful image for the initiate and layman alike. It also conforms visually to general underlying principles of arrangement that combine Śaiva items into groups of four (e.g., *caturmūrtitva*), eight (*aṣṭamūrti*) and twelve (e.g., *dvādaśajyotirliṅga*). Moreover, the eight heads on top, directed towards the eight points of the compass, create the idea of a powerful all-commanding deity. The image may have been the main idol of the BHK-I temple in which it was found.

When we look for a contemporary image that resembles the Mandhal Sadāśiva, at least in some of its outer aspects, the hybrid, spectacular, perhaps even slightly absurd image that was found near the entrance of the Devarānī Temple in Tala comes to mind (Plate XLII). It has to be admitted, though, that when we apply the principle of hierarchical vertical ranking of the tiers of heads/faces to this image, no clear organisational structure appears. There are five such tiers: the uppermost one is the single head that wears a turban (*uṣṇīṣa*) made up by serpent coils; the second tier consists of two bald, moustached faces on the breast; the third tier is a large round, moustached and apparently bald face that forms the belly of the figure; the fourth tier consists of four bald, grinning faces without moustaches on the thighs, in the front and on either side; the fifth tier is formed by two animal heads on the knees. It would seem that the last two faces represent lions. The image is further composed of various natural motifs, such as animals.

---

30 In a forthcoming publication (South Asian Archaeology 1995) I have tentatively applied the iconography given in the *Viṣṇudharmottarapurāṇa* to the present image.

The serpent coils of the *uṣṇīṣa* seem to end in two cobra hoods that flank the head on either side above the shoulders. The serpent motif returns in the coils which gird the neck and encircle the face-in-the-belly above and below; they form, as it were, a kind of *hāra*, *udarabandha* and *kaṭibandha*. The two bangles and the fingers of the left hand are modelled after snakes, the preserved thumb of the right hand shows the head of a snake. This right hand may have rested on a mace (*gadā*); the uppermost part of it is preserved. A large hood of a snake comes forward from the rear next to the left foot of the image and rises beside the leg; it is likely that a similar snake-hood rose along the right leg too, but is now missing. Various parts of the body are composed of different animals.[31]

The elongated, pierced ear lobes of the two faces on the breast are adorned by bells, the four faces on the thighs are without ornaments. The two frontal faces on the thighs are wreathed by a garland (or coil of a snake?), of which the central ornamentation (or protruding head?) has broken off. An alternative interpretation would conceive of the 'wreath' as two bent arms, the broken-off middle piece as hands in an *añjali* pose.

The conception underlying this deity and hence his identification remains a puzzle despite some similarities with the Mandhal Sadāśiva. If we count also the two *makara* heads, the image has twelve heads/faces. However, the relationship between them seems to be different from the one that underlies the Mandhal sculpture. Rather than a hierarchy of emanations (*vyūha*) these heads seem to represent various aspects of the deity. In view of the animals constituting and accompanying the image one could think of Paśupati, but this does not explain the five tiers of faces.

If, however, we compare the Tala image with descriptions of figures from Śiva's entourage, the *gaṇas* and *pramathas*, in Mahābhārata 9.44, we find many similarities, although their combination into one figure is unique and rather odd. Here it is said that a *gaṇa* may be large-bodied (*mahākāya*) and possessed of heavy limbs (*sthūlāṅga*); he may be shaven-headed (*muṇḍa*) or with matted hair (*jaṭila*); he may be monstruous (*virūpin*) and possessed of the forms of various animals (*anekaprāṇirūpin*); he may possess the face of a lion (*siṃhamukha*) and *makara*, or he may have a head in his belly (*udaratomukha*), or on his thighs (*jaṅghamukha*). The *gaṇa* may be naked (*nagna*) or hooded by a kind of snake (*ghoṇāsāvaraṇa*).

31 The nose is formed by a lizard, the hind-legs of which form the brows; both ears and their ornaments are represented by two peacocks with fanned tails; the eyes are modelled after the head of a frog-like animal that holds the eye-ball in its widely opened mouth (the nose and eyes of the frog-like animal are faintly visible on the eyelid); the moustache is made out of two fish, while the chin is formed by a crab. Both arms emerge from gaping *makara* mouths. The erect penis is formed by the neck, its glans by the head of a tortoise; the two fore-legs of this animal, together with the shell from which they protrude, form the scrotum.

In short, he may be deterrent (*śatrubhayaṅkara*), and this the Tala image at issue certainly is.[32] In want of any other clue, we tentatively propose considering the Tala image as a composite Śaiva *gaṇa* figure, who may have had an apotropaic function, protecting the Devarānī Temple.

Finally a general remark needs to be made about a feature common to both images compared and the Maheśvara one (Plates I & II), which, despite all differences, seems to belong to an indefinite local, i.e., tribal background. In this respect it may be of some importance to refer to a publication of Carl Schuster (1951), in which it is made clear that the motif of faces on the joints of the human body is very common and widespread among tribal cultures. The faces at the limbs of both images may derive from ancient tribal prototypes in which the joints of the human body were believed to be endowed with special significance, because they were considered to be knots in which the forces of the soul (or souls) were confined (Schuster 1951, 19 f.). Schuster adduces examples of joint-markings from East and South-East Asia, Oceania, the Western Pacific and the New World, i.e., Precolumbian America. The Tala sculpture as well as some of the sculptures of Mandhal seem to be informed by the same conception, which in both cases may indicate the still close links of the sculptors with their own tribal background and which may point to an environment on its way towards what is now called 'Hinduism.'

Plates IX & X
Rudra (Andhakāsurasaṃhāramūrti), Mandhal
(IX *front*, X *rear*)

Mandhal. Museum of the Dept. of AIHCA, University of Nagpur. Red-brown sandstone. 62 × 46 × 24 cm. c. 400 AD. Found under the floor of the brick temple of BHK-I. Lit.: Jamkhedkar 1991a, 200, Pl. 71; Shastri 1977–78, 145 f.

The two-armed image represents the anthropomorphic Śiva/Rudra as he has been described from the times of the *Śatarudrīya*[33] onwards: the formidable (*bhīma*) piercer (*nivyādhin*), short in stature (*vāmana*, *hrasva*), dwelling on the mountains (*giriśanta*) and wielding the bow (*dhanvan*). The bow became known as Pināka and its arrow was recognized by Upamanyu in his vision of Śiva as the terrible

32 MBh 9.44.51–110. Cf. Dhaky 1984, 248.
33 TaiSa 4.5.1–11; see Sivaramamurti 1976.

Pāśupata weapon.[34] Bow (*dhanus*) and arrow (*iṣu*, *śara*) are held in the left hand of the image. The other formidable weapon that was seen by Upamanyu is the lance (*śūla*), with its razor-sharp point (*atitīkṣṇāgra*),[35] 'that splits the whole world and vaporizes the great ocean.'[36] Patañjali *ad* P. 5.3.76 attributes the iron lance (*ayaḥśūla*) to the followers of Śiva (*śivabhāgavatas*), and it is this weapon that the god himself seems to clasp with his right hand in this image. Unfortunately, this attribute is broken off at the top and the bottom, but, to judge by the way it is held, it is likely that it is a pointed weapon, i.e., the *śūla*.[37]

The other characteristics of the image also conform to traditional Śaiva iconography. It has an intricate ascetic coiffure of matted strands (*jaṭājūṭa*). The round knob protruding from the left front side of his hair may be a skull (*kapāla*), which has been eroded almost beyond recognition; to its right is the crescent (cf. the skull and the crescent on the head of the Mansar Śiva, Plate XXXVII). The deity has a vertical third eye and earrings in the elongated ear lobes.[38] He wears a necklace (*ekāvali*), belly-band (*udarabandha*), bracelets (*valaya*), and the *upavīta* of the *snātaka* or *gṛhastha*—a band consisting of six strings of pearls (*muktāyajñopavīta*), similar to the ones worn by the Rāmagiri Trivikrama, Mansar Śiva and Ajanta Vajrapāṇi.[39] The band runs over the left shoulder crosses the breast obliquely, but is not continued on the reverse. The deity is clad in a tiger-skin (*vyāghracarman*)—the head being visible on the right thigh—which leaves the erect penis exposed.[40] In this

---

34 MBh 13.14.122–130; see above p. 72.

35 MBh 13.14.135.

36 MBh 13.14.131–132.

37 Shastri (1977–78, 145) identifies this attribute as the club (*lakuṭa*). The trident (*triśūla*) as an attribute of Śiva features already in the earliest representations of this god, especially on coins in the north-west of the sub-continent. Kreisel (1986, 22) concludes that it was probably a borrowing from the Hellenistic culture (the trident of Poseidon found on Hellenistic coins). On the other hand, Kreisel observes that 'die Darstellung des Dreizacks erscheint in Mathura erstmals in der Guptazeit, im Jahre 380/81 n. Chr., jedoch nicht als Attribut in Śivas Hand, sondern als Kult Symbol im Relief an der Gedenksäule der Māhadeva- oder Pāśupata-Sekte. [...] Erst aus der Spätguptazeit ist der Dreizack als Attribut einer Śivafigur der Mathura-kunst bekannt' (Kreisel 1986, 105). Equally late is the appearance of the *triśūla* as an attribute of Śiva in Sanskrit literature. The relatively late *Tīrthayātrāparvan* of the MBh associates the *triśūla* with the great god, Mahādeva (MBh 3.80.84; cf. MBh 12 App. 1 No. 28 l. 178; MBh 14.8.25), but in Upamanyu's and Kṛṣṇa's description of Śiva his weapon is the *śūla* (MBh 13.14.131, 151; 13.15.11). In retrospect, after the *triśūla* had replaced the original lance, the term *śūla* was and is often interpreted as 'trident.' This might be justifiable for later sources, but should be avoided in translating and interpreting Sanskrit sources dating from before the 7th century AD.

38 For the significance of the third eye see above n. 6 on p. 96.

39 Plates XXXIV A, XXXVII and XXXVIII A. For this type of *yajñopavīta* see Kane II, 293.

40 In contrast with the Maheśvara and Sadāśiva images (Plates I & VII), which represent the auspicious (*śiva*) side of the god and emphasize his celibacy (*brahmacarya*) by an *ūrdhvaliṅga* that is covered by a *dhotī*, the present image, showing his ferocious (*ghora*) side, depicts his sex bla-

respect the image may be compared with a sculpture that rests at the bottom of the eastern steps that lead up to the Jithānī Temple in Tala (Plate XLIII A), in which the scrotum and erect penis are very pronounced, although they are covered by the tiger-skin. The face of the tiger, flanked by two claws, is sculptured on the inner right thigh (Plate XLIII B), like in the Mandhal image.

The face of the Mandhal image is damaged, but the bulging eyes seem to look downward towards the imaginary target of the lance. It would seem that this target was pushed down by the left foot. This becomes clear when the image is seen from the rear: it shows a lifted left leg, the heel against his bottom, and toes pressing down something not shown. Evidently we are concerned with a so-called *saṃhāra-mūrti* which represents Śiva as a ferocious deity.[41] The victim is apparently forced into submission by the *śūla*. This would exclude the possibility of the image being a Kāmāntakamūrti, Kālārimūrti, or Tripurāntakamūrti. Since Śiva wears a tiger-skin, and there is no trace of an elephant, it would also follow that the image does not represent the Gajāsurasaṃhāramūrti. We therefore conjecture that the image depicts the victory over the demon Andhaka (Andhakāsurasaṃhāramūrti). It may, according to one (Vaiṣṇava) version, represent the moment when—after the demon had been hit by one of Rudra's arrows and the blood issuing from the wound had been drunk by the Mātṛkās and Śuṣkarevatī (the 'Shrivelled Revatī,' created by Viṣṇu at Śaṃkara's request)—Rudra plants his *śūla* in him and the demon surrenders and starts praising his victor.[42]

---

tantly. Cf. MBh 13.146.3–5: *dve tanū tasya devasya vedajñā brāhmaṇā viduḥ | ghorām anyāṃ śivām anyāṃ te tanū bahudhā punaḥ ||3|| ugrā ghorā tanūr yāsya so 'gnir vidyut sa bhāskaraḥ | śivā saumyā ca yā tasya dharmas tv āpo 'tha candramāḥ ||4|| ātmano 'rdhaṃ tu tasyāgnir ucyate bharatarṣabha | brahmacaryaṃ caraty eṣa śivā yāsya tanus tathā ||5||.*

41 Cf. MBh 13.146.7 where the name 'Rudra' is reserved for this form of the deity: *yan nirdahati yat tīkṣṇo yad ugro yat pratāpavān | māṃsaśoṇitamajjādo yat tato rudra ucyate ||7||.*

42 MP 179.5–39 (see also n. 59 on p. 115). Various versions of the Andhaka myth exist. They are discussed by Collins 1988, 57–65 in connection with the Andhakāsurasaṃhāra relief in the Elephanta cave temple. Discussing the story in the *Vāmanapurāṇa*, Collins 1988, 61 observes: 'The attribute of the lance, also alluded to in the *Mahābhārata*, is repeatedly mentioned here as the instrument of death or reform, and not the trident as found in the *Matsya-*, *Kūrma-* and *Liṅgapurāṇas*, or the mace of the *Harivaṃśa*; [...] This probably relates more closely to the Elephanta relief since a spear or lance, but not a trident, is used to destroy Andhaka in the similar relief at Ellora cave-temple 29.' Collins falls victim to the wrong translation of *śūla* by 'trident' in the cases of the *Matsya-* and *Liṅgapurāṇa* which both consistently read *śūla*; only the critical edition of the *Kūrmapurāṇa* alternates *śūla* with *triśūla* (see above n. 37 on p. 108).

PLATES XI & XII
NAIGAMEṢA, MANDHAL
(XI *front*, XII *rear*)

Mandhal. Museum of the Dept. of AIH-CA, University of Nagpur. Red-brown sandstone. 64 × 40 × 19 cm. c. 400 AD. Found under the floor of the brick structure of BHK-I. Lit.: Bakker, *forthcoming* a; Jamkhedkar 1991a, Pl. 70; Shastri 1977–78, 147 f.

This image represents another figure from Śiva's entourage. It concerns a deity with the head of a ram (*meṣa*) or goat (*chāga*), whose horns bend downwards around the ears. The face is partly damaged, but the right bulging eye appears to be that of an animal. The horns flank a thick head of hair which falls on to the shoulders in a check pattern. The deity wears a necklace (*ekāvali*), *yajñopavīta* (visible at the back), and simple bracelets (*valaya*). The *dhotī* covers an *ūrdhvaliṅga* and is rolled into a belt. Its rim is marked by two lines on the thigh. The spare cloth falls along both thighs. The legs of the image are broken off at the knees, but its two arms have been preserved. Its left hand rest on the top of his hip in a highly unnatural position (cf. the right lower hand of the Nandīśvara (?) image, Plate III), whereas the right hand holds a tapering shaft, probably of a spear (*śakti*), which reaches up to the right shoulder and is broken off at the left knee; it is more slender than the shaft in the hands of the Nandīśvara (?) and Rudra images (Plates III & IX) and is definitely not a *daṇḍa* as in the Naigameṣa image of Tala (Plate XLIV A).

The ram/goat-headed deity in Śiva's following is known as Naigameṣa (Naigameśa) or Naigameya and is closely related to the figure of Skanda. In the *Āraṇyakaparvan* of the *Mahābhārata* Skanda's father Agni metamorphosed into Naigameya for the sake of his son's entertainment, a figure that is characterised by having a 'goat face' and being blessed with much progeny.[43] *Mahābhārata* 3.217.11–12 adds that the goat-faced deity is intimately related to the sixth face of Skanda, a deity who, joined with the eight valiant sons of the Mātṛkās, forms a group of nine and who is therefore always venerated by them.[44] This goat-faced manifestation of Skanda is said to be a protector in battle, surrounded by maidens

---

43 MBh 3.215.23: *agnir bhūtvā naigameyaś chāgavaktro bahuprajaḥ | ramayāmāsa śailasthaṃ bālaṃ krīḍanakair iva* ||23||. SPBh 132.19 calls him 'Śiva's son' (*harātmajaḥ*); see n. 45 on p. 111.

44 MBh 3.217.11–12: *eṣa vīrāṣṭakaḥ proktaḥ skandamātṛgaṇodbhavaḥ | chāgavaktreṇa sahito navakaḥ parikīrtyate* ||11|| *ṣaṣṭhaṃ chāgamayaṃ vaktraṃ skandasyaiveti viddhi tat | ṣaṭśirobhyantaraṃ rājan nityaṃ mātṛgaṇārcitam* ||12||. See n. 59 on p. 115.

and sons.[45] *Mahābhārata* 1.60.23 describes Naigameṣa as being born from the back of Kumāra (Skanda). Simultaneously with him, Śākha and Viśākha were born, thus giving rise to a 'fourfold body' (*caturmūrti*): Skanda, Śākha, Viśākha, Naigameṣa.[46]

Though his exact relationship to Skanda thus remains obscure, it is evident that the 'ram/goat-headed god' is regarded as a ferocious deity with a protective, i.e. deterrent, nature. As such he is found *in situ* in Tala, where he protects the southern side of the entrance to the Devarānī Temple (Plate XLIV A). The Mandhal Naigameṣa may have had a similar function in the brick temple of BHK-I.

PLATES XIII & XIV
PĀRVATĪ, MANDHAL
(XIII *front*, XIV *rear*)

Mandhal. Museum of the Dept. of AIHCA, University of Nagpur. Red-brown sandstone. 68 × 39 × 21 cm. c. 400 AD. Found under the floor of the brick structure at BHK-I. Lit.: Divakaran 1984, 284; Jamkhedkar 1991a, 199, Pl. 80; Shastri 1977–78, 147 f.

This well-proportioned figure of a female ascetic combines sturdiness with female elegance and no doubt represents the Goddess in her yogic aspect, symbolized by her coiffure of matted hair which falls on to her back. A ribbed cord separates the hair from the forehead. The body is without ornaments.

The figure is two-armed; the right upper arm and hand are broken off, leaving only part of the right forearm, which is directed towards the front beside her hip, similar to the right arm of the Sadāśiva image. Under the right wrist a few beads

---

45 MBh 3.217.3: *sa bhūtvā bhagavān saṃkhye rakṣaṃś chāgamukhas tadā | vṛtaḥ kanyāgaṇaiḥ sarvair ātmanīyaiś ca putrakaiḥ ||3||*. SP$_{\text{Bh}}$132 describes how Śukra points out the prominent figures in the god's army to Andhaka prior to battle, among whom Naigameṣa appears mounted on a ram: *meṣam āsthāya balavān bāla eva vyavasthitaḥ | naigameṣa iti khyāta eṣo 'ndhaka harātmajaḥ ||19|| caturbhir eṣa putrais tu dṛśyate 'surahā vṛtaḥ |*.

46 MBh 1.60.23: *agneḥ putraḥ kumāras tu śrīmāñ śaravaṇālayaḥ ||22|| tasya śākho viśākhaś ca naigameśaś ca pṛṣṭhajaḥ |*. Van Buitenen translates *pṛṣṭhajaḥ* with 'as the last born.' Some MSS read, however, *pṛṣṭhataḥ* and this is also the reading of MBh 9.43.37, where they are said to be simultaneous (*kṣaṇena*) manifestations: *tato 'bhavac caturmūrtiḥ kṣaṇena bhagavān prabhuḥ | skandaḥ śākho viśākhaś ca naigameṣaś ca pṛṣṭhataḥ ||37||*. See also PPL p. 162, vs. 41; p. 212, vs. 27. Naigameṣa is together with his three brothers (i.e. Skanda, Viśākha and Śākha) called the son of Śiva in SP$_{\text{Bh}}$132.20; see n. 45 on p. 111. In SP$_{\text{Bh}}$132.52 the same quartet appears and Naigameṣa is mentioned as the 'goat-headed' one (*chāgamukha*; cf. SP$_{\text{Bh}}$150.26 *chāgavaktra*).

of the *akṣamālā* are still visible. Her left arm is kept straight downwards; the palm of the hand is turned to the front and grasps from behind a spherical object which may represent the *ghaṭa* or *kamaṇḍalu*.[47] The goddess wears a dress that is wrapped around her legs. Folds of the garment, which is held up by a double, twisted braid around the hips, fall along her right thigh (rear). Her legs are marked by two vertical pleats. A diaphanous upper garment passes over her left shoulder, revealing her full breasts.

With her attributes of asceticism and fertility the Goddess is the female counterpart of the Sadāśiva and Maheśvara figures. She represents the daughter of the mountain, Umā or Pārvatī, whose great *tapas* persuaded Śiva to marry her. A contemporary poet described her as follows.

> Firmly resolved she took off her necklace of pearls—the pendulous string had wiped off the paste of sandal wood—and put on a garment of bark, rose-coloured like the sun at dawn, the fabric of which was torn apart by the swelling of her breasts. (8)
>
> Matted locks, no less than well-decorated tresses of hair, made her face shine sweetly; a lotus does not appear beautiful only by swarms of bees, but also when weed sticks to it. (9)
>
> Her skin, where it was used to the cord of a girdle, was turned red when for the first time a braid made of three strands of *muñja* grass was fastened—the braid which she wore for the sake of her observance, and which, constantly, made her hair stand on end. (10)
>
> Her fingers no longer touched her lower lip, from which the red colour had disappeared, and they dropped the playing ball, which was reddened by the paint of her breasts; she gave her hand the rosary (*akṣamālā*) as a dear friend, while her fingers were wounded by the picking of blades of *kuśa* grass. (11)
>
> [...]
>
> Indefatigable, she herself raised the saplings by the flows from her breast that was the water pot (*ghaṭa*); not even Guha (i.e., Skanda) would be able to diminish (her) motherly love for them, her first-born sons. (14)[48]

The Goddess might have occupied a position to the left of the Sadāśiva image in the BHK-I temple.

---

47 Divakaran 1984, 284; Shastri 1977–78, 148.

48 *Kumārasaṃbhava* 5.8–11, 14.

PLATES XV & XVI
MĀTRKĀ, MANDHAL
(XV *front*, XVI *rear*)

Mandhal. Museum of the Dept. of AIHCA, University of Nagpur. Red-brown sandstone. 72 × 44 × 30 cm. c. 400 AD. Found under the floor of the brick structure of BHK-I. Lit.: Jamkhedkar 1991a, 200, Pl. 79; Shastri 1977–78, 148.

This sculpture is among the finest found in Mandhal. The goddess is seated on a throne which is supported by four delightfully carved lions at the corners, each wearing a necklace and showing a deterrent (*ugra*) face, like the deity herself.[49]

The most peculiar aspect of the image is the hairdo/head-dress. It consists of a combination of four elements. The hair at the temples has been smoothly gathered up and braided into a broad and long plait (*veṇibandha*) that falls down the back. The top of the head is covered by a lotus cap or rosette. At the end of the tapering plait, just above the *dhotī*, hangs an ornament in the form of a flagon, which is divided by a wavy furrow into an upper and lower half and which might be a (metal) bell. Along the temples at both sides of the braid a pitted roll curves around the ears, reaching till the shoulders. Unless the pits are meant to create the impression of matted hair—but the hair of the temples seems to be stiffly combed underneath the rolls—there is no inherent connection with the rest of the headdress. On the contrary, these 'rolls' look like horns, and this likeness is perhaps intended.[50] They reflect the horns of the Naigameṣa image, which are equally pitted, though much more eroded. It therefore appears likely that this female deity is, in some way, related to the figure of Naigameṣa.[51]

---

49 Cf. a capital of Eran (Williams 1982, Plate 124) or 'the finely carved rampant lions at the corners of the Vaibhāra base' (Williams 1982, 35, Plate 28).

50 In the end it is immaterial whether we conceive of these 'rolls' as hair or horn, both are *śiroruha*. What matters is that these 'rolls' are associated with horns and consequently with horned deities. In this way this image continues the tripartite hairdress style found in many (earlier) figurines (see e.g., Härtel 1993, 100 ff.), which is sometimes taken to symbolize youth (see e.g., the Kumāra image in Pal 1986, 269, which shows the so-called *śikhandaka*, a pony-tail like hair arrangement on the two sides of the head), but which in this image (and possibly also in the figurines mentioned in the following note) has acquired a more significant meaning.

51 The image invites comparison with a small female bust from Nanpur (in the vicinity of Nagardhan) with 'horn-like hair-do' (Jamkhedkar 1991b, 90, Fig. 12). In other respects also this figurine, kept in the Nagpur Central Museum, seems to be closely akin to the sculpture at issue. Compare, for instance, the curved lower lip of both sculptures. The upper left arm of the Nanpur figurine is preserved and its position could also have been that of the (missing) arm of the Mandhal image. A fracture on the upper arm of the Nanpur figurine indicates that something rested against it. Jamkhedkar identifies the Nanpur image 'from the posture and the head-dress'

Though her face is beautiful in its own way, with almond eyes and arched brows, her opened mouth shows fangs, thus expressing her fierce (*ugra*) character. She wears jewelled discs in the elongated pierced ear lobes (*ratnakuṇḍala*), a necklace of overlapping small discs (*niṣka*) and simple anklets (*nūpura*).

The deity sits in the *lalitāsana* posture. She has wrapped a cloth around her waist, pulled up at the loins. On the hips rests a broad waistband (*kaṭibandha*) which loops at both her sides, returns over the thighs and passes in front of her across the throne.[52] The left foot rests upon this band on the pedestal. Above the waist the body is naked. The goddess has full round breasts and two arms. The right arm is broken off at the elbow, the left arm at the armpit. The left hand is preserved, however, and rests upon the left thigh, the little finger touching the band. It would seem that the right arm held a spear (*śakti*)—or, less probable, a lance (*śūla*)—for, on the right upper arm traces remain of an attribute which rested against it and which extended downwards towards the left foot. The shaft of this weapon may have rested against the fractured surface at the end of the toes.

By her beauty, pose, ornamentation and braid on the one hand, and by the open mouth (*karāla*), horn-like hairdo and the fierce faces of the lions on the other hand, the image of this goddess conveys an ambivalent impression. Lack of attributes, however, means that it is difficult to determine the precise form of the goddess that is intended. The assumed weapon in the right hand, if a *śūla*, and the lions on the throne seem to point to Durgā; the deity, however, does not ride the lion, but only

---

as 'a figure of Durgā' (op. cit. 90), which identification, on account of what is said here, may be reconsidered. Another image of a female deity that may be relevant is the one found in Arambha, a minor Vākāṭaka site 72 km SW of Nagpur in the Wardha District. It is described as a 'mother goddess.' 'It has puffy nose and lips with prominent pout. [...] The braided hair deviced into two side buns has incised decoration of latticed diamond pattern, while the hair braided at the back has chevron motif. Almost identical heads of mother goddesses have been reported at Paunar and are attributed to the Vakatakas' (Nath 1991–92, 71, Fig. 4). For the Paunar figurine see Deo & Dhavalikar 1968, 110 (Plate XXV Nos. 1–2): 'The coiffure is curious and interesting and resembles a wig (*chūrṇa-kuntala*). The hair is parted in the middle and arranged in two large parallel rolls along the parting line on either side. This criss-cross pattern of the hair is indicative of its being secured in a net (*jālikā*). Cf. Gupta 1992, 145 about these findings in Paunar: 'One piece shows a male head while the second a female one (Fig. 14.1, 2). Both the sculptures are made of sandstone. The hair-styles and the horn-like ornamentation of these pieces show stylistic affinities with the Vākāṭaka sculpture of Durgā found in Māṇḍhaḷ' [i.e. the image at issue].

52 Compare the Goddess from Ālampur (Kṣemaṅkarī), illustrated in Divakaran 1984, 283, Pl. 240, who wears this type of band. Jamkhedkar 1991a, 211 n. 13: 'This characteristics [sic] which has an antiquity going back to at least second century A.D. is to be seen prominently in the western Indian sculptures.' Harle 1974, 40, describing the Mātṛkā goddesses of Besnagar, notes that, 'A scarf (?) appears to have been stretched across the laps of all the figures but only the ends, lying on the tops of the thrones, can still be seen.' One wonders whether this band or 'scarf' could not be a stylized version of the birth cloth depicted in some Lajjā Gaurī images (see below p. 134).

sits on a lion-throne (*siṃhāsana*).[53] None of the Mandhal images, nor any other Vākāṭaka image for that matter,[54] shows a *vāhana*. The descriptions of Durgā in contemporaneous literature, depicting her as a martial figure, hardly seem to apply to this image.[55] The Durgā images that occur in the Gupta period have as characteristic feature that the goddess *rides* the lion.[56] Finally the horn-like rolls which form part of her headdress seem to stand in the way of a straightforward identification as Durgā. The *lalitāsana* and *ugra* face are, on the other hand, common in images of the Mātṛkās. The *Āraṇyakaparvan* of the *Mahābhārata* describes how the maidens (*kanyās*) that were born from the impact of Indra's *vajra* on Skanda surround the latter in battle when he assumes his goat-faced form.[57] The same maidens turn to Skanda and ask him whether they may become the mothers (*mātaras*) of the world. Skanda replies: 'Certainly! As such you shall be of different nature, inauspicious and auspicious.'[58] Thereupon these 'world-mothers' adopt Skanda as their son (*putratva*). In addition, seven of them—viz., Kākī, Halimā, Rudrā, Bṛhalī, Āryā, Palālā, Mitrā—become each the mother of a very cruel and strong (*vīrya*) infant (*śiśu*).[59]

The identification of the image at issue as a mother goddess is reinforced by the braid (*veṇi*), which, when it is allowed to fall on the back, indicates that the woman is solitary or mourns the absence of her husband (*ekaveṇi*, see PW s.v.). As such it is known from other Mātṛkā images of the Gupta period and in keeping with the

---

53 Shastri 1977–78, 148 identifies the image as Durgā: 'khīṃsoṃ ke rūp meṃ bāhar nikle hue dāṃtoṃ se durgā kī bhayānaktā sūcit kī gayī hai |.'

54 Exceptions are the River Goddess (Ajanta) and the Gaṅgā image of Paunar (Plate XXIX), who both stand on the *makara*.

55 MBh 4 App.I No. 4 (D), ll. 1–51; MBh 6 App. I No. 1, ll. 7–32; HV App. I No. 20, ll. 361–375.

56 See e.g. Singh 1977, 154 f.; N. P. Joshi 1972, 70 f.; Williams 1982, 73 f., Plate 80. However, the Bilsaḍh image illustrated in Plate 80 and defined by Williams as 'Durgā seated on a lion' carries a child on her left thigh. It may be argued that an image of a two-armed, lion-riding goddess with a child in her lap represents a Mātṛkā figure rather than the 'Athenean' Durgā. Naturally all Mātṛkā figures can be seen as manifestations of Durgā.

57 See n. 44 on p. 110 and n. 45 on p. 111.

58 MBh 3.317.8: *so 'bravīd bāḍham ity evaṃ bhaviṣyadhvaṃ pṛthagvidhāḥ | aśivāś ca śivāś caiva punaḥ punar udāradhīḥ ||8||*. We take *pṛthagvidhāḥ* as a qualification of each mother as such, not as referring to different sorts of *mātṛkās*, as is the common interpretation.

59 MBh 3.217.1–11. Together with Skanda, presumably, these sons are called the 'Octet of Heroes' (*vīrāṣṭaka*). When the goat-faced form of Skanda is added they are known as 'the Nine' (*navaka*, see n. 44 on p. 110). These *kanyās/mātaras* were originally different from the Kṛttikās and the group of Mothers as a whole (see below n. 61 on p. 116); various groups of mother goddesses were synthesized *inter alia* into a group of mother deities that was created by Rudra to drink the blood of Andhaka: *pānārtham andhakāsrasya so 'sṛjan mātaras tadā | māheśvarī tathā brāhmī kaumārī mālinī tathā ||9||* etc. (MP 179.9–32, see also n. 42 on p. 109). The different origin and background of various groups of mother goddesses account for the great variety in their iconography.

nature of the *mātṛkās* as women whose husbands are absent. At least two of the seven Mātṛkā statues that were found in Besnagar (MP) have plaited hair (see Plate XLVII B).[60]

The above-mentioned (seven) mothers—despite their acquired motherhood actually the daughters or manifestations of Skanda—were associated, i.e. replaced by or fused with the six wives (Kṛttikās) of the seven seers; the latter had divorced their wives on the basis of the (false?) accusation that they had mothered Skanda, which, however, did not withhold them from asking Skanda to consider them as his mothers.[61] The ambivalent impression conveyed by the image is actually rooted in the complex, synthesized character of the figure of the Mātṛkā itself: she is a maiden (*kanyā*, *kumārī*), a mother (*mātṛ*), the embodiment of virtue (*dharmayukta*), as well as inauspicious (*aśiva*), bloodthirsty (*śoṇitapriya*), and feared as the dangerous snatcher, eater, 'grasper' (*graha*) of infants.

The *Bṛhatsaṃhitā* (58.56) states that the mother goddesses should be sculpted in accordance with their respective gods. Applied to the image at issue this would connect the deity with the figure of Naigameṣa. In this respect some images dating from the Kuṣāṇa period, preserved in the Archaeological Museum Mathura, may be of relevance.[62] It concerns female deities carrying a child and having the head of a goat. No matter what their origin may have been,[63] the *Matsyapurāṇa* does actually list a ram-headed goddess among the 'mothers' that were created by Rudra.[64]

60 Agrawala 1971, Fig. 20; cf. R. C. Sharma 1976, 53, Plates 39–42 (Mathura Museum Acc. Nos. F.6, 12.186; 17.1324).

61 MBh 3.219.3–6: *vayaṃ putra parityaktā bhartṛbhir devasaṃmitaiḥ* | *akāraṇād ruṣā tāta puṇyasthānāt paricyutāḥ* ||3|| [...] *skanda uvāca* | *mātaro hi bhavatyo me suto vo 'ham aninditāḥ* |. MBh 3.219 tells the interesting myth how the group of Mothers as a whole (*mātṛgaṇaḥ sarvaḥ*), which may refer to the Mothers mentioned in MBh 3.215.16–22, try to persuade Skanda to make them 'Mothers of the World,' instead of the maidens (including the seven mothers, Kākī etc.) who were just raised by him to that much coveted status.

62 Sculptures No. 00. E 2, L.D. 55; 00. E 3 (referred to in N. P. Joshi 1972, 55). In a casual remark Joshi (op. cit. 121) identifies sculpture 00. E 2 as 'the goat-headed deity Śaṣṭhī,' an identification taken for granted by Harper 1989, 59 f., although arguments for such an identification are altogether lacking. Panikkar 1997 [1996], 44 f. takes up a suggestion by V. S. Agrawala to identify these goat-headed Mātṛkās as the female counterpart of the Jaina deity Harinaigameṣin (see Panikkar 1997 [1996], Pls. 9 & 10). Our own interpretation of the image at issue follows a similar line of thought, though we take the goat-headed mother goddess as a generic folk deity who was associated to the Jaina as well as Hindu pantheons, the present image being an example of the latter case.

63 Joshi 1972, 62 (line drawing 55) remarks: 'In none of the lists the goat-headed goddess seems to have found any place, unless we take Śivā of Matsya (i.e., *Matsyapurāṇa*) as one of her synonyms. Her origin seems to be shrouded in the Jain mythology as the female counter-part of the goat-headed god Negameṣa. It may also not be of the place [sic] to mention that Negameṣa was one of the names of Kārtikeya.' Cf. N. P. Joshi 1989, 354; Panikkar 1997 [1996], 42–48.

64 MP 179.24: *gokarṇikājamukhikā mahāgrīvā mahāmukhī* | *ulkāmukhī dhūmaśikhā kampinī*

Agrawala discusses still another (Medieval) stone panel kept in the State Museum at Lucknow, which shows, in addition to a four-armed Śiva with matted hair (third figure from the left), 'six Mothers, each having a goat's head and carrying a child on their lap.'[65]

From the evidence surveyed we conclude that this Mandhal image represents a Mātṛkā figure, and as such she may be the counterpart of the goatish Naigameṣa 'rich in offspring.' It cannot be excluded that she carried a child (Skanda?) on her missing left arm, though the presence of a child is not a *sine qua non* for a Mātṛkā image.[66] The right arm might have held the weapon particularly associated with Skanda and related figures, i.e., the spear (*śakti*), similar to the one carried by Naigameṣa (Mandhal). Her position in the BHK-I temple may have been related to that of the latter image.

PLATES XVII & XVIII
BRAHMĀ, MANDHAL
(XVII *front*, XVIII *rear*)

Mandhal. Museum of the Dept. of AIHCA, University of Nagpur. Red-brown sandstone. 79 × 51 × 36 cm.
c. 400 AD. Found under the floor of the brick structure of BHK-I. Lit.: Jamkhedkar 1991a, 200, Pl. 75; Shastri 1977–78, 147.

The four-headed male deity is seated with folded legs on a lotus throne (*paṅkajāsana*); the feet cross each other rather clumsily in the front. The lotus throne consists of overlapping petals, which are plain except for a raised border and a slight central declivity. The image was probably two-armed; the left arm has broken off completely, the right arm just below the armpit. The left hand is preserved, however, and holds the ascetic's water jar (*kamaṇḍalu*) which rests on the left leg.

---

parikampinī ||24||.

65 Agrawala 1971, 82 (cf. Agrawala 1969, 57 pl. XXIII, Fig. 3). The same author discusses panel No. D–250 of the State Museum that is also discussed by Joshi. This Kuṣāṇa panel shows according to Joshi (1972, 122; cf. Joshi 1987, 165) 'a lion-headed female deity,' which according to Agrawala 1971, 81 f. is 'a goat-headed Mātṛkā.' The jar next to the Kārttikeya figure of the panel is interpreted by Agrawala as 'a ram-headed jar [which] may represent the *suvarṇakuṇḍa* from which Skanda was born.' For similar panels see also Bautze 1987.

66 For instance, not all the Mātṛkā statues of Besnagar seem to have been carrying a child (Plate XLVII). The fracture on the upper arm of the Nanpur figurine (see above n. 51 on p. 113), which shows similarities with the image at issue, could point to a child who leaned against his mother's arm.

The four heads all seem to have a *saumya* expression, though the mouth of the front face is somewhat damaged and hence distorted. The neck supporting the four heads nearly equals the shoulders in width, an aesthetically unfortunate solution. The joint ears and matted hairstyle are similar to that of the Maheśvara image (Plates I & II).[67] The deity is dressed as an ascetic and is without ornaments. A *yajño-pavīta* and the skin of a (black) antelope are worn over the left shoulder. A faint outline of what is possibly the head of the antelope can be seen on the left part of the breast.[68] The *dhotī* is held up by a braided belt that is wrapped thrice around the waist. Over the *dhotī*, covering the thighs and falling down at the back-side, is a circular skirt, which is marked by two incised concentric circles. Parallels of this type of lower, poncho-type, garment are unknown to me. One wonders whether it could have anything to do with the (Vedic) sacrifice.

The statue shows the distinguishing characteristics of the god Brahmā: four heads (which propound the four Vedas), the *kamaṇḍalu*, and a lotus seat.[69] Other features of the sculpture, viz. the *saumya* faces, antelope skin, and matted hair are assigned to the image of Brahmā in the *Viṣṇudharmottarapurāṇa*. The right hand may have held the rosary (*akṣamālā*).[70]

67 Cf. the Brahmā image in the collection of the Mathura Museum, Acc. No. 48,34.33 described in Siṃha 1982, 119, Pl. 87.

68 Cf. the image of Brahmā in the Viṣṇu Śeṣaśayana panel of the temple at Deogarh illustrated in Harle 1974, Pl. 103 and Siṃha 1982, 120 (Pl. 90). The antelope (*mṛga*) refers to the sacrifice (*yajña*) with which the figure of Brahmā (Prajāpati) is closely linked. Sacrifice is said to have changed into an antelope when it was chased by Rudra (AitBr 3.33.5; MBh 10.18.13, 12.274.34 f.).

69 *Bṛhatsaṃhitā* 58.41: *brahmā kamaṇḍalukaraś caturmukhaḥ paṅkajāsanasthaś ca* |.

70 VDhP 3.44.5–7: *brahmāṇaṃ kārayed vidvān devaṃ saumyaṃ caturmukham* | *baddha-padmāsanaṃ toṣyaṃ tathā kṛṣṇājināmbaram* ||5|| *jaṭādharaṃ caturbāhuṃ saptahaṃse rathe sthitam* | † *vāme nyastaṃ karatale* tasyaikaṃ doryugaṃ bhavet* † ||6|| *ekasmin dakṣiṇe pāṇāv akṣamālā tathā śubhā* | *kamaṇḍalur dvitīye ca sarvābharaṇadhāriṇaḥ* ||7|| *sarvalakṣaṇayuktasya śāntarūpasya pārthiva* | *padmapatradalāgrābhaṃ dhyānasaṃmīlite-kṣaṇam* ||8||. * According to the text quoted in Rao 1914 IV, 245: *vāme nyastetarakaraṃ*, which also makes little sense.

PLATES XIX & XX
VĀSUDEVA, MANDHAL
(XIX *front*, XX *rear*)

Mandhal. Museum of the Dept. of AIH-CA, University of Nagpur. Red-brown sandstone. 43 × 39 × 21 cm. c. 400 AD. Found under the floor of the brick structure of BHK-I. Lit.: Bakker 1993, 305; Jamkhedkar 1987b, 337 f.; 1991a, 200, Pl. 72; Jamkhedkar s.d., 111, Pl. III; Shastri 1977–78, 147.

This powerful bust of a male deity is sadly damaged. In view of the fractures at the back of the image, it appears almost certain that the deity had four arms. Only the front left upper arm is preserved. The image is broken off just below the middle. When whole it must have been a most imposing sculpture of a god who probably stood in *samabhaṅga* posture, about one meter in height. The bust is adorned by a *yajñopavīta*, and a necklace (*ekāvali*), while jewelled earrings (*ratnakuṇḍala*) rest on the collar bones. Snail-shell curls (similar to those of the Gaṇādhyakṣa image, Plates V & VI) fall on his shoulders. A faint impression of what seems to be a *śrīvatsa* mark is visible on the breast.[71]

The most conspicuous part of the sculpture, though, is the square *kirīṭamukuṭa*, which has a beautiful flower rosette at the rear. The lateral and front sides are adorned with smaller six-petalled rosettes, from the pericarp of which fall broad festoons. The four corners of these sides are also embellished with lotus petals which are connected by strands of pearls. The edges are lined by jewelled strings.[72]

On account of the square *mukuṭa* there can be little doubt that the deity represents Viṣṇu. In this respect the image invites comparison with the contemporaneous Viṣṇu image of Cave VI of Udayagiri (to the viewer's right (NW) of the entrance, Plate XLV A).[73] The four arms lend further support to this identification. The hands may have held his standard attributes, the mace (*gadā*) or sword (*asi*), the *cakra*, and the conch (*śaṅkha*), whereas the fourth hand may have shown the *varada-* or *śāntidamudrā*, similar to the Udayagiri image, though it is impossible to say whether the Mandhal Viṣṇu also was accompanied by *āyudhapuruṣas* as in Udayagiri.[74]

71 Cf. Shastri 1977–78, 147.

72 It has been suggested that the *mukuṭa* was originally taller (in accordance with those of some Gupta images), but this seems to be unlikely in view of the lightly indicated cross-bands connecting the corners of the front side.

73 Compare also the Viṣṇu head of Besnagar: Harle 1974, 36, Pls. 18, 19; and the standing Viṣṇus at Ramgarth Hill: Berkson 1978, 225 f., Fig. 5.

74 *Bṛhatsaṃhitā* 58.31, 32, 34: *kāryo 'ṣṭabhujo bhagavāṃś caturbhujo dvibhuja eva vā viṣṇuḥ* | *śrīvatsāṅkitavakṣāḥ kaustubhamaṇibhūṣitoraskaḥ* ||31|| *atasīkusumaśyāmaḥ pītāmbarani-*

We are obviously concerned with the High God of the Bhāgavatas, Vāsudeva. It has been argued above (p. 83) that this sculpture may have been the main idol of the temple on the Boṃgī Huḍkī hillock (BHK-II) and that the deity thereof may have been the god who was invoked in the Mandhal Plates of Rudrasena II under the name of Mondasvāmin (above p. 19), the 'Lord of Muṇḍā' (i.e. of Prabhāvatī Guptā). We have noted in that context that the description of Mondasvāmin as resting on the coils of Ananta on the ocean during his yogic sleep links the deity to Vāsudeva/Viṣṇu/Nārāyaṇa, but does not necessarily entail that the iconography of the image installed was in conformity with that invocation. The deity may have been worshipped by the two Sātvata communities that had settled in Mandhal or its vicinity.

PLATES XXI & XXII
SAṂKARṢAṆA (DHENUKĀSURAVADHAMŪRTI), MANDHAL
(XXI *front*, XXII *rear*)

Mandhal. Museum of the Dept. of AIHCA, University of Nagpur. Red-brown sandstone. 40 × 41 × 20 cm. c. 400 AD. Found under the floor of the brick structure of BHK-I. Lit.: Bakker 1992c, 17, Plate 6; Jamkhedkar s.d., 111 f., Pl. VI; Shastri 1977–78, 147.

The headless figure stands with his right leg slightly bent, which gives the image a certain air of prowess. Both legs are broken off below the knees, but the two arms are intact. The right arm is bent at the elbow and holds an indistinct attribute that is broken off above and below the hand. The left hand rests on the hip, holding an animal by its tail. The animal, the hind part of which is preserved, hangs against the left thigh. Its right hind leg and shank are clearly visible. Its tail curls around the hand.

The wrists are embellished by bracelets, and part of a necklace (*graiveyaka*) is visible atop the trunk; the latter is also adorned by a *yajñopavīta*. Below the necklace the vague outline of what could be a *śrīvatsa* mark is visible. The deity wears a *dhotī*—marked by two incisions just below the knees—which undergirds a big belly.

---

vasanaḥ prasannamukhaḥ | *kuṇḍalakirīṭadhārī pīnagaloraḥsthalāṃsabhujaḥ* ||32|| [...] *atha ca caturbhujam icchati śāntida eko gadādharaś cānyaḥ* | *dakṣiṇapārśve tv evaṃ vāme śaṅkhaś ca cakraṃ ca* ||34||.

The reverse of the sculpture is highly significant in that it shows the coils (*bhoga*) of a snake in the form of a horizontal figure eight.[75] The upper body of the snake, in low relief, rises perpendicularly from the coils along the back of the image and probably extended above the head, where its hoods may have formed a canopy.

This snake deity, who is evidently depicted in the act of slaying a demon in the form of an animal, can hardly be other than Saṃkarṣaṇa/Balarāma, Vāsudeva/Kṛṣṇa's elder brother, who killed Dhenuka in the palmyra grove. The *Harivaṃśa* describes this as follows.

> And again the demon, while he turned his head away, kicked the unarmed son of Rohiṇī (i.e. Balarāma) with both his hind feet against the breast. He took that ass-demon by those feet and, his head and shoulders dangling down, threw him on top of the palmyra (*tāla*) tree. The ass fell back to earth, mangled, with fractured neck, shanks and breast and his backbone broken, and along with him the *tāla* fruits fell.[76]

The animal in the relief, though seized by its tail rather than by its hind feet,[77] is the ass-demon Dhenuka. The god's right hand may have held the plough (*hala*, *lāṅgala*), the traditional attribute (later weapon) of Balarāma as an agricultural deity.[78] Saṃkarṣaṇa/Balarāma (also known as Halin, Rāma, or Bala(deva), see above n. 8 on p. 60), whose serpent nature is one of his hallmarks, is associated with the cosmic serpent Ananta or Śeṣa in the *Anuśāsanaparvan* of the *Mahābhārata*.[79] As such he is believed to be the incarnation of the serpent on which Viṣṇu Mondasvāmin is said to rest during his cosmic sleep. The image may therefore have been installed in the premises of the temple on top of the Boṃgī Huḍkī hillock along with his younger brother Vāsudeva.

---

75 HV 83.25–26: *nīle vasāno vasane pratyagrajaladaprabhe | rarāja vapuṣā śubhraḥ śaśīva ghanamālayā ||25|| lāṅgalenāvasaktena bhujagābhogavartinā | tathā bhujāgraśliṣṭena musalena ca bhāsvatā ||26||*.

76 *Harivaṃśa* 57.18–20; Entwistle 1987, 35.

77 Cf. the Devī grabbing the buffalo's tail rather than its hind legs in the image found in Nagardhan (Plate XXIX A).

78 See above n. 75 on p. 121. *Bṛhatsaṃhitā* 58.36: *baladevo halapāṇir madavibhramalocanaś ca kartavyaḥ | bibhrat kuṇḍalam ekaṃ śaṅkhendumṛṇālagauratanuḥ ||36||*.

79 MBh 13 App. I No. 16, ll. 105–112: *tasya caivāgrajo bhrātā sitābhranicayaprabhaḥ* | [105] *halī bala iti khyāto bhaviṣyati dharādharaḥ | triśirās tasya devasya śātakaumbhamayo drumaḥ | dhvajas tṛṇendro devasya bhaviṣyati rathāśritaḥ | śiro nāgair mahābhogaiḥ parikīrṇaṃ mahātmanaḥ | bhaviṣyati mahābāhoḥ sarvalokeśvarasya hi* | [110] *cintitāni sameṣyanti śastrāṇy astrāṇi caiva ha | anantaś ca sa evokto bhagavān harir avyayaḥ* |. See Joshi 1979, 17 ff.

Plates XXIII & XXIV
A Vṛṣṇi Hero (Sāmba?), Mandhal
(XXIII *front*, XXIV *rear*)

Mandhal. Museum of the Dept. of AIH-CA, University of Nagpur. Red-brown sandstone. 60 × 41 × 20 cm. c. 400 AD. Found under the floor of the brick structure of BHK-I. Lit.: Jamkhedkar 1991a, Pl. 68.

The standing, two-armed image, holds the stalk of a double-petalled lotus in its right hand. The stalk ends in a whorl of petals on which again rests a lotus bud with petals pointing upwards. The left hand has broken off. Judging from the fractured surface, it probably rested on the elevated hip holding a (rather short) attribute. The deity has highly arched brows. His hair is combed in fine wave-like tresses towards the left and right, which may have been thought to reflect the radiance of the sun. Locks fall on to the shoulder in a check pattern, as in the figure of Naigameṣa (Mandhal). Three pleats of the *dhotī*, which is held up by a *kaṭibandha*, fall between the legs; the spare cloth is gathered in folds at both sides. The upper part of the body is naked. The left leg is broken off at the middle of the thigh, the right leg just above the knee, where the rim of the *dhotī*, marked by two lines, is just visible. The deity is without *yajñopavīta*. Its ornaments are a necklace (*graiveyaka*), a bracelet, and earrings, which, like those of Vāsudeva and Gaṇādhyakṣa rest on his collar bones.

The ornaments and lotus attribute on the one hand, and the absence of matted hair, third eye and *ūrdhvaliṅga* on the other, make this a Vaiṣṇava image rather than a Śaiva one. To go any further is problematic. Judging by the sign at the pedestal, the staff of the Museum identified the image as Sūrya. This may be based on the lotus in the right hand, an attribute of the sun-god. Two early (Kuṣāṇa) images in the Mathura Museum show a deity with the bud of the lotus flower in the right hand, while the left hand holds a dagger.[80] This could have been the attribute in the left hand of the Mandhal image also. Eight features of Sūrya images of the Gupta period are listed by Joshi (1972, 27 f.), none of which is prominent in the present image. The image also does not show any non-Indian elements. It therefore is doubtful whether this sculpture really represents the sun-god.

In an article quoted above (p. 62) J. N. Banerjea has put the case that the Kuṣāṇa images of Mathura that are commonly identified as Sūrya, actually represent one of the Five Heroes (the Vṛṣṇi Pañcavīra), namely Sāmba, Vāsudeva's elder son. The sculpture at issue certainly gives the impression of a forceful, if not haughty deity,

---

80 Mathura Museum Nos. 12.269 and D.46, illustrated in Singh 1977, Pls. 52, 53; cf. R. C. Sharma 1976, 52, Fig. 38; Joshi 1972, 27 and line drawing 20. See also the Gupta Sūrya from Mathura in the Ashmolean Museum, Harle 1974, 44, Pl. 51.

which would accord well with a hero (*vīra*). Given the obscurity of the iconography of the Pañcavīra deities other than Vāsudeva and Saṃkarṣaṇa, it cannot be excluded that the image represents Sāmba's brother Pradyumna or the latter's son Aniruddha, who, like Sāmba, is associated with the sun.[81] We simply lack enough comparative material to decide the issue, but the presence in Mandhal of the two principal Vṛṣṇi deities, Vāsudeva and Saṃkarṣaṇa, and of two Sātvata communities seems to endorse Banerjea's hypothesis.

PLATE XXV A
AN UGRA HEAD, MANDHAL

Mandhal. Museum of the Dept. of AIH-CA, University of Nagpur. Red-brown sandstone. 21 × 16 × 18 cm. Last quarter of 4th century AD.

In addition to the nine images discussed above three loose male heads were found in the excavation of BHK-I. From Shastri's publications it cannot be deduced with certainty whether these heads were found also 'under the floor of the structure.'[82]

The head illustrated here belongs to the Śaiva pantheon. It expresses the terrifying (*ugra*) aspect of Maheśvara, in mythology often personified by Vīrabhadra,[83] later also by Bhairava (see above n. 7 on p. 96). In iconographic descriptions a head like this is sometimes designated as 'Aghora,' the ferocious face (*vaktra*) among the five Brahmans, i.e. of Sadāśiva. The head at issue appears to have belonged to an anthropomorphic representation of Śiva, not to a *liṅga*, hence the designation 'Vīrabhadra' or 'Bhairava' is preferable.

The face inspires terror. The mouth is open showing teeth and fangs. On the forehead is a horizontal third eye (see above n. 85 on p. 78). Strands of matted hair are combed back over the head. As far as we can determine the head is without ornaments. Compare, for instance, the description in the original *Skandapurāṇa* of the southern, ferocious form of Śiva.

> Then this good-looking woman (i.e. Tilottamā) bowed before his southern body. Thereupon a fiery head emerged from that Guru of the

81 Later iconographic descriptions in the Pāñcarātra Saṃhitās tend to depict these deities in an undistinctive Vaiṣṇava fashion.

82 That this was actually the case has been confirmed by an oral communication to the present author.

83 For Vīrabhadra see MBh 12 App. 1 No. 28, ll. 69–80: a monstrous figure, personifying Śiva's wrath, born from his face (*vaktra*) in order to destroy Dakṣa's sacrifice (cf. VāP 30.122–141).

Gods, possessed of the colour of a languid cloud laden with water, having a ferocious voice, with dreadful teeth shining (in an open mouth), and the corners of his eyes bloodshot and glittering. Next there issued from (this) southern face a heat more fierce than that of the sun and, with all the gods watching, it entered that most beautiful of (all) women.[84]

PLATE XXV B
NAGARDHAN, VIEW OF THE RĀMAGIRI

The village Nagardhan. Lit.: Bakker 1989a; 1989b; 1990; 1991; 1992a; 1992b; 1993; Hiralal 1908; Jamkhedkar 1985a; 1985–6; 1987a; 1987b; 1988; 1991b; 1992; Mirashi 1959; 1964; 1968; Venkataramayya 1963; Williams 1983.

It is by now commonly accepted that the site of the village Nagardhan and the adjacent villages of Hamlapuri and Nandapuri, situated about 6 km south of Ramtek Hill (Rāmagiri), is the ancient location of the Vākāṭaka site Nandivardhana. The hill is visible in the background.

PLATE XXVI
A KAVI, NAGARDHAN

Nagardhan. Nagpur Central Museum. Red sandstone. 27 × 20 × 12 cm. First half of 5th century AD. Lit.: Bakker 1993, pl. 20.3; Jamkhedkar 1991b, pl. 9.

This image is said to have been found in the Nagardhan area in 1987. It is hewn out of the dark red sandstone peculiar to the Ramtek-Nagardhan area. It has in common with the Mansar Śiva (Plate XXXVII) that it is a sculptured stele.

The two-armed seated figure, whose right forearm is broken off, holds a book in his left hand. We are here clearly concerned with an open *pothī*—the two folios

84 SP_{Bh}62.18–20 (reedited on the basis of Nepalese palm-leaf MSS by Y. Yokochi): *atha sā dakṣiṇāṃ mūrtiṃ praṇeme cārudarśanā | nirjagāma tadā dīptaṃ mukhaṃ suraguros tataḥ ||18|| vāribhārālasāmbhodarucimad bhīmanisvanam | karāladaśanodbhāsi dīptaraktāntalocanam ||19|| atyādityaṃ tatas tejo mukhān niḥsṛtya dakṣiṇāt | dṛśyamānaṃ suraiḥ sarvair viveśa pramadottamām ||20||*. Cf. above p. 73.

are separated by a groove—and not with a slate or writing board as, for instance, in the *lipiśālāsaṃdarśana* sculpture of the Peshawar Museum.[85] The fine diaphanous drapery is elegantly folded on the left shoulder forming a sort of epaulette. A lower garment partly covers his thighs. Though the figure has a slender waist, resembling the Narasiṃha of Ramtek (Plate XXXIII A), and in this respect deviates significantly from the stocky Mandhal images, the type of the face (the nose is mutilated) and curly hairstyle are similar to the images found in Mandhal (especially the Vāsudeva image, Plates XIX & XX), rather than to the Śiva of Mansar (Plate XXXVII). With the latter sculpture, however, it has a fillet and a string of pearls in common, which are braided into the hair and which fall to the left from the crown of the head, which is covered by a rosette-like decoration or lotus-cap such as is also known from other Vākāṭaka sculptures (see e.g., Plates XV, XXX B and XXXIII A). The figure wears a simple necklace and earrings, and the upper garment is worn by way of a *yajñopavīta*.

He casts a sidelong glance at the book in his hand, which is held open so that also the viewer is permitted to read its content, in principle at least. Jamkhedkar (1991b) is silent about the characters which are visible on the book and which form an as yet undeciphered two-lined inscription.[86]

85 Foucher 1905, 322–26; Salomon 1990, 262 ff.

86 In January 1997 I was finally permitted to inspect the image from close range. It turned out that the first line of the inscription contains six, the second line seven *akṣaras*. They have solid square headmarks of the type known from other Vākāṭaka inscriptions. The characters are turned towards the image, not towards the viewer. I have not yet succeeded in deciphering the inscription. Though some of the *akṣaras* are clearly legible the text as a whole does not (yet) make sense and this may explain Jamkhedkar's silence. It is not even clear whether the text refers to the figure portrayed or to the donor. Par acquit de conscience I present a photograph of the inscription.

The figure is seated in the *paryaṅka* pose also called *sattvaparyaṅkāsana*—the legs are not crossed and one foot is placed on the other thigh—a posture that is especially, but not exclusively, known from (later) South Indian images of saints and teachers like e.g. Rāmānuja.[87]

A possibly significant difference from the two seated Mandhal images (Plates XV and XVII) is that the Nagardhan figure does not sit on any sort of throne. This reminds us of a verse found in the 'Discussion of Propriety' (*Aucityavicāracarcā*) of Kṣemendra that the prolific writer from Kashmir attributes to a '(lost) work' of Kālidāsa, the *Kuntaleśvaradautya* ('The Mission to the Lord of Kuntala'), in which the poet observes, when the ambassador is refused a seat and is forced to sit on the ground,

> Here on earth rests Mount Meru, the crown of the mountains, and also the seven oceans have here laid down their heavy mass; this surface of the earth shines forth due to its being supported by the hoods of the Lord of the Serpents: here alone is a seat for people like us.[88]

The image lacks any distinctive features or attributes that would connect it unmistakably with a Hindu or Buddhist deity. The book and flower decoration on the head are too general to allow any such identification. On the other hand, the lack of *lakṣaṇas* and the fact that the figure sits on the ground in *paryaṅka* posture seem to point, rather than to a divine, to a 'human' figure such as a seer (*ṛṣi*), teacher (*ācārya*) or sage/poet (*kavi*), exceptional as this may be for a fifth century image.[89] The absence of ascetic characteristics seems to preclude the image representing a *sādhu*, *siddha* or any other world-renouncer as proposed by Jamkhedkar. Furthermore it is remarkable that the *pothī* is held in such a way that it is readable for the beholder, and this would exclude the possibility of the image representing a *ṛṣi* or any other sectarian *guru*, since the wisdom contained in their books is generally thought to be only accessible after initiation. The books held by Hindu deities like Brahmā[90] or Sarasvatī,[91] or semi-divine human teachers such as Lakulīśa or his dis-

87 Mallebrein 1984, 122; Coomaraswamy 1978, 113–115 (calling the posture *vīrāsana*), though here the right foot is placed on the left thigh and the sole of the left foot is turned upwards; cf. also an image of Lakulīśa in the Bhāratī Maṭha at Bhubaneswar: Donaldson 1987 III, 1095, 1320, Fig. 3476.

88 *iha nivasati meruḥ śekharaḥ kṣmādharāṇām iha vinihitabhārāḥ sāgarāḥ sapta cānye | idam ahipatibhogastambhavibhrājamānaṃ dharaṇitalam ihaiva sthānam asmadvidhānām ||*. Quoted from Mirashi & Navlekar 1969, 30 f. The *Śṛṅgāraprakāśa* of king Bhoja seems to suggest that the ambassador involved might have been Kālidāsa himself, sent to the Lord of Kuntala by king Vikramāditya (ibid. 31).

89 Apart from the famous Kuṣāṇa images of Mat, an early example of sculptural portraiture of secular figures is possibly found on a panel of Sagar (Stadner 1982, 132).

90 See e.g. van Lohuizen-de Leeuw 1964, 130, Fig. 28.

91 See e.g. the image from Mathura illustrated in Joshi 1972, Fig. 62.

ciples,[92] are closed and generally held vertically.

If we accept the hypothesis that the image represents a 'human' figure, the assumption that it depicts a *kavi* seems most plausible. There are two *kavis* who appear to have a special link with the Rāmagiri, at the foot of which the image was found. The *ādikavi* Vālmīki, who describes Rāma's perigrinations, and Kālidāsa, who describes the mountain in his *Meghadūta*. In the *Rāmāyaṇa*, as we have it, the Rāmagiri is not mentioned as such, but there are pieces of evidence from which one can argue that local tradition in the 4th and 5th centuries nevertheless associated the hill with a visit of Rāma (see above p. 64 and below p. 136 f.). One of these is furnished by Kālidāsa's *Meghadūta* (see above p. 86). Elsewhere we have given various arguments for the assumption that Kālidāsa maintained good relations with the court of the Vākāṭakas in Nandivardhana (Bakker 1993). Against identification of the image as Vālmīki speaks the fact that he holds a book in his hand, since we would have expected that the *Rāmāyaṇa* would have been sung by its author. Kālidāsa, on the other hand, possibly did make use of birch bark for his compositions. That there existed a tradition of Vālmīki images may follow from a prescription in the *Viṣṇudharmottarapurāṇa* to the effect that his image should be white, with an awe-inspiring head of matted hair, neither meagre nor fat but peaceful, like the image of Dattātreya.[93] Though the image at issue hardly conforms to the Purāṇa's description—notably the figure hardly shows marks of asceticism—an image of the legendary Vālmīki as the archetype of all *kavis* would a priori be more plausible than one of the historical poet, who lived shortly before or contemporaneously with the maker of the image.[94] For the time being no other conclusion seems justified than to conceive of the image as that of an unknown sage (*kavi*).

---

92 See e.g. an image in the Mathura Museum (No. 45.3211), described by R. C. Sharma (1976, 74) and illustrated in Kreisel 1986 (p. 251, Abb. 124) or the images illustrated in Donaldson 1987 III, 1319 ff. (Figs. 3471–3486).

93 VDhP 3.85.64–65: *gauras tu kāryo vālmīkir jaṭāmaṇḍaladurdṛśaḥ* | *tapasy abhirataḥ śānto na kṛśo na ca pīvaraḥ* ||64|| *vālmīkirūpaṃ sakalaṃ dattātreyasya kārayet* |.

94 The contemporary spectator, however, may have been reminded of the greatest poet of his time, when he saw the image of that much admired predecessor (*pūrvasūri*) 'who had forged the path,' if, indeed, the image represents Vālmīki: *athavā kṛtavāgdvāre vaṃśe 'smin pūrvasūribhiḥ* | *maṇau vajrasamutkīrṇe sūtrasyevāsti me gatiḥ* ||4|| (*Raghuvaṃśa* 1.4).

Plate xxvii
Viṣṇu, Nagardhan

Nagardhan. Nagpur Central Museum. Red sandstone. *c.* 30 cm (?). First half of 5th century AD. Lit.: Jamkhedkar 1987b, 339, photograph 32; Jamkhedar s.d., 109, Pl. II.

This head has been identified as that of Viṣṇu on account of its *kirīṭamukuṭa*. The fragment, made out of the dark red sandstone which gave Rāmagiri its other name, viz. Sindūragiri, was found in Nagardhan (Nandapuri). Its facial features deviate from the general idiom of the sculptures of the Vākāṭaka's of Nandivardhana. Obliquely set eyes, thin nose and delicate lips make quite a contrast, for instance, with the Mandhal Vāsudeva (Plate xix), yet are found again in some of the faces pictured in the Ajanta caves.[95] The cylindrical *mukuṭa* is remarkable. It seems to represent a crown that is wrapped by (metal?) strips studded with precious stones. The top is edged by a string of pearls.

Plate xxviii
Gaṇeśa, Nagardhan

Nagardhan, *in situ*. Red sandstone. 130 × 80 × 45 cm. First half of 5th century AD. Lit.: Jamkhedkar 1991a, 201, Pl. 81.

This broken image is found in a little (modern) shed/shrine situated half-way between the villages Nagardhan and Hamlapuri. The image has recently been 'restored' and coated with a protective layer. The 'restoration' has been far from successful and the coating prevents a good view of the subtle modelling of the sculpture.

On account of its style this sculpture may be regarded as belonging to the Vākāṭaka age. Its size, unusual for Gaṇeśa images of this period, agrees with the Vākāṭaka images of Ramtek Hill (Varāha and Narasiṃha).

The nude two-armed elephant-faced god is sitting in *sukhāsana* pose (cf. the Śiva of Mansar, Plate xxxvii). His trunk has broken off, but presumably turned towards his left hand, in which he may have held a bowl with cakes (*modakabhāṇḍa*). Both hands are missing, making it impossible to determine

95 Cf. a loose Viṣṇu head from Nachna, Williams 1982, Plate 163.

which attribute the right hand, which rested on the knee, once held. The knob of his tusk is seen to the proper right of the trunk; the same appears to be absent on the left side. The deity wears a wreath around the two knobs of his forehead and a necklace of beads encircles his neck. The image represents the god Gaṇeśa who emerged from the background of various traditions in the 4th century.[96] Robert Brown, who surveyed the evidence, came to the conclusion that,

> as early as ca. 400 AD images of Gaṇeśa functioned in a defined and sophisticated role within temple worship that involved his functions as remover of obstacles, as initiator for further worship, and probably as locus of wordly [sic] desire. This is indeed our "real" Gaṇeśa. [...] The earliest Gaṇeśa images, which tend to be two-armed, do not hold a tusk; nor do they appear to have a broken tusk. They hold the sweet cakes, usually placed in a bowl, in their left hands, but the attribute in their right hands varies considerably.[97]

A comparable image of roughly the same period is found in Udayagiri Cave VI—in a niche in the south-eastern side-wall of the verandah (Plate XLIV B)—though here Gaṇeśa is ithyphallic and sits in *lalitāsana*; his right hand is also sadly broken off. Like the Gaṇeśa of the Mathura Museum, the right hand of the Nagardhan Gaṇeśa might have held the *mātuluṅga*,[98] but, in view of the fact that the deity seems to have only one tusk, it cannot be excluded that the right hand held the (broken-off left) tusk, as does the Gaṇeśa of Tala (see Bakker 1994, Plate XIX). Like the latter, who protects a Śiva temple, or the Gaṇeśa of Udayagiri Cave VI, the Nagardhan Gaṇeśa may have been originally a guardian deity of the temple to which also the Viṣṇu (Plate XXVII) and Mahiṣamardinī (Plate XXIX A) images may have belonged

---

96 Jamkhedkar 1991a, 201 places this image in the 'category' of the Mandhal images.

97 Brown (ed.) 1991, 8. An image of Gaṇeśa of brown sandstone (21 × 5 cm), which possibly formed a part of a frieze, was found in the excavations in Mandhal. Another fragment (8.5 × 12.5 cm) may represent Gaṇeśa in *sukhāsana* posture. Both images are reported to have been found in BHK-II; they are kept in the Museum of the Department of AIHCA of the University of Nagpur. A small red sandstone image of Gaṇeśa (Vākāṭaka period), measuring about 8.5 × 5.0 cm, was found in the Paunar excavation (Deo & Dhavalikar 1968, 112 f., Pl. XXX Nos. 1 & 2): 'It has two hands of which the right one is missing; the left hand holding a bowl of sweets, is slightly raised. [...] Its two hands and the restrained use of ornaments is betoken of the early stage of development of the iconography of the god.' A temple of Gaṇeśa is mentioned in an inscription of Mādhavavarman Janāśraya (EI XXXVII, 125–130; see above n. 179 on p. 52).

98 Mathura Museum, No. 792; illustrated in Brown 1991, 206, Fig. 6. The *mātuluṅga* or *bījapūra* (Citrus medica Linn.), the seeds (*bīja*) of which are said to symbolize the atoms out of which the (material) world is built (see n. 10 on p. 97). The Mathura Gaṇeśa seems to be seated in *sukhāsana* posture like the Nagardhan image. A *vyālayajñopavīta* distinguishes him from the image at issue.

(see above p. 85).[99]

PLATE XXIX A
DEVĪ (MAHIṢĀSURAMARDINĪMŪRTI), NAGARDHAN

Nagardhan. Nagpur Central Museum. Red sandstone. 40 × 34 cm. First half of 5th century AD. Lit.: Bakker 1993b, Pl. 20.1.

There can be little doubt that this broken image of dark red sandstone represents the famous battle between the Goddess, Devī—also referred to in this context as Kauśikī/Vindhyavāsinī or Caṇḍikā/Ambikā (the first two names are used in the original *Skandapurāṇa*, see below; the latter two in the *Devīmāhātmya*)—and the demon (*asura*), who had assumed the form of a buffalo (*mahiṣa*). This myth is told in Sanskrit literature (as far as preserved) in the *Skandapurāṇa* that is found in early ninth-century Nepalese palm-leaf MSS and for which good reasons exist to believe that it represents the original text bearing this name, composed in the sixth or seventh century.[100] Textual descriptions are surprisingly late, if we realize that images of this fight began to appear in the Kuṣāṇa period. Though the *Skandapurāṇa* is probably a century or so later than the image at issue, it describes the conception underlying the image at issue more closely than the *Devīmāhātmya* which is probably of still later date.[101]

> As soon as the Mistress of Yoga, Vindhyavāsinī, learned about his arrival she went quickly to the place where that meanest of the demons was staying. Thereupon this demon, when he saw that Goddess, made a firm resolve and came running towards her, his eyes bloodshot with

99 Brown (ed.) 1991, 7 notices with respect to the Udayagiri Cave VI: 'It is difficult to know how these various images were worshiped; the cave curiously combines both Vaiṣṇavite and Śaivite deities, and its very small size would appear to argue against any extensive movement through space by devotees, such as circumambulation that we find used in later Hindu temples. Nevertheless, Gaṇeśa is clearly spatially paired with the mothers, as worshipers would have passed these deities first as they progressed toward the inner and most sacred area of the cave.'

100 See Adriaensen & Bakker & Isaacson 1994.

101 The *Devīmāhātmya*—dated by Coburn 1991, 13 ff. to the 6th century—appears to reflect a later iconography of this battle, in which the demon in anthropomorphic form is shown as coming forth from the mouth of his animal embodiment when he is struck by Devī's lance. Images informed by this feature are beginning to appear in the eighth century, first in Cave XV at Ellora (Mitterwallner 1976, 208) and then spread throughout North India (von Stietencron 1983, 134–36, Abb. 20–27).

anger. With raised tail and sharp-pointed horns, his breast swollen and his ears stiffly pricked up, he impetuously hurled himself upon the Goddess like a dark mountain, as it were, while his eyes were like red copper and *guggulu*.[102] When she saw that enraged buffalo attacking her, this son of the lord of the demons,[103] Kauśikī became angry, her large lovely eyes reddened, while she stood firmly, ready to kill the lord of the demons.

The son of the demon king, intoxicated by his extreme strength, assailed that Goddess: he butted his horn, unbendable like Śakra's bolt, into her breast, (which made) her necklace quiver. Then, after having withstood this blow of his, she took the buffalo by his horn with her hand and, after she had vehemently whirled him around, she furiously smashed him to the ground, while he was gasping for breath. She pulled the enemy of Indra up by his tail, placed her foot on his head with force, and taking her trident, she pierced his back, and quickly she made the demon give up the ghost. As soon as she had killed the buffalo, who had been swollen with pride, whose horn was hard like the thunderbolt and who resembled a dark cloud, Kauśikī, while being strewn from all sides by a shower of various kinds of flowers, returned to the mountain, into her own abode.[104]

---

102 The meaning seems to be that his eyes were bloodshot, i.e., red like copper (*tāmra*) and with great pupils, black like *guggulu* (the resin of the Commiphora mukul Engl.), i.e., they resembled a red copper censer holding black *guggulu* incense. I owe this interpretation to Dr J. Meulenbeld.

103 In the *Skandapurāṇa* myth of the Goddess's fight against several demons the buffalo seems to be an afterthought, as it were, and is connected to the main story (the fights against Sunda and Nisunda, and Sumbha and Nisumbha) by being called the son of the demon king Sumbha, whom she had just slain (SP_{Bh}66.18–35).

104 SP_{Bh}68.16–23 (text reedited by Ms Y. Yokochi on the basis of the Nepalese MSS): *vijñāya tasyāgamanaṃ yogeśā vindhyavāsinī | jagāma tvaritā tatra yatrāsau dānavādhamaḥ* ||16|| *atha dṛṣṭvā sa tāṃ devīṃ krodhād raktatarekṣanaḥ | abhyājagāma vegena yatnam āsthāya dānavaḥ* ||17|| *udvāladhis tīkṣṇaviṣāṇakoṭiḥ supīnavakṣāḥ kaṭhinordhvakarṇaḥ | abhyāpatad guggulutāmranetro javena devīm asitādrikalpaḥ* ||18|| *taṃ kauśikī vīkṣya tadāpatantaṃ daityendraputraṃ mahiṣaṃ saroṣam | cukrodha tāmrāyatacārunetrā sthitā dharaṇyām asurendrahantrī* ||19|| *abhyetya tāṃ dānavarājasūnur balena mattaḥ parameṇa devīm | abhyāhanad vakṣasi lolahāre śṛṅgeṇa śakrāyudhakarkaśena* ||20|| *viṣahya taṃ tasya tadā prahāraṃ jagrāha śṛṅge mahiṣaṃ kareṇa | udbhrāmya coccaiḥ paritaḥ saroṣā nyapātayad bhūmitale śvasantam* ||21|| *udgṛhya sā vāladhim indraśatroḥ kṛtvā ca pādaṃ śirasi prasahya | triśūlam ādāya bibheda pṛṣṭhe vyayojayac cāsubhir āśu daityam* ||22|| *kuliśakaṭhinaśṛṅgaṃ nīlajīmūtakalpaṃ mahiṣam atha nihatya prauḍhadarpaṃ tadānīm | vividhakusumavṛṣṭyā sarvataḥ kīryamāṇā dharaṇidharam agacchat kauśikī svaṃ nivāsam* ||23||. Cf. Devīmāhātmya 3.37–39: 'After she had thus spoken, she jumped and, got upon that great demon, she forced her foot upon him and struck his neck with the lance. Thereupon, pressed by her foot, he then came out of his own [i.e. the buffalo's] mouth, only half-way, checked by the power of the

Von Stietencron (1983, 128 ff.) distinguishes five iconographic types of *mahiṣa-mardinī* representations. The image at issue best conforms to his type no. 2, which is characterized by the Goddess pressing down the head of the buffalo with her (right) foot while her (left) hand lifts the hind-part of the animal by grabbing it by its hind-leg; her right arm drives the lance into the back of the animal. This type, represented by the Mahiṣamardinī of Udayagiri Cave VI (on the viewer's right of the entrance, see Plate XLV B), had emerged at the beginning of the fifth century during the reign of Candragupta II and was further developed in the image at issue. All the examples of this type presented by von Stietencron (Abb. 8 to 13) show the Goddesss with more than two arms, and there are reasons to believe that the goddess of the present image also possessed four (or more?) arms, though the sculpture is broken off above the waist, leaving only one left hand, by which she holds the tail.

The Nagpur Central Museum possesses still another, smaller, *mahiṣamardinī* image of yellow sandstone, found at the same site, measuring 32 × 13 cm. As far as the images can be compared, their iconography is very similar, though the carving of the red image is far superior. The yellow sandstone image preserves two arms, the left lower hand grabbing the tail of the animal and the lower right hand holding a sword upwards. Parallel to the sword, however, the lance (*śūla*) runs downwards, piercing the head of the animal. This *śūla*, of which the upper part has broken off, must have been held by the rear right hand. Both rear arms, however, have broken off at the place where they joined the front upper arms, as fractures indicate.[105]

When we reconstruct the iconography of the red sandstone image with the help of the yellow image, we may say that the image at issue conforms to a sub-type of type no. 2, in which the four-armed goddess lifts the animal by the tail (not by the hind-leg) and the *śūla* or *triśūla* is driven into the head (not into the back). The earliest specimen of this sub-type found by von Stietencron is the relief in Badami Cave 1, which dates from the last quarter of the 6th century AD (op. cit. Abb. 9). If our reconstruction is correct, we can push back the origin of this type of the *mahiṣa-mardinī* image by at least one century into the middle of the Gupta/Vākāṭaka period.[106]

Goddess. That great demon, only half come forth, continued fighting, (but) cutting off his head by her great sword the Goddess struck him down.'

105 Cf. the Mahiṣamardinī found in Ramgarth Hill (von Stietencron type no. 2) described by Berkson 1978, 232 (Figs. 12 & 12a): 'In her lower right [hand], she holds a sword, which points upwards, and with her upper right she holds the *triśūla*.'

106 There are at least three other images of this sub-type that are older than the Badami one. The Mandhal excavations (BHK-II) yielded a fragment of a little Mahiṣamardinī image of red sandstone (13.5 × 9.5 cm), which, though cruder, resembles the image at issue: the Goddess holds the animal by its tail, the *śūla* pierces the neck. Outside the Vākāṭaka area, mention should be made of a sculpture from Devihal (Sundara 1990, 222 f., Pl. XXVa; a four-armed image very similar to the Vākāṭaka ones) and an image found in Kunjuru (Karnataka) (Divakaran 1984, 287 (Plate

The beautifully carved image shows the Goddess with a lower garment which stretches around her right lifted leg, flares out behind the 'kneeling' buffalo till behind her left ankle and is wrapped around her hips in folds that cross each other in the front. *Nūpuras* embellish her ankles. Two long strings of pearls (*channavīra*) rest on her belly. On the head of the buffalo is an *āmalaka*-like decoration; if we transpose the iconography of the yellow image to the one at issue, it is here that the *śūla* (which has completely disappeared) entered the animal. The top left hand might have held a shield (as in the Bhumara relief, von Stietencron op. cit. Abb. 9) or a conch (as in the Badami relief, ibid. Abb. 10). The image may have adorned the temple in Nagardhan to which also the Gaṇeśa and Viṣṇu belonged.

PLATE XXIX B
LAJJĀ GAURĪ, NAGARDHAN

Nagardhan. Nagpur Central Museum. Fifth century AD.
Yellowish sandstone. 15 × 16 cm.

This yellowish sandstone tablet was found in Hamlapuri (together with four similar reliefs) in the Nagardhan area. It represents type no. 2 of the so-called Lajjā Gaurī images according to the typology developed by Janssen 1993.

> This type is characterized by the elongation of the torso to include breasts, yet the arms remain absent. Here we meet with extra figures next to the goddess: a devotee, a *liṅga*, a *vṛṣabha*, and/or a lion's head in various combinations. These images, mostly in stone, date from the third century onwards and are predominant in the Vākāṭaka area, especially in Vidarbha.[107]

The relief at issue shows the goddess of fecundity with a double-petalled lotus[108] in the place of her head, flanked by two icons, which are very much damaged, but which presumably represent the *liṅga* to the proper right of the lotus and a bull (*vṛṣa*) to the proper left. The goddess wears a *graiveyaka*, *channavīra*, *mekhalā*, and *nūpuras*. On both sides of her shins, what could be interpreted as two human faces adorned by necklaces, are visible. If this interpretation is correct these faces

252); a two-armed image stylistically different from the Vākāṭaka ones).

107 Janssen 1993, 464. Cf. Bolon's (1992, 11, 17 ff.) type II.

108 Cf. the Vṛṣṇi Hero, Plate XXIII.

(devotees, or the souls of future births, or peeping Toms?) would add a unique feature to the Lajjā Gaurī iconography (personal communication of Frans Janssen to the author).

Between the knees and the two icons in the upper corners are two discs, which in the Indian context may generally be thought to represent lotus rosettes. However, it might be appropriate to draw attention once again to the study of Carl Schuster. He observes that,

> among traditional designs showing correspondence between the Old World and the New, one of the most curious is the motive of a squatting human figure with a pair of disks occupying the spaces between the flexed elbows and knees. [...] For in both regions we find, often side by side with the motive of disks *between* the elbows and knees of crouching human figures, other representations with disk-like marks inscribed *upon* the elbows and knees, and sometimes upon other joints of the body as well. (Schuster 1951, 5)

This author (op. cit. 12) comes to the conclusion that 'the disks outside the body are really displaced joint-marks' (for the conception underlying such joint markings see above p. 107). In the sculpture at issue the elbows are substituted by the two icons that flank the lotus.

Research of Bolon (1992) and Janssen (1993) has made it plausible that the deity should be conceived as lying on her back with drawn up legs, her feet pointing outwards (*uttānapad*), a posture that is congruous with that of women giving birth.[109] Some similar plaques show a cloth on the thighs of the goddess, which is interpreted by Janssen as a 'special birth cloth (Pāli: *sotthiya coḷa*)' which 'covers the thighs and disappears behind the back.' This cloth is missing in the image at issue. The lotus 'replacing' the head is explained by Janssen by tracing the origin of these (half) anthropomorphized images back to the *pūrṇakalaśa*, as the relief from Karlapalem may illustrate.[110] The two additional icons of the bull and the *liṅga* are consistent with the overall symbolism of this tablet as an image of a goddess of fertility, worshipped by women for the sake of offspring.

---

109 Bolon 1992, 4: 'The pose of Lajjā Gaurī is ambiguous, but probably intentionally so since the pose of sexual receptivity and the pose of giving birth are the same. The human form and the intercourse/birth pose are used as a metaphor for creation. In turn human parturition is used in this image as a metaphor for divine creation.' op. cit. p. 6: 'As applied by Kramrisch the word *uttānapad* exactly describes this image. In *Ṛgveda* (X.72.4) it is said the Earth sprang from the *Uttānapad*, the Creative Agency or Productive Power. *Uttānapad* in Sanskrit means "one whose legs are extended in parturition." It is the "name of a peculiar creative agency." [...] The position of the body may be described as *uttāna*, which means "stretched out, lying on the back, sleeping supinely or with face upwards".'

110 Janssen 1993, pl. 34.4; cf. Divakaran 1984, 283; Bolon 1992, 11 ff.

PLATE XXX
TWO BHĀRARAKṢAKAS, NAGARDHAN

Nagardhan. Nagpur Central Museum. Red sandstone. 40 × 30 cm. First half of 5th century AD. Lit.: Jamkhedkar 1991a, 202 f., photo 88.

These two delightful sculptures, found in the Nagardhan area, must have formed part of a construction that they were meant to support and to guard, hence their designation as *bhārarakṣakas*, i.e. guardians (*rakṣaka*) that carry a burden (*bhāra*).[111] The stone, style and quality of craftsmanship suggest that this was the construction to which also the Gaṇeśa, Viṣṇu and Mahiṣamardinī sculptures may have belonged.

The corpulent figure of Plate XXX A is squatting while his hands rest on his knees for support, conveying the impression of being weighed down by the burden carried on the head. The modelling of the flesh resembles that of the Śiva of Mansar (Plate XXXVII) to such an extent that one is inclined to think that these images came from the same workshop (see above p. 78). A twisted band similar to the one of the Mansar Śiva girds the big belly just above the deep navel. Two large round earrings (*tāṭaṅka*) resting on the shoulders adorn the ears, and the wrists are embellished by simple bracelets, not unlike the ornaments worn by the Mansar Śiva. The surly face is crowned by a wealth of curly hair.

The figure of Plate XXX B supports his burden by leaning backwards on his left arm. The right arm, which has broken off, probably propped up its load, while the elbow may have rested on the drawn up right knee.[112] The figure wears a simple bracelet and necklace (*ekāvali*). The *yajñopavīta* consists of three twisted strings of pearls. Though the face is mutilated, it would seem that only the right ear wore an earring. In contrast with the other image, the head is bald, save a flower rosette that covers the crown. From behind the crown a string of pearls drops down, loops on the left shoulder and disappears behind the left ear. This ornament resembles in some respects the ones worn by the Mansar Śiva (Plate XXXVII) and the Kavi image (Plate XXVI).

111 This type of figures is generally classified as belonging to the *gaṇas*, who constitute Śiva's jolly but powerful host. They are also called '*bhāravāhaka*' or 'atlantes.'

112 Cf. one of the Tala Bhārarakṣakas, Bakker 1994, Plate XXII.

Plate XXXI A
Narasiṃha (miniature), Nagardhan

Nagardhan. Nagpur Central Museum. Yellowish-grey sandstone. 21 × 23 cm. 5th century AD. Lit.: Bakker 1991.

As far as can be ascertained, there have been found altogether at least nine miniature images that can be considered as reduced copies of the large Narasiṃha images in the Rudra- and Kevala-Narasiṃha Temples on Rāmagiri, for which see Plate XXXIII below. Four (or six, two missing?) of them were found in the Nagardhan/Hamlapuri area and are kept in the Nagpur Central Museum. The one illustrated here is the best preserved of this set and represents a rather faithful copy of the temple images. It appears that instead of ears the miniature has two lotus caps (or hair-knots?) similar to the central one on the crown of the head; it gives the impression of a *triśikhā* (three tufts of hair).

These miniature images were used on domestic altars and were probably produced en masse in the Rāmagiri region for devotees to bring home.

Plate XXXI B
Viṣṇupada, Nagardhan

Nagardhan. Private Collection. Yellowish-grey sandstone. c. 12 × 12 × 4 cm. 5th century AD. Lit.: Bakker 1991.

On this tablet of yellowish sandstone a pair of footprints is engraved in bas-relief, squared in by what may represent a railing or wall in the centre of a square 'platform,' which is, again, enclosed in an outer square. Above the (viewer's) left footprint a *gadā* is engraved, above the right one the *śaṅkha*, thus making the tablet undoubtedly a Viṣṇupada icon. In between the two footprints an enigmatic symbol is engraved. It consists of a vertical axis to which horizontal strokes, slightly turning upwards, are attached on both sides, rounded off in the apex, giving the impression of a tree.[113]

Elsewhere I have argued (Bakker 1991) that in the early centuries of the Christian era places on earth began to be considered as able to preserve the footstep of

---

113 Cp. Sharma 1990, Plate 39.

Viṣṇu Trivikrama. The epic references might at first have had hardly more than mythological significance, such as the Viṣṇupada in the Northern (Himalaya) mountains seen by Kṛṣṇa and Arjuna on their way to Śiva's abode (MBh 7.57.32), or the Viṣṇupada on Mount Kailāsa described by Garuḍa: 'Here (at Kailāsa) is the Viṣṇupada placed by the striding Viṣṇu when he bestrode the three worlds, O Brahmin, situated in the North' (MBh 5.109.19). As the quoted examples show, the Viṣṇupada was preferably situated on the top of hills or mountains, and this makes sense, since it may have its origin in the idea that the strides of Viṣṇu were taken along the *axis mundi*, represented by the primordial hill of Vedic cosmogony or in later Hinduism by a mountain in the centre of the inner continent (Jambūdvīpa), e.g., Mount Meru or Mandara, Mount Kailāsa or, for that matter, any mountain (see p. 142). The footprint of Viṣṇu thus represents the spot from where the second stride through the upper world was taken, a stepping-stone so to speak. At the same time these terrestrial representations of Viṣṇu's footstep may have been thought to share in the nature that characterizes especially Viṣṇu's highest step, viz. that of being the 'source of life.'[114]

The idea of Viṣṇu Trivikrama leaving a footprint behind on earth was extended to Viṣṇu in general and to his human incarnations in particular. There is literary evidence for the existence of Viṣṇu footprint shrines in the Gupta/Vākāṭaka age, but no such sanctuary has survived. Rāmagiri appears to be an example, as may be inferred from the evidence presented above (p. 64 f.).

The considerable number of miniature Narasiṃha images that have come to light (see above) indicates that it was quite common to have reduced copies of the main deities of Ramtek Hill installed in smaller altars for personal devotional purposes. It seems likely that the footprint plaque served a similar aim. The conclusion that it represents a miniature version of the central sanctuary of the hill appears natural.

Returning to the iconography of the tablet, it may be observed that in the light of what has been said above about the symbolism of the striding Viṣṇu, it would make perfect sense to include the symbol of the tree in the Viṣṇupada iconography. It represents the cosmic pillar (*skambha*), symbolized by the world tree that rose out of the primordial hill, along which Viṣṇu took his strides to separate heaven and earth (see above n. 33 on p. 66). This symbolism would be complete, if our hypothesis is correct, and we could assume that this tablet found at the foot of the hill represents the central shrine that once crowned the hill. The tradition that connected the hill with a visit of Rāma naturally saw in it the footprints of Raghupati.

---

114 See below n. 132 on p. 143. This seems already implied in ṚV 1.154.4: *yásya trī́ pūrṇā́ mádhunā padā́ny ákṣīyamāṇā svadháyā mádanti | yá u tridhā́tu pṛthivī́m utá dyā́m éko dādhā́ra bhúvanāni víśvā* ||4||, '[Viṣṇu] whose three steps, full of mead and unremittant, rejoice spontaneously, and who sustains the threefold world, earth and heaven, and all beings (therein), alone.'

PLATE XXXII A

VARĀHA (ENSHRINED), RĀMAGIRI

Rāmagiri, Varāha Maṇḍapa (*in situ*). Basalt stone. 174 × 250 × 96 cm. First quarter of 5th century AD. Lit.: Bakker 1989b, 88 f.; 1992b; Beglar 1873–74, 110 f. Jamkhedkar 1987a, 217, Figs. 2 & 3; 1987b, 339; 1988, 65, Plates 101 & 102; 1991a, 198, 202, Pl. 85; 1992, 160, Figs. 36 & 37. Jamkhedkar s.d., 111.

A large image of a boar is found in an open, square pavilion (*maṇḍapa*) on top of Ramtek Hill. The *maṇḍapa* is raised on a *jagatī* and consists of four square pillars (*rucaka*), connected by architraves that rest on bracket capitals. This part of the construction belongs to the Vākāṭaka period. The roof has been reconstructed by the Archaeological Survey with the help of old materials, such as a cover stone with a large lotus medallion (Jamkhedkar 1988, 65). The pavilion is similar to the central *catuṣkī* of the *garbhagṛhas* of the Narasiṃha Temples. The image of a boar installed in an open pavilion (instead of in a closed temple) is also found, for instance, in Khajuraho.[115]

The robust, true-to-life image of a boar is without decoration and does not have a hump on its neck (as later images usually have). Along the right side of its snout part of the bust of a female deity is preserved (height 34 cm). Her left arm clings to the tusk of the boar; her breast is bedecked with a *graiveyaka*. Beneath the animal, between his hind and front legs, coils of a serpent are sculpted in the stone of the floor. The hood of the serpent probably rose between the two front legs.[116]

The image represents Varāha, i.e., the incarnation of Viṣṇu as a boar. The female figure clinging to the tusk is the Goddess Earth (Pṛthivī Devī), who is rescued from the ocean or nether regions into which she had sunk. The snake beneath the boar is the cosmic serpent Śeṣa, who surports the universe and serves as a prop for Varāha.

The connection of the boar with the earth dates back to Vedic times.[117] Early Sanskrit literature identifies the cosmic boar with different deities, but the *Mahābhārata* lists him among the forms of Viṣṇu.[118] Various versions of the myth of Viṣṇu's transformation into a boar began to appear in the *Mahābhārata* and *Harivaṃśa*.[119] The core of the myth is that the earth (*pṛthivī*) had sunk down to the nether regions (*rasātala*) and that Viṣṇu lifted the earth (*pṛthivīdhara*) on his (single) tusk in order to restore the world order (*lokahitārtham*).

115 Zannas 1960, 180, Pl. CXXIV.

116 Cf. Zannas 1960, 180 and Pl. CXXVI.

117 E.g. TaiSa 7.5.1. Gonda 1954, 136 ff.

118 MBh 6.63.13, cf. MBh 12.337.36.

119 MBh 12.202; MBh 3 App. I No. 16, ll. 68–128 & No. 27, ll. 42–53; HV App. I No. 42, ll. 97–195.

> Thereupon (the Lord) turned into a boar (Varāha) of great lustre and possessed of one tusk, causing terror, as it were, due to his bloodshot eyes. And illuminating the (dark) smoke by his radiance, he expanded in that (nether) region. Having taken the earth upon his single shining tusk, he, the imperishable one, lifted (her) up, O hero, a thousand *yojanas*. And while she was being lifted, a trembling began, and all the gods were shaken, as well as the seers rich in *tapas*. The whole cosmos burst into lamentation, heaven and earth. Not a single god or human being stood firm.[120]

Śeṣa's role as Varāha's support does not feature explicitly in the early Sanskrit sources. The cosmic serpent, however, is already found in the famous Varāha panel in Udayagiri Cave V (Plate XLVI).[121] Later iconographic texts prescribe the presence of Śeṣa.[122]

In contrast with other early representations of Varāha,[123] the image at issue is completely theriomorphic and as such may be the earliest of its kind; the theriomorphic Varāha of Eran dates from at least half a century later.

It has long been recognized that the symbolism of the Varāha figure can serve well as a metaphor of royal glory.[124] When the next of kin of Pṛthivīṣeṇa I erected this sanctuary on the Rāmagiri for the sake of his merit, they may have envisaged a similar symbolism.[125] If this hypothesis is correct, the Varāha image can be dated around AD 400.

---

120 MBh 3 App. I No. 16, ll. 91–99.

121 Harle 1974, 35; Mitra 1963, 99; Patil 1948, 28. Apparently also in the Varāha panel in Badoh, where Śeṣa is accompanied by his wife (Berkson 1978, 225).

122 VDhP 3.79.2; MP 260.30.

123 Mathura Museum Acc. No. 65.15 (in R. C. Sharma 1976, Fig. 44); Los Angeles County Museum M.72.53.8 (in Pal 1986, 198); Udayagiri Cave V (Plate XLVI); Ramgarth Hill (in Berkson 1978, 216 ff., Fig. 4).

124 Asher 1983, 55 ff. See above p. 22. The Udayagiri Varāha may refer to Candragupta II's consolidation of the Gupta empire and the reverential position of the serpent Śeṣa in it may have meant to the contemporaneous beholder the subordinate status of the Nāgas, the Serpent kings of Padmāvatī and Vidiśā. Likewise the Varāha of Eran 'serves as a visual metaphor and Varāha's act as an allegory for Toramāṇa's usurpation of authority in Eran' (Asher 1983, 58).

125 Above p. 22; Bakker 1992b.

PLATE XXXII B
VARĀHA (LOOSE FIND), RĀMAGIRI

Rāmagiri. Nagpur Central Museum. Brown-red sandstone. 48 × 60 × 28 cm. First half of 5th century AD. Lit.: Bakker 1991, 30.

A much smaller version of the Varāha image that was discussed above is reported to have been found in front of the Rudra-Narasiṃha Temple on Rāmagiri. The sculpture is severly mutilated and only traces of the figure of Pṛthivī are preserved. The divine animal wears an *ekāvali*, which is not a feature of the large Varāha image.

PLATE XXXIII
NARASIṂHA, RĀMAGIRI
(A *front*, B *rear* (detail), C *right side* (detail))

Rāmagiri, Kevala-Narasiṃha Temple (*in situ*). Basalt stone. 200 × 204 × 102 cm. c. 450 AD. Lit.: Bakker 1989b (colour photograph); 1992a; 1992b; Jamkhedkar 1985–86; 1987a, Fig. 5; 1987b; 1988, 66 f.; 1991a, 198, 202, Pl. 84; 1992; Jamkhedkar s.d., 111; Soundara Rajan 1980, 180, Fig. 25.

A large image of Viṣṇu's man-lion incarnation, a human body with the head of a lion, occupies the *garbhagṛha* of the so-called Kevala-Narasiṃha Temple on Rāmagiri. An almost identical, but somewhat smaller image (measuring 198 × 198 × 62 cm) is found in the adjacent Rudra-Narasiṃha Temple (not illustrated). These temples have been restored by the Archaeological Survey and are described in detail in Jamkhedkar 1988, 66–68.

The god is seated in *mahārājalīlāsana* (≈ *sukhāsana*), the relaxed, gentle but sovereign pose of a king, his right knee pulled up, supporting lightly the right arm that holds the *cakra* (Plate XXXIII C), the symbol of royal power, dignity and sovereignty and as such the emblem of the Vākāṭaka kings who confessed the Bhāgavata faith. The lion face of the image, its mane falling on to the back, expresses a serenity that every devotee would wish his king or god to have. The well-shaped body with broad shoulders and slender waist is naked, but for a necklace, bracelets, a belly-band, and a *dhotī*, pulled up between the legs and held by a belt (Plate XXXIII B). On the crown of the head the deity wears a lotus-cap. Small fangs are visible in the corners of his mouth.

The present name of the temple assigns an iconographic appellation to the deity that became current only centuries after the carving of the image, but which nevertheless is appropriate to some extent, viz. that of Kevala-Narasiṃha (also named Girija Narasiṃha), which represents the man-lion god alone (*kevala*) without his demonic adversary Hiraṇyakaśipu. The Kevala form is said in the *Vaikhānasāgama* (quoted in Rao 1914 I.2 App. C, p. 33) to represent Narasiṃha as seated on a lotus with two or four arms; his hands may hold the *gadā* and/or *cakra*, whereas the other hand(s) rest(s) on the knee(s). A well-known early example of this iconographic type, though at least half a century later than the Rāmagiri specimen, is found in a *caitya* window of the Daśāvatāra Temple at Deogarh. Although the physiognomy of the latter image is very different from the Rāmagiri Narasiṃha, his sitting posture is the same. The Deogarh image has four arms, however, holding the *gadā* and *śaṅkha* in his rear hands (see Fig. 67 in Desai 1973). Another Narasiṃha image of this type of about the same period or somewhat later was found in Garhdhanora (see above p. 54).[126]

Like Varāha, the lion form features in the early lists of Viṣṇu's manifestations (e.g., MBh 12.337.36). The myth of Viṣṇu's descent as a man-lion in order to slay the demon Hiraṇyakaśipu first appears in the *Mahābhārata* and *Harivaṃśa*.[127]

There are indications that a lion-like deity had been worshipped in 'folk' religion before this deity was adopted by Bhagavatism and was turned into the man-lion. In one of the earliest lists of Viṣṇu's manifestations he is said to have adopted the 'lion' (*siṃha*) form rather than that of the 'man-lion' (MBh 6.63.13), and in one of his earliest representations in art he is depicted in full animal form.[128] As has been argued by, *inter alios*, Eschmann, Narasiṃha, in addition to the theriomorphic boar deity, has been the figure par excellence to accommodate non-Sanskritic, so-called 'tribal' deities within the Vaiṣṇava pantheon of the 'Great Tradition.'[129]

We are fortunate in having a lengthy inscription which was found in the wall of the Kevala-Narasiṃha Temple.[130] If the inscription belongs originally to this

---

126 Jamkhedkar s.d., 111 gives some intriguing information concerning Narasiṃha images that I have been unable to verify: 'More representations of life size from Gogaon (sic) (Gadchiroli District) [formerly part of Chandrapur District] and some from Bhatala in the vicinity Warora (Chandrapur district) are all of Vakataka period. Those from Gaogaon (sic) are probably on the site of a temple and those from Bhatala are by the side of a pond and part of a miniature shrine carved in live rock'(sic).

127 MBh 3 App. I No. 27, ll. 54–63; HV App. I No. 42A. See Hacker 1960, 25 ff.

128 The image found in Kondamotu, Guntur District (AP), described in Khan 1964. The only human part of this lion figure are his two rear hands (attached to the neck) holding *gadā* and *cakra*. Compare also the image of a squatting lion in the Los Angeles County Museum of Art (Pal 1986, 192).

129 Eschmann 1978, 106 f.; Bakker 1992a, 89 ff.

130 See Appendix I and Bakker & Isaacson 1993. The temple also contains two grafitti dating roughly from the same period—featuring the names of Śrīmadanalobha and Bharaka(ta?)nātha—and

temple (see above n. 94 on p. 30), the deity was called Prabhāvatīsvāmin, Lord of the World (Lokanātha), and installed in the sixties of the fifth century by Prabhāvatī's daughter Atibhāvatī (?) for the sake of transferring merit to her mother.

PLATE XXXIV
TRIVIKRAMA, RĀMAGIRI
(A *front*, B *lower part front* (detail))

Rāmagiri, *in situ*. Red sandstone. 178 × 119 cm. Third quarter of the 5th century AD. Lit.: Bakker 1989b; 1992b; Beglar 1873–74, 112; Cousens 1905, 42; Jamkhedkar 1985–86, Fig. 1 & 2; 1988, Plates 104–109; 1991a, 198, 201; Jamkhedkar s.d., 113, Pl. VII; Mirashi 1963, lx, Plate A; Soundara Rajan 1980, 181, Fig. 27; Williams 1983, 225 f., Plates 10–12, 15.

This severely damaged image of Viṣṇu striding through the universe stands in the open air a few metres to the east of the partly preserved *maṇḍapa* of a temple that is situated over 200 m to the north-east of the Varāha sanctuary. The temple, or what remains of it, has been described in detail in Jamkhedkar 1988, 65 f. The image faces west and probably still stands in its original location.

Viṣṇu's striding through the universe in three steps (*trivikrama*) is this god's most characteristic deed in the *Ṛgveda*, in which this is described as follows.

> Viṣṇu strode through this (universe); he placed down his foot in a threefold way. It (i.e., the universe) is collected in his dusty [footstep]. Three strides he strode, Viṣṇu, the invulnerable protector; thence he established the laws (of the universe).[131]

Kuiper gives the following cosmogonic interpretation of these three steps.

> In the beginning there was the undifferentiated primeval world consisting of the waters and the beginning of the primordial hill, which the cosmogonical boar had dug up out of the waters. Heaven still lay on the earth. By slaying Vṛtra, Indra rivets the hill, opens it, and 'props up' (*stabh-*) the sky: thereby the dual organisation of the cosmos is created. But at the same moment Viṣṇu 'strides out:' his first step corresponds to the nether world (which includes the earth), his second step

---

two short inscriptions from AD 1240 (see Bakker 1989a).

131 ṚV 1.22.17–18: *idáṃ víṣṇur ví cakrame tredhā́ ní dadhe padám̐ | sámūḷham asya pāṃsuré* ||17|| *trī́ṇi padā́ ví cakrame víṣṇur gopā́ ádābhyaḥ | áto dhármāṇi dhāráyan* ||18||.

> to the upper world, but his third step is a mystery, not perceptible to the human eye, for it corresponds to the totality of the opposed moieties, just as the thirteenth month stands for the totality of the preceding twelve months.[132]

Viṣṇu's act of striding through the universe became associated with the mythology of his dwarf (*vāmana*) incarnation. This descent was provoked by the arrogance of the mighty *asura* Bali. The *Mahābhārata* has the story.

> After the Lord had slain in this way the king of the Daityas, who was a killer of enemies, the lotus-eyed God (assumed) again another (form) for the benefit of the world, (viz. that of) Kaśyapa's illustrious issue carried in Aditi's womb. After (a pregnancy) of a full millennium, she gave birth to a superior infant: he resembled a rain-cloud (in colour), had luminescent eyes, and the stature of a dwarf.
>
> Then the illustrious Lord, having the body of a child, went to the sacrificial field of the king of the Dānavas, carrying a staff and a water pot, with matted hair and wearing the sacred thread, while the *śrīvatsa* mark adorned his breast; accompanied by Bṛhaspati he joined the sacrifice of Bali.
>
> When Bali saw that dwarf-like figure, he said cheerfully: 'I am glad to see you, O brahmin; tell me, what can I offer you?' Thus addressed by Bali the dwarf responded; having saluted him by saying 'Hail,' the God spoke to Bali while he smiled: 'O lord of the Dānavas, give me the earth that (is measured by) three steps of mine.' Bali gave (it) happily to the brahmin of infinite might.
>
> Thereupon the striding Hari (assumed) his most wonderful divine form and by three steps he, imperturbed, took at once possession of the earth. And the eternal God Viṣṇu gave the earth (back) to Śakra (i.e. Indra).[133]

The image at issue is not the earliest of its kind. Comparison is invited with the Gupta image in the Mathura Museum,[134] and the eight-armed image on a lintel of Pawaya.[135] The iconography of the Rāmagiri Trivikrama has been described by Mirashi.

132 Kuiper 1983, 53. In addition it may be noted, that Viṣṇu's highest footstep also represents the ultimate place in heaven, where the 'honey well' is, the sweet stream of which quickens the world: *víṣṇoḥ padé paramé mádhva útsaḥ* (ṚV 1.154.5; cf. ṚV 2.24.4). Von Stietencron 1972, 65 f.; see also above p. 137.

133 MBh 3 App. I No. 27, ll. 63–80.

134 Mathura Museum 70.58, published in IAR 1970–71, Plate LXXVIIIc.

135 Williams 1982, 53 ff., Plate 50.

> The god has a crown on his head, with a halo round his face. He wears the *kuṇḍalas* on his ears and a pearl-necklace with a large pendant round his neck. His *vaijayantī* garland is shown falling on both his legs. He wears an *udarabandha*. His lower garment, which is fastened at the waist with a girdle, hangs down in folds in front. His arms are now broken on both the sides, but their jewelled *aṅgadas* (armlets) can still be seen. His left foot is planted on the ground, while the right foot, which was raised to measure the sky, is now broken at the knee. The pose shows his determination to rescue the three worlds from the demon king Bali. The latter is standing in the *tribhaṅga* pose at the god's feet in an attitude of reverence. The image of his queen who was standing by his side is now very mutilated. In its original condition this panel must undoubtedly have been reckoned among the best products of the Vākāṭaka age.[136]

The deity had eight arms, all sadly broken off. He wears the double *muktāyajño-pavīta* which we have come across in the Rudra of Mandhal (Plates IX & X).[137] The figure of Bali (c. 74 cm in height), 'surpassed' by Viṣṇu's stride, also wears a *mukuṭa* and *aṅgadas*. Of the smaller figure to his proper left (his wife?), who may have leaned against Viṣṇu's left leg, only one foot, ankle and shin seem to remain (at least we were not able to descry more). To the right of king Bali another scene must have been depicted, which has, however, been completely obliterated.[138] According to the *Bṛhatsaṃhitā*, the eight-armed image of Lord Viṣṇu should hold in his right hands a sword, mace, arrow, and the fourth hand should show the *śāntida-* (= *varada-*) *mudrā*; in his left hands he should hold a bow, shield, discus, and conch.[139] This description does not fit the Pawaya Trivikrama (Williams 1982, 53), and whether it conforms to the image at issue is impossible to know. A significant feature of the Rāmagiri Trivikrama is the 'pleated' *śiraścakra* that encircles his head. Harle 1987 traces the origin of this type of adornment to the fan-shaped tufts at the end of the band holding the crown (*mukuṭa*). The Rāmagiri specimen could be among the earliest images showing this type of halo.

Like the sanctuaries of Varāha and Narasiṃha, the Trivikrama Temple may have

---

136 Mirashi 1963 (= CII V), lx.

137 These six strings of pearls have been almost completely erased at the front side of the image, but are still clearly visible at the rear (see Jamkhedkar 1988, Plate 109). Compare the Śiva of Mansar (Plate XXXVII).

138 Cf. the lintel from Pawaya, in which the Vāmana myth is depicted in several panels (Williams 1982, Plate 50). The right half of this sculpture was missing, but has been recovered recently. Its publication is foreseen by Rekha Morris.

139 *Bṛhatsaṃhitā* 58.33: *khaḍgagadāśarapāṇir dakṣiṇataḥ śāntidaś caturthakaraḥ* | *vāmakareṣu ca kārmukakheṭakacakrāṇi śaṅkhaś ca* ||33||.

been built for the spiritual benefit of a member of the Vākāṭaka dynasty. In view of the solar connotations of Viṣṇu Trivikrama,[140] it has been conjectured that this shrine was erected for the sake of the merit of the eldest son of Rudrasena II and Prabhāvatī, Divākarasena, who died before he had ascended the Vākāṭaka throne (Bakker 1992b). The Kevala-Narasiṃha Temple Inscription opens with a verse in praise of Viṣṇu-Trivikrama.

> He is victorious, whose ⟨colour resembles⟩ the depths of a water-laden rain-cloud, ⟨who⟩ [...] ⟨in the assembly of the gods⟩, the beauty of whose body expanded at the occasion of ⟨Bali's⟩ sacrifice, and who is looked at with gazes that tremble with fright ⟨by the wives of Diti's sons (i.e. the demons)⟩.[141]

If—though I consider this unlikely (see above n. 94 on p. 30)—this inscription belonged originally to the Trivikrama Temple, the image at issue should be considered as that of Prabhāvatīsvāmin. In either case it may date from the sixth decade of the fifth century.

PLATE XXXV A
VIṢṆU, RĀMAGIRI

Rāmagiri. Nagpur Central Museum. Basalt stone. 82 × 50 × 30 cm (exclusive pedestal). Second half of the 5th century AD (?). Lit.: Bakker 1989b, 93; Jamkhedkar 1988, 70, Plate 128; 1991a, 198, photo 99; 1992, 161, Fig. 45; Jamkhedkar s.d., 111.

This well-proportioned image, which is carved in the round, stands on a pedestal (10 × 50 × 30 cm), underneath which is a rectangular block of stone meant to fit into a socket. The image is reported to have been recovered from the debris in front of the little rock-cut temple of Kapaṭarāma (Jamkhedkar 1988, 70), which is possibly identical to the Guptarāma Temple mentioned in the (13th-century) Ramtek Stone Inscription of the time of Ramachandra.[142] No socket that matches the image could be detected in the temple, but the possibility cannot be ruled out that this is covered by the pedestal of the 18th century *liṅga* that is found in it today. However, it seems questionable whether the image at issue ever belonged to this temple. At least its

140 Gonda 1954, 60. Cf. Kuiper 1983, 41 n. 1.

141 Translation based on the revised edition, Appendix I vs. 1 (cf. Bakker & Isaacson 1993, 55).

142 Bakker 1989a, 494 (vs. 101)); see also the Mahānubhāva text *Sthānapothī* p. 5.

style does not tally with the other Vākāṭaka sculptures found on Rāmagiri and in the Nagardhan area.

The head and arms of the image are missing; the fractures at the left shoulder, however, seem to indicate that the deity was four-armed; it stands in *samabhaṅga* posture. On account of these features the image has been identified as that of Viṣṇu by Jamkhedkar (1991a, 198), which appears to be the most plausible interpretation. The deity wears a simple necklace and waist-belt. The lower left hand may have held the sash-like *dhotī*, the spare cloth of which is beautifully draped alongside both legs.

PLATE XXXV B
A DIKPĀLA (?), RĀMAGIRI

Rāmagiri. Nagpur Central Museum. Red sandstone. 107 × 50 cm. First quarter of 5th century AD. Lit.: Bakker 1989b, 86; Jamkhedkar 1988, 67, Plate 123; 1991a, 202, photo 87.

This is one of the two fragments of life-size images that were recovered from the debris around the Rudra-Narasiṃha Temple on Rāmagiri (Jamkhedkar 1988, 67). The present image is broken above the waist (the other one, not illustrated, is broken above the ankles). The figure rests on its left leg, while the right leg is slightly bent (*viṣamasthāna*?). Down along the right leg runs a long string reaching to under the right knee (*pralambahārī*), not unlike the one worn by the Paunar Gaṅgā (see Plate XXXIX B). Folds of the *dhotī* fall between the legs. Along his left leg the deity holds a long sword (*khaḍga*).[143]

The plan of the temple where the image was found is without parallel. Along its sides are 'ten projections: two at each of the four corners and one to either side, almost in the middle of each lateral wall. [...] Corresponding to eight of these projections, there are eight cisterns below the platform. The purpose of these and whether they formed part of the original plan is difficult to determine' (Jamkhedkar 1988, 67). Earlier we have conjectured that these 'projections' are pedestals on which images once stood (Bakker 1989b, 86). If this conjecture is correct, the image at issue may have been a protective (*pratihāra/dikpāla*) god, who belonged to the group of deities encircling the main image of Narasiṃha (*parivāradevatā*). The long sword points to an apotropaic function.

143 Jamkhedkar 1988, qualifies this attribute as a 'staff,' Jamkhedkar 1991a, 202 as a 'sword.'

PLATE XXXV C

MAKARA, RĀMAGIRI

Rāmagiri, Bhogarāma Temple (*in situ*). Red sandstone. 30 × 15 cm. Middle of 5th century AD. Lit.: Jamkhedkar 1985–86, Plate 5; 1988, 70, Plate 126.

This frieze of an imaginary aquatic monster, usually denoted as *makara* and sometimes equated with the crocodile, which animal might have served as one of its prototypes, is found in a dado (*antarapaṭṭa*) that forms part of the basal wall-mouldings (*vedībandha*) of the Bhogarāma Temple on Rāmagiri. It is fitted vertically (head downwards) at the end of the dado into the wall that separates the left (southern) *garbhagṛha* from the vestibule (*antarāla*). A similar, more worn image is found near the other cella. The frieze is edged by strings of alternating lozenges and elliptical forms, probably representing jewels, which are found throughout on Vākāṭaka monuments (Williams 1983, 220, 226). These strings of jewels border a vertical row of flower rosettes (*puṣpapaṭṭika*).

The *makara* resembles the terracotta relief kept in the Ashmolean Museum (Harle 1974, Plate 148). Around its neck it wears a kind of necklace, which is partly hidden by a flying mane. As is typical for this type of mythic animal, its tail ends in foliage.

The motif of the *makara*, which is ubiquitous in South- and South-East Asian art, is usually thought to express auspiciousness, symbolizing the primal source of life.[144]

PLATE XXXVI

GAṆAS, RĀMAGIRI

(A a Gaṇa, B a Nidhi)

Rāmagiri, Kevala-Narasiṃha Temple (*in situ*). Red sandstone. 35 × 24 cm. Middle of 5th century AD. Lit.: Bakker 1989b, 85, Fig. 7; Jamkhedkar 1987a, 218, Fig. 6; 1988, 67, Plate 116; 1991a, 201, photo 82; Williams 1983, 226, Plate 14.

---

144 Viennot 1958, 290; Coomaraswamy 1928 II, 47 ff. According to Darian 1976, 34, the symbolism of the *makara* has a darker side as well, representing 'the forces of envelopment, or reabsorption into the undifferentiate state.'

Two jambs of red sandstone containing each four dwarf-like figures set in rectangular niches one above the other flank the entrance of the Kevala-Narasiṃha Temple. There is a symmetry between the four figures on both jambs. The two bottom figures both shower coins, the two highest figures carry weapons, the northern one a mace, the southern a sword. The attributes of the two pairs of figures in between cannot be determined. Similar figures are found on the Trivikrama, Bhogarāma and Rudra-Narasiṃha Temples on Rāmagiri Hill. The images illustrated represent the bottom one (XXXVI B) and the third from the bottom (XXXVI A) of the southern jamb (viewer's right).

The short-legged figures have fleshy bodies, not unlike those of the two Bhārarakṣakas (Plate XXX). Both arms of the third-from-bottom figure (XXXVI A) are broken off near the elbow, but the left hand seems to have held a sash, which appears under the right upper arm and crosses the body obliquely; the pleated end of the sash falls to the ground parallel to the left leg. Corkscrew curls cascade on to his left shoulder. It would seem that only the left ear wears a large earring (*tāṭaṅka*), resting on the shoulder, similar to the ear-ornament of the Mansar Śiva (Plate XXXVII) and the Bhārarakṣaka (Plate XXX B). The only other ornament visible is a simple necklace of beads. Around the big belly the deity wears a braided band (*udarabandha*).

The dwarfish stature of these figures, along with their place next to the temple entrance, makes them *gaṇas* or *yakṣas* who function as guardians (of wealth). As such they are sometimes also denoted as *nidhis*, i.e. treasure(r)s. The latter designation applies in particular to the bottom figure (XXXVI B). He carries a money bag on his left shoulder, held by his left hand, which passes behind his back while his right hand holds its nozzle, from which coins are showered—a peculiar feature in view of the almost total absence of Vākāṭaka coinage.[145] Around the bag are two straps set with lozenges (diamonds). A thick bundle of coiled snail-shell curls stands out from the right side of his head (*pārśvamauli*). The figure also wears only an earring in his right ear; he is decorated by a necklace with pendant, bracelets and is clad in a *dhotī*, the edge of which is visible on the right thigh; the spare cloth hangs down along his left side.

---

145 See above p. 90.

PLATE XXXVII
ŚIVA, MANSAR

Mansar. National Museum, New Delhi (Acc. No. L–77/2). Red sandstone. 84 × 65 × 37 cm. First half of the 5th century AD. Lit.: Deo 1975–76; IAR (1972–73), 59, Plate XLII; *In the Image of Man*, p. 69 (colour photograph); Jamkhedkar 1991a, 203, Pl. 89; 1991b; Joshi 1984; Sarma 1992; Schastok 1981; Sivaramamurti 1976, Frontispiece; 1984; Williams 1983.

This splendid image was found (1972) among the debris of a brick temple that once crowned the so-called Hiḍimbā Tekḍī, a hillock to the east of the Village of Mansar, 5 km west of Ramtek (Rāmagiri), which we tentatively identified with the site of the Pravareśvaradevakulasthāna; the deity may therefore be assumed to be the Pravareśvara that was installed by king Pravarasena II in the second quarter of the fifth century (see above p. 87).

Two contrasting aspects of Śiva seem to inform the iconography of this image. This may appear, for instance, from the fact that the right elongated pierced ear lobe only contains a tiny ringlet such as worn by ascetics,[146] while the left ear is ornamented by a large earring (*tāṭaṅka*).[147] The hair is wrapped by spiring strands of matted hair into a *jaṭāmukuṭa*—resembling a turban (*uṣṇīṣa*) in some respects—from the centre of which curls cascade to the right side, bound by a fillet and a string of pearls, similar to the hair-ornament of the Kavi image from Nagardhan (Plate XXVI). The left side of the head is adorned by the symbol of death, the skull (*kapāla*). On top of the skull is a small lotus-flower rosette and the hind-part is adorned by festoons of pearls which fall from the pericarps of three tiny lotus flowers. Skull and *mukuṭa* are separated by a flower ornament;[148] the crescent, attached to the coils, shines above in the middle. The headband (*bhālapaṭṭa*) is rimmed by a string of beads (jewels).

The right upper hand holds the yogic attribute of the rosary (*rudrākṣa*), while the left upper hand holds the stalk of a (lotus) flower. The lower left hand is clenched in

---

146 Kreisel 1986, 126, Fig. 24; Lorenzen 1991, 2 f.

147 According to Sivaramamurti 1984, 190 this is 'proclaiming his eternal hermaphroditic form,' although there are no other signs of femininity to be found in the image. Cf. Kreisel 1986, 126 f. Though this distinction could be one of the symbolic layers underlying the image, the in our view main ambiguity of the image is not provoked by the male versus the female aspect of Śiva, but by his life-granting form versus his world-renouncing form. A similar asymmetry we find in the Gaṇa and Nidhi figures on the doorjamb of the Kevala-Narasiṃha Temple (Plate XXXVI), which may also express their ambiguous nature: auspicious, protective etc., and fearsome, violent etc.

148 According to Sarma 1992, 220 the 'eight favoured flowers (*aṣṭapuṣpikā*).' Cf. Sivaramamurti 1976, 113 and 1984, 190.

a fist (*muṣṭi*) and rests on the left, drawn up knee. The 'fist of the teacher' (*ācārya-muṣṭi*) is an old Indian symbol, known from the Buddhist tradition, referring to the doctrine known by the preceptor, which he teaches only to his most advanced students.[149] Kālidāsa in *Raghuvaṃśa* 15.21, on the other hand, speaks of the 'fist of death' (*kṛtāntasya muṣṭiṃ*), which could also be the meaning in the present image, viz. a symbol of the god's (destructive) power. In contrast, it seems that the right lower hand offers a precious thing to the (general) devotee. According to Sarma (1992, 220) this hand 'exhibits in the palm a laced ornament held up by the middle two fingers. [...] The way the *yajñopavīta* is shown flowing over the right hand [i.e. forearm, H.T.B.] and shoulder, indicates that the god is in the act of performing a *dāna* ceremony and the object is a precious ornament as shown in the palm which is in *varadamudrā*.' It would seem to me, however, that the hand shows an *añjali* of (lotus) flowers—similar to some of the flowers contained in the head ornament—by which the god offers life to his devotees.[150]

The two rear wrists wear bracelets with an ornamented clasp, the front wrists two simple bangles of beads. The deity wears an ornamented necklace, a twisted belly-band (*udarabandha*) and the double *muktāyajñopavīta* of the *snātaka* or *gṛhastha*, i.e. six strings of pearls—twisted 'with subtle irregularity' (Williams 1983, 228)—which are 'clasped by an ornamental leonine or *gajavyāla* head at the right and left sides very symmetrically arranged' (Sarma 1992, 220). While the anklet of the right foot is similar to the bangles, the left ankle is encircled by a *nāganūpura*.

The deity is naked but for a lower garment which passes between the legs over the front of the seat. He sits in the easy pose of *sukhāsana*, the back supported by a bolster on which his elbows rest.[151] Like the Kavi of Nagardhan (Plate XXVI) the image is a sculptured stele.

Though the third eye is absent—in the Mandhal images it also exclusively features as a characteristic of the *ugra* aspect (above n. 6 on p. 96)—there can be little doubt that the figure represents Śiva and not Kubera as was suggested by Schastok (1981, 108) and with whom he is compared by Williams (1983, viz. the Kayanpur Kubera). The mysterious smile raises the god above iconographic stereotypes; the combination of attributes defies the identification of the image as one specific form of Śiva.[152]

---

149 *Buddhist Hybrid Sanskrit Grammar and Dictionary*, s.v. For *ācariyamuṭṭhi* in the Pāli sources see *Critical Pāli Dictionary*, s.v.

150 Possibly the *aṣṭapuṣpikā*; see Pathak 1961, 17 f. Schastok 1981, 108 identifies it as a 'citron or fruit.'

151 The terms *sukhāsana* and *(mahā)rājalīlāsana* are mostly used indiscriminately, but we reserve the latter term for those figures who show more regalia on them.

152 Williams 1983, 227 n. 3: 'I have not found an exact parallel for this figure in iconography and thus cannot identify the specific form of Śiva.'

As has been noted above, the image rather comprises the two main aspects of the God of the Māheśvaras: the God of devotion (*bhakti*), who creates and sustains the universe (symbolized by the lotus and ornaments) and who by his grace safeguards the one who worships him (symbolized by the offered *añjali*), and the God who destroys all that belongs to the realm of space and time (symbolized by the skull and the snakes), who points the way out of the circle of birth and death only to him who shakes off his ignorance (symbolized by the fist?) by choosing the path of asceticism and mortification of the flesh (symbolized by the rosary and matted locks).

PLATE XXXVIII A
VAJRAPĀṆI, AJANTA

Ajanta Cave 19, *in situ*. 7th–8th decades of the 5th century AD. Lit.: The façade of Cave 19 has been described and depicted in many of the books and articles that deal with the Ajanta caves. Mirashi in CII V, lxxiii f., Plate N; Weiner 1977, 53, plates 19, 23; Williams 1983, 226 ff., Plate 19.

This large statue is found at the viewer's right of the *caitya* window in the façade of Cave 19. A similar figure adorns the opposite side of the window. The two figures evidently form a pair. This *caitya* hall (i.e. Ajanta Cave 19) was, together with the adjacent Cave 17, commissioned by a feudatory of the Vākāṭaka king of the Vatsagulma Branch, Hariṣeṇa, 'the moon among kings' (see above p. 35 ff.).

The resemblance of the figure at issue with the *gaṇa* of the Kevala-Narasiṃha Temple on Rāmagiri (Plate XXXVI A) and the Śiva of Mansar (Plate XXXVII) was first fully realized by Joanna Williams (1983, 226).

> The guardians of Ajantā Cave 19 are yet closer to the Manasar figure in the general quality of their carving. For example, the top of the chest shows the same small fold on either side below the armpit [cf. Plate XXX, H.T.B.], although such modelling is not apparent in the limbs, perhaps because of the guardian's greater stature. In general the Ajantā figure shows a similar richness of detail in head-dress and ornament, while it does not follow the unique style of coiled locks from which the Manasar figure's curls descend. The pearled band or *yajñopavīta* in both twists with subtle irregularity, as do many of the swags of pearls in the Ajantā paintings. Allowing for differences of iconography and position here, I find the two carvings similar in spirit, although the Ajantā carver did not show the extraordinarily inventive

> handling of detail that distinguishes the Manasar artist. (Williams 1983, 228)

There can be little doubt that the *gaṇa* of the Kevala-Narasiṃha Temple and the present image not only have stylistic and iconographic features in common, but also their function, viz. that of guardian (of wealth).

The Ajanta deity is more richly bedecked by ornaments. He wears a small *maṇi-kuṇḍala* in the (right) ear that is visible, an *ekāvali*, *graiveyaka*, *aṅgadas*, *valayas* and a double *muktāyajñopavīta*. The latter loops around the *udarabandha*. From his girdle a string of pearls drops on the right thigh. Folds of his *dhotī* fall between the legs, whereas the left hand holds the end of the cloth similar to the sash held by the Rāmagiri *gaṇa*. The corkscrew curls cascade onto the left shoulder. The head is surrounded by a halo (*śiraścakra*). The right hand holds what might be either a diamond (*vajra*) or the pointed end of a wand which, though it is without curved prongs, may also represent the *vajra*.[153] The right hand of the corresponding guardian figure on the left of the window shows the *kaṭakamudrā*, which indicates that he holds the lotus (*padma*), of which, possibly, the lowest part of the stem is preserved between the thumb and forefinger.[154] To the respective right and left of both guardians stand little devout figures (*gaṇa*), the (viewer's) right one carrying a garland.

Identification of the image at issue should show a coherence between the sculptures on either side of the window. Both belong to the class of protective deities (*yakṣa*) which were incorporated into popular Buddhism.[155] Their symmetry and resemblance may point to a complementary relationship. The richness of their ornamentation indicate that they are connected with wealth and treasures. In view of the attributes, the *padma* of the left, the *vajra* of the right figure, one may designate them Padmapāṇi and Vajrapāṇi, both well-known *yakṣa* figures.[156] The figure

---

153 The ambiguity of the term *vajra*, signifying diamond and thunderbolt, matches, as it were, the indistinctness of the attribute in its present state of preservation, of which only the 'adamantine' core remains.

154 Cf. the *yakṣa* of Amin (Coomaraswamy 1928 I, 39, Plate 7).

155 Coomaraswamy 1928 I, 37: Certainly 'the Yakṣa concept has played an important part in the development of Indian mythology, and even more certainly, the early Yakṣa iconography has formed the foundation of later Hindu and Buddhist iconography.'

156 Coomaraswamy 1928 I, 30 f.; Misra 1981, 120, 124. Similar considerations could lead, alternatively, to the two *yakṣa* brothers who likewise play a significant role within Buddhism, viz. Pūrṇabhadra and Maṇibhadra. That the latter *yakṣa* was important to the excavators of the Ajanta caves follows from a depiction of this *yakṣa* in Cave 17 'at the left of the verandah,' below which a painted epigraph is found reading *māṇibhadraḥ* (*Ajanta* III (1946), 97). Both *yakṣas* were the tutelary deities of merchant guilds and seem to have had a cult of their own (Misra 1981, 80–87). No doubt merchant guilds played a prominent role in the realization of the Ajanta project. Our knowledge of the iconography of *yakṣas* is, however, too poor to be more precise.

illustrated here represents the *yakṣa/bodhisattva* Vajrapāṇi.[157]

The Buddhistic context of the present image finds expression in 'the introduction of a Buddha image in the crest of the headdress of the *dvārapāla* to the left of the arch and what seems to be a *stūpa* in the crest of the figure at the right' as noticed by Weiner (1977, 53). This author continues,

> Functionally, the *dvārapālas* are descendants of the guardian *yakṣas* that are found on *toraṇas* and rails at older *stūpa* sites or *caitya* halls. [...] These *dvārapāla* figures guard the *stūpa* in the same way that *caurī* (fly whisk) bearers or *Bodhisattva* figures flank Buddha images. In fact, on the façade of the Viśvakarman *caitya* hall at Ellorā, their position on the gallery is occupied by Padmapāṇi and Vajrapāṇi.

Surprisingly, Weiner is silent about the attributes of both images, which, after all, suggest that we are here concerned with the same two Buddhistic acolytes. The *stūpa* in the crest of the right figure (illustrated here) reinforces our identification as Vajrapāṇi.[158]

PLATE XXXVIII B
A NIDHI, AJANTA

Ajanta Cave 21, *in situ*. 7th–8th decade of the 5th century AD.

The bottom of the right doorjamb of the entrance of Cave 21 contains a panel in which a dwarf-like figure showers coins from a bag held on his right shoulder, similar to the figure in the panel on the doorjamb of the Kevala-Narasiṃha Temple

---

Finally, one traditional feature of Maṇibhadra may be mentioned which might have some relevance: he is known as the one whose head-dress is to one side (*pārśvamauli*, Rām. 7.15.10). Mirashi in CII V, lxxiii identifies the two figures as 'Pañchika on the left and Pūrṇabhadra on the right.'

157 Coomaraswamy 1928 I, 31: 'Thus there was actually a Yakṣa Vajrapāṇi, not identical with Indra, but having an independent, pre-Buddhist cult; this Yakṣa became the Buddha's guardian angel and attendant, and finally came to be called the Bodhisattva Vajrapāṇi, who sometimes appears in Buddha triads, and is sometimes the object of separate worship.' The early iconography of Vajrapāṇi is beset with difficulties (Huntington 1989, 88 f.). On account of the presence of his counterpart Padmapāṇi (i.e. Avalokiteśvara) figures have been identified as Vajrapāṇi, even when they apparently do not hold the *vajra*.

158 Vajrapāṇi appears as a *dvārapāla* in Aurangabad Cave 6, having a *stūpa* as emblem in his headdress (Berkson 1986, 179, 182 f., 185). However, the little crest–*stūpa* was to become the hallmark of the *bodhisattva* Maitreya (Bhattacharya 1980, 100 ff.). Mainly on account of this Malandra (1993, 99 ff.) argues that several supposedly Vajrapāṇi figures in Ellora, being the counterparts of Avalokiteśvara figures, should actually be identified as Maitreya.

(above Plate XXXVI B). The sculpture, though apparently inspired by the Rāmagiri example, is clearly less subtle and detailed. The deity holds the nozzle of the bag with both hands. He does not havc thc one-sided coiffure of the Rāmagiri Nidhi. The only ornament that can be distinguished is a necklace.

PLATE XXXIX A
RIVER GODDESS, AJANTA

Ajanta Cave 16, *in situ*. 7th–8th decade of the 5th century AD.

Lit.: Mirashi 1963, lxvi; Spink 1975, Fig. 4; Viennot 1964, 13–19, Pl. 2a.

This image of the goddess rests on the capital of a pilaster to the (viewer's) left of the main doorway of the porch of Ajanta Cave 16. It is mirrored by a similar image to the right of the doorway. Visually these two images support the lintel above the door as two caryatids. In early Indian architecture this function is often performed by vegetation nymphs (*yakṣī*), denoted as *śālabhañjikās* (i.e. 'bending a branch of the śāla tree'). On the one hand, the branch of a (flowering) tree, which surrounds the head of the goddess as a kind of nimbus, is reminiscent of this prototype—part of the trunk seems to run in the corner of the niche behind the right arm; on the other hand, the fact that the figure stands on the aquatic *makara*, which has become very conspicuous, seems to mark her more specifically as a river deity (*nadī devatā*, Viennot 1964, 11). Ph. Vogel, followed by Coomaraswamy and Viennot, rightly has questioned, whether twin goddesses, both supported by *makaras*, who serve as architrave brackets (as in this instance), justify an identification as the individual goddesses Gaṅgā and Yamunā.[159]

The goddess stands graciously on the *makara*, her right leg bent before her left (*pādasvastika*?), while her right arm leans on the vertically turned tail of the animal. Her left forearm has broken off, but may have held a flower or fruit picked from the tree (Viennot 1964, 14). The sole of her right foot touches the trunk of the

159 Vogel 1925, 399: 'Evidemment les sculpteurs qui ornaient les caves d'Ajaṇṭā et d'Udayagiri ont imité le motif de la Yakṣiṇī *makara* qu'ils trouvaient sur les anciens monuments du bouddhisme. Peut-être n'ont-ils pas eu l'intention de représenter autre chose que des Yakṣiṇīs. Bientôt la présence du *makara*, l'animal aquatique par excellence, doit avoir suggéré aux croyants l'idée que c'étaient des déesses fluviales et, puisqu'elles apparaissaient toujours en couple, on aura vite fait d'y reconnaître le fleuve sanctissime, la Gaṅgā, avec sa sœur jumelle, la Yamunā. Cf. Fergusson & Burgess 1880, 304 where these deities are described as 'female figures standing on the heads of *makaras*.'

makara which is curled upwards. The goddess is naked, her girdle (*mekhalā*) exposing the mons Veneris. The ornaments that can be distinguished are a jewelled hair-ribbon (*keśabandha*), earrings (*kuṇḍalas*), a necklace (*hāra*), a *channavīra*, arm- and bracelets (*keyūra* and *kaṅkana*) and anklets (*nūpura*). On the sculpture remains of painting are preserved.

The excavation of Cave 16 was commissioned by Varāhadeva (probably the son of Hastibhoja), minister (*saciva*) of the Vākāṭaka king Hariṣeṇa of the Vatsagulma Branch, as appears from an inscription 'incised on the left-side wall at the extreme end outside the verandah' (CII V, 103). In it the cave is described as an abode (*layana*) in/on the mountain 'adorned with windows, doors, and pictures of celestial nymphs in beautiful galleries and on ledges, and so on, and ... with beautiful pillars and steps and a (Buddha) sanctuary built inside.'[160] Its architect (*sūtradhāra*) was named Yugadhara.[161]

PLATE XXXIX B
GAṄGĀ, PAUNAR

Paunar, Ashram of Vinobā Bhāve. Basalt stone. 166 × 65 × 31 cm. Early 6th century AD. Lit.: Deo & Dhavalikar 1968, Plate I; Gupta 1992, 148, Fig. 21; Jamkhedkar 1985b, Plate 117–118; 1991a, 206 f., Pl. 100, 101; 1991b, 92, Fig. 13; Mirashi 1963, lxxii, Plate D (I); Soundara Rajan 1980, 181, Fig. 29; Williams 1983, 230, Plate 23.

This image of the river goddess was discovered 'while digging in the courtyard of Vinōbājī's *āśrama*' (Mirashi in CII V, lxii). It is now installed in a niche within the Ashram. An inscription, reading '*gaṅgā bhagavati*' found beside her right knee, confirms the identification as Gaṅgā. The goddess stands on her traditional *vāhana*, the *makara*.

The two arms of the deity are broken off,[162] the right one above, the left one just below the bent elbow. A fractured surface at the left upper arm indicates that something must have rested against it that was held in the raised left hand. Another fracture next to the right upper leg may point to the place where her right hand may

---

160 CII V, 109 vs. 24: *gavākṣaniryūhasuvīthivedikā[sure]ndrakanyāpratimādyalaṅkṛtam* [|] *manoharastambhavibhaṅga* – ⌣ – [*ni*]*veśitābhyantaracaityamandiram* [||24||]. Alternatively the first compound may be interpreted (as is usually done) as '... with windows, doors, beautiful picture-galleries, ledges and images of girls of Indra's (paradise), and so on ...'.

161 According to an inscription on the right wall of Cave 16; see Dhavalikar 1968, 152.

162 Mirashi 1963, lxii thinks the image had originally four arms.

have been positioned. Apart from this conjectured position of the hand, however, there are no other indications that point to a small figure (*gaṇa*) standing at the side of the goddess.

The curls of hair fall to both sides; a string of pearls forms the parting, running over the crown of the head and ending in a pendant on her forehead. The goddess wore large earrings of which only a part remains (see Jamkhedkar 1991a, Pl. 100). Around her neck she wears an *ekāvali*, *niṣka*, *graiveyaka*, *vaikakṣa*, and a long string reaching to under her right knee (*pralambahārī*). The arms are ornamented by *keyūras* and *kaṅkanas*. A very fine diaphanous garment falling to the shins is pulled up between the legs, wrapped around the waist, and held up by an exquisite *mekhalā* consisting of strings of jewels and pearls. *Nūpuras* adorn her ankles.

Stylistically the image clearly belongs to the other Paunar figures with their slender elongated bodies. Joanna Williams compares the image with the Śiva of Mansar (Plate XXXVII) and Ajanta examples, but concludes 'for all these connections with the rest of Vākāṭaka and with Gupta art, the Pavnar Gaṅgā has a puzzling South Indian flavor,' though exact South-Indian counterparts cannot be adduced.[163]

The discovery of this image came too late to be included in the chef-d'oeuvre of Odette Viennot. If we try to accomodate this sculpture to the framework developed by this scholar, it could be compared with the images described in the second part of the volume under the heading 'Mahārāshṭra et Karṇāṭā A' (Viennot 1964, 120–123). Like these, the Paunar Gaṅgā does not convey the impression of having formed part of a doorframe construction; she may have been fixed to the wall at some distance from the entrance of the temple that was decorated by the panels discussed below.[164] In particular, the Paunar Gaṅgā may be compared with the river goddess outside the Rāmesvara cave temple (No. 21) in Ellora (Viennot 1964, Pl. 63a), despite differences such as that the latter is heavier (the 'South-Indian flavour' is absent) and stands on a lotus cushion on the back of the *makara*, which cushion is absent in the Paunar example. This absence may corroborate the relatively early date of the Paunar Gaṅgā.

---

163 Williams 1983, 231. See above p. 91. Cf. Jamkhedkar 1991a, 206: 'The very elongation of the figure with slender torso and very prominent breasts, a rather oval face but not very wide lips remind one of similar slender but elongated figures of Amaravati.'

164 Cf. Viennot 1964, 120: 'Gaṅgā et Yamunā de grandeur nature, l'une sur le *makara* et l'autre sur la tortue, se font pendant, contre le mur de part et d'autre à quelque distance du passage. Elles se présentent de face, jambes parallèles; le corps, très souplement fléchi, est en appui sur une jambe. Une *dhotī* de mousseline impalpable, retenue sur les hanches par une large ceinture à double pendentif ansé, voile leurs jambes.'

PLATE XL A
BALARĀMA (DHENUKĀSURAVADHAMŪRTI), PAUNAR

Paunar, Ashram of Vinobā Bhāve. Basalt stone. 156 × 90 cm. Early 6th century AD. Lit.: Gupta 1992; Jamkhedkar 1985, Plate 120; 1991a, 206, Pl. 97; Mirashi 1954; 1963, lx–lxii, Plate C; Williams 1983, 229, Plate 19.

In addition to quite a number of loose sculptures and parts thereof (for one of them see above Plate XXXIX B), eight panels were found in Paunar 'while digging in the fields round Śrī Vinōbājī's *āśrama* on the left bank of the river Dhām' (Mirashi 1963, lx). These panels are now placed in niches along a wall of the Ashram.

The scene on the panel at issue, described as 'killing of Vālī' by Mirashi, was again interpreted by Jamkhedkar (1985, 83), who describes it as follows.

> On the background of a palm-tree and two friendly male witnesses is shown Balarāma in *pratyālīḍha* posture, his left arm resting on his thigh. His right hand grabs the hindlegs of Dhenukāsura. Balarāma is about to fling the demon on to the tāla tree. On the palm-tree proper is shown the donkey-demon leaning over one of the branches. A human is shown fallen against the foot of the tree, his right hand on the head and left arm resting on the thigh, as though in swoon.

No doubt Jamkhedkar's identification of the main figure as Balarāma is correct. He is adorned by a necklacc and belly-band and wears a loin-cloth. The tall figure behind him to his proper right has placed his right hand on his hip and the other on the shoulder of the smaller (male) figure to his left. The tall (right) figure in the background, who wears a necklace, may be Kṛṣṇa, the second smaller figure could be one of the cow-herds (*gopa*) who, according to the *Harivaṃśa*, lived in the *tāla* wood, but were terrorized by the donkey and his mates (HV 57.25). Jamkhedkar (1985, 83) and Gupta (1992, 147) distinguish 'the forepart of an ass' on the leaves of one of the *tāla* trees. If this is the case (the present writer fails to see it) it would imply that the panel illustrates more than just one moment in the myth.

First we see Balarāma grabbing the donkey's hind legs; secondly, the donkey is hurled on to the *tāla* tree; the third moment may be represented by the human figure sitting on the ground behind Balarāma's left leg. Differently from the myth as told in the *Harivaṃśa* 57, *Viṣṇupurāṇa* 5.8, and *Bhāgavatapurāṇa* 10.15.20–40, it would seem that the panel tells us that the donkey, the cruel demon named Dhenuka who had the body of an ass,[165] fallen back to earth and fatally wounded, assumed his

165 HV 57.12ab: *dāruṇo dhenuko nāma daityo gardabharūpavān* |.

anthropomorphic form, just as the buffalo demon, when slain by the Devī, assumed a 'human' form.[166] This interpretation is reinforced by the myth as told in Bhāsa's *Bālacarita*. Though here it is Kṛṣṇa (Dāmodara) who kills the donkey, the latter is said to have changed back into his proper *dānava* (= anthropomorphic?) form before he breathed his last.[167]

PLATE XL B
KṚṢṆA (PLAYING WITH THE MOON), PAUNAR

Paunar, Ashram of Vinobā Bhāve. Basalt stone. 146×122 cm. First half of 6th century AD. Lit.: Gupta 1992; Jamkhedkar 1985, Plate 122; Mirashi 1954, Fig. II; Williams 1983, 229, Plate 17.

This panel was interpreted by Mirashi (1954, 4) as 'the birth of Rāma. The prominent male figure is Daśaratha who has taken the baby in his hands and is looking affectionately at him.' Though he casts doubts on Mirashi's interpretation, Jamkhedkar (1985, 84) does not propose an alternative. Joanna Williams (1983, 229) surmises that it 'may represent Vasudeva transporting the baby to Gokul.' In our view the probably correct identification has been proposed by Chandrashekhar Gupta, who describes the panel as follows.

> The main figure standing in the centre facing right (head mutilated) is shown carrying a child. Two persons are standing on his either [sic] side and a female attendant is seated in the *Garuḍakrama* posture, holding an oval object in her hands in the lower right corner. One of the male figures is an attendant holding the staff of an umbrella and the other is some elderly person in the *varadamudrā*. The scene is described [by Mirashi] as Daśaratha receiving Rāma, brought to him by the female attendant, after the birth. The child does not appear to be a newly born one. On the other hand he looks like a 2–3 years old boy. It can be identified with the story of Kṛishṇa's obstinacy for getting the moon. The oval object in the hands of the female attendant

166 See *Devīmāhātmya* 3.38–39. As we have seen above (n. 104 on p. 131), this appearance of the demon in anthropomorphic form at the moment he is killed is a comparatively late feature in the Mahiṣamardinī iconography. Williams 1983, 229 interprets this sitting figure as a 'spectator,' which is quite unlikely. Jamkhedkar and Gupta do not give an interpretation.

167 *Bālacarita* III, ll. 86–89: *tatra tālavane dhenuko nāma dānavo gardabhaveṣaṃ gṛhītvāgataḥ | tatas tam api jñātvā bhartṛdāmodareṇa tasya vāmapādaṃ gṛhītvotkṣipya pātitāni tālaphalāni | so 'pi dānavo bhūtvā tata eva mṛtaḥ ||*.

> can be identified as a mirror or a pot filled with water to reflect the image of the moon to satisfy Kṛishṇa. (Gupta 1992, 146 f.)

This theme is known from the devotional poetry of the Alvars.[168] It became widespread in North India through the poetry of the *Sūrasāgara* (*Sabhā* 809).

> Again and again, Yaśodā coaxes:
> 'Come, Moon! Moon, my little one's calling you!
> He's going to eat honey and fruit and nuts and sweets,
> and he might give you some too!
> He 'll play with you in his hand, and he won't
> even drop you once;
> Just come down and live in this bowl of water
> I 've got here in my hand ...'
> She set the bowl upon the ground, and took him
> and showed him the moon;
> And Sūr's Lord laughed and dipped his two hands
> again and again and again.[169]

I have been unable to trace this theme in early Sanskrit literature.[170] At variance with Sūrdās' description, the infant Kṛṣṇa in the Paunar relief is held by Nanda, while Yaśodā kneels in front of him to hold the mirror. The two male bystanders in the background may be inhabitants of Gokula.

The apparent unfamiliarity of the classical Northern tradition with the theme and its (later) occurrence in the devotional poetry of the South endorses our argument that the art of Paunar owed its origin to the southern dynasty of the Viṣṇukuṇḍins which succeeded the Vākāṭakas of Nandivardhana; the latter had been orientated towards the culture of the (Gupta) North throughout, as our essay may have demonstrated.

---

168 Notably from the poetry of Periyāḻvār (9th century); the theme became formalized in the *piḷḷaitamiḻ* (Hardy 1983, 406).

169 Translation Bryant 1978, 170.
bāra-bāra jasumati suta bodhati, āu caṃda tohiṃ lāla bulāvai |
madhu-mevā-pakavāna-miṭhāī, āpuna khaihai, tohiṃ khavāvai |
hāthahiṃ para tohiṃ līnhe khelai, naiku nahīṃ dharanī baiṭhāvai |
jala-bāsana kara lai ju uṭhāvati, yāhī maiṃ tū tana dhari āvai |
jalapuṭa āni dharani para rākhyau, gahi ānyau vaha caṃda dikhāvai |
sūradāsa prabhu haṃsi musakyāne, bāra-bāra doū kara nāvaiṃ |.

170 A literary image that comes close to what seems to be expressed in the panel at issue was found in Līlāśuka Bilvamaṅgala's *Kṛṣṇakarṇāmṛta*, Additional Verses (ed. by Frances Wilson, p. 227): *ghaṭodakeṣu pratimāśaśāṅkaṃ vilokya kṛṣṇo navanītabuddhyā* | *ādātum antar nihitāgrahastaḥ pāyāt tadaprāptisamākulo naḥ* ||. Līlāśuka probably also hailed from South India.

Appendices

Vākāṭaka inscription in the Kevala-Narasiṃha Temple on Ramtek Hill

APPENDIX I

The Kevala-Narasiṃha Temple Inscription

(second revised edition)

( ) reading uncertain
⟨ ⟩ editorial addition
◁ vowel part of syllable
◇ consonant part of syllable
⏑ , – and ⏓ : metrical quantity of illegible syllables

---

1 ⟨sa ja⟩(ya)ti sajalāmbudodarā⟨bha⟩(s),
(su)⟨rasa⟩miti ◇rasarājya – na – ⏓ |
⟨ba⟩(l)⟨i⟩(ma)khasamayaidhitāṅga(śo)⟨bho⟩,
⟨ditijavadhū⟩bhayalo⟨la⟩dṛṣṭi(dṛ)⟨ṣṭa⟩ḥ ||1||

(dū)⟨re⟩ṇa ⟨rā⟩jar(ṣ)iSA⟨MUDRAGUPTAḤ⟩,
⏓ – ⏑ – – ⏑ ⏑ – ⏑ – ⏓ |
⏓ – ⏑ – – ⏑ ⏑ – ⏑ – ⏓,
⏓ – ⏑ – – ⏑ ⏑ – ⏑ – ⏓ ||2||

[one verse possibly lost]

2 (tī)⟨kṣṇa⟩(pra)bhāvodgata(pā)da(pī)⟨ṭha-⟩,
(pra)⟨bhā⟩(dh)ṛti(sphā)la(na) – ñci – ◇r ⏓ |
yasyottamāṅgair bbalayo kriyant⟨e⟩,
(pā)de ⟨sa⟩cūḍāmaṇibhir nṛ⟨pāṇām⟩ ||3||

ta(s)yodadhiprānta ⏑ l◁ ⏑ – ⏓,
⏓ – ⏑ – – ⏑ ⏑ – ⏑ – ⏓ |
⏓ – ⏑ – – ⏑ ⏑ – ⏑ – ⏓,
⏓ – ⏑ – – ⏑ ⏑ – ⏑ – ⏓ ||4||

[one verse possibly lost]

---

1. Metre Puṣpitāgrā.

1d. Conjecture *ditijavadhū* proposed by Ms Y. Yokochi.

2–20. Metre Upajāti.

4a. Possibly *palāyamānām* to be construed with hypothetical *senām* in the following pādas.

3 ⟨yā d⟩(e)vateva pratipūjya⟨mān⟩(ā),
pitur gṛ⟨hītā⟩ (pra)ti(ṣ)i(ddha)⟨śakteḥ⟩ |
⟨kanyā yay⟩au vṛd(dhi)ka(ṃ) ⟨sāna⟩lasya,
prājyājyasiktasya śikheva ⟨śuddhā⟩ ||5||

tāṃ – ⏑ nābhyunnata – ⏑ – ⏓ ,
⏓ – ⏑ – – ⏑ ⏑ – ⏑ – ⏓ |
⏓ – ⏑ – – ⏑ ⏑ – ⏑ – ⏓ ,
⏓ – ⏑ – – ⏑ ⏑ – ⏑ – ⏓ ||6||

[*one verse possibly lost*]

4 tayoḫ kramād āhatala(kṣaṇeṣ)u,
jāteṣu ⟨putreṣu guṇā⟩nvite(ṣu) |
y⟨avīya⟩sī candra(ma)saḫ (p)ra(bh)⟨eva⟩,
⟨sā⟩ MUṆḌAnāmnī tana(yā) (ba)⟨bhūva⟩ ||7||

⏓ – ⏑ (lekhā)mi ⏑ – ⏑ – ⏓ ,
⏓ – ⏑ – – ⏑ ⏑ – ⏑ – ⏓ |
⏓ – ⏑ – – ⏑ ⏑ – ⏑ – ⏓ ,
⏓ – ⏑ – – ⏑ ⏑ – ⏑ – ⏓ ||8||

[*one verse possibly lost*]

5 sadaiva devas trisamudranāthas,
sa CANDRAGUP(T)A(Ḫ paripū)rṇ̣ṇa⟨v⟩(ṛ)ttaḥ |
⟨dadau prajā⟩nām adhi(pa)s su⟨tāṃ tā⟩ṃ,
śrī(RU)⟨DRA⟩SENĀYA (g)⟨u⟩ṇā⟨karāya⟩ ||9||

(ve) – ⏑ – (lī) ⏑ ⏑ – ⏑ – ⏓ ,
⏓ – ⏑ – – ⏑ ⏑ – ⏑ – ⏓ |
⏓ – ⏑ – – ⏑ ⏑ – ⏑ – ⏓ ,
⏓ – ⏑ – – ⏑ ⏑ – ⏑ – ⏓ ||10||

[*one verse possibly lost*]

6 sudurvvahāṃ rājyadhuraṃ samagrāṃ,
dhurandharasy(e)⟨va⟩ supuṅgavasya |
⟨prajādhipa⟩(syā) ⏑ ⏑ – ⏑ – ⏓ ,
⟨GHA⟩ṬO⟨TKA⟩CO nāma suto ⟨babhūva⟩ ||11||

⏓ m aṅganāpā ⏑ ⏑ – ⏑ – ⏓ ,
⏓ – ⏑ – – ⏑ ⏑ – ⏑ – ⏓ |
⏓ – ⏑ – – ⏑ ⏑ – ⏑ – ⏓ ,
⏓ – ⏑ – – ⏑ ⏑ – ⏑ – ⏓ ||12||

[*one verse possibly lost*]

7 tām bhāgineyīm atha rājarājo,
dṛ(ṣ)⟨ṭvā⟩⏑ – – ⏑ ⏑ veśmalakṣmī⟨m⟩ |
⏓ – ⏑ – – ⏑ ⏑ – ⏑ – (d)y◁⟨◇⟩,
⟨u⟩pāsya pāṇigrahaṇaṃ cakāra ||13||

devendra(dha)n– ⏑ ⏑ – ⏑ – ◇(ya)m,
amā⟨tya⟩– – ⏑ ⏑ – ⏑ – ⏓ |
⏓ – ⏑ – – ⏑ ⏑ – ⏑ – ⏓ ,
⏓ – ⏑ – – ⏑ ⏑ – ⏑ – ⏓ ||14||

[*one verse possibly lost*]

8 śuddhair vvacobhir vviduṣāṃ man⟨ā⟩(ṃ)⟨si⟩,
⟨pr⟩ī⟨nāti nīlā⟩mburuhekṣaṇā(nām) |
⏓ – ⏑ – – ⏑ ⏑ – ⏑ – ⏓ (s),
sādhūn dhanaughair yyaśasā ca lokān ||15||

(sa) – ⏑ – – ⏑ ⏑ – ⟨ma⟩hīpa,
⏓ – ⏑ – – ⏑ ⏑ – ⏑ – ⏓ |
⏓ – ⏑ – – ⏑ ⏑ – ⏑ – ⏓ ,
⏓ – ⏑ – – ⏑ ⏑ – ⏑ – ⏓ ||16||

[*one verse possibly lost*]

9 tasmin kadācit kamanīyarūpe,
⏓ – ⏑ – – ⏑ purandareṇa |
(t◁) – ⏑ (y◁) – ⏑ ⏑ – (s sa)mānāṃ,
bhrātā balāt svaṃ gṛham ā(ni)nāya ||17||

⏓ – ⏑ – – ⏑ ⏑ – ⏑ – ⏓ ,
⏓ – ⏑ – – ⏑ ⏑ – ⏑ – ⏓ |
⏓ – ⏑ – – ⏑ ⏑ – ⏑ – ⏓ ,
⏓ – ⏑ – – ⏑ ⏑ – ⏑ – ⏓ ||18||

[*one verse possibly lost*]

10 tatraiva yān yān manujendrapu(t)rī,
⟨yatnān sva⟩dha⟨rmapra⟩savān akā⟨rṣ⟩īt |
⏓ – ⏑ – – ⏑ ⏑ – ⏑ – ⏓,
⏓ – (ṇa teṣāṃ) ⏑ ⏑ bhāgam etaṃ ||19||

⏓ – ⏑ – – ⏑ ⏑ – ⏑ – ⏓,
⏓ – ⏑ – – ⏑ ⏑ – ⏑ – ⏓ |
⏓ – ⏑ – – ⏑ ⏑ – ⏑ – ⏓,
⏓ – ⏑ – – ⏑ ⏑ – ⏑ – ⏓ ||20||

[*one verse possibly lost*]

11 PRABHĀVATISVĀMINAṂ ca, lokanā⟨tha⟩m a(th)ā(la)⟨ye⟩ |
puṇyam akṣayam uddiśya, (mā)⟨tuḥ⟩ ⏓ ⏓ ⟨a⟩k⟨ā⟩raya⟨t⟩ ||21||

⏓ ⏓ ⏓ ⏓ ⏓ ⏓ ⏓ ⏓, jagadut⟨pa⟩(tti)nā ⏑ ⏓ |
⏓ ⏓ ⏓ ⏓ ⏓ ⏓ ⏓ ⏓, ⏓ ⏓ ⏓ ⏓ ⏑ – ⏑ ⏓ ||22||

⏓ ⏓ ⏓ ⏓ ⏓ ⏓ ⏓ ⏓, ⏓ ⏓ ⏓ ⏓ ⏑ – ⏓ |
⏓ ⏓ ⏓ ⏓ ⏓ ⏓ ⏓ ⏓, ⏓ ⏓ ⏓ ⏓ ⏑ – ⏑ ⏓ ||23||

[*one verse possibly lost*]

12 sudarśanaṃ taḍāgaṃ ca, deva(ñ) caiva sudar⟨śana⟩m |
kadalīvāṭakagrāme, kārayit⟨v⟩ĀTI⟨BHĀ⟩VATĪ ||24||

⏓ ⏓ ⏓ – (pī)takeśā, puṇyam u⟨ddiśya⟩– ⏑ ⏓ |
⏓ ⏓ ⏓ ⏓ ⏓ ⏓ ⏓ ⏓, (pā) ⏓ ⏓ ⏓ ⏑ – ⏑ ⏓ ||25||

⏓ ⏓ ⏓ ⏓ ⏓ ⏓ ⏓ ⏓, ⏓ ⏓ ⏓ ⏓ ⏑ – ⏓ |
⏓ ⏓ ⏓ ⏓ ⏓ ⏓ ⏓ ⏓, ⏓ ⏓ ⏓ ⏓ ⏑ – ⏑ ⏓ ||26||

[*one verse possibly lost*]

13 arddhaṃ brahmārppa⟨ṇaṃ⟩ puṇyaṃ, ◇ṛ ⏓ ⏓ ⏓ ṇa⟨śāli⟩nī |
mātāpitṛbhy⟨ām arddhaṃ ca⟩, ⏓ ⏓ ⏓ ⏓ ◇kr⟨i⟩yodbhavam **||** 27||

jagatas (sth)i⟨t⟩isaṅhārakāraṇasyā⟨m⟩itauja⟨saḥ⟩ |
(ā)rṣ⟨a⟩(d)◁ ⏓ ⏓ ⏓ ⏓ ⏓ ⏓, ⏓ ⏓ ⏓ ⏓ ⏑ – ⏑ ⏓ ||28||

21–34. Metre Śloka.

21d. Possibly *mātuḥ śubham akārayat* or *mātuḥ svayam akārayat*.

⏓ ⏓ ⏓ ⏓ ⏓ ⏓ ⏓ ⏓, ⏓ ⏓ ⏓ ⏓ ⏑ – ⏓ |
⏓ ⏓ ⏓ ⏓ ⏓ ⏓ ⏓ ⏓, ⏓ ⏓ ⏓ ⏓ ⏑ – ⏑ ⏓ ||29||

[*one verse possibly lost*]

14 prāsādaṃ dayi – – tur, vvicintya tam aśāśvatam |
mātur eva samuddi⟨śya⟩, ⟨pu⟩ṇyaugham aghavarjjitā ||30||

śil⟨ā⟩ ⏓ ◇(śi)lasaṅ⟨k⟩āśaṃ, (ci)rā(ya) ⏑ ⏑ – ⏑ ⏓ |
⏓ ⏓ ⏓ ⏓ ⏓ ⏓ ⏓ ⏓, ⏓ ⏓ ⏓ ⏓ ⏑ – ⏑ ⏓ ||31||

⏓ ⏓ ⏓ ⏓ ⏓ ⏓ ⏓ ⏓, ⏓ ⏓ ⏓ ⏓ ⏑ – ⏑ ⏓ |
⏓ ⏓ ⏓ ⏓ ⏓ ⏓ ⏓ ⏓, ⏓ ⏓ ⏓ ⏓ ⏑ – ⏑ ⏓ ||32||

[*one verse possibly lost*]

15 ālokasthāyinī(ñ ce)māṅ, kīrttim prakhyāpayiṣyatā |
tayā ⟨pari⟩gṛhī⟨te⟩na, tadājñānuvidhā⟨yin⟩ā ||33||

kāvya⟨ṃ ma⟩haj jay(a) ⏓ (daṃ), ⏓ ⏓ ⏓ ⏓ ⏑ gena (ca) |
⏓ ⏓ ⏓ ⏓ ⏓ ⏓ ⏓ ⏓, ⏓ ⏓ ⏓ ⏓ ⏑ – ⏑ ⏓ ||34||

[*one or two verses possibly lost*]

30a. *dayitādhātur* conjectured in Bakker & Isaacson 1993, 54.

Appendix II

Genealogy

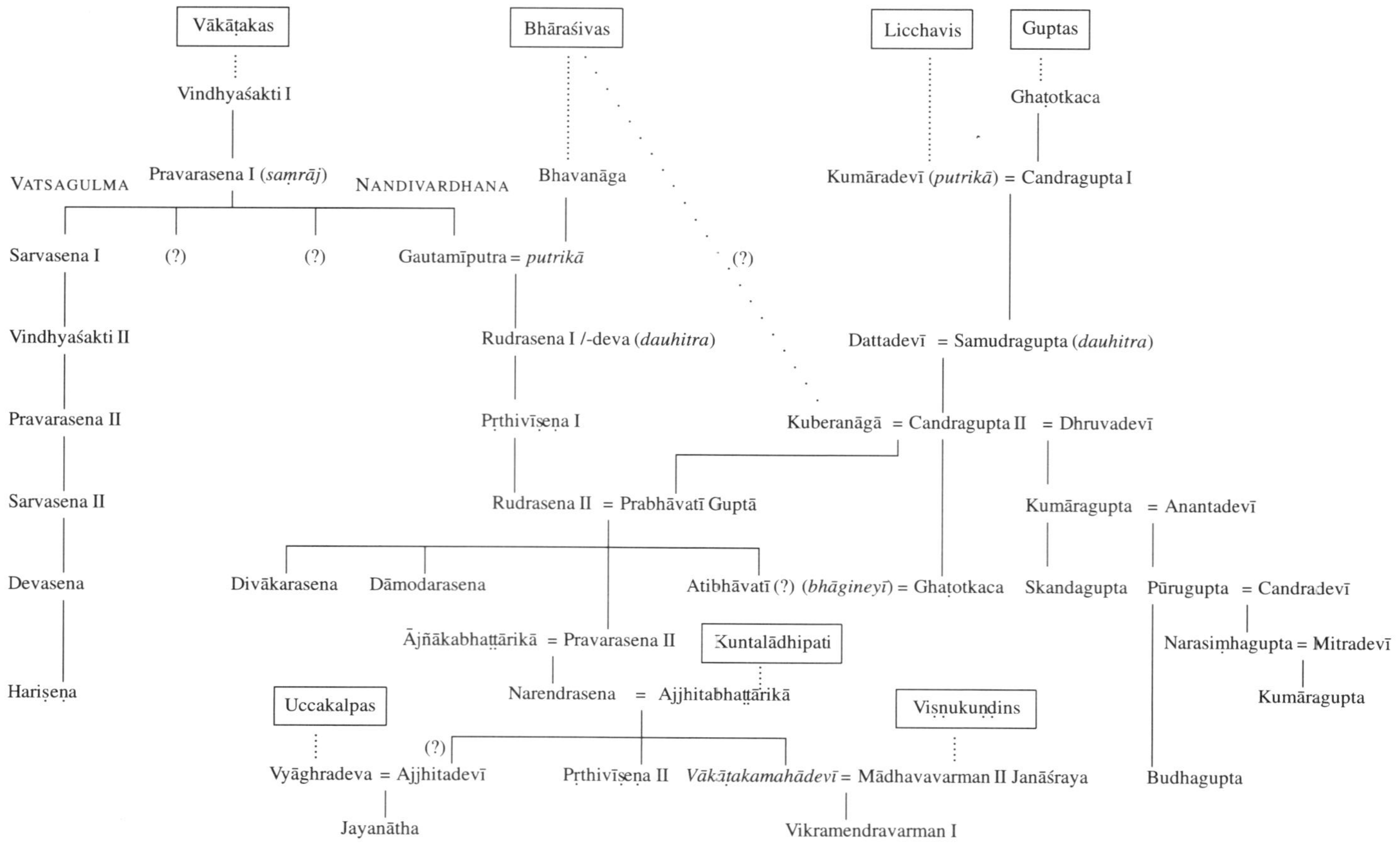

Vākāṭakas
Vindhyaśakti I
Pravarasena I (*saṃrāj*)
Vatsagulma
Nandivardhana
Sarvasena I
(?)
(?)
Gautamīputra = *putrikā*
Vindhyaśakti II
Pravarasena II
Sarvasena II
Devasena
Hariṣeṇa
Bhāraśivas
Bhavanāga
(?)
Rudrasena I /-deva (*dauhitra*)
Pṛthivīṣeṇa I
Rudrasena II = Prabhāvatī Guptā
Divākarasena
Dāmodarasena
Atibhāvatī (?) (*bhāgineyī*) = Ghaṭotkaca
Ājñākabhaṭṭārikā = Pravarasena II
Narendrasena = Ajjhitabhaṭṭārikā
Kuntalādhipati
Uccakalpas
Vyāghradeva = Ajjhitadevī
(?)
Jayanātha
Pṛthivīṣeṇa II
Vākāṭakamahādevī = Mādhavavarman II Janāśraya
Vikramendravarman I
Viṣṇukuṇḍins
Licchavis
Guptas
Ghaṭotkaca
Kumāradevī (*putrikā*) = Candragupta I
Dattadevī = Samudragupta (*dauhitra*)
Kuberanāgā = Candragupta II = Dhruvadevī
Kumāragupta = Anantadevī
Skandagupta
Pūrugupta = Candradevī
Narasiṃhagupta = Mitradevī
Kumāragupta
Budhagupta

APPENDIX III

Outline of Vākāṭaka Chronology*

AD 275–335	Rule of Pravarasena I in Kāñcana(kā) (Bundelkhand).
AD 335–360	Rule of Rudrasena I.
AD 350 / 360	Samudragupta vanquishes alliance of Nāgas and Vākāṭakas. Migration of Vākāṭakas to Vidarbha; settlement in Vatsagulma and Nandivardhana.
AD 360–395	Rule of Pṛthivīṣeṇa I in Nandivardhana.
AD 360–400	Rule of Vindhyaśakti II in Vatsagulma.
AD 376–415	Rule of Candragupta II in Āryāvarta.
c. 388	Wedding of Rudrasena II and Prabhāvatī Guptā.
AD 395–405	Rule of Rudrasena II in Nandivardhana.
AD 400–450	Rule of Pravarasena II and Sarvasena II in Vatsagulma (subordinate to Nandivardhana).
AD 405–419	Prabhāvatī Guptā acting monarch of the Vākāṭakas of Nandivardhana.
AD 415 / 419	Wedding of Prabhāvatī Guptā's daughter (Atibhāvatī?) with uncle Ghaṭotkaca.
AD 415–454	Ghaṭotkaca Gupta viceroy in Vidiśā.
AD 415–454	Rule of Kumāragupta in Āryāvarta.
AD 419–422	Rule of Dāmodarasena in Nandivardhana.

* With only a few certain (absolute) dates to go by, presenting a chronology is a very hazardous affair. The following dates are therefore to be considered to be merely conjectural and are to be qualified by 'about'-s and question marks, which have been omitted only not to encumber the schedule too much. In cases where I found it particularly bold to pin down an event in a certain year I have prefixed a *circa* (c.). The following dates are inferred from a reasoned reconstruction of the sequence of events that makes up Vākāṭaka history.

AD 422–457	Rule of Pravarasena II in Nandivardhana/Pravarapura.
c. AD 443	Death of Prabhāvatī Guptā.
AD 445	First intrusion of Pravarasena II into Gupta territory (Tripurī).
AD 450–460	Rule of Devasena in Vatsagulma.
AD 454–455	Succession war in the Gupta kingdom between Ghaṭotkaca and Skandagupta, resulting in death of Ghaṭotkaca and accession of Skandagupta in AD 455. Pravarasena intervenes in Gupta civil war, marches on Malwa (Vidiśā) and brings his sister (Atibhāvatī) back to Nandivardhana.
AD 455–469	Rule of Skandagupta in Āryāvarta.
AD 456/457	Building of the Kevala-Narasiṃha Temple on the Rāmagiri and a storage reservoir Sudarśana in Kadalīvāṭaka.
AD 457-461	Independent rule of Narendrasena in Nandivardhana.
AD 457–470	Drain of officials and craftsmen from Nandivardhana to Vatsagulma.
Śaka 380 = AD 457/8	Building of storage reservoir Sudarśana in Hisse-Borala near Vatsagulma.
AD 460–478	Rule of Hariṣeṇa in Vatsagulma.
c. AD 461–462	Hariṣeṇa subjects Aśmaka, Anūpa and Nandivardhana.
AD 461–475	Narendrasena rules in Nandivardhana, subordinate to Vatsagulma.
c. AD 462	Beginning of the excavation of Ajanta Cave XVI.
c. AD 465	Beginning of the excavation of Ajanta Caves XVII and XIX.
AD 470–490	Rule of Uccakalpa king Vyāghradeva in Kāñcana(kā) (Nachna).
AD 470–518	Rule of Viṣṇukuṇḍin king Mādhavavarman II Janāśraya.
c. AD 475	Pṛthivīṣeṇa II succeeds Narendrasena in Nandivardhana.

AD 478–480	Aśmaka subdues Vatsagulma; Anūpa and Nandivardhana assert independence.
AD 478–495	Independent rule of Pṛthivīṣeṇa II in Nandivardhana.
c. AD 493	War between Pṛthivīṣeṇa II and Nala king Bhavadattavarman. Viṣṇukuṇḍin king Mādhavavarman II Janāśraya comes to the help of the Vākāṭakas.
AD 495–518	Viṣṇukuṇḍin king Mādhavavarman II Janāśraya rules over Vākāṭaka estate (Vidarbha).
AD 518/19	Nala king Arthapati Bhaṭṭāraka, grandson of Bhavadattavarman, conquers Nandivardhana.

Bibliography & Indexes

Bibliography

Abbreviations

ABORI	Annals of the Bhandarkar Oriental Research Institute
AitBr	*Aitareyabrāhmaṇa*
ASI	Archaeological Survey of India
ASWI	Archaeologial Survey of Western India
AV	The Age of the Vākāṭakas (Shastri 1992)
BhG	*Bhagavadgītā*
BhP	*Bhāgavatapurāṇa*
BS	*Bṛhatsaṃhitā* (Varāhamihira)
BSOAS	Bulletin of the School of Oriental and African Studies
CII	Corpus Inscriptionum Indicarum
EI	Epigraphia Indica
EITA	Encyclopaedia of Indian Temple Architecture
HV	*Harivaṃśa*
IAR	Indian Archaeological Review
IHQ	Indian Historical Quarterly
IIJ	Indo-Iranian Journal
IRP	Indological Research Papers (Mirashi 1982)
JAOS	Journal of the American Oriental Society
JESI	Journal of the Epigraphical Society of India
JIH	Journal of Indian History
JISOA	Journal of the Indian Society of Oriental Art
JNSI	Journal of the Numismatic Society of India
JRAS	Journal of the Royal Asiatic Society
KūP	*Kūrmapurāṇa*
LiP	*Liṅgapurāṇa*
MBh	*Mahābhārata*, Critical Edition
MP	*Matsyapurāṇa*
PPL	*Purāṇapañcalakṣaṇa*
PW	*Sanskrit Wörterbuch*. St Petersburg 1855–1875. 7 Bde
Rām.	*Rāmāyaṇa*, Critical Edition
RGH	Reappraising Gupta History (Chhabra *et alii* 1992)
ṚV	*Ṛgveda*
ŚBr	*Śatapathabrāhmaṇa*
Sel. Ins.	Select Inscriptions (Sircar 1942)
SI	Studies in Indology (Mirashi 1960–62)

ŚiP	*Śivapurāṇa*
SP	*Skandapurāṇa* (original text of that name, see SP_{Bh})
SP_{Bh}	*Skandapurāṇa*, edit. by K. P. Bhaṭṭarāī
SŚP	*Somaśambhupaddhati* (Brunner-Lachaux 1963)
TaiĀ	*Taittirīyāraṇyaka*
TaiBr	*Taittirīyabrāhmaṇa*
TaiSa	*Taittirīyasaṃhitā*
VāP	*Vāyupurāṇa*
VDhP	*Viṣṇudharmottarapurāṇa*
VmP	*Vāmanapurāṇa*
WZKSA	Wiener Zeitschrift für die Kunde Südasiens

References

Abhinavagupta

Parātrīśikālaghuvṛtti. Edit. by Jagaddhara Zādoo Shāstri. Srinagar 1947. Kashmir Series of Texts and Studies No. LXVIII.

Tantrāloka. With Commentary by Rājānaka Jayaratha. Edit. with notes by M. R. Shāstrī and M. K. Shāstrī. Allahabad 1918–1938. 12 vols. Kashmir Series of Texts and Studies.

Adriaensen, R. & H. T. Bakker & H. Isaacson

1994 Towards a Critical Edition of the Skandapurāṇa. in: IIJ 37, 325–331.

Agrawal, Ashvini

1989 Rise and Fall of the Imperial Guptas. Delhi.

Agrawala, R. C.

1969 *Kṛittikā* cult in early Indian sculpture. in: Lalit Kalā 14, 56–57.

1971 Mātṛkā Reliefs in Early Indian Art. in: East and West XXI, 79–89.

Agrawala, Vasudeva S.

1966 Śiva Mahādeva. The great God [An exposition of the symbolism of Śiva]. Varanasi.

Ajanta IV

1955 Ajanta. The colour and monochrome reproductions of the Ajanta Frescoes based on photography. With an explanatory Text by G. Yazdani and Appendices on the Painted and Incised Inscriptions by N. P. Chakravarti and B. C. Chhabra. Part IV: Text. London, etc. [→ Yazdani 1930–55].

Allan, John

1914 Catalogue of the coins of he Gupta Dynasties and of Śaśāṅka, king of Gauḍa. London. A Catalogue of the Indian coins in the British Museum.

1936 Catalogue of the coins of Ancient India. London. A Catalogue of the Indian coins in the British Museum.

Altekar, A. S.

1957 The Coinage of the Gupta Empire (and its imitations). Varanasi. Corpus of Indian Coins Vol. 4.

1959 The Position of Women in *Hindu Civilization* from prehistoric times to the present day. Second edition: Delhi.

Amarakośa

The Amarakośa with the unpublished South Indian Commentaries *Amarapadavivṛti* of Liṅgaśūrin and the *Amarapadaparijāta* of Mallinātha. Crit. ed. with Introduction by A. A. Ramanathan. Madras 1971–83. 3 vols. The Adyar Library Series Vol. 101.

Archaeologial Survey of Western India

Vol. IV. Report on the Buddhist Cave Temples and Their Inscriptions. Being part of the fourth, fifth and sixth seasons operations of the Archaeological Survey of Western India 1876–77, 1877–78, 1878–79. By Jas. Burgess. Supplementary to the Volume on "The Cave Temples of India." London 1883.

Aryan, K. C.

1980 The Little Goddesses (Mātṛkās). New Delhi.

Asher, Frederick M.

1983 Historical and Political Allegory in Gupta Art. in: B. L. Smith (ed.) 1983, 53–66.

Avasthi, R.

1975 Two unique Sadāśiva images of Khajuraho. in: JIH 53, 211–215.

Bajpai, K. D.

s.d. Sagar through the ages.

Bajpai, K. D. & S. K. Pandey

1977 Malhār 1975–77[8]. Sagar.

Bakker, Hans T.

1986 Ayodhyā. Groningen. Groningen Oriental Studies I.

1987 Reflections on the Evolution of Rāma Devotion in the Light of Textual and Archaeological Evidence. in: WZKSA XXXI, 9–42.

1989a The Ramtek Inscriptions [I]. in: BSOAS LII.3, 467–496.

1989b The Antiquities of Ramtek Hill (Maharashtra). in: Journal of South Asian Studies 5, 79–102.

1990 Ramtek: An Ancient Centre of Viṣṇu Devotion in Maharashtra. in: H. T. Bakker (ed.), The History of Sacred Places in India as Reflected in Traditional Literature. Panels of the VIIth World Sanskrit Conference Vol. III. Leiden, 62–85.

1991 The Footprints of the Lord. in: D. L. Eck & F. Mallison (eds.), Devotion Divine. Bhakti Traditions from the Regions of India. Studies in Honour of Charlotte Vaudeville. Groningen, 19–37.

1992a Throne and Temple. Political Power and Religious Prestige in Vidarbha. in: H. T. Bakker (ed.), The Sacred Centre as the Focus of Political Interest. Groningen, 83–100.

1992b Memorials, Temples, Gods, and Kings. An Attempt to Unravel the Symbolic Texture of Vākāṭaka Kingship. in: A. W. van den Hoek, D. H. A. Kolff, M. S. Oort (eds.), Ritual, State and History in South Asia. Essays in Honour of J. C. Heesterman. Leiden etc., 7–19.

1992c The Manbhaus' Seat on Ramtek Hill. in: R. S. McGregor (ed.), Devotional Literature in South Asia: Current Research, 1985–88. Cambridge, 11–25.

1993 A Newly Found Statue from Nagardhan. in: A. J. Gail & G. J. R. Mevissen (eds.), South Asian Archæology 1991. Stuttgart, 303–311.

1994 Observations on the History and Culture of Dakṣiṇa Kosala (5th to 7th centuries AD). in: Nalini Balbir & J. K. Bautze (eds.), Festschrift Klaus Bruhn. Reinbek, 1–66.

1996 Pārvatī's Svayaṃvara (Studies in the Skandapurāṇa I). in: WZKSA XL, 5–43.

forthcoming a An Enigmatic Giant from Tala. in: L. S. Nigam (ed.), On the Image of Śiva from Tālā.

forthcoming b Rāma's Footstep: The Tradition of Rāmagiri. in: Proceedings of the XIIth International Rāmāyaṇa Conference. Leiden, August 28–30, 1995.

Bakker, Hans & Harunaga Isaacson

1993 The Ramtek Inscriptions II: The Vākāṭaka Inscription in the Kevala-Narasiṃha Temple. in: BSOAS LVI.1, 46–74.

Banerjea, Jitendra Nath

1942 The Holy Pañcavīras of the Vṛṣṇis. in: JISOA X, 65–68.

1944 Images of Sāmba. in: JISOA XI, 129–134.

1945–46 Hindu Iconography. I Viṣṇu. in: JISOA XIII (1945), 55–129. II Vyūhas and Vibhavas of Viṣṇu. in: JISOA XIV (1946), 1–74.

1948 Sūrya. Ādityas and the Navagrahas. in: JISOA XVI, 47–100.

1956 The Development of Hindu Iconography. Calcutta. [Reprinted by Munshiram Manoharlal, third edition: New Delhi 1974].

1968 Religion in Art and Archaeology (Vaiṣṇavism and Śaivism). Lucknow. Dr. Radha Kumud Mookerji Endowment Lectures, University of Lucknow 1961–62.

Banerji, Rakhal Das

1924 The Temple of Śiva at Bhumara. Calcutta. Memoirs of the ASI XVI.

Bautze, J.

1987 A Note on two Mātṛkā Panels. in: M. Yaldiz & W. Lobo (eds.), Investigating Indian Art. Museum für indische Kunst. Berlin, 25–30.

Beglar, J. D.

1873–74 Report of a Tour in the Central Provinces 1873–74: Ramtek. in: ASI Reports by Alexander Cunningham and others (Old Series) VII, 109–115.

Berkson, Carmel
1978 Some New Finds at Ramgarth Hill, Vidisha District. in: Artibus Asiae XL.2/3, 215–232.
1986 The Caves at Aurangabad. Early Buddhist Tantric Art in India. Text and Photographs by Carmel Berkson. Ahmedabad/New York.

Bhagavadgītā
The Bhagavad Gītā translated and interpreted by Franklin Edgerton. Cambridge (Mass.) 1972.

Bhandarkar, R. G.
1913 Vaiṣṇavism, Śaivism and Minor Religious Systems. Strassburg. Grundriss der Indo-Arischen Philologie und Altertumskunde III.6.

Bhāsa
Bhāsanāṭakacakram. Plays ascribed to Bhāsa. Original thirteen texts in Devanāgarī. Critically edited by C. R. Devadhar. Poona, 1962.

Bhattacharya, Gouriswar
1977 Nandin and Vṛṣabha. in: ZDMG Suppl. III.2 (XIX. Deutscher Orientalistentag, Freiburg), 1545–1567.
1980 Stūpa as Maitreya's Emblem. in: A. L. Dallapiccola & S. Zingel-Avé Lallemant (eds.), The Stupa. Its Religious, Historical and Architectural Significance. Wiesbaden, 100–111. Beiträge zur Südasienforschung 55.
1989 Deva: Caturmukha-Pañcamukha: Brahmā and Śiva: Śilpa-śāstras and art-objects. in: A. L. Dallapiccola (ed.), Shastric Traditions in Indian Arts. Stuttgart. 2 vols. Vol. I, 51–70.

Bolon, Carol Radcliffe
1992 Forms of the Goddess Lajjā Gaurī in Indian Art. Pennsylvania.

Brown, Robert L.
1991 Ganesh. Studies of an Asian God. New York.
1991a Gaṇeśa in Southeast Asian Art: Indian Connections and Indigenous Developments. in: R. L. Brown (ed.), Ganesh. Studies of an Asian God. New York, 171–233.

Brunner-Lachaux, Hélène
1963 Le rituel quotidien dans la tradition śivaïte de l'Inde du Sud selon Somaśambhu. *Somaśambhupaddhati.* Première Partie. Traduction, Introduction et Notes. Pondichéry. Publications de l'Institut Français d'Indologie No. 25.

Bryant, Kenneth E.
1978 Poems of the Child God: Structures and Strategies in the Poetry of Sūrdās. Berkeley/Los Angeles.

Buddhist Hybrid Sanskrit Grammar and Dictionary
Vol. II Dictionary. By Franklin Edgerton. New Haven 1953.

Burgess, James
1883 = Archeaological Survey of Western India, Vol. IV.
1970 The Rock Temples of Ajanta. Second edition: New York.

Chhabra, B. Ch. & P. K. Agrawala & Ashvini Agrawal & Shankar Goyal (eds.)
1992 Reappraising Gupta History for S. R. Goyal. New Delhi.
Coburn, Thomas B.
1991 Encountering the Goddess. A Translation of the Devī-Māhātmya and a Study of Its Interpretation. New York. SUNY Series in Hindu Studies.
Collins, Charles Dillard
1988 The Iconography and Ritual of Śiva at Elephanta. New York.
Coomaraswamy, Anand K.
1928 Yakṣas. I & II. Washington. [Reprinted by Munshiram Manoharlal, Delhi 1980.]
1978 Catalogue of the Indian Collections in the Museum of Fine Arts, Boston. Delhi (reprint).
Corpus Inscriptionum Indicarum
1888 Vol. III. Inscriptions of the Early Gupta Kings and their Successors. Edited by J. F. Fleet. Calcutta. [= CII III (1888)].
1981 Vol. III. Inscriptions of the Early Gupta Kings. Revised by Devadatta Ramakrishna Bhandarkar. Edited by Bahadurchand Chhabra & Govind Swamirao Gai. New Delhi. [= CII III].
1963 Vol. V. Inscriptions of the Vākāṭakas. Edited by Vasudev Vishnu Mirashi. Ootacamund. [= Mirashi 1963].
Cousens, H.
1905 Ramtek. in: Archaeology. Progress Report of the Archaeological Survey of Western India for the year ending 30th June 1905, 41.
Critical Pāli Dictionary
Begun by V. Trenckner. Revised, continued, and edited by Dines Andersen and others. Copenhagen 1924–.
Cunningham, Alexander
1871–87 Archaeological Survey of India. Reports by ~ and others. (Old Series). Simla, Calcutta. 23 vols.
Dallapiccola, Anne Libera (ed.)
1989 (In collaboration with Christine Walter-Mendy and Stephanie Zingel-Avé Lallemant). Shastric Traditions in Indian Arts. I Texts. II References and Documentation. Wiesbaden. 2 vols. Beiträge zur Südasienforschung 125.
Daṇḍin
Daśakumāracarita. Text with Sanskrit Commentary, Various Readings, A literal English Translation, Explanatory and Critical Notes, and an Exhaustive Introduction [by] M. R. Kāle. Fourth edition: Delhi 1966.
Darian, Steven
1976 The Other Face of the Makara. in: Artibus Asiae 38, 29–34.
Dasgupta, S. N. & S. K. De
1947 A History of Sanskrit Literature, Classical Period. Vol. 1. Calcutta.
Davis, Richard H.
1991 Ritual in an Oscillating Universe. Worshiping Śiva in Medieval India. Princeton.

DeCaroli, Robert
1995 An Analysis of Daṇḍin's Daśakumāracarita and its Implications for both the Vākāṭaka and Pallava Courts. in: JAOS (1995), 671–678.
Deglurkar, G. B.
1982 Maṇḍhal Yethīl Aṣṭamūrti Pratimā. in: Vidarbha Saṃśodhana Maṇḍaḷa Vārṣika.
1983 Tripurāntaka Śivamūrti. in: Vidarbha Saṃśodhana Maṇḍaḷa Vārṣika.
1992 Vilakṣaṇa Śiva's. in: Purātan 8, 29–31.
Deo, S. B.
1975–76 A Unique Sculpture from Mansar (Maharashtra). in: Journal of the Andhra Historical Research Society (Sri Mallampalli Somasekhara Sarma Commemoration Volume) Vol. XXXV, 275–277.
Deo, S. B. & J. P. Joshi (eds.)
1972 Pauni Excavations (1969–70). Nagpur.
Deo, Shantaram Bhalchandra & Madhukar Keshav Dhavalikar
1968 Paunar Excavation (1967). Nagpur.
Desai, Devangana
1973 Iconography of Vishnu (in Northern India, Upto The Mediaeval Period). New Delhi.
1984 Placement and Significance of Erotic Sculptures at Khajuraho. in: M. W. Meister (ed.), Discourses on Śiva. Bombay, 143–155.
1988 Sadāshiva Catushpāda Images of Khajuraho. in: Purātattva.
Dev, Krishna
1988 Pāṇḍuvāṃśīs of Śrīpura and Nalas. Varieties of North Indian Style: Dakṣiṇa Kōsala style, c. late sixth–early eighth century AD. in: EITA II.1, 219–250.
Devīmāhātmya
Devī-Māhātmyam. The Glorification of the Great Goddess. (Edit. by Vasudeva S. Agrawala) Ramnagar, Varanasi 1968.
Dhaky, M. A.
1984 Bhūtas and Bhūtanāyakas: Elementals and their Captains. in: M. W. Meister (ed.), Discourses on Śiva. Bombay, 240–256.
Ḍhavaḷīkar, Madhukar Keśava
1966 Pavnār yethīl Andhakāsuravadhamūrtī. in: Vidarbha Saṃśodhana Maṇḍaḷa Vārṣika, 49–58.
1968 New Inscriptions from Ajaṇṭā. in: Ars Orientalis VII, 147–153.
1973 Ajanta: A Cultural Study. Poona.
Divakaran, Odile
1984 Durgā the Great Goddess: Meanings and Forms in the Early Period. in: M. W. Meister (ed.), Discourses on Śiva. Bombay, 271–288.
Donaldson, Thomas E.
1987 Hindu Temple Art of Orissa. Vol. III. Leiden. Studies in South Asian Culture XII.

Encyclopaedia of Indian Temple Architecture
1988 North India. Foundations of North Indian Style. c. 250 BC–A.D. 1100. Edited by M. W. Meister, M. A. Dhaky, K. Deva. Delhi. 2 Vols. [= EITA Vol. II Pt. 1].

Entwistle, A. W.
1987 Braj. Centre of Kṛṣṇa Pilgrimage. Groningen. Groningen Oriental Studies III.

Eschmann, A.
1978 The Vaiṣṇava Typology of Hinduization and the Origin of Jagannātha. in: A. Eschmann, H. Kulke, G. Ch. Tripathi (eds.), The Cult of Jagannath and the Regional Tradition of Orissa. New Delhi, 99–117.

Fergusson, James & James Burgess
1880 The Cave Temples of India. London.

Foucher, A.
1905 L'Art Gréco-bouddhique du Gandhâra: Étude sur les origines de l'influence classique dans l'art bouddhique de l'Inde et de l'Extrême-Orient. Paris. Publications de EFEO V.

Ghosh, A. (ed.)
1989 An Encyclopaedia of Indian Archaeology. Vol. 1: Subjects. Vol. 2: A Gazetteer of explored and excavated sites in India. New Delhi. 2 vols.

Gonda, J.
1954 Aspects of Early Viṣṇuism. Utrecht. [Reprinted by Motilal Banarsidass, New Delhi 1969].
1970 Viṣṇuism and Śivaism. A Comparison. London.
1977 Medieval Religious Literature in Sanskrit. Wiesbaden. A History of Indian Literature Vol. II Fasc. 1.

Govinda, L. G.
1979 Tibet in Pictures. Volume I, Expedition to Central Tibet. Berkeley.

Goyal, S. R.
1967 A History of the Imperial Guptas. With a Foreword by R. C. Majumdar. Allahabad.
1988 Gupta aur Vākāṭaka Sāmrājyoṃ kā Yuga. Meerut.

Granoff, Phyllis
1979 Maheśvara/Mahākāla: a Unique Buddhist Image from Kaśmīr. in: Artibus Asiae XLI, 64–82.

Gupta, Chandrashekhar
1992 Paunar under the Vākāṭakas. in: AV, 119–153.

Gupta, Parmeshwari Lal
1974–79 The Imperial Guptas. Vol. I (Sources, Historiography & Political History). Vol. II (Cultural History). Varanasi. 2 vols.

Gupte, Ramesh Shankar & B. D. Mahajan
1962 Ajanta, Ellora and Aurangabad Caves. Bombay.

Hacker, Paul
1960 Prahlāda. Werden und Wandlungen einer Idealgestalt. Beiträge zur Geschichte des Hinduismus, Teil I & II. Wiesbaden. Akademie der Wissenschaften und der Literatur in Mainz. Abhandlungen der geistes- und sozialwissenschaftlichen Klasse, Jahrgang 1959 Nrs. 9, 13.

Hara, Minoru
1958 Nakulīśa–Pāśupata–Darśanam. in: IIJ II, 8–32.

Haracaritacintāmaṇi
Edit. by Śivadatta and Kāśīnāth Pāṇḍurang Parab. Bombay 1897. Kāvyamālā 61.

Hardy, Friedhelm
1983 Viraha-Bhakti. The Early History of Kṛṣṇa Devotion in South India. Oxford, New York.

Harivaṃśa
The Harivaṃśa being the Khila or supplement to the Mahābhārata. For the first time critically edited by P. L. Vaidya. Poona 1969–71. 2 vols.

Harle, J. C.
1974 Gupta Sculpture. Indian Sculpture of the Fourth to the Sixth Centuries A.D. Oxford.

1987 The 'Pleated' *Śiraścakra*. in: N. Rao (ed.), Kusumāñjali. C. Sivaramamurti Commemoration Volume II. Delhi, 234–237.

Harper, Katherine Anne
1989 Seven Hindu Goddesses of Spiritual Transformation. The Iconography of the Saptamatrikas. Lewiston/Queenston/Lampeter. Studies in Women and Religion Vol. 28.

Harṣacarita
of Bāṇa. Edited by P. V. Kane. Bombay 1918. [Reprint: Delhi 1965].

Härtel, Herbert
1993 Excavations at Sonkh. 2500 years of a town in Mathura District. With contributions by Hans-Jürgen Paech and Rolf Weber. Berlin.

Harting, Nicolaas Ubbo
1922 Selections from the *Baudhāyana-Gṛhyapariśiṣṭasūtra*. Amersfoort. Ph. D. Thesis, Rijksuniversiteit Utrecht.

Hiralal, Rai Bahadur
1908 A Visit to Ramtek. in: Indian Antiquary 37, 202–208.

Huntington, John C.
1989 Mathurā Evidence for the Early Teachings of Mahāyāna. in: D. M. Srinivasan (ed.), Mathurā. The Cultural Heritage. New Delhi, 85–92.

Huntington, Susan L.
1985 The Art of Ancient India. Buddhist, Hindu, Jain. With Contributions by John C. Huntington. New York, Tokyo.

In the Image of Man
The Indian perception of the Universe through 2000 years of painting and sculpture. Hayward Gallery, London 1982. Catalogue.

Jaiswal, Suvira

1967 The Origin and Development of Vaiṣṇavism (Vaiṣṇavism from 200 BC to AD 500). Delhi.

Jamkhedkar, A. P.

1985a Buddhist Bronzes from Ramtek. in: Lalit Kalā 22, 13–19.

1985b Narrative Sculptures from Paunar: A Reappraisal. in: A. Gay (ed.), Indian Epigraphy. New Delhi, 83–86.

1985–86 Ancient Structures. in: Mārg (Maharashtra. Religious and Secular Architecture) XXXVII No. 1, 25–36.

1987a A Newly Discovered Vakataka Temple at Ramtek, Dist. Nagpur. in: Nagaraja Rao (ed.), Kusumāñjali. C. Sivaramamurti Commemoration Volume I. Delhi, 217–223.

1987b Vaiṣṇavism in the Vakataka Times. in: Ratan Parimoo (ed.), Vaiṣṇavism in Indian Arts and Culture. New Delhi, 335–341.

1988 Beginnings of North Indian Style: Early Vidarbha Style, c. AD 350–500. Vākāṭakas (Main Branch). in: EITA II.1, 59–72.

1991a Vākāṭaka Sculpture. in: R. Parimoo *et alii* (eds.), The Art of Ajanta. New Perspectives. New Delhi, Vol. 1, 194–212.

1991b The Vakataka Area and Gupta Sculpture. in: K. Khandalavala (ed.), The Golden Age. Gupta Art—Empire, Province and Influence. Bombay, 85–92.

1992 Discovery of Vākāṭaka Temple at Ramtek. in: AV, 155–164.

s.d. Iconography of Vishnu in Maharashtra (From earliest times to 10th Cent. A.D.).

Janssen, Frans H. P. M.

1993 On the Origin and Development of the so-called Lajjā Gaurī. in: A. J. Gail & G. J. R. Mevissen (eds.), South Asian Archaeology 1991. Stuttgart, 457–472.

Joshi, M. C. & S. K. Gupta (eds.)

1989 King Chandra and the Meharauli Pillar. Meerut. Kusumanjali Problems of Indian History Series 1.

Joshi, N. P.

1972 Catalogue of the Brahmanical Sculptures in the State Museum, Lucknow. Part 1. Lucknow.

1979 Iconography of Balarāma. New Delhi.

1984 Early Forms of Śiva. in: M. W. Meister (ed.), Discourses on Śiva. Bombay, 47–61.

1987 Mātṛkā Figures in Kuṣāṇa Sculptures at Mathura. in: M. Yaldiz & W. Lobo (eds.), Investigating Indian Art. Museum für indische Kunst, Berlin. Berlin, 159–171.

1989 Early Jaina Icons from Mathurā. in: D. M. Srinivasan (ed.), Mathurā. A Cultural Heritage. New Delhi, 332–367.

Kālidāsa
The Complete Works of Kālidāsa. The text in Sanskrit and Prakrit edited with Introduction. Ed. by V. P. Joshi. Leiden 1976.

Kane, P. V.
1930–62 History of Dharmaśāstra (Ancient and Mediaeval Religious and Civil Law in India). Poona. 5 vols. Government Oriental Series, Class B, No. 6.

Kauṣītaki Brāhmaṇa
with the Vyākhyā of Udaya. Hrsg. von E. R. Sreekrishna Sarma. Bd. 1–3. Wiesbaden 1968–1976. Verzeichnis der Orientalischen Handschriften in Deutschland, Supplementband 9, 1–3.

Khan, Abdul Waheed
1964 An Early Sculpture of Narasimha (man-lion incarnation of Vishnu found from the coastal Andhra along with Pañca Vīras). Hydarabad.

Khandalavala, Karl
1991 The Chronology of Caves 16, 17, 19, 26, 1 and 2 at Ajanta and the Ghatotkacha Cave. in: R. Parimoo *et alii* (eds.), The Art of Ajanta. New Perspectives. New Delhi, Vol. I, 105–129.

Kolte, V. B.
1965 Hisse-Borālā Inscription of Vākāṭaka King Devasena. in: G. T. Deshpande & A. M. Shastri (eds.), Mirashi Commemoration Volume. Nagpur, 372–387.

1971–72 Dvitīya Pṛthivīṣenācā Māhurjharī tāmrapaṭ. in: Vidarbha Saṃśodhana Maṇḍaḷa Vārṣika, 53–77.

Kramrisch, Stella
1928 The Vishṇudharmottara. Part III. A Treatise on Indian Painting and Image-Making. Second revised and enlarged edition, Calcutta 1928.

1981 The Presence of Śiva. Princeton.

Kreisel, Gerd
1986 Die Śiva-Bildwerke der Mathurā-Kunst. Ein Beitrag zur frühhinduistischen Ikonographie. Stuttgart. Monographien zur indischen Archäologie, Kunst und Philologie Vol. 5.

Krishna, Nanditha
1980 The Art and Iconography of Vishnu-Narayana. Bombay.

Kuiper, F. B. J.
1979 Varuṇa and Vidūṣaka. On the Origin of the Sanskrit Drama. Amsterdam, etc. Verh. d. Kon. Ak. v. Wet., Afd. Letterkunde, NR, deel 100.

1983 Ancient Indian Cosmogony. Essays selected and introduced by John Irwin. Edit. by John Irwin. Delhi.

Kūrmapurāṇa
The Kūrma Purāṇa. Crit. Edit. by Anand Swarup Gupta. Varanasi 1971.

Laine, James W.
1989 Visions of God: Narratives of Theophany in the Mahābhārata. Vienna. Publications of the De Nobili Research Library 16.

Lienhard, Siegfried
1984 A History of Classical Poetry Sanskrit–Pali–Prakrit. Wiesbaden. A History of Indian Literature, III Fasc. 1.
Līlāśuka Bilvamaṅgala
Kṛṣṇakarṇāmṛta. The Love of Krishna. Edit. with an Introduction [and Translation] by Frances Wilson. Philadelphia 1975. Haney Foundation Series 14.
Liṅgapurāṇa
Liṅgapurāṇa of Kṛṣṇa Dvaipāyana Vyāsa, with Sanskrit commentary *Śivatoṣiṇī* of Gaṇeśa Nātu. Edit. by J. L. Shastri. Delhi, etc. 1980.
Lohuizen-de Leeuw, J. E. van
1964 Indische Skulpturen der Sammlung Eduard von der Heydt. Beschreibender Katalog. Museum Rietberg, Zürich.
Longhurst, A. H.
1924 Pallava Architecture Pt. I (Early Period). Simla. Memoirs of the ASI No. 17.
Lorenzen, David N.
1991 The Kāpālikas and Kālāmukhas. Two Lost Śaivite Sects. Revised edition, Delhi [1st ed. 1972].
Malandra, Geri H.
1993 Unfolding a Maṇḍala. The Buddhist Cave Temples at Ellora. Albany.
Mallebrein, Cornelia
1984 Skulpturen aus Indien. Bedeutung und Form. Staatliches Museum für Volkenkunde, München.
Manu
Bharuci's Commentary on the Manusmṛti (The Manu-Śāstra-Vivaraṇa, books 6–12). Text, Translation and Notes. Vol. I. The Text edited by J. Duncan M. Derrett. Wiesbaden 1975. 2 vols. Schriftenreihe des Südasien-Instituts der Universität Heidelberg Band 18.

Mānava-Dharma Śāstra [Institutes of Manu] with the Commentaries of Medhātithi, Sarvajñanārāyaṇa, Kullūka, Rāghavānanda, Nandana, and Rāmachandra. And an Appendix by Vishvanāth Nārāyan Mandlik. With a Foreword by Albrecht Wezler. Delhi 1992 [first edition: 1886].
Matsyapurāṇa
Śrīmad Dvaipāyanamunipraṇītaṃ Matsyapurāṇam. Ed. by Hari Nārāyaṇa Āpṭe. Poona 1907. Ananda Ashrama Series 54.
Maxwell, Thomas S.
1982 The Five Aspects of Śiva (in Theory, Iconography and Architecture). in: Art International XXV, 41–57.

1984 Nānd, Parel, Kalyānpur: Śaiva Images as Meditational Constructs. in: M. W. Meister (ed.), Discourses on Śiva. Bombay, 62–81.

1988 Viśvarūpa. Delhi, etc. Oxford University South Asian Studies Series.

Meister, Michael W. (ed.)
1984 Discourses on Śiva. Proceedings of a Symposium on the Nature of Religious Imagery. Edited and with an Introduction by ~. Bombay.

Mirashi, Vasudev Vishnu
1954 Pravarapura, an Ancient Capital of the Vākāṭakas. in: Sarūpa Bhāratī or the Hommage of Indology being Dr Lakshman Sarup Memorial Volume. Hosiarpur, 1–9. [Reprinted in: SI II, 272–284].
1959 Meghadūta mẽ Rāmagiri arthāt Rāmṭek. Nagpur. Vidarbha Saṃśodhana Maṇḍala Granthamālā No. 12.
1960–62 Studies in Indology. Nagpur. 3 vols. [Volume 3 'Ancient Indian Coins' = Nagpur University Research Series, 2]
1963 Inscriptions of the Vākāṭakas. Ootacamund. Archaeological Survey of India. Corpus Inscriptionum Indicarum Vol. V.
1964 Ramagiri of Kalidasa. in: JIH XLII Pt. 1, 131–143.
1968 Ramagiri in Jaina Literatur. in: Shri Mahavira Jaina Vidyalaya Golden Jubilee Volume Pt. I. Bombay, 124–129.
1982 Indological Research Papers. Vol. I. Nagpur.

Mirashi, V. V. & N. R. Navlekar
1969 Kālidāsa. Date, Life, and Works. Bombay.

Mishra, Ram Swaroop
1971 Inscriptions of the Early Gupta Kings and their Successors. Varanasi.

Misra, O. P.
1989 Iconography of the Saptamātrikās. Delhi.

Misra, Ram Nath
1981 Yaksha Cult and Iconography. New Delhi.

Mitra, Debala
1963 Varāha-Cave of Udayagiri—An Iconographic Study. in: Journal of the Asiatic Society 5, 99–103.

Mitra, Haridas
1958 Gaṇapati. in: Viśva-Bhāratī Annals Vol. VIII. Santiniketan, 1–120.

Mitterwallner, Gritli von
1976 The Kuṣāṇa type of the Goddess Mahiṣāsuramardinī as compared to the Gupta and Mediaeval Types. in: German Scholars on India. Contributions to Indian Studies. Edit. by the Cultural Department of the Embassy of the Federal Republic of Germany. New Delhi, Vol. II, 196–213.

Mukherjee, B. N.
1980 A Note on the Hisse-Borala Inscription of the Time of Vakataka Devasena. in: JESI VII, 3–5.

Mukhopadhyaya, K. Bh. S.
1951 The Tripura Episode in Sanskrit Literature. in: Journal of the Ganganatha Jha Research Institute (Allahabad) Vol. VIII.4, 371–395.

Nagpur District Gazetteer
Central Provinces District Gazetteers. Nagpur District. by R. V. Russell. Bombay 1908.
Revised Edition 'Maharashtra State Gazetteers.' Bombay 1966.

Narain, A. K.
1991 Gaṇeśa: A Protohistory of the Idea and the Icon. in: R. L. Brown (ed.), Ganesh. Studies of an Asian God. New York, 19–48.

Nath, Amarendra
1991–92 Arambha: A Vākāṭaka Site in Vidarbha. in: Purātattva 22, 69–74.

Newid, Mehr-Ali
1990 Remarks on Śataghnī and Paṭṭiśa, two old Indian weapons. in: South Asian Archaeology 1987. Rome, 628–641.

Nigam, L. S.
1993 The Image of Śiva from Tala: Issues in Identification and Interpretation of the Symbols therein. in: Heritage of India: Past and Present. Essays in Honour of Prof. R. K. Sharma. Delhi, 225–234.
1994 Antiquity of Garh-Dhanora (Bastar) and Debris Clearance of Viṣṇu Image Mound. in: Purātan 9, 71–73.

Nigam, M. L.
1987 Early Iconography of Viṣṇu in Andhra Region. in: R. Parimoo (ed.), Vaiṣṇavism in Indian Arts and Culture. New Delhi, 342–351.

Pal, Pratapaditya
1986 Indian Sculpture. Volume I circa 500 B.C.–A.D. 700. A Catalogue of the Los Angeles County Museum of Art Collection. Vol. I. Berkeley, Los Angeles and London.

Panikkar, Shivaji K.
1997[1996] Saptamātṛkā Worship and Sculptures. An Iconological Interpretation of Conflicts and Resolutions in the Storied Brāhmanical Icons. New Delhi 1997 [= 1996].

Pargiter, F. E. (ed.)
1913 The Purāṇa Text of the Dynasties of the Kali Age with Introduction and Notes. London, etc.

Pāśupatasūtra
With the *Pañcārthabhāṣya* of Kauṇḍinya. Edit. by R. Ananthakrishna Sastri. Trivandrum 1940. TSS CXLIII.
Pāśupata Sūtram with Pañcārtha-Bhāṣya of Kauṇḍinya. Translated with an Introduction on the history of Śaivism in India by Haripada Chakraborti. Calcutta 1970.

Patañjali
The *Vyākaraṇa-Mahabhāṣya* of Patañjali. Edit. by F. Kielhorn. Bombay, 1892–1909. 3 vols. [Revised edition: K. V. Abhyankar. Poona 1962–72.]

Pathak, V. S.
1960 History of Śaiva Cults in Northern India from Inscriptions (700 A.D. to 1200 A.D.). Varanasi.

Patil, D. R.
1948 The Monuments of the Udaygiri Hill. Gwalior.
Patil, N. B.
1980–81 Aurva—a mythical form of fire motif in the Mahābhārata. in: Journal of the Oriental Institute XXX, 13–19.
Pattabiramin, R. Z.
1971 Sanctuaires rupestres de l'Inde du Sud. I Āndhra. Pondichéry. Publications de l'Institut Français d'Indologie 42.1.
Pollock, Sheldon
1993 Rāmāyaṇa and Political Imagination in India. in: Journal of Asian Studies 52.2, 261–297.
Purāṇapañcalakṣaṇa
Das Purāṇa Pañcalakṣaṇa. Versuch einer Textgeschichte von Willibald Kirfel. Leiden 1927.
Ramesh, K. V. & S. P. Tewari
1990 A Copper-Plate Hoard of the Gupta Period from Bagh, Madhya Pradesh. ASI, New Delhi/Mysore.
Rao, Gopinatha T. A.
1914 Elements of Hindu Iconography. Madras. [Reprinted by Paragon Book Reprint Corp., New York 1968 in 2 volumes, 4 parts.]
Rao, Lakshman K. V.
1924 The Telugu Academy Plates of Vishṇukuṇḍin = Mādhavavarma III. A.D. 594. in: Journal of the Department of Letters, University of Calcutta. Vol. XI, 31–62.
Raven, Ellen M.
1994 Gupta Gold Coins with a Garuḍa-Banner. Samudragupta–Skandagupta. Groningen. 2 vols. Gonda Indological Studies I.
Raychaudhuri, Hemchandra
1936 Materials for the Study of the Early History of the Vaishnava Sect. Calcutta.
Rāykvār, Girdhārīlāl
1989 Bilāspur jile kī Śaiv pratimāẽ. in: Purātan 6, 187 f.
Rāykvār, G. L. & R. K. Siṃha
1994 [Plate found at Junawanī (Malhār)]. in: Purātan 9.
Ṛgveda
Hymns of the Rig-Veda in the Samhita and Pada texts. Reprinted from the Editio Princeps by F. Max Müller. Varanasi 1965. 2 vols.
Risbuḍ, Ānand Kumār
1984 Tālā Gāṃv kā Śiva-Mandir. in: Purātan 1, 58–61.
Sādhanamālā
Edit. with an Introduction and Index by Benoytosh Bhattacharyya. Baroda 1925–28. 2 vols. Gaekwad's Oriental Series.
Salomon, Richard
1990 New Evidence for a Gāndhārī origin of the Arapacana Syllabary. in: JAOS 110.2, 255–273.

Sanderson, Alexis
1988 Śaivism and the Tantric Traditions. in: Stuward Sutherland *et alii* (eds.), The World's Religions. London, 660–704.
Sankaranarayanan, S.
1977 The Vishṇukuṇḍis and Their Times (An Epigraphical Study). Foreword T. V. Mahalingam. Delhi.
Sārdhatriśatikālottarāgama
Sārdhatriśati-Kālottarāgama. Edit. by N. R. Batt. Pondichéry 1979. Publications de l'Institut Français d'Indologie No. 61.
Sarma, I. K.
1992 Some Unique Representations of Śiva of the Vākāṭaka Period. in: AV, 219–224.
Śatapathabrāhmaṇa
The Çatapatha-Brâhmaṇa in the Mâdhyandina-Çâkhâ with extracts from the commentaries of Sâyana, Harisvâmin and Dvivedaganga. [Edit.] by Albrecht Weber. Leipzig 1924. [Reprinted: Varanasi 1964].
Sāyaṇa Mādhava
Sarvadarśanasaṃgraha. Edited with an exhaustive Hindi Commentary, Copious Appendixes and Anglo-Hindi Introductions by Uma Shankar Sharma 'Rishi'. Varanasi 1964. Vidyabhawan Sanskrit Granthamala 113.
Schastok, Sara
1981 A Sixth-Century Kubera Image from Mandasor. in: Anand Krishna (ed.), Chhavi-2. Rai Krishnadasa Felicitation Volume. Benares, 105–108.
Schuster, Carl
1951 Joint Marks. A possible Index of Cultural Contact between America, Oceania and the Far East. Amsterdam. Koninklijk Instituut voor de Tropen. Mededeling No. XCIV, Afd. Culturele en Physische Anthropologie No. 39.
Select Inscriptions
Select Inscriptions bearing on Indian History and Civilization. Edit. by Dines Chandra Sircar. Volume I: Calcutta 1942 [2nd edition: Delhi/Madras 1965]. Volume II: Delhi 1983.
Seshadri, M.
1963 Mahiṣāsuramardinī. Images, Iconography and Interpretation. in: Half Yearly Journal of the Mysore University, N.S. Section A (Arts), Vol. XXII.2, 1–28.
Shah, Priyabala
1958–61 *Viṣṇudharmottara-purāṇa.* Third Khaṇḍa. Vol. I: Text, Critical Notes etc. Vol. II: Introduction, Appendices, Indexes etc. A study on a Sanskrit Text of Ancient Indian Arts. Baroda. 2 vols. Gaekwad's Oriental Series 130 & 137.
Shah, U. P.
1984 Lakulīśa: Śaivite Saint. in: M. W. Meister (ed.), Discourses on Śiva. Bombay, 92–102.
Sharma, Brijendra Nath
1976 Iconography of Sadāśiva. New Delhi.

Sharma, R. C.
1976 Mathura Museum and Art (A Comprehensive Pictorial Guide Book). Mathura.
Sharma, Savita
1990 Early Indian Symbols. Numismatic Evidence. Delhi.
Shastri, Ajay Mitra
1970 Some Observations on the Hisse-Borala Inscription of Vākāṭaka Devasena. in: Proceedings of the Indian History Congress 31st Session 1969. Varanasi, 47–55.
1975–76 Māṇḍhal Copper Plate Charter of Pravarasēna II, Year 16. in: EI XLI, 68–76.
1977–78 Māṇḍhaḷ Utkhanan. in: Vidarbha Saṃśodhana Maṇḍaḷa Vārṣika, 142–174.
1984–86 Fresh Epigraphic Evidence on the Vākāṭakas. in: Nagpur University Journal 35, 130–164.
1987 Early History of the Deccan. Problems and Perspectives. Delhi.
1991 The Mūdigere Plates of Siṁhavarman and Vākāṭaka-Kadamba Relations. in: C. Margabandhu *et alii* (eds.), Indian Archaeological Heritage. Shri K. V. Soundara Rajan Festschrift. Delhi. 2 vols. Vol. 1, 317–319.
1992 The Age of the Vākāṭakas. Edit. by A. M. Shastri. New Delhi. [= AV].
1992a Vākāṭaka Coins. in: AV, 285–294.
1994 [1995] Anantaśayana Viṣṇu: earliest epigraphic evidence. in: ABORI 75, 111–120.
1995 Inscriptions of the Śarabhapurīyas, Pāṇḍuvaṁśins and Somavaṁśins. Part I: Introduction. Part II: Inscriptions. Delhi. 2 vols.
1995a Nachnā-kī-talāi and Ganj inscriptions of the time of Vākāṭaka Pṛithivīsheṇa – some observations. in: JESI XXI, 1–13.
1996 Śaka Era. in: Indian Journal of History of Science 31, 67–88.
Shastri, Ajay Mitra & Chandrashekhar Gupta
1977–78 Yawatmal Plates of Pravarasēna II, Year 26. in: EI XLII, 30–34.
1985 Dvitīya Rudrasenācā Māṃḍhaḷa tāmrapaṭ. in: Bh. L. Bhoḷe (ed.), Saṃśodhanācī Kṣitije. Dr V. Bh. Kolte Amṛtamahotsava Gauravagraṃtha. Nagpur, 223–229.
Sherrier, Julian
1993 Śiva in Gandhāra. in: A. J. Gail & G. J. R. Mevissen (eds.), South Asian Archaeology 1991. Stuttgart, 617–624.
Shrimali, Krishna Mohan
1987 Agrarian Structure in Central India and the Northern Deccan (c. AD 300–500). A Study of Vākāṭaka Inscriptions. Delhi.
Siṃha, Rāhul Kumār
1989 Bilāspur jile ke prācīn Śiva Mandir. in: Purātan VI, 169–170.
Siṃha, Śrībhagavān
1982 Guptakālīn Hindū Deva-Pratimāẽ. Hindu Iconography of the Gupta Period. Prathama Khaṇḍa. New Delhi.

Singh, Sheo Bahadur
1977 Brahmanical Icons in Northern India. [A study of images of five principal deities from earliest times to circa 1200 A.D.]. New Delhi.
Sinha, Kanchan
1979 Kārttikeya in Indian Art and Literature. Delhi.
Sircar, D. C.
1942 = Sel. Ins. I.
1967 Studies in the Society and Administration of Ancient and Medieval India. Vol. I Society. Calcutta.
Śivapurāṇa
Śrīśivamahāpurāṇa. Venkatesvara Press, Bombay, VS 2011 (= AD 1954).
Sivaramamurti, C.
1974 Nataraja in Art, Thought and Literature. Delhi. National Museum.
1976 Śatarudrīya: Vibhūti of Śiva's Iconography. New Delhi.
1984 Forms of Śiva in Sanskrit Sources. in: M. W. Meister (ed.), Discourses on Śiva. Bombay, 182–190.
Skandapurāṇa
Skandapurāṇasya Ambikākāṇḍaḥ. [Edit.] Kṛṣṇa Prasāda Bhaṭṭarāī. Kathmandu 1988. Mahendra Ratnagrantha Series 2. [= SP_{Bh}].
Smith, Bardwell L. (ed.)
1983 Essays on Gupta Culture. Delhi, etc.
Soundara Rajan, K. V.
1980 Art of South India – Deccan. Delhi.
Spink, Walter M.
1966 Ajantā and Ghatotkacha: a preliminary analysis. in: Ars Orientalis VI, 135–155.
1968 Ajaṇṭā's Chronology: The Problem of Cave Eleven. in: Ars Orientalis VII, 155–168.
1972 Ajanta: A Brief History. in: P. Pal (ed.), Aspects of Indian Art. Leiden, 49–58.
1975 Ajantā's Chronology: the Crucial Cave. in: Ars Orientalis X, 143–169.
1976–77 Bāgh: A Study. in: Archives of Asian Art XXX, 53–84.
1981a Ajanta's Chronology: Politics and Patronage. in: J. G. Williams (ed.), Kalādarśana. American Studies in the Art of India. Leiden, 109–126.
1981b Ajaṇṭā's Chronology: Cave 1's Patronage and Related Problems. in: A. Krishna (ed.), Chhavi-2. Rai Krishnadasa Felicitation Volume. Benaras, 144–157.
1991 The Archaeology of Ajaṇṭā. in: Ars Orientalis XXI, 67–94.
Srinivasan, Doris Meth
1990 From Transcendency to Materiality: Para Śiva, Sadāśiva, and Maheśa in Indian Art. in: Artibus Asiae L.1–2, 108–142.

Stadtner, Donald M.
1976 Sirpur to Rajim: the Art of Kosala during the Seventh Century. Unpublished Ph. D. Thesis, University of California, Berkeley.
1980 A Sixth-Century A.D. Temple from Kosala. in: Archives of Asian Art 33, 38–48.
1982 Nand Chand and a Central Indian Regional Style. in: Artibus Asiae 43, 129–136.

Stern, Ph.
1972 Colonnes indiennes d'Ajantā et d'Ellora. Paris. Publications du Musée Guimet. Recherches et Documents d'art et d'archéologie XI.

Sthānapothī
Prastāvanā, Mūḷa Pothī, Sthānasūcī, Kaṭhīṇa śabdāṃca kośa ityadīsahita saṃpādilelā. [Edit. by] Viṣṇu Bhikājī Kolte. Malkapur 1976.

Stietencron, Heinrich von
1969 Bhairava. in: ZDMG Supplementa I. (XVII. Deutscher Orientalistentag vom 21. bis 27. Juli 1968 in Würzburg. Teil 3). Wiesbaden, 863–871.
1972 Gaṅgā und Yamunā. Zur symbolischen Bedeutung der Flussgöttinen an indischen Tempeln. Wiesbaden.
1983 Die Göttin Durgā Mahiṣāsuramardinī. Mythos, Darstellung und geschichtliche Rolle bei der Hinduisierung Indiens. in: Visible Religion, Annual for Religious Iconography, Vol. II, 118–166.

Sundara, A.
1990 An Early Kadamba Mahisamardini Sculpture from Devihal. in: K. V. Ramesh *et alii* (eds.), Indian History and Epigraphy. Dr. G. S. Gai Felicitation Volume. Delhi, 222–224.

Sūradāsa
Sūrasāgara. Edit. by Nandadulāre Vājapeyī. Kashi VS 2033–35 [= AD 1976–78] (5th printing).

Śvetāśvataropaniṣad
in: Eighteen Principal Upaniṣads. Vol. I. Edit. by V. P. Limaye & R. D. Vadekar. Poona 1958.

Taittirīyabrāhmaṇa
Edit. by Rajendralal Mitra. Calcutta 1859–1890. 3 vols. Bibliotheca Indica.

Taittirīyāraṇyaka
Taittirīyāraṇyakam. With the Commentary of Sāyaṇācārya. Edit. by Rājendralāl Mitra. Calcutta 1871. Bibliotheca Indica LII.

Taittirīyasaṃhitā
Die Taittirîya-Saṃhitâ. Hrsg. von Albrecht Weber. Theil 1–2. Leipzig 1871–72. Indische Studien XI–XII.

Thaplyal, Kiran
1972 Studies in Ancient Indian Seals. A study of North Indian Seals and Sealings from circa third century BC to mid-seventh century AD. Lucknow.

Trautmann, Thomas R.
1972 Licchavi-Dauhitra. in: JRAS (1972), 2–15.
Trivedi, Harihar Vitthal
1957 Catalogue of the Coins of the Nāga Kings of Padmāvatī. Gwalior.
Varāhamihira
Bṛhatsaṃhitā of Varāhamihira. With English Translation, Exhaustive Notes and Literary Comments by Ramakrishna Bhat. Delhi, etc. 1981–82. 2 vols.
Vāyupurāṇa
[Edit. by the Pandits of the Anandashrama]. Poona 1983. [Reprint of the Poona 1905 ed.].
Venkataramayya, M.
1963 Ramagiri of Kalidasa. in: JIH XLI, 62–92.
Viennot, Odette
1958 Le Makara dans la décoration des monuments de l'Inde ancienne: positions et fonctions. in: Arts Asiatiques V.3, 183–206 & V.4, 272–292.
1964 Les divinités fluviales Gaṅgā et Yamunā aux portes des sanctuaires de l'Inde. Paris.
Vimalasūri
Paumacariyam with Hindi Translation. Edit. by H. Jacobi. Sec. ed. revised by Punyavijayaji. Translated into Hindi by Shantilal M. Vora. Introduction by V. M. Kulkarni. Varanasi 1962–68. 2 vols. Prakrit Text Society Series Nos. 6 and 12.
Viṣṇudharmottarapurāṇa
Ed. by Kṣemarāja-Śrīkṛṣṇadāsa. Venkatesvara Press, Bombay, VS 1969 (= AD 1912).
Third Khaṇḍa → Shah 1958–61.
Vogel, J. Ph.
1925 Gaṅgā et Yamunā dans l'iconographie brahmanique. in: Études Asiatiques, publiées à l'occasion du vingt-cinquième anniversaire de l'EFEO, tôme II, 385–402.
Weiner, Sheila L.
1977 Ajaṇṭā: Its Place in Buddhist Art. Berkeley/Los Angeles/London.
Williams, Joanna Gottfried
1982 The Art of Gupta India. Empire and Province. Princeton.
1983 Vākāṭaka Art and the Gupta Mainstream. in: B. L. Smith (ed.), Essays on Gupta Culture. Delhi, 215–233.
Yazdani, G. *et alii*
1930–55 Ajanta. The Colour and Monochrome Reproductions of the Ajanta Frescoes Based on Photography. London. 4 vols. [= *Ajanta*].
Zannas, Eliky
1960 Khajuraho. Text and Photographs by Eliky Zannas. With a Historical Introduction by Jeannine Auboyer. 's-Gravenhage.

Index

abhayamudrā, 72, 96, 105
Abhinavagupta, 69
    Parātrīśikālaghuvṛtti, 70
    Tantrāloka, 69
ācāryamuṣṭi, 150
    ācariyamuṭṭhi, 150
    fist, 150
Accabhallikā, 20
Acyutanandin, 10, 11
Aditi, 143
Āditya, 61, 62
Ādityavardhana, 50
Aghora, 70, 78, 123
Agni, 110
agrahāra, 20, 21
ahiṃsā, 61
Ahmadnagar, 35
Aihole, 98
Airikiṇa, → Eran
Ajanta, 36–38, 40–42, 44, 45, 50, 58, 78, 88–89, 91, 108, 115, 128, 151–156
    Plateau, 14
Ajjhitabhaṭṭārikā, 28, 45, 49
Ajjhitadevī, 47, 49
Ājñākabhaṭṭārikā, 24
ākāśa, 104
Akola District, 14
akṣamālā, 112, 118
    rosary, 96, 105, 112, 118, 149, 151
    rudrākṣa, 149
alābupātra, 95
Ālampur, 114
Alexander, 37
    Romance, 37
Allahabad
    Pillar Inscription, 10
Alvars, 159
āmalaka, 133
Amarāvatī, 24
Amaravati (A.P.), 91, 156
Ambikā, 130
Āmbloda, 48
Amin, 152
amṛta, 72, 95, 105
Ananta, → Śeṣa
Anantavarman, 40
Andhaka, 109, 111, 115
    Andhakāsurasaṃhāramūrti, 109
Āndhra, 34, 35
Andhra Pradesh, 46, 53, 85
aṅgada, 144, 152
Aniruddha, 20, 59–61, 123
añjali, 106, 150, 151
antarāla, 43, 147
antarapaṭṭa, 147
antardeśa, 102
antelope, 72, 118
    mṛga, 118
Anūpa, 28, 38, 39, 45, 50
Aparānta, 34
Aragrāmakā, 20, 21
Arambha, 114
Arjuna, 137
arrow, → *iṣu*
Arthapati, 54, 55
Āryā, 115
Āryāvarta, 11
Ashmolean Museum, 122, 147
asi, → sword
Aśmaka, 15, 35, 37–39, 41, 45, 50
Aśoka, 18
ass, → donkey
aṣṭamūrti, 81, 97, 105
aṣṭapuṣpikā, 149, 150
Aśvamedha, 10, 46

Atibhāvatī, 17, 30, 31, 142
[Ati]candrā, 36
Atimārga, 67
Aurangabad, 153
Avalokiteśvara, 153
Avanti, 34, 35, 38, 39, 50
avatāra, 21, 22, 30, 62, 64, 65
Avidheya, 15, 28
axis mundi, → *skambha*
ayaḥśūla, → *śūla*
āyudhapuruṣa, 119

Bābbaikā, 20
Badami, 98, 132, 133
Badoh, 139
Bagh, 38–40, 50
Baghelkhand, 48, 49
Balarāma, 20, 30, 31, 60, 62–64, 121, 157–158
  Baladeva, 60
  Halin, 121
Bali, 19, 30, 63, 143–145
Balkhar, 39
Bappa, 32, 33
Bāppadeva, 33
Bappaka, 32, 33
Bāppārya, 32
Baroda District, 68
Basarh, 26
Basim, → Vatsagulma
Bastar District, 53–55
battle-axe, → *paraśu*
Baudhāyana
  Gṛhyapariśiṣṭasūtras, 75
Bembal, 56
Beṇṇā, → Wainganga
Beṇṇātaṭasthāna, 53, 88
Besnagar, 43, 60, 114, 116, 117, 119
  Vidiśā, 22, 26, 27, 47, 60, 139
Bhāgavata, 19, 20, 25, 58, 59, 65, 69, 70, 78, 79, 120
  Bhagavatism, 141
  faith, 16, 59–66, 140
bhāgineyī, 27
Bhairava, 74, 75, 78, 96, 98, 101, 123
bhakti, 61, 151
bhālapaṭṭa, 95, 102, 149
Bhandara District, 18, 56
Bharaka(ta?)nātha, 141
bhārarakṣaka, 78, 84, 135, 148
Bhāraśiva, 9–10, 20, 46, 75
Bhāsa, 158
  Bālacarita, 158
Bhāskaravarman, 40
Bh(ā)śrutasvāmin, 29
Bhatala, 141
Bhātkulī, 24
Bhavadattavarman, 54–56
Bhavanāga, 9, 15, 20, 46
Bhavvirāja, 41
Bhima river, 15, 35, 39
bhindipāla, 99
Bhir District, 35
Bhita, 13
Bhitari, 25–27, 31
BHK-I, 76–78, 80–83, 105, 111, 112, 117, 123
BHK-II, 78, 80, 81, 84, 120, 129, 132
bhoga, 19, 64, 121
  serpent coils, 19, 105, 106, 120, 121, 138, 149
Bhogarāma, 30
Bhogarāma Temple, 30, 43, 63, 64, 86, 147, 148
Bhoja
  Śṛṅgāraprakāśa, 126
Bhojakaṭa, 24
Bholāhuḍkī Tekḍī, 80, → BHK-I
Bhonsle, 87
Bhubaneswar
  Bhāratī Maṭha, 126
Bhuluṇḍa, 19
Bhumara, 48, 133
Bhūteśvara, 71
Bidar, 33
Bidar District, 33
bījapūra, 129
Bilsaḍh, 115
birth cloth, 114, 134
boar, → Varāha

bodhisattva, 78, 153
Boṃgī Huḍkī, 78, 80, 83, 120, 121, → BHK-II
book, → *pothī*
Boppadeva, 33
bow, → *dhanus*
Brahmā, 14, 67, 72, 77, 117–118, 126
  Prajāpati, 63, 118
brahmacārin, 96, 103
brahmacarya, 108
brahmamantras, 69, 70, 74
brahman, 70
Brahmans, 70, 74, 103, 104, 123
brahmasūtra, 104
Bṛhalī, 115
Bṛhaspati, 143
Buddha, 42, 43, 153, 155
Buddhabhadra, 41
Buddhism, 45, 78, 152, 154
Buddhist, 40, 45, 46, 58, 59, 67, 85, 89, 150
Budhagupta, 47, 48
buffalo, → *mahiṣa*
bull, → *vṛṣabha*
Bundelkhand, 12–14, 17, 28, 47–50

caitya, 89, 141, 151
cakra, 20, 22, 25, 52, 90, 119, 140, 141
  discus, 144
Cakrapāṇi, → Viṣṇu
Cālukya, 58
Canakā, → Kāñcana(kā)
Caṇḍikā, 130
Candra(bhāgā), → Chandra river
Candragupta I, 9
Candragupta II, 11, 12, 15–17, 27, 39, 46, 65, 85, 132, 139
Candrāvatī, 46
Carmāṅka, → Chammak
caturmukhaliṅga, → *liṅga*
caturmūrtitva, 73, 96, 105
caturvaktra, 98
caturvyūha, → *vyūha*
catuṣkī, 42, 43, 138
chāga, 110
  goat, 110, 116
  goat-faced, 110, 115
  goat-headed, 110, 111, 116, 117
Chammak, 23, 24, 32
  Carmāṅka, 24
Chandra river, 23
  Candra(bhāgā), 24
Chandrapur, 56
  District, 141
channavīra, 133, 155
child, 115–117, 143, 158
Cikkambu[rī], → Cīkmārā
Cīkmārā
  Cikkambu[rī], 18
club, → *lakuṭa*
coins, 9, 11, 23, 26, 44, 45, 51, 55, 56, 64, 90, 148, 153
conch, 90, 119, 133, 144
  śaṅkha, 119, 136, 141
cosmic pillar, → *skambha*
crescent, 71, 108, 149
Culla, 54
curls, 120, 135, 149, 151, 156
  corkscrew, 148, 152
  snail-shell, 99, 119, 148

dagger, 122
Dahrasena, 34
Dakṣa, 123
Dakṣiṇāpatha, 11, 41
Dāmodara, 158
Dāmodarasena, 17, 22, 23, 30, 34
dāna, 150
daṇḍa, 68, 72, 77, 97, 98, 110
  staff, 67, 68, 72, 97, 98, 143, 146
Daṇḍa, 68, 98
Daṇḍin, 37, 38, 50
  Daśakumāracarita, 37, 38, 40
Dantimukhasvāmin, 52
Daśaratha, 158
Daśāvatāra Temple, → Deogarh
datrima, 10
Dattātreya, 127
dauhitra, 9, 10
dāyāda, 40

Deogarh, 85, 91, 118, 141
Daśāvatāra Temple, 141
Deotek, 18, 52
Devakī, 26, 60
Devarānī Temple, → Tala
Devasena, 28, 31, 34, 39
Devī, 58, 121, 130–133, 138, 158
Devihal, 132
Devīmāhātmya, 130, 131
Dham river, 25, 56, 89–91, 157
dhanus, 108
bow, 71, 107, 108, 144
Dharādhipa, 36
Dhāraṇa *gotra*, → *gotra*
dharma, 14, 17, 24, 44, 60, 61, 67, 116
dharmamahārāja, 33, 58
Dhenuka, 121, 157
Dhenukāsura, 157
dhotī, 75, 95, 96, 98, 100, 108, 110, 113, 118, 120, 122, 140, 146, 148, 152, 156
Dhule District, 34
Dhūmrākṣa, 64
Dhūmreśvara, 64
dhvaja, 66
dikpāla, 146
dīkṣā, 67
dīkṣita, 96
Diṇḍi, 100
discus, → *cakra*
Divākarasena, 16–17, 22, 30, 145
Ḍoṅgar Maudā, 19
donkey, 157, 158, → Dhenuka
ass, 121, 157
duḥkhānta, 66, 67, 69
Durgā, 114, 115
dūtaka, 33
dvādaśajyotirliṅga, 105
dvārapāla, 84, 153
dvyāmuṣyāyaṇa, 10

earring, → *kuṇḍala*
ekāvali, 99, 108, 110, 119, 135, 140, 152, 156
ekaveṇi, → *veṇi*
Ekavīra, 37
Elephanta, 109
Ellora, 109, 130, 153, 156
Erai river, 56
Eran, 27, 47, 113, 139
Airikiṇa, 27

fangs, 72, 78, 100, 114, 123
fist, → *ācāryamuṣṭi*
flower rosette, 99, 119, 135, 147, 149
footprint, 21, 22, 24, 56, 64–66, 86, 136, 137
pādamūla, 22, 23, 65

gadā, 72, 97, 106, 119, 136, 141
mace, 62, 72, 106, 109, 119, 144, 148
Gadchiroli, 141
Gajāsurasaṃhāramūrti, 109
gajavyāla, 150
gaṇa, 44, 68, 72, 77, 78, 98–101, 106, 107, 135, 147–149, 151, 152, 156
Gaṇādhyakṣa, 77, 81, 99–101, 119, 122
gaṇapa, 100, 101
Gaṇapatināga, 11
gandhakuṭī, 36, 89
Gandhara, 101
Gaṇeśa, 84, 85, 90, 128–130, 133, 135
Vināyaka, 52
Gaṅgā, 9, 92, 115, 146, 154–156
Ganges, 14, 29
Ganj, 47, 48
garbhagṛha, 30, 64, 80, 82, 83, 138, 140, 147
Gārgya, 68
Garhdhanora, 54, 56, 141
Garuḍa, 27, 137
Gauri, 50
Gautama *gotra*, → *gotra*
Gautamīputra, 9, 10, 13
Gautamīputra (Vṛṣadhvaja), 13
ghaṭa, 77, 112
Ghaṭotkacagupta, 17, 26–28, 30
Ghaṭotkaca Cave, 40, 42

ghora, 108
Girinagara, → Junagaḍh
goat, → *chāga*
Godavari, 35, 45, 55
Goddess, 58, 73, 111, 112, 114, 130, 131, 133, 138, → Devī
River Goddess, 115, 154–155
Gogaon, 141
Gokula, 158, 159
Goṇḍārya, 32
Gonds (Koṇḍs), 24
Gopad river, 48
gotra, 12, 20
Bhāradvāja, 32
Dhāraṇa, 12, 16, 29
Dhāraṇi, 12, 29
Gautama, 32
Kāśyapa, 88
Vājikauśika, 32
Vatsa, 32
Viṣṇuvṛddha, 10
Govindavarman Vikramāśraya, 46
graha, 116
graiveyaka, 101, 120, 122, 133, 138, 152, 156
Great Tradition, 141
gṛhastha, 108, 150
guggulu, 131
Gujarat, 32, 68
Gulwada, 42
Guntur District, 46, 141
Gupta Era, 39, 48, 50
Guptarāma Temple, 42, 86, 87, 145
Kapaṭarāma, 42, 86, 145

hair
matted, → *jaṭila*
hala, 121
Halimā, 115
Halin, → Balarāma
Hamlapuri, 84, 124, 128, 133, 136
hāra, 106, 155
Hari, → Viṣṇu
Harinaigameṣin, 116
Harisāmba, 36
Hariṣeṇa, 28, 31, 33–41, 45, 49, 50, 52, 58, 89, 151, 155
Hāritī, 58
Hāritīputra, 58
Harivarman, 48
Hastibhoja, 34, 155
Hastin, 48
Hiḍimbā Tekḍī, 42, 78, 87, 88, 149
Hinduism, 20, 46, 58, 107, 137
Hinganghat Taluk, 53
Hiraṇyakaśipu, 141
Hiraṇyānadīvāsaka, 56, 88
Hisse-Borala Inscription, 32, 33
horn, 110, 113–115, 131
huḍḍukkāra, 69
Hūṇas, 27, 28

Indra, 44, 115, 131, 142, 143, 153, 155
Śakra, 131, 143
Indrapura, 46
Īśāna, 70, 104
iṣu, 108
arrow, 71, 72, 107–109, 144

Jabalpur, 25
jagatī, 83, 138
Jaina, 116
jālikā, 114
Jambūdvīpa, 137
Jambūmārga, 68
jaṭājūṭa, → *jaṭila*
jaṭāmukuṭa, → *mukuṭa*
jaṭila, 72, 106
jaṭājūṭa, 102, 108
matted hair, 72, 95, 96, 98, 99, 102, 106, 111, 113, 117, 118, 122, 123, 127, 143, 149
matted locks, 112, 151
jaya, 51
Jayabala, 29
Jayanātha, 47
jayaśāsana, 51, 90
jigīṣu, 51
Jithānī Temple, → Tala
joint-mark, 107, 134

Junagaḍh, 27, 28, 30, 31, 64
District, 32
Girinagara, 30–32

Kadalīvāṭaka, → Kelāpur
Kadamba, 31
Kailāsa, 137
Kaimur Range, 48
Kākī, 115, 116
kalaśa, 72, 77, 95, 102
pūrṇakalaśa, 134
Kālidāsa, 64, 84, 126, 127, 150
Kuntaleśvaradautya, 126
Kumārasaṃbhava, 98, 112
Meghadūta, 63, 64, 85, 86, 127
Raghuvaṃśa, 127, 150
Kaliṅga, 34, 35
Kāmān, 104
kamaṇḍalu, 77, 112, 117, 118
kambugrīva, 100
Kaṃsa, 26, 27, 60
Kāñcana(kā), 12, 13
Canakā, 12, 13
Kaṇḍariyā Mahādeva Temple, → Khajuraho
kaṅkana, 155, 156
kanyā, 115, 116
Kānyakubja, 68
kapāla, 108, 149
skull, 79
kapardin, 71
Kapaṭarāma, → Guptarāma Temple
Kapilavimala, 68
Kapileśvara, 68
karāla, 100, 114
Kārī-talāī, 48
Karlapalem, 134
Karnataka, 33, 132
Kārohaṇa, → Karvan
Kārtavīrya, 72
Kārttikeya, → Skanda
Karvan, 68
Kārohaṇa, 68
Kāyārohaṇa, 68
Kaśyapa, 12, 143
kaṭakamudrā, 152
kaṭibandha, 96, 100, 101, 106, 114, 122
kaṭihasta, 97
Kauṇḍarāja, 24
Kauṇḍinya, 69, 75
Kauruṣya, 68
Kauśika, → Kuśika
Kauśikī, 130, 131
kavi, 84, 124–127, 135, 149, 150
Kayanpur, 150
Kāyārohaṇa, → Karvan
Kelāpur, 31
Kadalīvāṭaka, 31, 32, 88
keśabandha, 102, 155
Kesarabeda, 54
Keselakagrāma, 54
Keskal, 54
Kevala-Narasiṃha, 141
Temple, 30, 42–44, 86, 136, 138, 140, 144, 148, 149, 151–153
Inscription, 11, 12, 17, 21, 26–29, 31, 32, 64, 141, 145
keyūra, 155, 156
khaḍga, → sword
Khajuraho, 104, 138
Archaeological Museum, 104
Kaṇḍariyā Mahādeva Temple, 104
Khammam District, 53
Khandesh, 34, 37, 39
Khoh, 48
kirīṭamukuṭa, → *mukuṭa*
Kondamotu, 141
Koṇḍarāja, 24
Koraput District, 53, 54
Kosala, 29, 34, 35, 40
Dakṣiṇa Kosala, 54, 55
Kosalā, 29, 39, 51, 53
Kṛṣṇa, 20, 26, 27, 30, 31, 36, 60, 62–64, 67, 72, 91, 108, 121, 137, 157–159
Kṛṣṇa river, 15, 46
Kṛṣṇadāsa, 36, 38
Kṛtayuga, 23
Kṛttikā, 101, 115, 116
Kṣemendra

Aucityavicāracarcā, 126
Kubera, 150
Kuberanāgā, 11, 12, 15, 16
Kumāra, → Skanda
Kumāradevī, 9
Kumāragupta I, 17, 23, 25–29, 39, 47, 64–66
Kumāragupta II, 47
Kumāragupta III, 47
kumārī, 116
kuṇḍala, 144, 155
earring, 99, 108, 119, 122, 125, 135, 148, 149, 155, 156
maṇikuṇḍala, 152
ratnakuṇḍala, 114, 119
Kunjuru, 132
Kuntala, 15, 31, 34, 35, 39, 45, 49, 126
Kūrma, 63
Kurnool District, 46
Kurudumbhaka, 20
kuśa grass, 67, 112
Kuṣāṇa, 62, 78, 104, 117, 122, 126
period, 116, 130
Kuśika, 68
Kauśika, 68
Kusumadhanvan, 40

Lajjā Gaurī, 58, 114, 133–134
Lakṣmaṇa, 65
Lakṣmaṇa Temple, 64, 86
Lakulīśa, 13, 68, 81, 85, 126
Nakulīśa, 67, 68
lakuṭa, 68, 97, 100, 108
club, 13, 97, 100, 108
lalitāsana, 114, 115, 129
lance, → *śūla*
lāṅgala, 121
Lāṭa, 34, 35
Licchavi, 9
Līlāśuka Bilvamaṅgala, 159
Kṛṣṇakarṇāmṛta, 159
liṅga, 20, 64, 68, 69, 73–75, 82, 87, 103, 104, 123, 133, 134, 145
caturmukhaliṅga, 75, 97, 103, 104
pañcamukhaliṅga, 103
ūrdhvaliṅga, 72, 75, 98, 100, 108, 110, 122
lion, 59, 90, 105, 106, 113–115, 117, 133, 140, 141
lion-throne, 115
siṃhāsana, 115
siṃha, 141
locks, 100, 122, 151
matted, → *jaṭila*
Los Angeles
County Museum, 139, 141
lotus, 72, 112, 113, 117, 119, 122, 133, 134, 138, 141, 149–152, 156
cap, 125, 136, 140
double-petalled, 122, 133
flowers, 62
lotus throne, 117, 118
paṅkajāsana, 117
lotus-eyed, 143
padma, 152
Lucknow
State Museum, 117

mace, → *gadā*
Mādhavavarman II Janāśraya, 46, 51, 52, 55–57, 129
Mādhavavarman III, 55
Mādhavavarman IV, 51
Madhunadī, 24
Madhya Pradesh, 53, 54
Magadha, 9
Mahābhairava, 13, 96
Mahābhārata
Nārāyaṇīya, 60, 62, 67
Tīrthayātrāparvan, 108
Mahādeva, → Śiva
Mahākāla, 76
Mahānubhāva, → Manbhaus
Sthānapothī, 145
Mahāpuruṣa, 23
Mahārājādhirāja, 16
mahārājalīlāsana, → *sukhāsana*
Mahāsadāśiva, 104
Mahāsena, 13
Mahbubnagar District, 46, 91

Maheśa, 96, 103
Maheshwar, 38, 39
Māheśvara, 13, 14, 20, 25, 59, 66–70, 72, 74–76, 78, 79, 96, 97, 104, 151
  faith, 66–79
  theology, 105
Maheśvara, 13, 14, 25, 58, 67, 68, 70, 72–77, 81, 82, 95–99, 101–105, 107, 108, 112, 118, 123
mahiṣa, 130
  buffalo, 58, 121, 130–133, 158
Mahiṣamardinī, 58, 84, 85, 129, 132, 135, 158
Māhiṣmatī, 38, 45, 50
Mahurjhari, 53
Maisada, 31
Maisava, 31
Maitrakas, 50
Maitreya, → Mitra
Maitreya (Bodhisattva), 153
makara, 106, 115, 147, 154–156
Mālava, → Malwa
Mallikārjuna, 46
Malwa, 17, 27–29, 34, 38, 39, 45, 47, 50
  Mālava, 29, 39, 51, 53
Māmalapuram, 66
Mānāṅka, 15, 41
Mānapura, 15
Manbhaus, 64
maṇḍapa, 30, 35, 42, 43, 52, 138, 142
  mukhamaṇḍapa, 80, 83
Mandara, 66, 137
Mandasor, 101
Mandhal, 14, 18–21, 23, 24, 31, 39, 53, 60, 62, 74–76, 78–84, 88, 90, 95–126, 128, 129, 132, 144, 150
  excavations, → BHK-I, BHK-II, MDL-I, MDL-II
Maṇibhadra, 152, 153
maṇikuṇḍala, → *kuṇḍala*
man-lion, → Narasiṃha
Mansar, 25, 42, 76, 78, 87–88, 90, 128, 149–152
  Śiva of, 78, 79, 108, 124, 125, 128, 135, 144, 148, 151, 156
Manu
  first man, 63
Mat, 126
Mathura, 59, 60, 62, 68, 98, 108, 122, 126, 129
  Museum, 116, 118, 122, 127, 129, 139, 143
Mātṛkā, → mother goddess
Mātṛviṣṇu, 47
mātuluṅga, 98, 129
Maudā, 19
MDL-I, 80
MDL-II, 76, 77, 80–82, 97, 99, 101
Meharauli
  Pillar Inscription, 65
Mekalā, 29, 39, 51, 53
mekhalā, 133, 155, 156
Meru, 126, 137
meṣa, 110
  ram, 110, 111, 116
  ram-headed, 117
Miregaon, 21, 22, 24
Mitra, 68
  Maitreya, 68
Mitrā, 115
Mitravarman, 38
modakabhāṇḍa, 128
Mogalrājapuram, 92
Mondasvāmin, 18, 19, 83, 84, 120, 121
mons Veneris, 155
mother goddess, 58, 114, 116
  mātaras, 115
  mātṛ, 116
  Mātṛkā, 43, 58, 77, 99, 109, 110, 113–117
moustache, 96, 98, 102, 104–106
mṛga, → antelope
mukhamaṇḍapa, → *maṇḍapa*
Muktādevī Temple, → Mūsānagar
muktāyajñopavīta, → *upavīta*
mukuṭa, 119, 128, 144, 149
  jaṭāmukuṭa, 149

kirīṭamukuṭa, 119, 128
Muṇḍā, 16, 19, 120
muṇḍa, 95, 106
muṇḍin, 67, 96
śipiviṣṭa, 71
vyuptakeśa, 71
muñja grass, 112
Murwara, 48
Mūsānagar, 102
Muktādevī Temple, 102

Nachna (Nachnā-kī-talāī), 12, 13, 47–49, 100, 128
Pārvatī Temple, 49
Nāga (dynasty), 9, 11, 12, 15–17, 20, 27, 57, 139
Nāga (Serpent)
Dhāraṇa, 12
Nāgabhaṭa, 39
Nāgadatta, 11
nāganūpura, → *nūpura*
Nagara, 56
Nagardhan, 13, 25, 59, 65, 66, 75, 78, 84–85, 113, 121, 124–137, 146, 149, 150
Nāgārjunakoṇḍa, 43, 91
Nāgasena, 10
Nagod District, 48
Nagpur, 18, 23, 25, 80, 81, 84, 85, 89, 114
Central Museum, 76, 81, 82, 84, 95, 100, 113, 132, 136
Museum of Dept. of AIHCA, 76, 81–84, 89, 129
Naigameṣa, 77, 97, 110–111, 113, 116, 117, 122
Naigameya, 110
Negameṣa, 116
Nakulīśa, → Lakulīśa
Nala, 53–57
nāla, 95
Nalanda, 47
Nanda, 159
Nandapuri, 124, 128
Nandin, 72, 76, 98, 99
Nandīśvara, 77, 81, 97–100, 110
Nandivaktra, 75, 97
Nandivardhana, 11, 14, 21, 23, 25, 28, 30, 31, 33, 42, 44, 50, 52–55, 58, 59, 64, 84, 86–88, 124, 127, 128, 159
Branch, 10, 40
Nannarāja, 41
Nanpur, 113, 117
Nārada, 60
Narasiṃha, 30, 42, 43, 54, 59, 63, 64, 86, 125, 128, 136–137, 140–142, 146
Girija, 141
man-lion, 22, 140, 141
Narasiṃhagupta Bālāditya I, 47
Narasiṃhavarman II, 37
Narataṅgavāristhāna, 88
Nārāyaṇa, 19, 60, 72, 120
Nārāyaṇarāja, 23
Nārāyaṇīya, → *Mahābhārata*
Narendra, 29, 40
Narendrasena, 24, 28, 29, 35, 39, 40, 42, 45–47, 49, 52, 53
Narindarāja, 24
Narmada, 12, 14, 19, 25, 27, 28, 38, 39, 47, 52, 57
Revā, 57
National Highway No. 7, 14, 16, 85
National Museum, 78
Negameṣa, → Naigameṣa
nidhi, 44, 148, 149, 153–154
Nīlalohita, 71
Nimar District, 39
Niṣadha, 54
niṣka, 114, 156
niskala, 103
Nisumbha, 131
Nisunda, 131
Nītiśāstra, 50
nūpura, 114, 133, 155, 156
nāganūpura, 150

Orissa, 53, 54

pādamūla, → footprint

pādasvastika, 154
Padma, 64
padma, → lotus
Padmapāṇi, 152, 153
Padmapura, 20
Padmāvatī, → Pawaya
Paithan, → Pratiṣṭhāna
Palālā, 115
Pallava, 37
Pāñcarātra, 60, 62, 67, 69, 102
    Saṃhitā, 123
pañcārtha, 67, 68
Pañcavīra, → Vṛṣṇi
Pañcika, 153
Pāṇḍavas, 29
Pāṇḍu, 29
Panna District, 12
para, 103
Paramabhaṭṭāraka, 12, 28, 29, 39
Paramabhaṭṭārikamahāvihāra, 46
Parameśvara, 70, 74
Para Śiva, → Śiva
paraśu, 72, 100
    axe, 77
    battle-axe, 13, 100
    paraśvadha, 100
Paraśurāma, 63, 72
paraśvadha, → *paraśu*
parivāradevatā, 146
Parivrājaka, 48
pārśvamauli, 148, 153
pārśvasūtra, 104
Pārvatī, 71, 77, 95, 111–112
paryaṅka, 126
    sattvaparyaṅkāsana, 126
Pāśupata, 13, 67–69, 71, 79, 108
    vrata, 67, 69
    weapon, 72, 108
Paśupati, 69, 71, 106
Pāṭaliputra, 40
Pathari, 99
Patur, 95
Paunar, 25, 56, 81, 89–92, 114, 115, 129, 146, 155–159
    excavations, → PNR-I
Pauni, 18, 59
Pawaya, 9, 11, 60, 143, 144
    Padmāvatī, 9, 11, 60, 139
Penganga, 23
penis, 72, 75, 76, 98, 100, 106, 108, 109
Periyāḻvār, 159
Peshawar Museum, 125
Phukudumbhaka, 20
pilgrimage, 54
Pināka, 72, 107
piṇḍa, 9
PNR-I, 89
Poseidon, 108
pothī, 84, 124, 126
    book, 125
Prabhāvatī Guptā, 12, 13, 15–17, 21, 22, 24, 25, 29, 30, 34, 52, 54, 57, 64–66, 83–85, 120, 142, 145
Prabhāvatīsvāmin, 30, 88, 142, 145
pradakṣiṇā, 73
pradakṣiṇāpatha, 42, 81, 83
Pradyumna, 20, 36, 59–61, 123
Prajāpati, → Brahmā
pralambahārī, 146, 156
pralambapādāsana, 43
pramathas, 72, 106
pratihāra, 146
Pratiṣṭhāna, 45
pratyālīḍha, 157
Pravarapura, 25, 31, 87–89, 91
Pravarasena I, 9, 10, 12, 33, 40, 46, 58
    Pravīra, 10, 12
Pravarasena II, 13–15, 22–26, 28–34, 39, 51, 53, 56, 78, 81, 84, 87, 88, 91, 149
Pravarasena II (Vatsagulma), 31, 33
Pravareśvara, 23, 25, 79, 88, 149
Pravareśvaradevakulasthāna, 23, 25, 88, 149
Pravīra, → Pravarasena I
Prayāga, 9, 54
Pṛthivī, 138, 140
Pṛthivīsamudra, 53
Pṛthivīṣeṇa I, 11, 13–15, 20, 22, 52, 139

Pṛthivīṣeṇa II, 13, 28, 29, 39, 40, 47, 49–53, 55–57, 81, 88, 92
puṇya, 24
Puṇyavarman, 37, 40
Pūrṇabhadra, 152, 153
Pūrugupta, 47
Puruṣa Hymn, 95
Puṣkarī, 54–56
puṣpapaṭṭika, 147
Puṣyamitras, 26
putrikā, 10

Raipur Museum, 54
rājalīlāsana, → *sukhāsana*
ram, → *meṣa*
Rāma, 21, 44, 63–65, 86, 91, 92, 127, 137, 158
Rāmacandra Temple, 86
Rāmagiri, 14, 18, 21–25, 30–32, 42–44, 53, 54, 59, 62–66, 78, 83–88, 108, 124, 127, 128, 136–149, 151, 152, 154
  Ramtek Hill, 11, 12, 14, 25, 26, 29, 84, 124, 128, 137, 138
  Ramtekri, 85
  Sindūragiri, 128
Rāmagiristhāna, 51, 65, 86–88
Rāmagirisvāmin, 24, 65, 86
Rāmagupta, 27
Rāmaliṅgasvāmin, 52
Rāmānuja, 126
Rāmāyaṇa, → Vālmīki
Rāmeśvara Cave Temple, 156
Ramgarth Hill, 99, 119, 132, 139
Ramtek, 25, 85, 124, 125, 149
  Stone Inscription, 145
Ramtek Hill, → Rāmagiri
Rāṣṭrakūṭa, 15, 41, 91
ratnakuṇḍala, → *kuṇḍala*
ratnavalaya, → *valaya*
Ravi, 36
Ravisāmba, 36, 38
Revā, → Narmada
Revatī, 109
riktha, 9
River Goddess, → Goddess
rosary, → *akṣamālā*
Ṛṣīka, 37
rucaka, 43, 138
Rudra, 68–72, 75, 77, 96, 98, 107–110, 115, 116, 118, 144
Rudrā, 115
Rudradeva, 11
rudrākṣa, → *akṣamālā*
Rudra-Narasiṃha Temple, 22, 30, 42, 43, 86, 136, 138, 140, 144, 146, 148
Rudrasena I, 9–11, 13, 14, 18, 20, 96
Rudrasena II, 14–19, 21, 22, 30, 31, 34, 52, 53, 60, 83, 120, 145
Rukmiṇī, 24
Russek Collection, 96, 104

Sadāśiva, 70, 74, 75, 77, 81, 83, 95, 101–108, 111, 112, 123
Sadyojāta, 70, 97
Sagar, 126
Sāgaradattā, 40
Sahya Mountain, 36
Śaivala, 64
Śaiva Siddhānta, 70, 103
Śaka Era, 32, 46
sakala, 96, 103
Sāketa, 9
Śākha, 111
Śakra, → Indra
śakti, 72, 110, 114, 117
  spear, 72, 110, 114, 117
śālabhañjikā, 154
samabhaṅga, 119, 146
Sāmba, 20, 36, 59, 60, 62, 83, 122, 123
Śambhu, 23, 25, 104
Śambūka, 64
saṃhāramūrti, 109
Śaṃkara, 72, 73, 109
Saṃkarṣaṇa, 20, 30, 59–64, 83, 120–121, 123
Sāṃkhya, 61, 67, 69
samrāj, 10, 14
Samudragupta, 9–12, 14, 15, 27, 39, 47

Samudrapura, 53
sāndhāra, 42, 49
Sankarpur, 48
śaṅkha, → conch
Śaṅkhasvāmin, 29
Śaṅkhika, 20
śāntidamudrā, 119, 144
sapiṇḍa, 17, 40
Saptamātṛkā, 84
Śarabha, 29
Śarabhapur, 29
Śarabhapurīya, 29, 40, 54, 55
Saragrāmakā, 20
Sarasvatī, 126
Śarvanātha, 48
Sarvasena I, 10, 14
Sarvasena II, 17, 31, 33
Śaṣṭhī, 116
Satara District, 52
Śatarudrīya, 71, 107
Sātavāhana, 14, 18
Satpura Range, 14, 38, 85
Śatrughnarāja, 24
Sātvata, 20, 21, 25, 31, 59–64, 123
saumya, 74, 118
Śaurisāmba, 36
Sāyaṇa Mādhava, 67, 68
Selluddraha, 20
senāpati, 33
Seoni Plateau, 23
serpent, 19, 72, 106, 121, 126, 138, 139
  coils, → *bhoga*
  snake, 72, 100, 106, 138, 151
Śeṣa, 121, 138, 139
  Śeṣaśayana, → Viṣṇu
  Ananta, 18, 120, 121
shell script, 87
shield, 133, 144
Siddhanātha Cave, 42, 86
Sidhi District, 48
śikhandaka, 113
siṃha, → lion
Siṃhavarman, 31
Sindūragiri, → Rāmagiri
śipiviṣṭa, → *muṇḍa*
śiraścakra, 144, 152
Sītā, 21, 85
Śivā, 116
Śiva, 20, 23, 25, 46, 58, 67–70, 72–79, 81, 85, 87, 88, 96–98, 100–106, 108–112, 117, 123, 129, 135, 137, 149–151
  Andhakāsurasaṃhāramūrti, → Andhaka
  Hara, 44
  Kālārimūrti, 109
  Kāmāntakamūrti, 109
  Mahādeva, 75, 77–79, 97, 108
  Para Śiva, 103
  Sthāṇu, 71, 73
  Tripurāntakamūrti, 109
Śivadharma, 69
Śivamegha, 13
Siwani, 23
skambha, 66, 137
  axis mundi, 137
  cosmic pillar, 66, 137
Skanda, 72, 77, 104, 110–112, 116, 117
  Guha, 112
  Kārttikeya, 101, 104, 116, 117
  Kumāra, 101, 111, 113
Skandagupta, 25–31, 47, 64
Skandapurāṇa
  original, 74, 130, 131
Skandavarman, 55
skull, → *kapāla*
snake, → serpent
snātaka, 108, 150
Śoḍāsa, 60
Soma, 36
Son river, 48
spear, → *śakti*
śrāddha, 40
Śrīkaṇṭha, 67, 68
Śrīmadanalobha, 141
Śrīparvata, 46
Śrīparvatasvāmin, 46
Śrīśaila Hills, 91
śrīvatsa, 119, 120, 143
staff, → *daṇḍa*

Sthālakanagara, → Thalner
Sthāṇu, → Śiva
stūpa, 18, 87, 91, 153
Subandhu, 39, 50
Sudarśana, 30–33
Suketuvarman, 32
sukhāsana, 128, 129, 140, 150
  (mahā)rājalīlāsana, 22, 140, 150
Śukra, 111
śūla, 25, 72, 77, 97, 98, 108, 109, 114, 132, 133
  ayaḥśūla, 108
  lance, 25, 72, 76, 97, 98, 108, 109, 114, 130–132
Sumbha, 131
Sunda, 131
Sura, 31
Śūrabala, 29
Suraśmicandra, 47
Sūrdās, 159
  Sūrasāgara, 159
Sūrya, 62, 122
Sūryasvāmin, 88
Śuṣkarevatī, 109
sūtradhāra, 155
Svāmideva (Gautama *gotra*), 32
Svāmideva (Vatsa *gotra*), 32
Svāmilladeva, 32, 33
Śvetāsvatara, 70
sword, 18, 62, 100, 119, 132, 144, 146, 148
  asi, 119
  khaḍga, 146

Tala, 105–107, 109–111, 129, 135
  Devarānī Temple, 105, 107, 111
  Jithānī Temple, 109
tāla, 121, 157
tapas, 64, 70, 112, 139
Tapi river, 34, 38
tāṭaṅka, 135, 148, 149
Tatpuruṣa, 70, 97
tejas, 74
Tewar, 25
Thalner, 33, 34, 37, 39
  Sthālakanagara, 34
third eye, → *tryakṣa*
tiger-skin, → *vyāghracarman*
Tilottamā, 73, 74, 123
Tīrthayātrāparvan, → *Mahābhārata*
Toramāṇa, 139
toraṇa, 153
Traikūṭakas, 32
tree, 66, 121, 136, 137, 154, 157
tribal, 107, 141
tribhaṅga, 144
Trikūṭa, 34, 35, 55
Triple City, 72
Tripurī, 25
Tripurīvāsaka, 25, 56, 88
triśikhā, 136
triśūla, 68, 99, 108, 109, 132
  trident, 99, 108, 109, 131
Trivikrama, 30, 63, 64, 66, 108, 137, 142–145, → Viṣṇu
  Temple, 30, 86, 144, 145, 148
tryakṣa, 74, 96
  third eye, 78, 98, 104, 108, 122, 123, 150
  three eyes, 71
Tumain, 26
tusk, 129, 138, 139

Uccakalpa, 13, 48
  dynasty, 47
Uchahara, 48
udarabandha, 106, 108, 144, 148, 150, 152
Udayagiri, 19, 22, 84, 85, 119, 129, 130, 132, 139, 154
ugra, 71, 74, 77, 78, 96, 104, 113–115, 123, 150
  head, 76, 77, 123–124
Ujjain, 45
  Ujjayinī, 68
Umā, 67, 68, 73, 96, 112
  Umāvaktra, 75
Upamanyu, 71, 72, 107, 108
Upamitavimala, 68
Upamiteśvara, 68

upavīta, 96, 100, 101, 108
    muktāyajñopavīta, 108, 144, 150, 152
    upavītin, 71
    vyālayajñopavīta, 72, 129
    yajñopavīta, 72, 98, 100, 108, 110, 118–120, 122, 125, 135, 150, 151
Upendragupta, 38
ūrdhvaliṅga, 96, → *liṅga*
uṣṇīṣa, 96, 105, 106, 149
    uṣṇīṣin, 71, 95, 96, 102, 103
uttānapad, 134

vāhana, 87, 98, 115, 155
vaijayantī, 144
vaijayika dharmasthāna, 88
vaikakṣa, 156
Vaikhānasāgama, 141
Vaiśravaṇa, 40
vajra, 115, 152, 153
Vajrapāṇi, 108, 151–153
valaya, 108, 110, 152
    ratnavalaya, 101
Vālī, 157
Valkhā, 19, 28, 39
Vallabhī, 50
Vālmīki, 127
    Rāmāyaṇa, 63–65, 91, 98, 127, 153
Vāmadeva, 70
Vāmana, 30, 63, 64, 143, 144
vāmana, 71, 78, 107
Vaṃśagiri, 65
Vaṃśasthapura, 65
Vanavāsī, 15
varadamudrā, 72, 119, 144, 150, 158
Varāha, 19, 22, 30, 43, 63, 85, 86, 128, 138–142
    boar, 138, 139, 141, 142
    Temple, 22, 86, 144
Varāhadeva, 15, 34, 36, 38, 42, 45, 155
Varāhamihira
    Bṛhatsaṃhitā, 116, 118, 119, 121, 144
Varhaḍī Talāō, 82
Varman dynasty, 48
vāsaka, 56, 88
Vasantabhānu, 37
Vasudeva, 60, 158
Vāsudeva, 19, 20, 30, 59–63, 78, 83, 119–123, 125, 128
Vasundharā, 40
vāṭaka, 88
Vatsa *gotra*, → *gotra*
Vatsagulma, 11, 14, 20, 21, 28, 31–35, 42, 44, 50, 51, 58, 59
    Basim, 14, 32
    Branch, 10, 15, 17, 31–33, 40, 151, 155
Vatsarāja, 29
vedībandha, 147
Velpuru, 52
Vembāravāsaka, 56
veṇi, 115
    ekaveṇi, 115
    veṇibandha, 113
vetra, 98
Vidarbha, 14, 15, 41, 44, 45, 55–57, 90, 91, 133
Vidiśā, → Besnagar
vihāra, 38, 43, 46, 89
vikrama, 100
Vikramāditya, 126
Vikramendravarman I, 46
Vikramendravarman II, 32, 46
Vimalasūri
    Paümacariya, 64
Vināyaka, → Gaṇeśa
Vindhya, 11–13, 15, 16
Vindhyaśakti I, 10, 12, 13, 33, 40
Vindhyaśakti II, 10, 58
    Vindhyasena, 10, 11, 14, 15, 31
Vindhyavāsinī, 130
Vinobā Bhāve Ashram, 90–92, 155, 157
Vīrabhadra, 101, 123
vīrāsana, 126
vīrāṣṭaka, 115
Viśākha, 111
viṣamasthāna, 146
Viṣṇu, 13, 18–22, 30, 31, 54, 56, 58,

62–66, 78, 83–87, 91, 99, 109, 119–121, 128, 129, 133, 135, 137, 138, 140–146
Śeṣaśayana, 19, 118
Anantaśayana, 19, 92
Bhagavat, 52, 58, 61, 65, 66
Cakrapāṇi, 20
Hari, 60
Viṣṇukuṇḍin, 37, 46, 51, 54–57, 90–92, 159
Viṣṇupada, 66, 85, 136–137
Viṣṇuvarman, 31
Viśruta, 37
Viśvakarman, 153
Vrātyas, 71
vṛṣabha, 71, 98, 133
bull, 71, 72, 82, 87, 90, 98, 133, 134
Vṛṣadhvaja, 13, 76, 77
Vṛṣṇi, 20, 59, 60, 62, 123
Hero, 82, 83, 122–123, 133
Pañcavīra, 59, 122, 123
Vṛtra, 142
vyāghracarman, 108
tiger-skin, 72, 108, 109
Vyāghradeva, 13, 47–52
vyāla, 72
vyālayajñopavīta, → *upavīta*
Vyāsa, 72
vyūha, 62, 102, 106
caturvyūha, 102, 103
vyuptakeśa, → *muṇḍa*

Waghora river, 42, 89
Wainganga, 14, 17, 18, 23, 53, 56, 85, 88
Beṇṇā, 14
Wardha District, 53, 89, 114
Wardha river, 23
Warora, 141

Yādava, 59, 60
Yādava dynasty, 64, 65, 82
yajña, 118
yajñopavīta, → *upavīta*
yakṣa, 64, 78, 85, 148, 152, 153
yakṣī, 154
yakṣiṇī, 154
Yama, 97
Yamunā, 47, 154, 156
Yaśodā, 159
Yaudheya
coins, 101, 104
Yoga, 67, 69
yoga, 67, 69, 73, 96
yogin, 68, 76, 79, 96, 98, 100, 102–104
yoni, 82
Yudhiṣṭhira, 14, 44
Yugadhara, 155
yuvarāja, 10, 16, 17, 30

Index of Quotations

Aitareya Brāhmaṇa
3.33.5, 118
Amarakośa
III 3.89, 40

Bālacarita
III, ll. 86–89, 158
Bhagavadgītā
4.5–8, 63
7.19, 60
11.24, 62
11.30, 62
11.50, 60
18.74, 60
19.57, 60
Bhāgavatapurāṇa
10.15.20–40, 157
Bṛhatsaṃhitā
58.31, 119
58.32, 119
58.33, 144
58.34, 119
58.36, 121
58.41, 118
58.56, 116

Chāndogya Upaniṣad
3.17.6, 60

Daśakumāracarita
p. 208, 40
Devīmāhātmya
3.37–39, 131
3.38–39, 158

Gṛhyapariśiṣṭasūtras (Baudhāyana)
II.16–17, 75

Haracaritacintāmaṇi
4.74–76, 99
Harivaṃśa
1.88.32, 24
57, 157
57.12ab, 157
57.18–20, 121
57.25, 157
83.25–26, 121
App.I No. 20, ll. 361–375, 115
App.I No. 42, ll. 97–195, 138
Harṣacarita
p. 50, ll. 18f., 11

Kauṣītaki Upaniṣad
1.3–4, 61
Kṛṣṇakarṇāmṛta
Add. Verses, p. 227, 159
Kumārasaṃbhava
3.41, 98
5.8–11, 112
5.14, 112
Kūrmapurāṇa
1.11.26–27, 102

Liṅgapurāṇa
1.18.22, 102

Mahābhārata
1.60.23, 111
1.203.22–26, 73
1.210.12, 60
3.80.84, 108
3.81.86–87, 65
3.130.7–8, 65
3.215.16–22, 116
3.215.23, 110
3.217.1–11, 115
3.217.3, 111
3.217.11–12, 110

3.219.3–6, 116
3.317.8, 115
3 App.I No. 16, ll. 68–128, 138
3 App.I No. 16, ll. 91–99, 139
3 App.I No. 27, ll. 42–53, 138
3 App.I No. 27, ll. 63–80, 143
4 App.I No. 4 (D), ll. 1–51, 115
5.101.16, 12
5.109.19, 65, 137
6.63.13, 138, 141
6 App.I No. 1, ll. 7–32, 115
7.57.32, 65, 137
7.173.83–85, 73, 97
7.173.83, 75
7.173.92, 73
9.43.37, 111
9.44, 106
10.18.13, 118
12.29.31, 65
12.202, 138
12.274.34f., 118
12.321–339, 60
12.322.19, 60
12.323.10–11, 61
12.326.1ff., 60
12.326.17–46, 61
12.326.35–43, 61
*12.326.851**, 63
12.327.78, 61
12.332.13–18, 61
12.336.31, 60
12.337.36, 63, 141
12.337.62, 68
12 App.1 No. 28, ll. 69–80, 123
12 App. 1 No. 28 l. 178, 108
13.14.99–102, 73
13.14.101, 97
13.14.115–118, 71
13.14.119–126, 72
13.14.122–130, 108
13.14.131–132, 108
13.14.131–140, 72
13.14.131, 108
13.14.135, 108
13.14.141–146, 72
13.14.144, 98
13.14.150–153, 72
13.14.151, 108
13.15.4, 67, 96
13.15.11–12, 72
13.15.11, 97, 108
13.15.13–14, 72
13.16.2, 67
13.16.6, 67
13.16.13–65, 72
13.17.30–150, 72
13.128.1–6, 73
13.128.3–6, 73, 96, 102
13.146.3–5, 109
13.146.6, 97
13.146.7, 109
13.146.8, 79
13.146.15–18, 73
13.146.16–18, 97
13 App.I No. 16, ll. 105–112, 121
14.8.25, 108
Manu
3.11, 10
9.104, 10
9.105, 10
9.132, 9
9.156, 10
Bhāruci *ad 9.132*, 9
Medhātithi *ad 9.132*, 9
Matsyapurāṇa
179.5–39, 109
179.9–32, 115
179.24, 116
260.30, 139
Meghadūta
1, 63, 85
12, 63, 64, 86

Pāṇini
Patañjali *ad*
2.2.24, 60
2.2.35, 60
3.1.26, 60
3.2.111, 60
4.1.114, 60

5.3.76, 108
Parātrīśikālaghuvṛtti
p. 7 ll. 18–21, 70
Pāśupatasūtra
1.9, 68
5.40, 69
Kauṇḍinya *ad 1.9*, 75
Kauṇḍinya *ad 5.40*, 69
Paümacariya
40.16, 65
Purāṇapañcalakṣaṇa
p. 162, vs. 41, 111
p. 212, vs. 27, 111

Raghuvaṃśa
1.4, 127
15.21, 150
Rāmāyaṇa
1.75.11–12, 63
7.15.10, 153
7.16.13–14, 98
Ṛgveda
1.22.17–18, 142
1.114.1, 71
1.114.5, 71
1.154.4, 137
1.154.5, 143
1.155.1, 66
2.24.4, 143
2.33, 71
7.21.5, 75
10.72.4, 134
10.99.3, 75

Sarvadarśanasaṃgraha
Ch. 6, p. 161 ll. 1–6, 67
Śatapatha Brāhmaṇa
1.8.1, 63
7.5.1.5, 63
14.1.2.11, 63
Śivapurāṇa
Vāyavīya Saṃhitā
10.29, 102
Skandapurāṇa (original)
Bhaṭṭarāī edition (SP_{Bh})
33.9, 102
62.1–26, 74
62.12, 74
62.16–24, 74
62.18–20, 124
66.18–35, 131
68.16–23, 131
132, 111
132.19, 110
132.20, 111
132.52, 111
150.26, 111
167.128–149, 68
our edition (SP)
23.6–10, 101
Sthānapothī
p. 5, 145
Sūrasāgara
Sabhā 809, 159
Śvetāśvatara Upaniṣad
4.9–10, 70
6.7, 70
6.21, 70

Taittirīya Āraṇyaka
10.43–47, 70
Sāyaṇa *ad 10.43–47*, 70
Taittirīya Brāhmaṇa
1.1.3.5, 63
Taittirīya Saṃhitā
4.5.1–11, 71, 107
4.5.1, 71
4.5.2–3, 71
4.5.2, 71
4.5.3, 71
4.5.5, 71
4.5.7, 71
4.5.11, 71
7.1.5.1, 63
7.5.1, 138
Tantrāloka
Jayaratha *ad 8.157f.*, 69

Vāyupurāṇa
23.220–24, 68

23.223, 68
30.122–141, 123
97.1–2, 59
Viṣṇudharmottarapurāṇa
3.44.5–7, 118
3.48.1–3, 70
3.48.3–6, 75, 104
3.48.5, 96
3.48.11–13, 97
3.48.11, 96
3.73.15cd–17, 99
3.79.2, 139
3.85.64–65, 127
Viṣṇupurāṇa
5.8, 157

Yajurveda
Vājasaneyī Saṃhitā
IX.39, 71
XXXIX.8, 71

Plates

Mandhal: male head medallion

Mandhal: Maheśvara, *front*

PLATE II

Mandhal: Maheśvara, *rear*

Mandhal: Nandīśvara (?), *front*

PLATE IV

Mandhal: Nandīśvara (?), *rear*

Mandhal: a Gaṇādhyakṣa, *front*

Mandhal: a Gaṇādhyakṣa, *rear*

Mandhal: Sadāśiva, *front*

Mandhal: A, Sadāśiva, *rear*

B, Sadāśiva, *right side*

Mandhal: Rudra Andhakāsurasaṃhāramūrti, *front*

PLATE X

Mandhal: Rudra Andhakāsurasaṃhāramūrti, *rear*

Mandhal: Naigameṣa, *front*

Mandhal: Naigameṣa, *rear*

Mandhal: Pārvatī, *front*

Mandhal: Pārvatī, *rear*

Mandhal: Mātṛkā, *front*

Mandhal: Mātṛkā, *rear*

Mandhal: Brahmā, *front*

Mandhal: Brahmā, *rear*

Mandhal: Vāsudeva, *front*

Mandhal: Vāsudeva, *rear*

Mandhal: Saṃkarṣaṇa Dhenukāsuravadhamūrti, *front*

Mandhal: Saṃkarṣaṇa Dhenukāsuravadhamūrti, *rear*

Mandhal: a Vṛṣṇi Hero (Sāmba?), *front*

Mandhal: a Vṛṣṇi Hero (Sāmba?), *rear*

A, Mandhal: an Ugra Head

B, Nagardhan, view of the Rāmagiri

Nagardhan: a Kavi, *front*

Nagardhan: Viṣṇu

Nagardhan: Gaṇeśa

Nagardhan: A, Devī Mahiṣāsuramardinīmūrti

Nagardhan: B, Lajjā Gaurī

Nagardhan: A, a Bhārarakṣaka

Nagardhan: B, a Bhārarakṣaka

Nagardhan: A, Narasiṃha (miniature)

Nagardhan: B, Viṣṇupada

PLATE XXXII

Rāmagiri: A, Varāha, *enshrined*

Rāmagiri: B, Varāha, *loose find*

Rāmagiri: A, Narasiṃha, *front*

B, Narasiṃha (bottom), *rear* (detail)

C, Narasiṃha (*cakra*), *right side* (detail)

Rāmagiri: A, Trivikrama, *front*

B, Trivikrama, *lower part front* (detail)

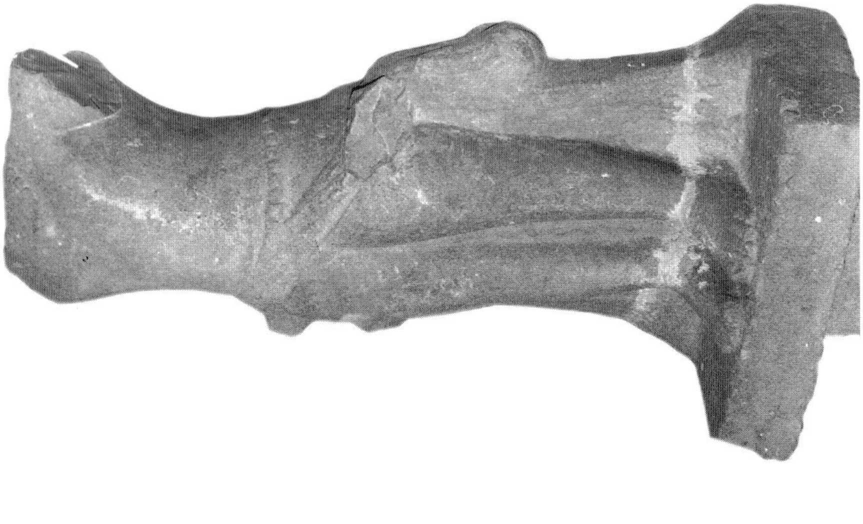

Rāmagiri: A, Viṣṇu

Rāmagiri: B, a Dikpāla (?)

Rāmagiri: C, Makara

Rāmagiri: B, a Nidhi

Rāmagiri: A, a Gaṇa

Mansar: Śiva

(left) Ajanta (Cave 19): A, Vajrapāṇi
(below) Ajanta (Cave 21): B, a Nidhi

A, Ajanta (Cave 16): River Goddess

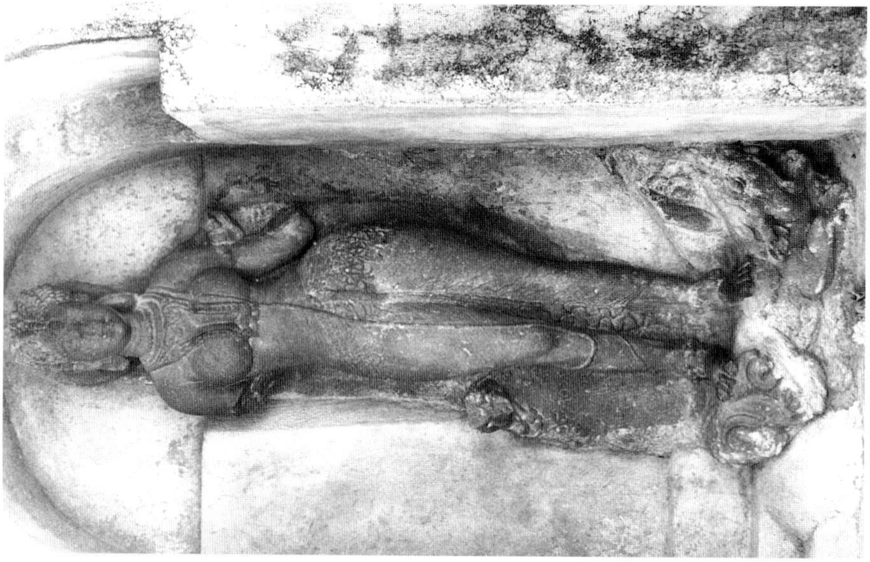

B, Paunar: Gaṅgā

Paunar: A, Balarāma Dhenukāsuravadhamūrti

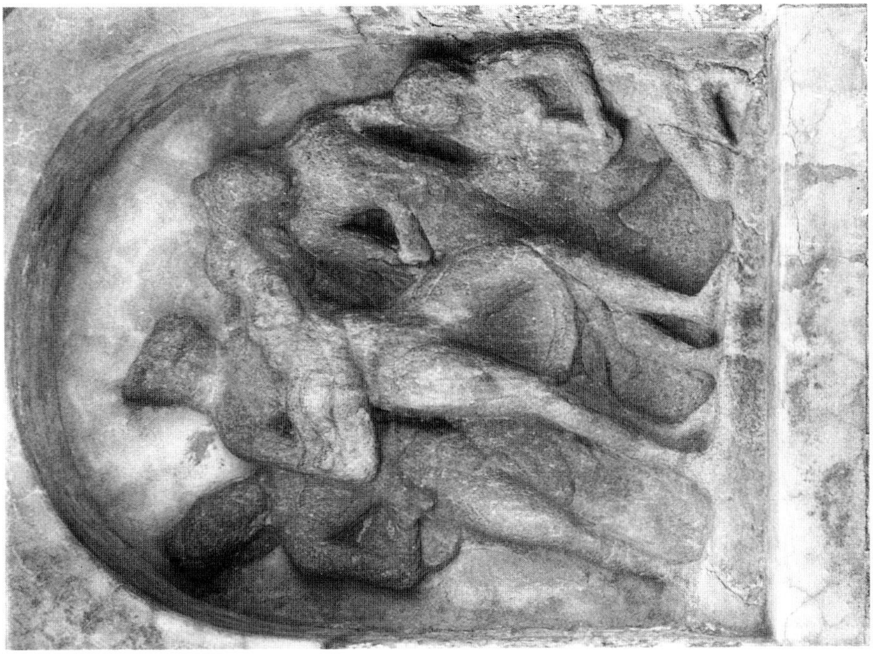

Paunar: B, Kṛṣṇa playing with the moon

Mathura: A, Maheśa, *front*

B, Maheśa, *rear*

Tala: a Gaṇa

Tala: A, Rudra, *front*

B, Rudra, *front* (detail)

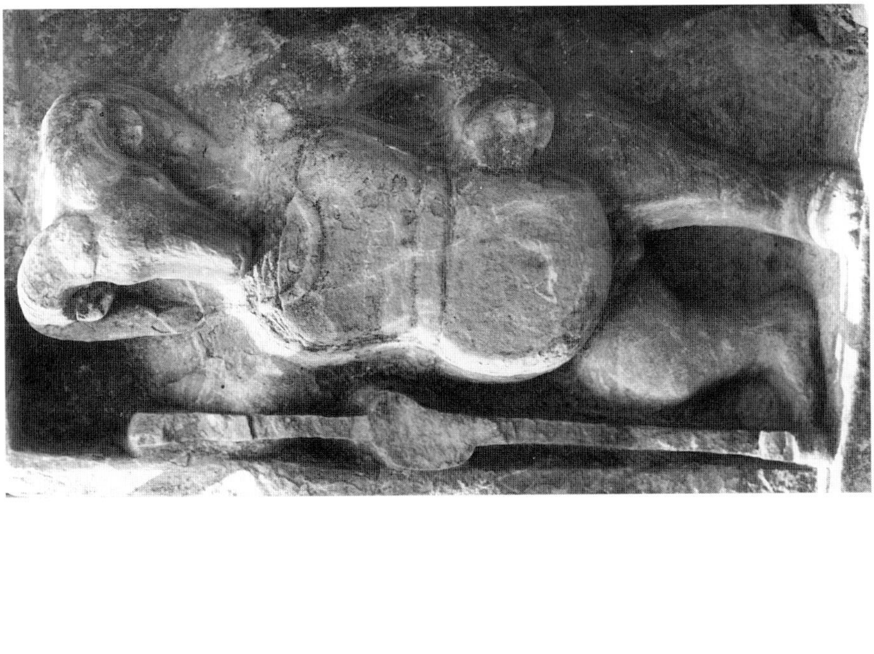

A, Tala: Naigameṣa

B, Udayagiri (Cave 6): Gaṇeśa

Udayagiri (Cave 6): A, Viṣṇu

Udayagiri (Cave 6): B, Devī Mahiṣāsuramardinī

PLATE XLVI

Udayagiri (Cave 5): Varāha

PLATE XLVII

Besnagar: A, Mātṛkās, *front*

B, Mātṛkās, *rear*

Maps

CHINA
NEPAL
PAKISTAN
BANGLADESH
PUNJAB
RAJASTHAN
DOAB
SAURASTRA
MALWA
ANUPA
MEKALA
MAGADHA
BIHAR
BENGAL
KOSALA
VIDARBHA
ORISSA
ASMAKA
MAHARASTRA
ANDHRA
Arabian Sea
Bay of Bengal
Jhelum
Chenab
Sutlej
Indus
Ganga
Yamuna
Chambal
Ghaghara
Brahmaputra
Narmada
Tapi
Godavari
Wainganga
Thanesvar
Dehli
Mehrauli
Ahiccharta
Mathura
Bilsadh
Jankhat
Lucknow
Saketa
Bhitargaon
Mandor
Jodhpur
Pawaya
Prayaga
Kausambi
Gadhwa
Bhitari
Varanasi
Mundesvari
Bhita
Patna
Rajgir
Bodh Gaya
Bhinmal
Nagari
Chitor
Udaipur
Mukundara
Mahua
Nachna ki Talai
Samalaji
Mandasor
Vidisha
Devnimori
Tripuri
Ahmedabad
Ujjain
Calcutta
Bagh
Mahismati
Tala
Mallar
Junagarh
Mansar
Ramtek
Thalner
Nagpur
Raipur
Sirpur
Mandhal
Rajim
Paunar
Ghatotkaca
Ajanta
Basim
Ellora
Bembal
Garhdhanora
Aurangabad
Paithan
Bombay
Manapura
0 200 km
0 100 miles
Betwa
Ken
BUNDELKHAND
Panna
Nagod
Satna
Rewa
Mahua
Deogarh
Bhumara
Nachna
Unchehara
Sankargadh
Tumain
Ramgarth Hill
Eran
Nand Chand
Bina
Marhia
Khoh
Sakhor
Badoh-Pathari
Kunda
Son
Udayagiri
Vidisa (Besnagar)
Tigowa
Shankarpur
Bhopal
Jabalpur
Sanci
Narmada
0 100 km
0 50 miles

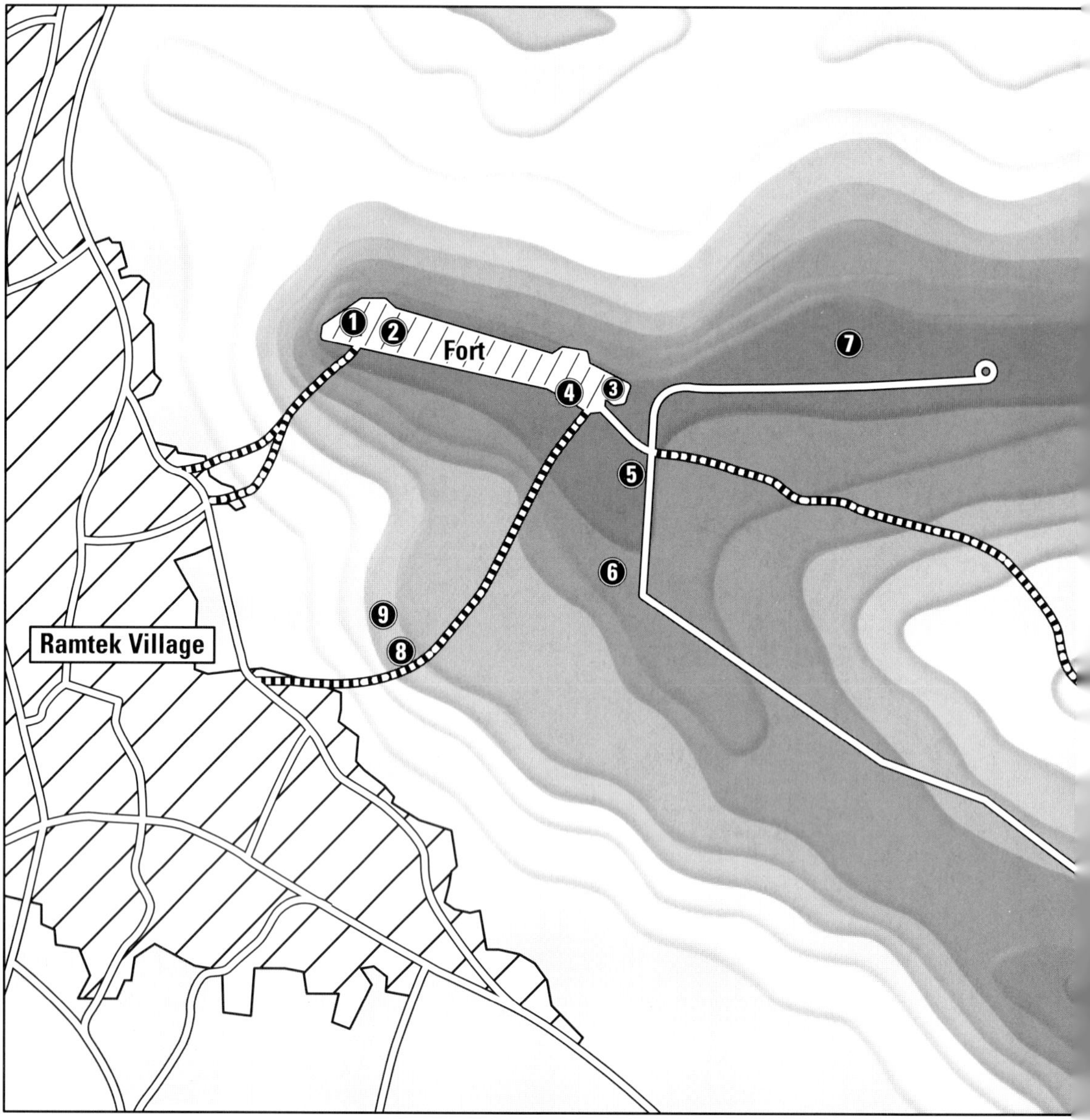

Ramtek Hill/Rāmagiri

scale 1:61

1 Rāmacandra Temple (Yādava)
2 Lakṣmaṇa Temple (Yādava)
3 Varāha Temple
4 Bhogarāma Temple
5 Rudra-Narasiṃha Temple
6 Kevala-Narasiṃha Temple
7 Trivikrama Temple
8 Kapaṭa/Gupta-Rāma Templ
9 Siddhanātha Cave

1 : 2.000.000

0 50 100 km

100 - 150 metres
150 - 300 metres
300 - 450 metres
450 - 600 metres
600 - 900 metres
900 - 1200 metres

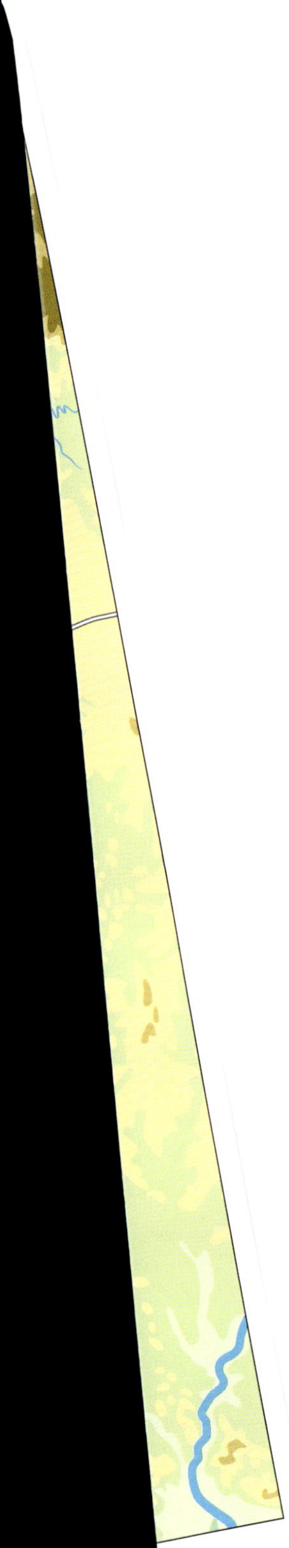